DECOLONISING SOCIAL WORK IN FINLAND

Racialisation and Practices of Care

Edited by
Kris Clarke, Leece Lee-Oliver and
Satu Ranta-Tyrkkö

First published in Great Britain in 2025 by

Policy Press, an imprint of
Bristol University Press
University of Bristol
1-9 Old Park Hill
Bristol
BS2 8BB
UK
t: +44 (0)117 374 6645
e: bup-info@bristol.ac.uk

Details of international sales and distribution partners are available at
policy.bristoluniversitypress.co.uk

© Bristol University Press 2025

The digital PDF versions of the Introduction and Chapter 10 are available Open Access and distributed under the terms of the Creative Commons Attribution-NonCommercial-NoDerivatives 4.0 International licence (https://creativecommons.org/licenses/by-nc-nd/4.0/) which permits reproduction and distribution for non-commercial use without further permission provided the original work is attributed.

British Library Cataloguing in Publication Data
A catalogue record for this book is available from the British Library

ISBN 978-1-4473-7142-7 hardcover
ISBN 978-1-4473-7143-4 paperback
ISBN 978-1-4473-7144-1 ePub
ISBN 978-1-4473-7145-8 ePdf

The right of Kris Clarke, Leece Lee-Oliver and Satu Ranta-Tyrkkö to be identified as editors of this work has been asserted by them in accordance with the Copyright, Designs and Patents Act 1988.

All rights reserved: no part of this publication may be reproduced, stored in a retrieval system, or transmitted in any form or by any means, electronic, mechanical, photocopying, recording, or otherwise without the prior permission of Bristol University Press.

Every reasonable effort has been made to obtain permission to reproduce copyrighted material. If, however, anyone knows of an oversight, please contact the publisher.

The statements and opinions contained within this publication are solely those of the editors and contributors and not of the University of Bristol or Bristol University Press. The University of Bristol and Bristol University Press disclaim responsibility for any injury to persons or property resulting from any material published in this publication.

Bristol University Press and Policy Press work to counter discrimination on grounds of gender, race, disability, age and sexuality.

Cover design: Nicky Borowiec
Front cover image: iStock/ leningrad1975

Bristol University Press and Policy Press use environmentally responsible print partners.

Contents

List of figures		v
Notes on contributors		vi
Acknowledgements		xi
Introduction		1
Kris Clarke, Leece Lee-Oliver and Satu Ranta-Tyrkkö		

PART I	Exploring coloniality in the Finnish social work field	
1	Between a rock and hard place: discussing Sámi issues in contemporary Finland – a conversation with Ánneristen Juuso *Ánneristen Juuso (Anni-Kristiina Juuso)*	35
2	Welfare state nationalism, family reunification and forced migrants' strategies to surpass structural violence *Camilla Nordberg, Joa Hiitola, Hanna Kara and Maija Jäppinen*	49
3	Contesting universalism in Finnish health and social services: experiences of migrant parents with a disabled child *Eveliina Heino, Hanna Kara and Annika Lillrank*	66
4	Homonationalism and talking back in Finnish social work with non-heterosexual people with refugee backgrounds *Inka Söderström*	85
5	Social workers' perceptions on structural challenges for minorities' social care *Kati Turtiainen and Merja Anis*	105
6	Deconstructing racialised and cultural otherisation with young people through pluralistic arts-based social work *Enni Mikkonen*	125

PART II	Naming and confronting epistemic and structural injustice	
7	Silence so loud it hurts: racialisation, erasure and future-building in Finnish social work *Koko Hubara*	147
8	Transcultural mental health as the colonisation of racialised bodies: a personal insight *Fadumo Dayib and Kris Clarke*	161
9	Emergent healing spaces: decolonising healing and wellness in Finland *Wambui Njuguna*	182
10	Intersectional knowledge practices in academia from marginal positions: *testimonios* from researchers of colour in Finland *Smarika KC, Priscilla Osei and Kris Clarke*	195

PART III	**Reimagining caring and social work futurities**	
11	Counter-archiving as a decolonial pedagogy of collective care *Lena Sawyer, Kris Clarke and Nana Osei-Kofi*	217
12	Post-professional social work? Decolonising social work professionalism through the engagement of community health workers *Saana Raittila-Salo*	237
13	Decolonising mindfulness, mindful decolonisation and social work futurities *Michael Yellow Bird and Holly Hatton-Bowers*	256

Conclusion 270
Kris Clarke, Leece Lee-Oliver and Satu Ranta-Tyrkkö

Index 274

List of figures

6.1	Deconstructing racialised and cultural otherisation with youths from asylum-seeking backgrounds through arts-based methods in social work research	139
11.1	'The Iron Well' (also called 'The Five World Parts')	222
11.2	Leap	224
11.3	Chinatown plaque	230
11.4	The Bing Kong Association	231

Notes on contributors

Merja Anis is Professor of Social Work at the University of Turku, Finland. Her research and teaching topics are social work with migrants and ethnic minorities and child and youth social work.

Kris Clarke is Professor of Social Work at the Faculty of Social Sciences at the University of Helsinki. Her research interests centre on decolonisation, structural social work, LGBTQ+ issues in social work and the significance of place and social memory. She is currently working on a study about the history of the AIDS epidemic in Central California.

Fadumo Dayib is a doctoral student in social work at the University of Helsinki, Finland. She is also a public health expert with almost two decades of experience in public health, clinical care, economic empowerment, gender and development.

Holly Hatton-Bowers is Associate Professor and Early Childhood Extension Specialist at the University of Nebraska-Lincoln. Her scholarship focuses on how to uplift and cultivate mental health, emotional well-being and social-emotional development among caregivers, helping professionals, families and young children. These programmes include the use of strategies that cultivate reflective practice, social-emotional learning, resilience, mindfulness and compassion. She is committed to addressing issues of systemic inequities in early care and education, and brings these issues to the forefront of her work. Currently, she is Principal Investigator for an Administration Children and Families Head Start University Partnership Grant aiming to research the implementation of the Nebraska Extension Cultivating Healthy Intentional Mindful Educators programme (CHIME) settings using community-based participatory methods.

Eveliina Heino is University Lecturer at the Faculty of Social Sciences at the University of Helsinki. Her research has focused on diversity, migration and social and health services. Currently she is working on research related to consequences of the COVID-19 pandemic.

Joa Hiitola is University Lecturer and Director of Gender Studies at the University of Oulu, Finland. They have also received the title of Adjunct Professor (Docent) in Social and Public Policy from the University of Eastern Finland and in Social Work from the University of Jyväskylä, Finland. Their research includes intersectional feminist family studies, migrant integration, interpersonal violence, forced migration studies, citizenship scholarship and, most recently, family separation of forced migrants.

Koko Hubara is a Master of Social Work and currently studying for a PhD in comparative literature. She's an arts advisor, author, translator and creative writing teacher with a focus on race, gender, class, mothering and daughtering.

Maija Jäppinen is Assistant Professor of Social Work at the University of Helsinki and scientific co-leader of the Helsinki Practice Research Centre (HPRC). Her research focuses on social work practices, especially in child and family services, and migration, diversity and multilingualism. She is part of an ethnographic research project 'Ordering the "Migrant Family" – Power Asymmetries and Citizenization in Restructuring Welfare Bureaucracies' (2017–23). In 2023–24, she is also leading a research project on interaction skills in child and family social work, and a sub-project on transnational child protection.

Ánneristen Juuso (Anni-Kristiina Juuso) is a Sámi woman, reindeer herder, actress, lawyer and doctoral researcher in law. Her doctoral project examines the role of the Truth and Reconciliation Commission as an institution and whether and how such types of commission contribute to the realisation of the right of Indigenous peoples to self-determination. She lives in the Karesuando area in the corner of northern Sweden and north-western Finland, which is the heart of Sápmi (also known as Sámi land). In addition to her primary career in acting, she works as a lawyer focusing on Indigenous and human rights law. Ánneristen has worked on issues concerning the Truth and Reconciliation Commission since 2017 both in Norway and Finland.

Hanna Kara is University Lecturer in Social Work at the University of Helsinki and as a postdoctoral researcher at Åbo Akademi University. She has researched social work with migrant families and linguistic diversity in social services in Finland, and the transnational migration of Latin American women in Mexico and Spain. She has written, for example, on public service interpreting in social services, research ethics, transnational family relations, transnational daughtering, intersectionality, (in)visibility, belonging and time.

Smarika KC is a doctoral researcher in social work at the University of Helsinki. Her research interests are inequalities in ageing, identity construction, intersectionality, migration and well-being. She has a Master's in Advanced Development in Social Work from the University of Lincoln, UK. She has more than five years of work experience in the international development sector in the Global South.

Leece Lee-Oliver (Blackfeet/Choctaw) is a decolonial scholar and activist whose work is dedicated to understanding how Native American, Indigenous and marginalised peoples experience and respond to national policies and societal beliefs that pose challenges to their sovereignty, safety and security. Her teaching and writing reflect the transgressive political work of Third World liberation scholars. Leece's scholarship pays homage to the legacies of resistance emergent in strategically marginalised communities and highlights how Native Americans draw on cultural traditions to address anti-'Indian' violence and promote and protect sovereignty today. The heart of her work examines US and colonial laws to explore genocidal state violence and today's epidemic rate of violence against Native American women and girls, most notably in the Missing and Murdered Indigenous Women, Girls and People (MMIWGP) pandemic. Leece is Chair of the Board of Directors of the Fresno American Indian Health Project, where her work serves to support Indigenous-based wellness and education practices for 'urban Indian' and California Native Americans. Leece is an Associate Professor of American Indian Studies and Women's, Gender and Sexuality Studies, and Director of American Indian Studies at California State University, Fresno.

Annika Lillrank is Senior Lecturer Emerita in Social Work at the Swedish School of Social Science, University of Helsinki, Finland, and Adjunct Professor (Docent) of Social Work and Health Care at Jyväskylä University, Finland.

Enni Mikkonen is a postdoctoral researcher in social work at the University of Lapland, Finland. She is currently studying Whiteness and racialised structures in social work professionalism in the Nordic and South-Asian contexts. Her doctoral dissertation (2017) addressed social change processes in the position of women in Nepalese rural communities. She has recently worked in various interdisciplinary research projects combining arts-based methods and service design with social work, particularly regarding the questions of the social integration and immigration of young people. Her research interests focus on social work professionalism; hegemonic epistemologies; decolonial feminist solidarity; transnational and pluriversal social work approaches; Global South–North collaboration; and ethnography and arts-based methods in social work.

Wambui Njuguna is a yoga and meditation teacher operating at the crux of yoga, intersectional feminism and social and racial equity. Wambui's motive is to uphold a culture in wellness spaces that operate from a justice-oriented lens for both personal and collective liberation.

Camilla Nordberg is Associate Professor in Social Policy at Åbo Akademi University in Finland. She has conducted research in the fields of migration and welfare, focusing on issues of citizenship, social justice and street-level institutional encounters. She is the project leader of 'Ordering the "migrant family": power asymmetry work and citizenisation in welfare professional bureaucracies', funded by the Academy of Finland, and of 'Language diversity and vulnerability in social work in the era of digitalisation', funded by the Ministry of Social Affairs and Health. She is also an affiliated researcher at the Centre of Excellence in Research on Ageing and Care at the University of Helsinki.

Priscilla Osei is a Ghanaian photographer pursuing a doctoral degree in social work at the University of Helsinki. Her dissertation engages with Black motherhood, parenting, social work and socio-economic development throughout the Finnish African diaspora. She founded Studiopeee, a creative place in Helsinki that focuses on capturing the beautiful moments of immigrant families. Her creative praxis is invested in documenting the Black diaspora in Finland.

Nana Osei-Kofi is Professor of Women, Gender, & Sexuality at Oregon State University. As a critical feminist scholar, her research employs two lines of enquiry centred on justice and the politics of difference. One line of enquiry focuses on structural shifts in higher education in the service of equity and access through curriculum transformation, change leadership and faculty development. The second line of enquiry centres on the experiences and conditions faced by people of African descent in Europe generally, and Sweden specifically, which is the subject of her forthcoming book with Northwestern University Press, tentatively titled *AfroSwedish Places of Belonging*.

Saana Raittila-Salo is a doctoral researcher at the University of Helsinki, Finland, and Visiting Researcher at the University of the Witwatersrand, South Africa. Her current research focuses on informal caregiving for older people of Mozambican-background living with cognitive difficulties in rural South Africa. Her research interests include social network analysis, care studies, Indigenous and popular social work, and community-driven interventions in resource-poor settings.

Satu Ranta-Tyrkkö is Lecturer at the Faculty of Humanities and Social Sciences, University of Jyväskylä, Finland. She has been interested in post- and decolonial social work, local global continuums, and interfaces and confluences of social work and art, as well as environmental issues, throughout her research career. Recently, she has worked especially on issues of social and ecological sustainability, social work futures and eco-social work.

Lena Sawyer is a teacher and researcher, mother, daughter, granddaughter, friend and human being trying to move through this world and understand, learn and make a positive contribution. She is a University of California, Santa Cruz Cultural Anthropologist by training who teaches in the Department of Social Work in Gothenburg, Sweden.

Inka Söderström is a doctoral researcher in social work at the University of Helsinki, Finland. Their doctoral dissertation focuses on social work with queer people with refugee backgrounds in Finland. It deals with questions of borders, heteronormativity and Whiteness in social work, as well as anti-oppressive social work practice. Inka has earlier worked as a social worker with refugees and asylum seekers in Finland, and they are engaged in queer communities and social justice activism in Helsinki.

Kati Turtiainen is Senior Lecturer and Adjunct Professor (Docent) of Social Work in the University of Jyväskylä, Finland. After graduating in social work, she has practised social work and worked as Director of Migrant Services. Currently, she is responsible for the master's degree training in the University Consortium Chydenius. During her work career, she has participated in various national and international development and research projects concerning social work with forced and voluntary migrants. She is the author of three books and various research papers.

Michael Yellow Bird is Dean and Professor, Faculty of Social Work, University of Manitoba and a member of the MHA Nation (Mandan, Hidatsa and Arikara) in North Dakota, US. He has held faculty appointments at the University of British Columbia, Kansas, Arizona State, Cal Poly Humboldt and North Dakota State University. His research focuses on colonisation, decolonisation, healthy Indigenous ageing, mindfulness, Arikara ethnobotany and traditional agriculture, and the cultural significance of Rez dogs. He is the author of numerous scholarly articles and the co-editor of four books: *For Indigenous Eyes Only: the Decolonization Handbook* (2005); *For Indigenous Minds Only: a Decolonization Handbook* (2012); *Indigenous Social Work around the World: Towards Culturally Relevant Education and Practice* (2008); and *Decolonizing Social Work* (2013). He is the co-author of two books: *A Sahnish (Arikara) Ethnobotany* (2020) and *Decolonizing Holistic Pathways Towards Integrative Healing in Social Work* (2021). He is co-authoring two books, *Arikara Traditional Agriculture* and *Decolonizing the Social Work Curriculum*. His most recent articles include, 'Enacting decolonial contemplative mentorship: meditations on the legacy of Plenty Fox' (in press), 'The cultural determinants of healthy indigenous aging' (2022) and 'Molecular decolonization: an indigenous microcosm perspective of planetary health' (2020).

Acknowledgements

No book is created in isolation and this volume has had the support of many gracious and supportive people who guided us through the many obstacles to publication.

We thank Pigga Keskitalo, H. Monty Montgomery and Michael Yellow Bird for inspiring conversations that launched the concept of the book.

Barzoo Elianssi, Lenore Manderson and Bob Pease generously gave their time to read our work and provided solid feedback which sharpened the manuscript.

We also wish to acknowledge all of the authors who wanted to be part of this collection but faced insurmountable challenges to complete their manuscripts due to the pandemic. Your work is important, and we hope that you find the right place to publish it.

We are grateful to Kath Browne, who encouraged us after we faced a wall of rejection. We would have given up without this push across the finish line.

Finally, we thank our fabulous editor, Isobel Bainton, who took on this project and brought it to fruition.

Introduction

Kris Clarke, Leece Lee-Oliver and Satu Ranta-Tyrkkö

Decolonising Social Work in Finland: Racialisation and Practices of Care coalesces a transnational community of social workers, educators, advocates and scholars to identify the long-term impact of coloniality extant in Finnish social work practices and to envision how diverse practices might move us towards deeply needed decolonised futures. Studies of coloniality are often located in the lands and systems of former empires or colonised territories, but what about small nations that have histories enmeshed in complex social relations that shape-shifted as both coloniser and colonised? How can we theorise the ongoing legacy of coloniality in the Nordic social welfare systems, often seen as the most progressive in the world? This book centres the case of Finland, a country on the periphery of Northern Europe, to explore how social welfare structures and social care practices reinforce coloniality at the intersection of racialisation and belonging. The contributions in this edited book bring nuance and complexity to understanding how coloniality and racialisation are intrinsically linked in the contemporary welfare society, and it points to some possible avenues of decolonial transformation.

Decolonising social work reflects a diversity of theories, policies and practices that aim to interrogate, challenge and fundamentally upend knowledge systems and institutions mired in coloniality (for example, Rowe, Baldry and Earles, 2015; Gray, Coates, Yellow Bird and Hetherington, 2016; Pyles, 2017; Fortier and Hon-Sing Wong, 2019; Clarke and Yellow Bird, 2021; Madew, Boryczko and Lusk, 2023; Niigaaniin, MacNeil and Ramos-Cortes, 2023). Decolonial theories and practices are heterogeneous, expansive and extensive. They have lineages in every continent and stretch back decades, and while they have similarities across borders, decolonial theorisations are deeply implanted in place and local histories of coloniality (for example, Quijano, 2007; Mignolo, 2009; Loftsdóttir and Jensen, 2012; Hino, 2020; Velez and Turana, 2020; Ciofalo et al, 2022; Funez-Flores et al, 2022).

As Sylvia Tamale (2020: 13) points out, decolonisation implies a rupture or undoing and therefore starts by fundamentally recognising how entrenched colonial structures pervade every aspect of our 'common sense' and how we see the world. In terms of social work, decolonisation challenges us to question our systems of knowledge and expertise, as well as how we practice. To go beyond what Linda Tuhiwai Smith (2021) called 'colonising knowledge' also requires centring diverse knowledge systems, not simply as alternatives but as key ontologies and epistemologies that can inform social work. Further, decolonising means assuming the responsibility of challenging how interlocking systems of oppression lay at the heart of how we conceptualise social work as a profession and practice. In this book, authors utilise diverse research theories, place-based knowledge, critical auto-ethnography and qualitative research studies to shed light on how the comfort of familiar threads of consciousness simultaneously ensure and deny the existence of colonial modes of social organising and control.

Starting points

The genesis of the book came from a memory that Kris has carried from a doctoral seminar at the University of Tampere, Finland, back in the 1990s. She was among a small group of international and Finnish students who had just started postgraduate studies in social work with great excitement. One day a guest lecturer opened his talk by declaring that "we in Finland have nothing to learn from African social work". The statement was jarring on many levels, not least that university should be a place where curiosity reigns. Around the same time, fellow doctoral student Satu attended a meeting of social work scholars, practitioners and students who shared an interest in global social work, where someone was proudly introduced as *the* person who brought child protection to Africa – as if before his visit no practices existed to ensure child welfare on the continent. Besides indifference to global structural inequalities that stem from the era of colonialism and imperialism and the deployment of racialisation as a tool of social control, these vignettes illustrate how colonial social work knowledge, expertise and professional ancestry continue to inform social work perspectives (Clarke, 2021).

In Finland, a certain attitude of disinterest is often directed towards people other than White-passing Finns (beyond questioning who they are, why they are here and what they think of Finland). This habit precludes learning from their knowledges and insights, especially when they are from non-Western and Indigenous contexts, even in cases of when social workers are explicitly tasked to support a person on their own path to wellness. On the surface level of Finnish culture, however, Finns are seen as liberal and open-minded and they are accustomed to receiving a positive response globally. Who would not want to learn about Finnish achievements in primary education, gender equality, information technology or universal welfare services? Rather than taking these kinds of attitudes as mere gusts of patriotism, our standpoint is that they reflect and enforce the broader hegemonic cultural undercurrent of Finnish society, which casts Finnishness as synonymous with the West as in the classic binary between 'the West' and 'the rest', or 'us' and 'others'. And, indeed, the parliamentary elections of 2023 produced a coalition between the conservative party and the extreme ethno-nationalist right. The fact that horrifically racist comments in public blog posts from earlier years were made by several members of the new Finnish government reflects perhaps a new stage where openly racist and pro-Nazi sympathies have come out of the shadows and into the mainstream. While it is significant that many politicians and business leaders have taken an anti-racist stance, it is equally worth noting that many of them have emphasised their concern about the harm caused to Finland's national brand more than the everyday experience of racialised people in Finland.

Colonialism and imperialism were justified with precisely similar ideas, as history reflects, that seizing the land, wealth and labour of *othered* people called for a reasoned vindication that reinforced the need for such appropriation. European overseas colonialism, which started in the late 15th century, and reached its zenith between the latter half of 19th century and World War I, was rationalised by spreading the 'good word' of Christianity and civilising 'the uncivilised' (on colonialism's civilising mission, see Kiernan [1995], or Mann [2004]). Even the enslavement of peoples forced into colonial subjecthood, seen in the transatlantic slave trade and genocidal campaigns against Indigenous peoples, was condoned by colonisers through laws and church precepts like the Doctrine of Discovery, government policies that fomented the inevitability of Manifest Destiny, and philosophies such as the White Man's Burden that were popularised, for example, in the poetry of Rudyard Kipling and recited in myriad children's lessons and stories.

The late Edward Said (Said, 1979) identified and described the mental and philosophical framework that undergirded notions of the innate superiority of Europe and (White) Europeans in relation to non-Europeans as Orientalism (1979). Said argued that Western knowledge about the 'Orient' (the Middle East, North Africa and Asia) was not neutral but immersed in asymmetrical power dynamics related to colonialism. It was based on growing a sense of White superiority, where the difference between colonisers and the colonised could be systematically maintained at the most intimate level – as members of a common humanity. From an Orientalist perspective, those deemed colonial subjects fell towards the bottom of the racial hierarchy, with similarities to, yet vastly different from those cast at the top of the hierarchy.

Already in the late 18th century, naturalist and zoologist Johannes Blumenbach organised a human hierarchy relegating all peoples on the planet into five categories, with Caucasians at the top. In it, he reified the notion that all persons are subject to their own biological determinism, occupying a rung on the ladder ranging from savage to civilised. Human difference, over centuries, thus became equivalent to subjugation. For had the colonised and colonisers become equals, colonialism would have lost its raison d'etre (Mann, 2004). Unequal social relationships were further produced and naturalised through the power structures of Whiteness and racism, in essence utilising certain physical and cultural attributes to reinforce power relations and subjectivities beyond categorisations such as class and gender and in ways that classified whole peoples in geographic regions as lesser than the colonisers (Fanon, 1967; Wallerstein, 2004a; Seikkula and Hortelano, 2021).

Besides the actions claimed (and by many Europeans genuinely believed) to be beneficent to the colonised, colonialism and imperialism were substantially about making economic profit and creating a huge gap in the power differentials between colonisers and their newly claimed colonised states (for example, McLeod, 2000: 7). Accordingly, what the colonisers articulated as liberation and modernisation often meant exploitation and oppression from the viewpoint of the colonised. However, maybe then, just as now with the contemporary thumb-twiddling over embarking on truly effective climate change mitigation measures, reasoning from the West and Western-aligned countries is again guided by strategic visions that conflate wishful thinking with a lack of critical self-reflection, and a cunning eye for economic and ideological gain.

The system of colonialism, and the resulting socio-economic and political structures, leaves colonial subjects with formidable structural and economic barriers and social ideologies that hold them in place. Layers deep, the colonised world of the past centuries would find themselves hard-pressed to develop their own countries, regions and homelands, as colonisers' claims to vast regions, undiscovered territories and whole continents and peoples, lands and waters were continuously subjected to new statuses and conceptualisations – as property of the colonising authority (Memmi, 1991; Muthu, 2003). When colonial territories eventually took on the appearance of independence, the divide remained between settler colonial subjects and the colonised. In sum, the newly autonomous status of the colonised did not necessarily alter their relationship to the coloniser. Following Walter Rodney (1982), a more accurate view of the process, or project, of colonialism could be understood best with his phrase 'how Europe undeveloped Africa'. Harvey Kaye (1995: 16–18) has further noted that in Europe the 'benefits of imperialism were most unequally distributed by region and class', making visible the ways in which the racism and violence of colonialism and imperialism cast its logics and brutalities in European life as well. The use of racialisation by colonising forces as a means for human subjugation left its imprint on the ways in which human difference would continue to shape European life and nationalist perspectives into the future.

Nowadays colonialism and imperialism as direct political control and economic exploitation are largely overlaid by corporate expansion and political systems that operate well outside of the view of the general public, though their various political, economic, cultural, ideological and epistemic legacies live on even in the systems of welfare and care (for example, Hunter, 2021). Often with sophisticated overwriting that employs oppressive models of racialisation articulated through state logics, their existence is identifiable in the ways that privilege is extended to some over others. Reconfigured racial tropes that retain what Blumenbach saw as biological determinism, for example, minoritise some people and uphold the ostensible success of mainstream hegemonic cultural bodies through concepts that range from meritocracy to wilful ignorance (for example, Au et al, 2016; Joseph, 2019).

Conceptually, coloniality (as extended from colonialism) refers to the global structures of power that stem from the colonial era in economy, culture and knowledge production, and that continue shaping the current world (Quijano, 2000, 2007; Mignolo, 2012; Keskinen, Seikkula and Mkwesha, 2021: 49). More than creating processes in which the colonised become independent from colonisers, decoloniality, to situate the process of decolonisation in the contemporary, is about identifying and strategically dismantling the complex legacies of colonialism in the present in order to achieve liberation and create futures for all peoples, emancipated from racist thinking and structures. These efforts must include eradicating internalised colonial mindsets by creating new social systems where liberation is prioritised.

Another, partially overlapping, umbrella term for decolonisation is often thought to be postcolonialism. Discursively, postcolonial studies cover a spectrum of interpretations of colonialism and its consequences, aimed at making theoretical sense of how something is *because of* and *after* the onset of colonialism (Hutcheon, 2003: 18–19, italics original). As a term, however, postcolonialism has raised plenty of criticism, not least for terminologically obscuring the continuing influence of racialised and colonial hierarchies on our perceptions of the world, sustaining Eurocentrism, dissolving into generalities and overly focusing on identities and cultural representations (Goss, 1996; Keskinen, Seikkula and Mkwesha, 2021: 50). In this book, the choice to use the term decolonising is due to its action-oriented aims. In addition to recognising, criticising and deconstructing still-existing colonial structures and practices, decolonising is also about seeking and producing alternatives – the goal being liberation, empowerment and equality.

Why decolonise, why now, why in Finland?

Presuming that these days colonialism and imperialism have already been quite thoroughly discussed, and that Northern Europe is promoted as relatively peripheral to colonial practices, what contemporary sense does it make to address decolonisation in a Nordic country such as Finland? Was not life in the North at times harsher than in the colonies itself? The standpoint of this book is that decolonisation serves, at last, to raise awareness and inspire action for several reasons: (1) Actual Nordic involvement in colonial practices is under-theorised and unacknowledged in scholarly and political discourses;[1] (2) Nordic societies colonised Indigenous societies during their own efforts of nation-formation; and (3) Nordic societies at-large internalised the tenets of a colonial hegemonic world view of European superiority, and thus the racialised and gendered inequalities and biases intrinsic to it. Therefore, contemporary practices, policies and attitudes exhibit the inherent continuum between colonial racialisation and normative Finnish society, thus creating the marginalisation of people with 'non-Western' ethnic identities, even when they are native Finns, and refugees and immigrants. Given that social work is a point of entry for people facing social, economic, political and (in the case of refugees) medical precarity, and that social work is considered a social justice practice especially in democratic nations, all of these points have important ramifications in the fields of social rights and care.

Discussions of decolonising social work first began to appear in the early 2000s (for example, Sinclair, 2004; Razack, 2009; Waterfall, 2009) as scholars, specifically critical Indigenous scholars, such as Michael Yellow Bird (1999), began to articulate that the very structures intended to 'help' were further oppressing many people. The volumes edited by Mel Gray, John Coates and Michael Yellow Bird (2008, 2016) gave breadth and depth to developing the concepts of Indigenous knowledges and active decolonisation in social work. This work spawned a variety of events like the Liberation Healing Conference at California State University, Northridge (Almeida, Melendez and Paez, 2015), reinventions of social work programmes like the University of Johannesburg in South Africa (Rasool and Harms-Smith, 2021), discussions on the decolonisation of social work ethics (Sewpaul and Henrickson, 2019) and new approaches to transdisciplinary practice, such as Boston Liberation Health Group (Martinez and Fleck-Henderson, 2014). Public health and medicine have also begun to explore the need for decolonisation in medical care (Marya and Patel, 2021) and health research (Krusz et al, 2020). In Finland, Satu Ranta-Tyrkkö (2010, 2011) wrote about the need for postcolonial analysis in social work already over a decade ago, though there has been little response in the Finnish social and healthcare field.

Even though relatively peripheral in Europe, Nordic societies played an active part in broader regional and global power relations, including colonial and imperial processes (Keskinen et al, 2009; Vuorela, 2009; Ranta-Tyrkkö, 2011; Keskinen, 2021: 69). Certain Nordic areas, such as Greenland or the *Sápmi* (the Sámi land) in Northern Fennoscandia, and their people were in various and divergent ways targets of colonisation (Loftsdóttir and Jensen, 2012; Lehtola, 2015). In spite of the great effort of Sámi peoples to bring public attention to the impacts of Nordic expansion in their homelands and lives, the internal colonisation and the resulting pressure placed on the Sámi have only recently been acknowledged and considered in academic research (for example, Lehtola, 2015, 2022: 157–88; Kuokkanen, 2022). It is clear from these newer investigations that the Finnish state-supported settler colonial practices in the Sámi areas are effectively forcing many of the Indigenous Sámi to become stationary, restricting access to the broader expanses of land and waters they were accustomed to, and forcing them to reside in fixed dwellings (Lehtola, 2015: 25). In more recent times, various infrastructure projects have worked as 'persuasive colonialism' by expanding public institutions, such as healthcare services, postal services and police in the Sámi communities, thereby eventually 'nationalising' the Sámi homelands (Massa, 1994: 262–3; Lehtola, 2015: 29).

The Roma in Finland were also targets of repressive assimilative legislation, policies and practices (Keskinen, 2021). Though there has been some debate on the origins of the Roma community, there is scholarly consensus that Finnish Roma always saw themselves as a distinct group from the mainstream community (Rekola, 2023). Consequently, Pyykkönen (2015) points out how Finnish administrative techniques towards ethnic minorities shifted in the 19th century as the national romantic movement, a form of cultural activism often described as a 'national awakening', gained stem. While the Roma were first subject to the Finnish administrative law on vagrancy, techniques of governance changed to directly controlling the bodies of the Roma through deportation, involuntary labour and forced settlements (Pulma, 2006). Ethnic minorities thus became increasingly negatively 'culturalised' as comparisons were drawn between those seen as being 'on the margins of the nation and its civilisation' and racialised White Finns (Pyykkönen, 2015).

Overseas, Nordic countries and individuals also are deeply implicated in various colonial enterprises. Denmark and Sweden (the only independent Nordic countries throughout the era of colonialism) had colonies of their own. Some people with a Finnish background migrated and settled in North America, Australia, South Africa and other areas where they participated in perpetuating land theft against Indigenous people, an opportunity rendered possible by the broader settler colonial structures of power and the ideologies that the burgeoning Nordic societies embraced (Keskinen, 2021: 75; Merivirta, Koivunen and Särkkä, 2021). Denmark, as a seafaring nation, took advantage of and exploited the triangle trade that carried enslaved peoples, sugar and cotton across the North Atlantic. Nordic peoples participated in colonial practices as missionaries, shipmasters, military personnel, engineers and academics. These colonial connections were important to Nordic economies as sources of knowledge, as well as of raw materials, such as cotton, and for developing a system of exporting goods. Sweden, for example, produced the iron chains used in slave ships, and Finland made tar, which was needed to maintain sailing ships (Ranta-Tyrkkö, 2011: 29–30). Most commonly, Finns' involvement in colonialism took place 'at home, in everyday situations. Finns circulated, shared, adopted, adapted and created colonial discourses: texts, scientific studies, objects, imagery and artifacts' (Merivirta, Koivunen and Särkkä, 2021: 6). In sum, while the degree of Nordic colonial involvement varied from country to country, many participated and profited from the colonial practices that produced Europe as a global centre (Loftsdóttir and Jensen, 2012: 1; Keskinen, 2021). Despite the long durée of colonial practices, somehow each of these Nordic nations holds a special political positionality as the world's neutral powers. This status further complicates decolonial efforts to call attention to and address the erasure and impacts of their inherent coloniality.

As previously noted, although Nordic societies have been reluctant to take accountability for their role in colonialism, where major imperial powers such as Britain or France assume centre stage (Jensen, 2009: 164), Nordic societies did indeed embrace the hegemonic, inherently racist world view of colonialism, taking it by and large as natural and 'universally' accepted (Vuorela, 2009). As an ideological undercurrent, the colonial world view has informed attitudes towards non-European others, paving the way for patronising, disparaging and, at times, hostile attitudes and representations, rather than equality. Nonetheless, by emphasising their perceived outsider and neutral positions, Nordic societies have been able to envision and portray themselves as liberal bystanders, at worst, to racism and the dehumanising colonial and imperial practices of other nations. In this line of thought, it is assumed that since there has been little contact with colonised people of colour in Nordic societies, then there has been little racist behaviour, and consequently no racism to deal with. If anything, Finns have been appalled to see their own history as a negatively racialised peoples, represented as being among the 'Yellow' race in the European racial theories of late 19th and early 20th century. When racial classifications changed to also include Eastern Europeans as quite White, Finns were gradually Whitened, which shows how racial categorisations are fluid and change over time (Ignatiev, 1995; Keskinen, 2021: 76–7).

Overall, Nordic societies have been uninterested in their colonial legacies and slow to acknowledge racism as a long-standing cultural and structural undercurrent, and not merely individual bad behaviour (for example, Keskinen et al, 2009; Keskinen, 2021: 70). Not long ago, even research proposals on racism were routinely evaluated as irrelevant on the basis that 'there is no racism' in Nordic society for it to be researched (personal communication with a Nordic social work professor whose research plan was in question). Still in the spring of 2022, a local Finnish newspaper reported a story about an anguished grocery store customer in Satu's former municipality of residence, Pirkkala, who called police after seeing Janette Grönfors, a Roma woman, behind the store's cash counter (Ellilä, 2022). The customer simply could not absorb the fact that the Roma woman wearing the store's vest was a shop assistant on duty. Ironically, the same Roma woman had been unable to finish her studies because she never managed to get an internship to complete the practical training period required to complete her degree. As these kinds of experiences attest, equality in Nordic societies may appear to be a myth, rather than a default value, especially for those excluded from, or contesting, hegemonic Nordic imaginaries and understandings of society.

The previously discussed conceptualisation of Nordics as outsiders rather than directly engaged in colonialism has enabled the notion of 'Nordic exceptionalism' to emerge and assert an image of Nordics as peace-loving, rational, conflict resolution-oriented do-gooders in ways that resonate globally (Loftsdóttir and Jensen, 2012). The ostensible certainty of Nordic exceptionalism serves as a beacon of democratic respectability and reifies early colonial formations that aggregate Whiteness with civility. Backed up with relatively generous development aid funding, the seemingly neutral position has facilitated positive international roles for Nordic countries in the international arena, including political engagement in various anti-imperial and anti-racist activities since the 1970s. Indeed, there have been social justice movements in Finland like *prosenttiliike* (the per cent movement) of the 1980s, which called for Finland to increase its development aid to the level recommended by the United Nations. Many members donated 1 per cent of their salary to development cooperation in solidarity with the Global South. When Kris first started at the University of Tampere, for example, she studied with students from the African National Congress that were funded by the Finnish government. At the same time, hosting students and intellectuals from colonised nations or making donations to development projects may effectively push Nordic involvement in colonialism, accountability and decolonisation-as-necessary even further away from the national consciousness (Puar, 2007; Morgensen, 2011).

In the end, there is no denying the fact that there are many taken-for-granted practices and patterns of thought that carry discriminatory elements in the Nordic societies. Sometimes it takes a child to point these out. Satu, for instance, was happy to eventually find a Finnish children's book, *Metkat menopelit* (*Funny Set of Wheels*, WSOY, 2010) with diverse (not only White) human characters. While the book is joyful and fun to read, one illustration leaves the reader troubled. On a double-page spread presenting a train and its passengers, the one and only seated Black passenger has non-cushioned sides in his seat, whereas the seats of the other, White travellers are nicely soft, and can be stroked by a small reader. Confused, Satu's child asked why that one person did not have a soft seat like the others. Indeed, why not? Maybe the technical explanation for the inferior seat of the Black passenger is that the picture happens to be situated close to the spine of the book, its softness thus difficult to make out. The fact that this seat has a racialised passenger may be a mere accident, though hard to imagine given the rigorous inspection that publishing editors and illustrators painstakingly give to materials before they go to press. The trouble is that too often those who do not fit into the norm of Whiteness are presented in inferior positions, which implicitly and explicitly inform readers where they belong (for a historical analysis on normalising imperialist world order and colonialism in children's literature, see Merivirta, 2021). Likewise, people who are aware of colonial legacies and who take a decolonial mind to the art and practice of literature would notice such marginalising acts like placing the only person of colour in a position where their representation also situates them as differential beings tied to distinct aesthetics.

Hegemonic Whiteness in the Finnish context

As we have previously discussed, normative Whiteness has been central to mainstream notions of Finnishness and national identity. Those not fitting into the (narrow) norm of Whiteness have been and are still today easily interpreted as foreigners, or dubious and different in some nefarious way (such as the Sámi, the Roma, refugees, immigrants and other categories of not fitting in). Even if this kind of stance is suggested to originate from a world view consisting of clear-cut and stable national units associated with a natural land area untethered to other peoples and cultures (Assmuth et al, 2021: 17), the presupposition is at odds with historical realities. Nordic histories, among others, show that national borders keep changing, people can be scattered across several states or be stateless and people mix and migrate. In the past, many people emigrated from Nordic countries to areas of colonial conquest in search of better lives, and tens of thousands of Finns, sometimes annually, moved to Sweden as late as the 1960s and 1970s seeking a better quality of life or economic opportunities. Hence, the concepts of migration and desire do not reside outside of the hegemonic national consciousness.

In contemporary discussions on migration in Finland, however, the term migrant has often been used to convey the implicit notion that immigrating refugees, asylum seekers and racialised migrants lack the drive and means to achieve the threshold of living among Finnish peoples. They are dehumanised and deemed, before and after arrival, as financial and educational burdens who need external support to find and achieve even a modicum of dignity and a place in Finnish society. At the same time, for the prosperous, those recognised as key experts in their fields and holders of the 'right' passport, crossing borders in the European Union and the Nordic countries is rarely a problem. No matter how robust the efforts of members of racially marginalised groups to overcome barriers and fully participate in Nordic societies, studies indicate that systemic unconscious bias reinforces structures of discrimination, not only against ethnic minorities, but also against people with gendered or non-normative identity factors (Huuki and Juutalainen, 2016; Liebkind, Larja and Brylka, 2016; Ahmad, 2020). Noting the simultaneous acute labour shortage in many fields, and layers of need throughout the ageing Finnish society, a dividing line is drawn between those assumed to be resourceful and/or culturally unchallenging for Finns and those assumed to be somehow too different or opportunistic. The most restrictive, and sometimes even insurmountable, immigration and asylum policies seem to be reserved for truly distressed migrants only (for example, Assmuth et al, 2021: 8, referencing Hiitola and Pellander, 2019). It is from the latter 'kind' of migrants that the European Union (including the exceptional Nordics) protects itself with walls, radars and armed patrols, while preaching about human rights to the world in other arenas.

Notwithstanding the previously mentioned histories of emigration, contemporary discussions on migration in Finland have largely focused on the potential problems of current immigration, particularly when imagining non-White newcomers. Immigration is often viewed, first and foremost, as a problem of national security and economic stability. These assumptions emerge from a prominent national narrative that is rooted in hierarchical colonial structures of power that reproduce racist attitudes regarding racialised immigrants in every arena from politics to media to literature. Consequently, this problem-oriented mode of speech, which easily extends to other racialised and othered groups in Finland, has eroded the sense of security of some members of Finnish society (Assmuth et al, 2021: 12–13). Moreover, it probably also reflects nebulous White fears of change combined with a longing for what felt like less complex times. Nostalgia, a key part of national exceptionalism, ventures to imagine society's past as simple and agreeable; it is a conceptualisation that is well aligned with the conception of Nordic benevolence and a time when, in reality, minoritised peoples lacked visibility in the mainstream culture and conscience and 'knew their place'. Fears and prejudices have political currency, which partly explains the emergence and success of political parties such as the Finns Party (*Perussuomalaiset*) in Finland or Swedish Democrats (*Sverigedemokraterna*) in Sweden. Whatever one's side in these discussions, paying attention only to the present may hide the fact that the rhetoric is neither tied to nor a consequence of migration alone but, rather, is rooted in racist and racialised notions about ostensible outsiders, alongside the naturalised merit of White Nordic citizenry, and has a long history in Finnish and other Nordic societies (Seikkula and Keskinen, 2021: 13).

In the Nordic countries, many of the White-majority population still find the notion that White is a skin colour or related with privilege to be novel ideas. As Keskinen, Mkwesha and Seikkula (2021) argue, many people racialised as White are often not accustomed to dealing with racialised hierarchies, or to acknowledge their own position within them. Likewise, many find doing so to be uncomfortable, and may react with uneasiness, self-pity, annoyance and, even, accusations. In addition to excusing racism with White innocence, White tears and White ignorance, this kind of White fragility can delay or prevent tackling racism and critical analyses of power (Keskinen, Mkwesha and Seikkula, 2021: 62). Part of the pain may be that acknowledging racism leads to seeing the many positional advantages that come along with Whiteness in a critical light (for example, Seikkula and Hortelano, 2021: 149).

Deconstructing colonial and racist structures of power requires understanding how they have evolved and been maintained. Against the historical continuities of oppression, exploitation and discrimination that colonialism, imperialism and racism have both directly and indirectly enforced, working to deconstruct them in the present should be vital to any society striving to be just and democratic. Therefore, decolonising is everyone's task, and not something to be left solely to those racialised and othered, though their insights are astute and needed. As Seikkula and Hortelano (2021: 150) argue, while anyone can practise racism in everyday life, anyone can also learn to recognise and resist racism. Colour-blindness, a popular but misconceived notion that associates racism with phenotypic difference, in other words the surface of the skin (that is, colour), became a point of action which invited peoples, businesses and societies to adopt the practice of overlooking or being indifferent to human physical differences. Ideally, ignoring how we look would achieve anti-racism and enable individuals and institutions to overcome inequality. However, the profound implications of race ideologies and racial formations, in reality, create complex mental frameworks upheld by long-standing beliefs in racial difference, which only serve to maintain these interlocking systems of oppression (Omi and Winant, 1994; Seikkula and Hortelano, 2021).

If one of the enemies of combating racism and other colonial legacies in contemporary societies is White people's fear of losing the positional advantages that they are accustomed to, then the challenge is not only individual and societal, but also deeply embedded in the structures of the globalised economy and hegemonic positions of power. In Northern societies, a similar demand to adjust to the rules and power structures that protect the interests of dominant groups are imposed on those considered 'other', such as migrants or refugees. The trouble with demands such as 'when in Finland, do as Finns do' is that newcomers often face barriers to their becoming, in this sense, Finnish in multiple nuanced ways. As Tobias Pötzsch's research (2020) in Finland and Canada shows, (White) fears of real integration are embedded in the various structural and institutional arrangements of migrant integration programmes to the extent that they often impede the critical citizenship of migrants in complex and subtle ways. The newcomers are managed in ways that de facto protect the interests of dominant groups, whereas truly enabling the equal involvement and self-management of the othered groups requires giving them voice and learning from their views and experiences.

Introduction

Today, the Global North is an increasingly political rather than geopolitical location (Santos, 2015: 10). In the global division of resources, the Global North (and the Nordics as part of it) continues to utilise cheap resources such as raw materials, labour and food from societies facing the ongoing structures of coloniality to its own benefit and at environmental and social costs to the Global South. In today's Global North, maintaining an upper hand and taking care of one's own competitiveness intersects with the coloniality of thought, knowledge and being, leaving the descendants of colonised nations the subjects of those in power in today's Global North (Lugones, 2007; Quijano, 2000). Illustrative of the latter is, for example, the use of seasonal migrant labour, such as berry and vegetable pickers, as well as more permanent workers in sectors where labour shortages prevail, such as in transport and care. Their contracts and conditions commonly force workers to come without their families and be ready to go back once they are no longer needed or productive.

As Bob Pease (2017) writes, global forces shape professions like social work; thus the problems that social workers and other social professionals address are often not solvable within national borders alone. While the nation-state context, its status quos and service infrastructures have long served as the taken-for-granted institutional frameworks to comprehend and deal with the issues at stake in social and care work, it is high time to take a critical distance from the kind of (methodological) nationalism that this has entailed. The same applies to social work research. In a globally interconnected world, social work must remain adaptive and attuned to the structural inequalities that spread within and across countries, in order to avoid reinforcing the already existing inequalities and vulnerabilities mapped onto world systems through colonial ideology (Wallerstein, 2004b).

Moreover, tackling these inequalities is not possible by focusing on social work's traditional, often marginalised, or low-income clients or service-user groups alone. In the case of the currently spiralling climate and ecological crises, for example, an urgent and major task is to confront and limit the internalised prerogative of the affluent sectors of humanity, political powers and corporations, the majority of which are situated comfortably in the Global North, to consume more than their share of the planetary resources. Under these conditions, anti-immigrant and racialised rhetorics spread, with little differentiation, over both those who seek asylum and those seeking work. As such, racialising asylum seekers and immigrants looking for gainful employment through the deployment of political rhetoric obscures the point and scale of the challenges at stake and ahead despite their political currency and real need for peaceful, constructive solutions. A fundamental tenet of social work, to advocate for the equality of all peoples, contends that we are all together, interconnected, and interdependent on planet Earth and to each other, a fact which even the privileged cannot eternally escape despite the expansive resources to protect and secure themselves and their descendants.

Pluriversalising knowledge production

Clarke and Yellow Bird (2021: 34) point out, 'How we exist in the world is interwoven with how we know the world.' Capitalist extractivism, structural racism and colonial systems provide the context to hierarchical systems of knowledge production. Our academies are grounded in class, race and gender privilege maintained by admissions gatekeepers, through biased standardised exams and legacy enrolment. Further, our educational systems are imbued with what Midgley (1981) called 'professional imperialism'; namely, the attempt of Western social workers to 'universalise' their own social work knowledge to the world, which our personal memories in the beginning of this chapter highlighted. The professional histories instilled in students continue to mirror the dominant structures of power. One example of this is that the global story of the social work profession continues to focus on early White female professionals in the US, such as Jane Addams and Mary Richmond, even in places as disparate as India, China and South Africa. Today, a great deal of feminist research recounts the ways in which racialisation and the belief in White saviourism deeply informed much of the work of White suffragists and feminists (Newman, 1999; Lee-Oliver, 2019). Likewise, though there are increasing efforts in social work research to trouble these universalising histories (for example, Coles, Netting and O'Connor, 2018; Chapman and Withers, 2019), the enduring dependence on these founding figures reflects the persistent racialised misperceptions of, at best, or the refusal to acknowledge, at worst, comparable Global South social work ancestors (Clarke, 2021).

As Suoranta and Ryynänen (2016: 137) point out, 'academic research is one of the machineries that maintain and renew the hegemonic position of Western knowledge'. In other words, much academic research has for long been either openly or implicitly Northern, stemming from and being specific to the Global North, even when disseminated globally and claimed to be universally applicable (Connel, 2007). Social work is no exception. A central goal of Western social work, after all, has been 'to synthesise the various theories and practices that aimed at the improvement of the self and society and the maintenance of order' (Howe, 1994: 519). It is therefore no wonder that knowledge production that challenges and deconstructs coloniality (Keskinen, Seikkula and Mkwesha, 2021: 51) must take place both inside and outside of academic circles, particularly in social movements, public scholarship and through artistic activities in order to arrive at liberatory praxes. Decoloniality ensures that theory and praxes are community informed and place-based. Social work practice, research and education are not politically neutral arenas, even when disguised as such (Pease, 2017: 222). For a field claiming to promote global justice, a necessary critical skill is the ability to recognise and acknowledge its own complicities – specific to time and place – with the perpetuation of inequalities, including processes such as colonialism (Haug, 2015, referenced in Pease, 2017: 222).

By resisting coloniality, and the lingering frameworks of colonialism, and acknowledging and claiming space for diversity in the present, it is important to recognise that decolonisation is not a fixed process, but rather a call to be adaptive and develop new, dynamic knowledge projects and collective ways of learning and contributing (Connell, 2014). Rather than aspiring to the universal, a decolonial standpoint is that knowledge must be pluriversal (Escobar, 2018) and involve people from diverse backgrounds in its making (Keskinen, Seikkula and Mkwesha, 2021: 67). As Reiter (2018: 7) argues: 'This world has space for many ways of explaining it and making sense of it. To think that the Western way of thinking about and understanding the world is the only one is ignorant.' Pluriversality resists the epistemic violence of colonial exceptionalism that sees only one kind of empirical world and is open to a myriad of scientific traditions and languages (Harding, 1998: 40).

Decolonisation is also about 'the reconstruction of knowledge' that was suppressed by colonialism (Connell, 2014). In general, due to the globally adopted hegemonic position of Northern perspectives, even those outside of Northern academia are forced to become fluent in the language and master its theories and concepts as a condition to use their own voices on 'global' academic platforms. In the case of this book, some of the publishers we initially approached were hesitant about our wish to also include authors who are not primarily academics, but who work actively on decolonisation and culturally responsive social work practices in their communities, despite their effectiveness. We have argued that it is critical to include voices that also bring pluriversality and experiential knowledge to the foreground and challenge the dominance of Western scholarly discourses and the social work practices that they produce.

Margaret Kovach (2021: 158) underlines that it is important not only to bring racialised and Indigenous bodies into the academy but emphasises that diverse knowledges must also transform ways of knowing through relational work aimed at decolonising 'the exclusive domain of knowledge creation'. Articulating a critical research agenda centred on racialised and Indigenous voices, according to Māori scholar Linda Tuhiwai Smith (2021), reinforces self-determination and resists the further dehumanisation and colonisation of racialised and Indigenous people through academic research. Following Patricia Hill Collins (2008: 8), resistance to the omission, trivialisation and depoliticisation of racialised experiences and perspectives as knowledge production is the first step towards empowerment (Dotson, 2015). Hence, incorporating a pluriversalist standpoint also requires acknowledgement of and the need for action on reparations: epistemologically, materially and spiritually. Thus, globally, holistic culturally responsive social work praxes should be in the service of the wellness of peoples, which includes their sovereignty, bodies and contexts.

Genuine integration requires adjustments for all parties, not only from the newcomers or those whose othering has been customary (Pötzsch, 2020). In this sense, the body of work produced by Indigenous and decolonial scholars on how to frame inclusive and pluriversal research agendas could be educative and even vital to the development of the social work profession (for example, Waziyatawin and Yellow Bird, 2005; Kovach, 2021; Smith, 2021).

Decolonising social work in context

Histories of social work are intertwined with the historical processes of colonialism and imperialism, as well as the struggles against them (Ioakimidis and Wylie, 2023). Social work emerged as a profession in the late 19th century, the period when European colonialism was at its height and was heavily influenced by both social control and social (also anti-imperial) activism (for example, Ranta-Tyrkkö, 2010: 92–103). On the one hand, social work has deep roots in social activism, specifically challenging unfair labour laws, poor public health, the disempowered position of women and children, as well as promoting education and supporting immigrants. On the other hand, it has also operated within structures of White supremacy and colonialism, collaborating with the removal of Indigenous children to boarding schools, the imposition of heteronormativity, the institutionalisation of people perceived as 'not normal', control of reproduction through racial hygiene praxes and efforts to repress and erase diverse cultures among immigrants (Lavalette and Ioakimidis, 2011; Ioakimidis and Trimikliniotis, 2020; Sudenkaarne and Blell, 2021). Indeed, the genesis of the police in much of the Global North coincided with the formation of social work and the two professions have continually intersected throughout history, particularly when managing 'troublesome' or unhoused populations (Gasche and Holler, 2021; Dettlaff et al, 2023). The early roots of Western social care were also embedded in a patchwork of rhetoric and logic grounded in laws that stigmatised poor people, workhouses and saviourism that emerged from Church-based activities that were anchored in local contexts.

The social work profession has sought to develop a methodological reproduction of the 'hard' sciences through 'evidence-based practice' (Soydan, 2014). By striving for recognition and status within this paradigm, social work reveals that its view of professionalism is infused with modernity's positivist illusion of detachment in working relationships, neutrality, social worker-as-expert, universal laws and empiricism, and the separation of the professional from the personal (Sewpaul, 2010). It is also premised on holding the 'right knowledge', commonly understood as objectively produced academic knowledge in Western/Northern contexts, and the marginalisation or epistemicide of other knowledges. In so doing, it has been firmly embedded in what Aníbal Quijano (2000) terms the 'colonial matrix'; namely, hegemonic control over four interrelated domains: the economy; authority and social institutions; gender and sexuality; and subjectivity and knowledge. This dominant 'expert' model of social work has thus been exported globally through colonialism, missionisation, saviourism, extractivism and the European/North American undertaking to subdue Indigenous peoples in their respective homelands through imposing colonised ways of knowing and acting (Sewpaul and Hölscher, 2004).

Though the colonial record leaves evidence of the mechanisms applied to manage human difference, especially as is found in the Doctrine of Discovery and thereafter, a deeper understanding of decolonisation remains elusive to many who seek to democratise institutions and transnational, and inter-sovereign, relationships. For the purposes of pluriversal social work, it is important to acknowledge that while decolonial projects take up the aim of an epistemological revolution, the argument in fact is not against professionalism per se. Rather, decoloniality is critical of the reification of positivist professionalism and exceptionalism. In affluent Global North societies, such professionalism risks not taking accountability by apolitically maintaining carceral control over racialised and Indigenous communities through the veneer of following agency protocols. These types of practices maintain a distance between social workers and those in the vulnerable populations they serve (Sewpaul and Henrickson, 2019: 1473).

A similar distancing may also arise between the often middle-class, university-educated, social work labour force and the many diverse and complex vulnerable populations they serve. The distance can be reinforced when social work education does not challenge students to develop a critical and reflective stance to the structural inequalities that position service users differently from them. National identity in many Global North nations has been framed by marginalising communities based on processes of othering. In other words, contrasting the ideal corporeal citizen with those excluded from this category has occurred through Orientalist practices, scientific racism, heteronormativity and eugenics (Said, 1979; Butler, 1990; Kelley, 2000; Hagren, 2022). Social work education must challenge these binaries of 'us' and 'them' that have been projected corporeally onto diverse populations, not only based on perceived race, but also sexual orientation, gender expression, class, religion and ability by pluriversalising its knowledge production and practices.

By the 20th century, in Finland, eugenics (also known as race hygiene) was quite influential in systems of care. It emerged at a time when democracy (in the sense of 'one person, one vote') took root in Finland, which had gained independence from Russia. In the context of emerging independence and sovereignty, there were growing anxieties about the burgeoning population growth of 'others' in the nation. Eugenics thus was constructed as a health intervention and used to sterilise and isolate individuals represented systematically as 'subnormal' in institutions (Hemminiki, Rasimus and Forssas, 1997: 1876). Finnish sterilisation laws were in force between 1935 and 1970. Coercive sterilisation was initially aimed at those deemed 'mentally incompetent' and was supported through political and institutional rhetoric that perpetuated fears of the 'degeneration' of Finns. This dissociative practice enabled racism to be obscured through protective orders to distance the Finnish citizenry from those inferior peoples ostensibly affected by 'feeble-mindedness', alcohol abuse, poor hygiene, laziness and a lack of proper Christian beliefs (Seeman, 2007). It should come as no surprise, then, that Roma women were disproportionately subjected to sterilisation orders, particularly in the period between 1960 and 1970 (Mattila, 2018). The concerns that drove eugenics in Finland easily morphed into fears about 'unproductive' people that threatened to drain the welfare state (Spektorowski and Ireni-Saban, 2013). Sudenkaarne and Bell (2021) characterise the Finnish welfare state as 'haunted' by the legacy of eugenics. Nowadays, this haunting reality emerges in structural racism and fears about a diminishing White Finnish population, also known in radicalised nationalist groups as 'the great replacement'. Both the state rhetoric and social fears that centre the need to prevent the loss of Finnishness concentrate on hegemonic Whiteness and are couched in everyday subtle and obvious ways of excluding diverse service users. Just as social work in the US, for example, has been critiqued for its uneasy historical and ongoing alliance with the police, and aligned as a carceral rather than justice-oriented practice, Nordic social work likewise has had its own long-standing engagement with eugenic (or race hygiene) medicine.

Given the recent globalised and multi-variant illuminations of resistance against systematic violence and state tactics of oppression, the resurgence of interest in social work history and contemporary practices also reflects a timely need to drill down into the colonial matrices of White supremacy that have shaped the profession from its inception. Wright, Carr and Akin (2021) argue that the ways that social work history has been taught to students reinforces colonial ideas that Whites have been the doers while BIPOC (Black, Indigenous, People of Colour) populations have been the dependent recipients of their efforts to reform and bring about social change. It reflects a saviour mentality that justice for marginalised peoples happens because modern, liberal citizens make the effort to democratise their institutions. Unless the professionals within social work, and the policy makers who shape it, begin a deep examination of the roots of the profession, and take into account that colonial systems are most clearly defined by White supremacy, it will continue to replicate systems of human difference and differential treatment in its practices, in its knowledge production and its reinvention of social structures. Unravelling metanarratives of social work through a close examination of colonial history and coloniality, therefore, lends a future orientation towards a transformative social work profession.

Why futures matter

Along with the reasons that we have already highlighted, we have elaborated colonialism and its impacts, as well as decolonisation in and beyond social work, because we strongly believe this to be crucial for imagining and building just futures in social work and care. At a time when there is no dearth of dystopic scenarios, including ever increasing polarisation, catastrophic ecological crises and a growing scarcity of resources, our political systems are simultaneously creating a greater need for social work and care and removing the resources to provide such care. In spite of obvious power differentials, our collective futures are 'incredibly contested' and 'saturated with conflicting social interests' (Urry, 2014: 3). We contend that if social work wants to remain faithful to the moral and ethical value base it claims, then the preferable, and really the only, futures worth striving for are the ones that are inclusive and worth living – for all. To generate new outcomes requires learning from various pasts, including the colonised and marginalised ones, and on that basis not only 'developing ways of understanding how past, present and future are mutually intertwined' (Urry, 2014: 7), but also striving towards a more inclusive and equal world that embraces and builds upon situated knowledge systems and coalitional engagement. At the 1952 Bandung Conference, when world powers came together to imagine futures not under the oppressive force of First World nations, a commitment was made to acknowledge coalitional engagement and mutual respect as cornerstones to building prosperity without human subjugation as a mechanism. Similarly, we find our global communities at yet another turning point, surrounded by the silencing threats of White supremacist domination, seeking to move towards thriving liberation and diversity.

While futures tend to end up being different from what was imagined or planned, the capacity to imagine and own futures matters, to the extent that a central element of power is the power to determine, out of a myriad of ways, how the future is imagined, materialised and distributed (Urry, 2014: 17). From a social work perspective, the question is whether and how social work can promote inclusive futures with credible and positive roles, and a promise of care, for a diverse array of people. However, there is no denying the existing path dependencies: 'different social futures are fateful for people's lives in the present' (Urry, 2014: 7). As our lives are still today influenced by colonial legacies, in other words the presence of coloniality, this book argues for the necessity to decolonise both to recognise and rework our embeddedness in the coloniality of systems, knowledge and being, as well as for the sake of the futures of social work and care.

Until now, efforts to incorporate pieces of diverse knowledge or ideas into social work praxes have been limited or they have been appropriative. Curtis and Morley (2019) argue that greater critical reflection is needed in social work to safeguard against integrating alternative practices without reinscribing colonial, individualised interventions under different guises. Thus, the question is not what decolonisation can add to what we already know, but rather what can decolonisation do to transform social work practices into the tools that we need to create real change? What can social work do to level out the existing polarisations in the society? And how could social work, on its part, promote dismantling the entanglement of the affluent in exploitative and destructive relationships with nature and the Global South? These and related questions are pertinent to the chapters that fill these pages. Examining the implications of social work and care as systematically and practically entwined with coloniality make comprehensible and give impetus to complex decolonial praxes, especially as it seems that future dividing lines will deepen between those who hold egalitarian participatory agendas, and those lining up with right-wing, anti-globalisation, anti-liberal and anti-environmentalist standpoints (for example, Blühdorn and Deflorian, 2021). Each author in this book demonstrates a commitment and praxis that unpacks as it reimagines the future of social work through the lens of justice. Our future visions have powerful social consequences, and the time to work with them, as well as finding the desired ways to achieve them, is now.

Kara Keeling (2019: 15) has asserted that we need a 'reinvigorated concept of knowledge production—as an imaginative, scholarly enterprise (that) ... engages with existing academic work and other knowledges and that involve the body as well'. When tensions build through growing contradictions between the current historical moment and the webs of meaning attached to institutions and systems, then radical imaginaries emerge that create new ways of knowing, organising and transforming. While the radical imaginary can easily be dismissed as utopian or pie-in-the-sky, such visions are critical to seeing beyond the colonised mind of the present to contemplating a different tomorrow.

Emerging movements such as Afrofuturism, Indigenous and Asian futurism together with complex constellations of global queer, multiracial and trans identities use speculative fiction, comics, art and technology to create new visions and aesthetics of a future where BIPOC people are not exoticised as others, and where they are firmly centred in narratives. Radical change, in other words, requires a radical imaginary that can not only creatively re-envision different structures of social existence, but also understand the past in new ways to enact transformation. The current explosion of texts and discussions on decolonisation around the globe perhaps represents such a transformational historical moment.

The structure of the book

In this volume, we examine our current realities and practices before considering some ways to transform future practices of social work. In many of these contributions, an important part of the process of approaching the topic is a critical unpacking of colonial and White supremacist views of care that bear the phenomenological markers of coloniality. The work herein observes and questions the intellectual hegemony of the metropole, and its broad institutional underpinnings, including universities but extending far beyond them into professions, governments, corporations and communities of practice. In this book, the authors represent practitioners, scholars and experts whose unique contributions and voices, in and of themselves and as a whole, provide not only insights and critiques, but also practised epistemological social work methods that envision and create justice-oriented outcomes.

This book is constructed in three parts. The first part, 'Exploring coloniality in the Finnish social work field', outlines the structures, policies and practices that constitute coloniality in Finnish social work. The second part, 'Naming and confronting epistemic and structural injustice', presents racialised voices that often go unheard about the barriers they face in Finnish society as students and practitioners. Finally, the third part, 'Reimagining caring and social work futurities', opens up diverse approaches to co-creating and envisioning decolonising social work education, practices and ways of thinking.

Part I: 'Exploring coloniality in the Finnish social work field'

The book opens with 'Between a rock and hard place: discussing Sámi issues in contemporary Finland – a conversation with Ánneristen Juuso'. In an interview with the editors, Juuso, a Sámi woman, reindeer herder, actor, lawyer and doctoral researcher in law discusses the possibilities and problematics of decolonisation, and Indigenous erasure within the construct of a benevolent Finland.

Camilla Nordberg, Joa Hiitola, Hanna Kara and Maija Jäppinen then explore the complexity of the family reunification process for forced migrants resident in Finland. Their case studies illustrate how the layers of street-level welfare bureaucracy reinforce the welfare state nationalism of Finnish immigration policies. They illustrate the enormous emotional and financial pressures of navigating administrative barriers by forced migrants, which not only reduces their ability to integrate into Finnish society but also profoundly affects their fundamental wellbeing. Forced migrants trapped in a state of constant longing and rejection present significant challenges to frontline social workers, who reflect the ambivalence of fulfilling their ethical responsibilities and utilising their professional expertise while carrying out Finnish migration policies.

Eveliina Heino, Hanna Kara and Annika Lillrank examine universal services for disabled children in the Finnish context where cultural homogeneity is often constructed as synonymous with equality. Analysing the accounts of two migrant parents who have a disabled child reveals systemic limitations in Finnish social and healthcare services. They show how responsibility for ensuring universal access to services falls heavily on frontline workers, producing arbitrary practices rather than structures of inclusion.

Inka Söderström investigates homonationalist and colonial meaning-making processes through the stories of queer people with a refugee background and their social workers. In closely examining these stories, Söderström shows how social workers use the homophobia and oppression in refugees' countries of origin to construct Finland as a superior, discrimination-free queer haven. Queer people with a refugee background, nonetheless, talk back to these totalising discourses by narrating alternative stories of their countries of origin and current circumstances. Söderström calls for breaking the tyranny of the single story through listening as a decolonial praxis.

Kati Turtiainen and Merja Anis utilise Iris Marion Young's concepts of the social connection model for building justice-oriented social work that centres the role of responsibility. Through an analysis of social workers' discussions and texts on child welfare and child protection issues, Turtiainen and Anis demonstrate how power dynamics operate on the client-professional level, especially when clients are othered as linguistic or cultural minorities. Most importantly, they indicate how social workers could intervene to take responsibility for structural injustice and shift inequitable outcomes.

Enni Mikkonen presents a rich case study of an arts-based intervention with racialised and otherised young people with an asylum-seeking background aimed at building on the youth's agency while addressing structural racism and bias. Mikkonen shows how arts-based methods can provide decolonised entry points for deconstructing cultural and racialised otherisation and empowering youth.

Part II: 'Naming and confronting epistemic and structural injustice'

Koko Hubara offers a personal essay on her journey through Finnish social work as a Brown native Finn former client, student of social work and practitioner. Drawing on her experience, she presents a deep reflection on the role of race in contemporary Finnish social work education and practice, and offers solutions so that the social work field could free itself from the shackles of colonialism.

Fadumo Dayib reflects on her experience working in the mental health system, while Kris Clarke collaborates in outlining colonial genealogies of ethnopsychiatry and transcultural mental health care. They argue that these conceptualisations perpetuate colonialism by othering, incarcerating, controlling and medicalising the racialised bodies that come into contact with it. The confluence of structural and epistemic injustice in the Whiteness of Finnish mental health services underserves racialised people resident in Finland.

Wambui Njuguna explores her journey through wellness advocacy and care in southern Finland as a practitioner of colour. She discusses the challenges of creating healing spaces for BIPOC people in a wellness landscape filled with cognitive dissonance and colour-blindness. Njuguna talks frankly about how difficult it is to initiate decolonising wellness events within communities with complex identities.

Smarika KC, Priscilla Osei and Kris Clarke discuss epistemic injustice in the Finnish discipline of social work through the critical self-reflection method of *testimonio*. Clarke, the supervisor of doctoral students Smarika and Priscilla, opens the chapter by outlining the concepts of epistemic injustice and intersectionality. The students then present their own *testimonios* about their own experiences as students of colour resident in Finland, and they discuss why they see their research is significant to Finnish social work and the Finnish academy.

Part III: 'Reimagining caring and social work futurities'

Lena Sawyer, Kris Clarke and Nana Osei-Kofi explore the value of city walking as a method of counter-archiving in social work education. They argue that centring people and our bodies in encounters with physical and public space creates decolonial pedagogical forms for grappling with the context of place and how the legacy of colonialism continues, through signs that signify coloniality of power. They closely examine case studies in Sweden and California to show how city walking was used with groups to explore how colonialism lives in our present day.

Saana Raittila-Salo outlines lay people's social work through a case study of community health workers in Mozambique. Arguing that Indigenous community health workers have deep experiential knowledge of the social environment, Raittila-Salo sees the concept of lay people's social work as one way to reframe Indigenous, popular and culturally relevant community practices as social work, thus challenging the dominance of colonial Eurocentric definitions of the profession and confronting professional imperialism.

Michael Yellow Bird and Holly Hatton-Bowers offer the final chapter in the book by exploring how decolonising the mind can build resilience, as well as support social work values and healing practices. Yellow Bird and Hatton-Bowers argue that decolonising mindfulness by intentionally including ethical principles and spirituality in praxis is necessary for sustained systemic changes within the social work field. They underline the key importance of practices acknowledging the historical violence and harm social work has contributed to Black, Indigenous and People of Colour (BIPOC), which is challenging, often painful work, but central to healing and change.

We then offer a Conclusion as a challenge to take up the promise of decolonisation, to reimagine and re-envision how social work could function in Finland.

Note

[1] It should be noted that there are more discussions on colonial legacies in the Finnish public sphere. The Finnish Broadcasting company (YLE) have developed some podcast series, such as 'At Caribbean slave markets or mines in Congo – stories of Finnish colonialism [*Karibian orjamarkkinoilla ja Kongon kaivoksilla – suomalaisen kolonialismin tarinat*], https://areena.yle.fi/podcastit/1-65173734, and 'Chapters of the history of racism [*Lukuja rasismin historiasta*], https://areena.yle.fi/podcastit/1-50821999. YLE has increasingly provided content that addresses these issues.

References

Ahmad, A. (2020) 'Ethnic discrimination against second-generation immigrants in hiring: empirical evidence from a correspondence test', *European Societies*, 22(5): 659–81.

Almeida, R., Melendez, D. and Paez, J.M. (2015) 'Liberation-based practice', in *Encyclopedia of Social Work*, Oxford University Press.

Anderson, B. (2006) *Imagined Communities: Reflections on the Origin and Spread of Nationalism*, London: Verso.

Assmuth, L. et al (2021) 'Johdanto: Muuttoliikkeet arjen turvallisuuden tutkimuksen kohteena', in L. Assmuth et al (eds), *Arjen turvallisuus ja muuttoliikkeet*, Tietolipas 269, Helsinki: Suomalaisen Kirjallisuuden Seura, pp 7–28.

Au, W., Mayorga, E., Dumas, M. and Dixson, A. (2016) 'Meritocracy 2.0: high-stakes, standardized testing as a racial project of neoliberal multiculturalism', *Educational Policy (Los Altos, Calif.)*, 30(1): 39–62.

BlackDeer, A.A. (2023) 'Unsettling feminism in social work: toward an indigenous decolonial feminism', *Affilia*. https://doi.org/10.1177/08861099231193617

Blühdorn, I. and Deflorian, M. (2021) 'Politicisation beyond post-politics: new social activism and the reconfiguration of political discourse', *Social Movement Studies*, 20(3): 259–75.

Butler, J. (1990) *Gender Trouble: Feminism and the Subversion of Identity*, London: Routledge.

Castoriadis, C. (1997) *The Imaginary Institution of Society*, Cambridge, MA: MIT Press.

Chapman, C. and Withers, A.J. (2019) 'A violent history of benevolence', in *A Violent History of Benevolence*, Toronto: University of Toronto Press.

Ciofalo, N., Dudgeon, P., and Nikora, L.W. (2022) 'Indigenous community psychologies, decolonization, and radical imagination within ecologies of knowledges', *American Journal of Community Psychology*, 69(3–4): 283–93.

Clarke, K. (2022) 'Reimagining social work ancestry: toward epistemic decolonisation', *Affilia*, 37(2): 266–78.

Clarke, K. and Yellow Bird, M. (2021) *Decolonising Pathways Towards Integrative Healing in Social Work*, London: Routledge.

Coles, D.C., Netting, F.E. and O'Connor, M.K. (2018) 'Using prosopography to raise the voices of those erased in social work history', *Affilia*, 33(1): 85–97.

Collins, P. (2008) *Black Feminist Thought: Knowledge, Consciousness, and the Politics of Empowerment*, London: Routledge.

Connell, R. (2007) *Southern Theory: The Global Dynamics of Knowledge in Social Sciences*, Cambridge: Polity Press.

Connell, R. (2014) 'Using southern theory: decolonising social thought in theory, research and application', *Planning Theory*, 13(2): 210–23.

Curtis, C. and Morley, C. (2019) 'Banging the same old colonial drum? Moving from individualising practices and cultural appropriation to the ethical application of alternative practices in social work', *Aotearoa New Zealand Social Work*, 31(2): 29–41.

Dettlaff, A.J., Abrams, L.S. and Teasley, M.L. (2023) 'Interrogating the carceral state: re-envisioning social work's role in systems serving children and youth', *Children and Youth Services Review*, 148: 106920.

Dotson, K. (2015) 'Inheriting Patricia Hill Collins's Black Feminist epistemology', *Ethnic and Racial Studies*, 38(13): 2322–8.

Ellilä, T. (2022) 'Romani Janette Grönfors aloitti työt kaupan kassalla Pirkkalassa – heti ensimmäisessä iltavuorossa asiakas soitti poliisin paikalle: "Tiesin, että tästä tulee myrsky"', *Aamulehti*, 30 April.

Escobar, A. (2018) *Designs for the Pluriverse: Radical Interdependence, Autonomy, and the Making of Worlds*, Durham, NC: Duke University Press.

Fanon, F. and Sartre, J.-P. (1967) *The Wretched of the Earth*, trans. C. Farrington, London: Penguin.

Fortier, C. and Hon-Sing Wong, E. (2019) 'The settler colonialism of social work and the social work of settler colonialism', *Settler Colonial Studies*, 9(4): 437–56.

Fúnez-Flores, J.I., Díaz Beltrán, A.C. and Jupp, J. (2022) 'Editorial introduction: inter-epistemic dialogues with decolonial thought from Latin America and the Caribbean', *Educational Studies (Ames)*, 58(5–6): 575–80.

Gasche, M. and Holler, M. (2021) 'Selective memories: Finnish state policy toward Roma in the 1930s and 1940s in its European context and post-war perception', *Journal of Finnish Studies*, 24(1–2): 94–111.

Goss, J. (1996) 'Postcolonialism: subverting whose empire?', *Third World Quarterly*, 17(2): 239–50.

Gray, M., Coates, J., Yellow Bird, M. and Hetherington, T. (2016) *Decolonizing Social Work*, London: Routledge.

Hagren, K. (2022) 'Othering in discursive constructions of Swedish national identity, 1870–1940', *Critical Discourse Studies*, 19(4): 384–400.

Harding, S. (1998) *Is Science Multicultural? Postcolonialisms, Feminisms, and Epistemologies*, Bloomington, IN: Indiana University Press.

Haug, E. (2015) 'Critical reflections on the emerging discourse of international social work', *International Social Work*, 48(2): 126–35.

Hemminki, E., Rasimus, A. and Forssas, E. (1997) 'Sterilisation in Finland: from eugenics to contraception', *Social Science and Medicine*, 45(12): 1875–84.

Hiitola, J. and Pellander, S. (2019) 'The alien child's best interest ignored: when notions of gendered parenthood meet tightening immigration policies', *NORA-Nordic Journal of Feminist and Gender Research*, 27(4): 245–57.

Hint, A. (2020) 'Expatriating the universal: a decolonial imagination beyond authentic "Asia"', *International Quarterly for Asian Studies*, 50(3–4).

Howe, D. (1994) 'Modernity, postmodernity and social work', *British Journal of Social Work*, 24(5): 513–32.

Hunter, S. (2021) 'Decolonizing white care: relational reckoning with the violence of coloniality in welfare', *Ethics and Social Welfare*, 15(4): 344–62.

Hutcheon, L. (2003) 'Postcolonial witnessing – and beyond: rethinking literary history today', *Neohelicon*, 30(1): 13–30.

Huuki, T. and Juutilainen, S. (2016) 'Mapping historical, material and affective entanglements in a Sami woman's discriminatory experiences in and beyond Finnish boarding school', *Education in the North*, 23(2): 3–23.

Ignatiev, N. (2012) *How the Irish Became White*, London: Routledge.

Ioakimidis, V. and Trimikliniotis, N. (2020) 'Making sense of social work's troubled past: professional identity, collective memory and the quest for historical justice', *The British Journal of Social Work*, 50(6): 1890–908.

Ioakimidis, V. and Wyllie, A. (2023) *Social Work's Histories of Complicity and Resistance: A Tale of Two Professions*, Bristol: Policy Press.

Jensen, L. (2009) 'Scandinavia: a peripheral centre', *Kult* (special issue: Epistemologies of Transformation: The Latin American Decolonial Option and its Ramifications), (6): 165–6.

Joseph, E. (2019) 'Discrimination against credentials in Black bodies: counterstories of the characteristic labour market experiences of migrants in Ireland', *British Journal of Guidance and Counselling*, 47(4): 524–42.

Kaye, H.J. (1995) 'Introduction: imperialism and its legacies', in H.J. Kaye (ed) *Imperialism and its Contradictions*, New York: Routledge, pp 1–22.

Keeling, K. (2019) *Queer Times, Black Futures*, New York: New York University Press.

Kelley, R. (2000) 'A poetics of anticolonialism', in A. Césaire (ed) *Discourse on Colonialism*, New York: Monthly Review Press.

Keskinen, S. (2021) 'Kolonialismin ja rasismin historiaa Suomesta käsin', in S. Keskinen, M. Seikkula and F. Mkwesha (eds) *Rasismi, valta ja vastarinta Suomessa: Rodullistaminen, valkoisuus ja koloniaalisuus Suomessa*, Helsinki: Gaudeamus, pp 69–84.

Keskinen, S. Mkwesha, F. and Seikkula, M. (2021) 'Teoreettisen keskustelun avaimet – rasismi, valkoisuus ja koloniaalisuuden purkaminen', in S. Keskinen, M. Seikkula and F. Mkwesha (eds) *Rasismi, valta ja vastarinta Suomessa: Rodullistaminen, valkoisuus ja koloniaalisuus Suomessa*, Helsinki: Gaudeamus, pp 45–68.

Keskinen, S., Tuori, S., Irni, S. and Mulinari, D. (eds) (2009) *Complying with Colonialism: Gender, Race, and Ethnicity in the Nordic Region*, Farnham: Ashgate.

Kiernan, V.G. (1995) 'Imperialism and its contradictions', in H.J. Kaye (ed) *Imperialism and its Contradictions*, New York: Routledge.

Kovach, M. (2021) *Indigenous Methodologies: Characteristics, Conversations, and Contexts* (2nd edn), Toronto: University of Toronto Press.

Krusz, T., Davey, T., Wiggington, B. and Hall, N. (2020) 'What contributions, if any, can non-indigenous researchers offer toward decolonizing health research?', *Qualitative Health Research*, 30(2): 205–16.

Kuokkanen, R. (2011) *Reshaping the University: Responsibility, Indigenous Epistemes, and the Logic of the Gift*, Vancouver: UBC Press.

Kuokkanen, R. (2020) 'Reconciliation as a threat or structural change? The truth and reconciliation process and settler colonial policy making in Finland', *Human Rights Review*, 21(3): 293–312.

Kuokkanen, R. (2022) 'All I see is White: the colonial problem in Finland', in J. Hoegaerts, T. Liimatainen, L. Hekanaho and E. Peterson (eds) *Finnishness, Whiteness and Coloniality*, Helsinki: Helsinki University Press, pp 291–314.

Lavalette, M. and Ioakimidis, V. (2011) 'International social work or social work internationalism? Radical social work in global perspective', in M. Lavalette (ed) *Radical Social work Today: Social Work at the Crossroads*, Bristol: Policy Press, pp 135–52.

Lee-Oliver, L.M. (2019) 'Situating Native American studies and red feminisms: sustaining ethnic studie', *Ethnic Studies Review*, 42(2): 196–209.

Lehtola, V.-P. (2015) 'Sámi histories, colonialism, and Finland', *Arctic Anthropology*, 52(2): 22–36. https://muse.jhu.edu/article/612132

Lehtola, V.-P. (2022) 'Driving around with Aunt Máret: historical consciousness of the Sámi in transition', in S. Valkonen, A. Aiko and S.-M. Magga (eds) *The Sámi World*, London: Routledge, pp 479–93.

Liebkind, K., Larja, L. and Brylka, A. (2016) 'Ethnic and gender discrimination in recruitment: experimental evidence from Finland', *Journal of Social and Political Psychology*, 4(1): 403–26.

Loftsdóttir, K. and Jensen, L. (2012) 'Introduction: Nordic exceptionalism and the Nordic "others"', in K. Loftsdóttir and L. Jensen (eds) *Whiteness and Postcolonialism in the Nordic Region: Exceptionalism, Migrant Others and National Identities*, Farnham: Ashgate, pp 1–11.

Lugones, M. (2007) 'Heterosexualism and the colonial/modern gender system', *Hypatia*, 22(1): 186–219.

Madew, M., Boryczko, M. and Lusk, M. (eds) (2023) *Decolonized Approaches to Human Rights and Social Work*, London: Springer Nature.

Mann, M. (2004) '"Torchbearers upon the path of progress": Britain's ideology of a moral and material progress in India. An introductory essay', in H. Fischer-Tiné and M. Mann (eds) *Colonialism as Civilising Mission: Cultural Ideology in British India*, London: Anthem Press, pp 1–26.

Martinez, D.B. and Fleck-Henderson, A. (eds) (2014) *Social Justice in Clinical Practice: A Liberation Health Framework for Social Work*, London: Routledge.

Marya, R. and Patel, R. (2021) *Inflamed: Deep Medicine and the Anatomy of Injustice*, New York: Penguin.

Massa, I. (1994) *Pohjoinen luonnonvalloitus: Suunnistus ympäristöhistoriaan Lapissa ja Suomessa*, Helsinki: Gaudeamus.

Mattila, M. (2018) 'Sterilisation policy and Gypsies in Finland', *Romani Studies*, 28(1): 109–39.

McLeod, J. (2000) *Beginning Postcolonialism*, Manchester: Manchester University Press.

Memmi, A. (1991 [1957]) *The Colonizer and the Colonized*, trans. H. Greenfeld, Boston, MA: Beacon.

Merivirta, R. (2021) 'Colonialism, race, and White innocence in Finnish children's literature: Anni Swan's 1920s' serial "Uutisasukkaana Australiassa"', in R. Merivirta, L. Koivunen and T. Särkkä (eds) *Finnish Colonial Encounters: From Anti-Imperialism to Cultural Colonialism and Complicity* (Cambridge Imperial and Post-colonial Studies Series), London: Palgrave Macmillan, pp 171–97.

Merivirta, R., Koivunen, L. and Särkkä, T. (eds) *Finnish Colonial Encounters: From Anti-Imperialism to Cultural Colonialism and Complicity* (Cambridge Imperial and Post-colonial Studies Series), London: Palgrave Macmillan.

Midgley, J. (1981) *Professional Imperialism: Social Work in the Third World*, Portsmouth, NH: Heinemann.

Mignolo, W. (2009) 'Epistemic disobedience, independent thought and decolonial freedom', *Theory, Culture and Society*, 26(7–8): 159–81.

Mignolo, W. (2012) 'Decolonizing western epistemology/building decolonial epistemologies', in A.D. Isasi-Diaz and E. Mendieta (eds) *Decolonizing Epistemologies: Latina/o Theology and Philosophy*, New York: Fordham University Press, pp 19–43.

Mignolo, W. (2017) 'Coloniality is far from over, and so must be decoloniality', *Afterall*, 43(1): 38–45.

Morgensen, S.L. (2011) 'The biopolitics of settler colonialism: right here, right now', *Settler Colonial Studies*, 1(1): 52–76.

Muthu, S. (2003) *Enlightenment Against Empire*, Princeton, NJ: Princeton University Press.

Newman, L.M. (1999) *White Women's Rights: The Racial Origins of Feminism in the United States*, Oxford: Oxford University Press.

Niigaaniin, M., MacNeill, T. and Ramos-Cortez, C. (2023) 'Decolonizing social services through community development: an Anishinaabe experience', *Community Development Journal*, 58(2): 225–46.

Omi, M. and Winant, H. (1994) *Racial Formation in the United States : From the 1960s to the 1990s*, London: Routledge.

O'Sullivan, N. (2019) 'Walking backwards into the future: Indigenous wisdom within design education', *Educational Philosophy and Theory*, 51(4): 424–33.

Pease, B. (2017) 'Undoing privilege in social work: implications for critical practices in the local and global context', in M. Livholts and L. Bryant (eds) *Social Work in a Glocalised World*, London: Routledge, pp 216–27.

Pötzsch, T. (2020) 'Critical perspectives on social inclusion in integration education programs for adult migrants', doctoral dissertation, University of Helsinki, HELDA. http://urn.fi/URN:ISBN:978-951-51-6191-8

Puar, J. K. (2007) 'Introduction: homonationalism and biopolitics', in *Terrorist Assemblages: Homonationalism in Queer times*, Durham, NC: Duke University Press, pp 1–36.

Pulma, P. (2006). *Suljetut ovet. Pohjoismaiden romanipolitiikka 1500-luvulta EU-aikaan* [Closed doors. Nordic Roma policy from the sixteenth century to the EU era], Helsinki: SKS.

Pyles, L. (2017) 'Decolonising disaster social work: environmental justice and community participation', *British Journal of Social Work*, 47(3): 630–47.

Pyykkönen, M. (2015) 'Ethically ethnic: the ethno-culturalisation of the moral conduct of the Sámi and the Roma in the governance in Finland between the 1850s and 1930s', *Journal of Political Power*, 8(1): 39–59.

Quijano, A. (2000) 'Coloniality of power and Eurocentrism in Latin America', *International Sociology*, 15(2): 215–32.

Quijano, A. (2007) 'Coloniality and modernity/rationality', *Cultural Studies (London, England)*, 21(2–3): 168–78.

Ranta-Tyrkkö, S. (2010) *At the Intersection of Theatre and Social Work in Orissa, India. Natya Chetana and its Theatre*, Acta Unviersitatis Tamperensis 1503, Tampere: Tampere University Press. http://urn.fi/urn:isbn:978-951-44-8003-4

Ranta-Tyrkkö, S. (2011) 'High time for postcolonial analysis in social work', *Nordic Social Work Research*, 1(1): 25–41.

Rasool, S. and Harms-Smith, L. (2021) 'Towards decoloniality in a social work programme: a process of dialogue, reflexivity, action and change', *Critical African Studies*, 13(1): 56–72.

Razack, N. (2009) 'Decolonising the pedagogy and practice of international social work', *International Social Work*, 52(1): 9–21.

Reiter, B. (2018) *Constructing the Pluriverse: The Geopolitics of Knowledge*, Durham, NC: Duke University Press.

Rekola, T. (2023) 'A double-edged sword: the impact of military service on "zigenare" and "tattare" in Finland, c.1743–1809', *Social History (London)*, 48(2): 232–58.

Rodney, W. (1982) *How Europe Underdeveloped Africa* (rev edn), Washington DC: Howard University Press.

Rowe, S., Baldry, E. and Earles, W. (2015) 'Decolonising social work research: learning from critical Indigenous approaches', *Australian Social Work*, 68(3): 296–308.

Said, E. (1979) *Orientalism* (Vintage Books edn), New York: Vintage.

Santos, B. (2015) *Epistemologies of the South: Justice Against Epistemicide*, Boulder, CO: Paradigm.

Satka, M. and Harrikari, T. (2008) 'The present Finnish formation of child welfare and history', *British Journal of Social Work*, 38(4): 645–61.

Seeman, M. (2007) 'Sterilisation of the mentally ill during the years of World War II in Finland', *International Journal of Mental Health*, 36(1): 58–66.

Seikkula, M. and Hortelano, P. (2021) 'Arjen rasismi ja rasisminvastaisuus arjessa', in S. Keskinen, M. Seikkula and F. Mkwesha (eds) *Rasismi, valta ja vastarinta Suomessa: Rodullistaminen, valkoisuus ja koloniaalisuus Suomessa*, Helsinki: Gaudeamus, pp 147–61.

Sewpaul, V. (2010) 'Professionalism, postmodern ethics and the global standards for social work education and training', *Social Work [Maatskaplike Werk]*, 46(3).

Sewpaul, V. and Henrickson, M. (2019) 'The (r)evolution and decolonisation of social work ethics: the global social work statement of ethical principles', *International Social Work*, 62(6): 1469–81.

Sewpaul, V. and Hölscher, D. (2004) *Social Work in times of Neoliberalism: A Postmodern Discourse*, Hatfield: Va Schaik Publishers.

Sinclair, R. (2004) 'Aboriginal social work education in Canada: decolonising pedagogy for the seventh generation', *First Peoples Child and Family Review: A Journal on Innovation and Best Practices in Aboriginal Child Welfare Administration, Research, Policy and Practice*, 1(1): 49–61.

Soydan, H. and Palinkas, L.A. (2014) *Evidence-based Practice in Social Work: Development of a New Professional Culture*, London: Routledge.

Spektorowski, A. and Ireni-Saban, L. (2013) *Politics of Eugenics: Productionism, Population, and National Welfare*, London: Routledge.

Sudenkaarne, T. and Blell, M. (2021) 'Reproductive justice for the haunted Nordic welfare state: race, racism, and queer bioethics in Finland', *Bioethics*, 36(3): 328–35.

Suoranta, J. and Ryynänen, S. (2016) *Taisteleva tutkimus* (2nd edn), Helsinki: Into.

Tamale, S. (2020) *Decolonization and Afro-Feminism*, Ottawa: Daraja Press.

Tuhiwai Smith, L. (2021) *Decolonising Methodologies: Research and Indigenous Peoples*, London: Bloomsbury.

Urry, J. (2014) *What Is the Future?*, Cambridge: Polity.

Velez, E.D. and Tuana, N. (2020) 'Toward decolonial feminisms: tracing the lineages of decolonial thinking through Latin American/Latinx feminist philosophy', *Hypatia*, 35(3): 366–72.

Vuorela, U. (2009) 'Colonial complicity: the "postcolonial" in a Nordic context', in S. Keskinen, S. Tuori, S. Irni and D. Mulinari (eds) *Complying with Colonialism: Gender, Race, and Ethnicity in the Nordic Region*, Farnham: Ashgate, pp 19–33.

Wallerstein, I. (2004a) 'Cultures in conflict: who are we? Who are the others?', *Journal of the Interdisciplinary Crossroads*, 1(3): 505–21.

Wallerstein, I. M. (2004b) *World-systems Analysis: An Introduction*, Durham, NC: Duke University Press.

Waterfall, B.F. (2009) 'Decolonising Anishnabec social work education: an Anishnabe spiritually infused reflexive study', doctoral dissertation, University of Toronto, Library and Archives Canada, Bibliothèque et Archives Canada, Ottawa.

Waziyatawin, A.W. and Yellow Bird, M. (2005) *For Indigenous Eyes Only: A Decolonisation Handbook*, Santa Fe: School of American Research.

Wright, K., Carr, K.A. and Akkin, B.A. (2021) 'Whitewashing of social work history: how dismantling racism in social work education begins with an equitable history of the profession', *Advances in Social Work*, 21(2/3): 274–97.

WSOY (2010) *Metkat menopelit*, from French original *Mes Transports à Toucher* (Éditions Milan, 2009) translated into Finnish by E. Melasuo, Helsinki: WSOY.

Yellow Bird, M.J. and Chenault, V. (1999) 'The role of social work in advancing the practice of Indigenous education: obstacles and promises in empowerment-oriented social work practice', in K.G. Swisher and J. Tippeconnic (eds) *Next Steps: Research and Practice to Advance Indian Education*, Charleston, WV: ERIC Publications, pp 201–35.

PART I

Exploring coloniality in the Finnish social work field

1

Between a rock and hard place: discussing Sámi issues in contemporary Finland – a conversation with Ánneristen Juuso

Ánneristen Juuso (Anni-Kristiina Juuso)

Here the editors, Kris Clarke and Satu Ranta-Tyrkkö, discuss how colonialism has long been erased in Finland with Ánneristen Juuso (Anni-Kristiina Juuso). Leece Lee-Oliver sent Ánneristen questions, which she answered in writing. We have included Leece's questions with the conversation to better integrate the themes of the text.

We open this book by acknowledging the original Indigenous inhabitants of northern Finland. The Indigenous Sámi reside in Sápmi as one people that stretch across four countries: Norway, Sweden, Finland and Russia (Kola Peninsula). The total population of Sámi is 100,000, with approximately 10,000 Sámi resident in Finland. The Sámi are the only Indigenous people in the European Union. While this book is not grounded in Indigenous Sámi histories, perspectives and world views, our point of departure is that the themes of erasure and coloniality, which are developed in this book, have deep roots in the Finnish nation-building history that emerge from the long history of coexistence with Sámi peoples.

Finland is often depicted through the geographical imaginary as a maiden, with the north being the head and right arm (the other arm was lost in the Second World War to then Soviet Union), the middle being the waist, and with southern Finland being covered by the maiden's skirt. The figure of the maiden has been a recurrent presence in Finnish art and literature reinforcing the notion of Finnishness as Whiteness and purity. The allegory of the maiden, who is almost always portrayed as young, pale and blonde, has been used throughout Finnish history as a nation-building exercise. The problematic use of this image, infused as it is with historically misogynist and racist ideologies, also maintains exclusionary views of belonging rooted in territory.

The following discussion took place online in February 2023. Ánneristen participated from her home in north-western Finland; Satu and Kris joined from their homes in southern Finland, some 1,000 km south of Ánneristen's place. Leece Lee-Oliver sent questions from her home in the territories of the Yokuts and Mono people in what is now called the San Joaquín Valley of California. The conversation illuminates the layers of Finnish society while exploring how one Sámi person's lived experience reflects the challenges to Indigenous sovereignty and self-determination as they are impacted by the Finnish governmental system and social ideologies framed by coloniality.

The interview offers a deep historical and contemporary analysis of the deracination of Sámi peoples and the intentional and strategic formation of a hegemonic Finnish national identity, a process that renders Indigenous rights and knowledge invisible. The phenomena of Finnish coloniality, and its denial, sets the context for othering immigrants and refugees who also face erasure, othering and enforced dependency.

Ánneristen: You know the map of Finland and the one arm that Finland has? I live here in the arm. And I need to emphasise that I am not a spokesperson for all the Sámi. I can only speak on behalf of myself. In the case of Indigenous peoples, it is often assumed that one person speaks on behalf of everybody, but we are not any different than others in that regard because we are all individuals and as a people, very heterogeneous. This is why one Indigenous individual's voice is not the 'all of us' voice.

Kris: I remember what really struck me when I spent some time up in Enontekiö (one of the northernmost municipalities in Finland and part of Sápmi) was the landscape and the ways people were living in it. I'm just wondering if you'd like to speak to that.

Ánneristen: To answer your question, you have to put yourself in the context of today and also in history. I come from a Sámi reindeer herding family; and as far back as we can track and know our history, every one of us has been reindeer-herding Sámi: all of my ancestors, my whole family. About the Sámi people, we like to say that we are one people in four different countries. But actually, we are focused on the area where we live: our reindeer, our territories, our winter and summer pastures, our history and family. So in a way, speaking about one people in four different countries is ... a mantra because the reality is much more colourful and complex. We, the Sámi, have been coping and managing to survive throughout our history. So that's why our alliance is local in a way. The Karesuando area, which is on both sides of the river on the border of Sweden and Finland, is the place where I'm at home, where my family comes from, where my history comes from, where I get my identity, my language, my way of thinking of life. For me as a member of a Sámi reindeer-herding family and, of course, through the reindeer as animals and the connection with nature, the connection with the land is essential. For example, I don't know anybody here who likes wintertime – it's snow-filled, dark and cold. Whereas people in Helsinki always marvel that "oh, you have snow!" But nobody in my big Sámi family likes winter and snow and darkness because it's all about reindeer, about their survival. Wintertime is not easy for people. Even if reindeer are Arctic animals and evolved to cope with the cold, they struggle with over a metre of snow cover or frozen ground. Nowadays, with climate change, the winters are not like they used to be. At its worst it can be a struggle for eight months. Because it's so long, wintertime is also a kind of a mental struggle with nature, with the climate and with weather. So, there's nothing nice with snow and winter.

Kris: So, how has the struggle changed with climate change?

Ánneristen: It's not so easy to say exactly how the climate has changed because it varies from winter to winter, from year to year, from summer to summer. The Sámi people have lived with nature, by nature and in connection with nature. We have read the signs of nature like how winter's going to be, when the snow is going to melt. Nowadays, those old signs that we have used to read are hardly legible anymore. The winters have become windier, and they've gotten longer than before. Before, we had winter from October to April, then the snow melted and we had summer, and it was warm and not so rainy. Now the first snow can come already in September. Then it can melt and rain. Then it snows again. Back and forth with snowing and then melting. It can freeze the ground if it doesn't dry properly in between these changes of weather. And we have hard winds nowadays, all year around. These are all the signs of climate change. But not only weather changes, climate change impacts on the vegetation, biota and nature in full and we see the impacts here in the north already – everything is connected.

Kris: But you also said that it's always been a history of coping, so how did people cope through centuries?

Ánneristen: Well, it has been, I suppose, for all Indigenous peoples, all about coping and surviving. We are peoples living with and from nature. Like the elders say, we have not had any schools; everything we've learned, we've learned by doing it. Like self-made people, huh? So, it's coping because you have to when living with and by nature and being dependent on it. There's nobody you can ask. You don't find a book about how to do things and so on. Of course, nowadays, the young Sámi reindeer herders have access to all the knowledge of everybody else. They have their snowmobiles, ATVs and the internet. The world has changed and we're changing. Our way of thinking has also changed. I've been thinking that the trouble with decolonising and resisting colonial things is that we have grown up with these modern things, so we hardly recognise them as distinct from us anymore. We are so tied with modernisation. And modern structures go hand-in-hand with various kinds of colonising structures. A conceptual question is: what does it mean for an Indigenous people to modernise? To survive is also to modernise, and we perhaps would not survive without changing with the world.

Kris: It's sort of about how past and present structures of colonialism are intertwined with what knowledge is considered relevant. Do you have any thoughts about this?

Ánneristen: It's a tricky question, isn't it? I don't like the word decolonise, decolonisation or decolonised, because in my opinion, decolonisation is not possible anymore. We are colonised. Colonisation is so deep in the structures, and it's already hit the Indigenous peoples. They've been colonised so that they don't even recognise that they've changed their way of thinking and living. They've lost the connection with the Sun Our Father and the Earth Our Mother as our earlier generations still had a genuine connection. How do you decolonise if the connection is gone?

We have lost a great deal of the connection with nature because the whole world has modernised and industrialised rapidly. Of course, the Sámi, I suppose, have maintained some secret of survival because we are coping, we have survived somehow. But nowadays, the younger generations live their life as modern Sámis. They live in the modern world. They can do whatever they want. They may not know our history. But without knowing our ancestors' history, our family's history, the connection with our roots is somehow not that tight or honest anymore. I received a question about Sámi peoples' future: Is it bright or is it dark? In my brutally honest opinion, the Sámi way of being that I hold dear to my heart … we've lost the game. The future is not going to be that bright. While the language in general will survive somehow, the Sámi language that originates from nature, what if nobody knows nature? If a Sámi doesn't know nature, then the Sámi language disappears and becomes the 'new' Sámi language. For example, the youngsters don't know the traditional Sámi reindeer-herding words or the words connected with nature, mountains or rivers because they've not used those words. They've been to the mountains briefly for a day to ride snowmobiles, or ATVs in the summertime, and then back home to play video games or use social media. So, they are lacking the connection. The Sámi-ness that I hold dear is going to be less and less and then it's only going to be a memory. Well, this also belongs to life: people, they come and go as waves in the sea. It's ok, it's part of life.

Leece: Could you reflect more on Finnish institutions and services for Sámi peoples? Do the Sámi have access to any culturally appropriate forms of social work support?

Ánneristen: In the Constitution of Finland (section 17, subsection 3), the Sámi people are recognised as Indigenous people having the right to develop and maintain their own language and culture as well as the right to use the Sámi language before the authorities. As stipulated in section 121, subsection 4 of the Constitution, the Sámi have cultural and linguistic self-government in their own home area, which is defined as the three northernmost municipalities, Enontekiö, Utsjoki and Inari, along with the northernmost part of Sodankylä municipality. The

Sámi parliament is the official representative institution of the Sámi people in Finland. The status that the Sámi are given in the Constitution obliges and enables the Sámi to receive social services in their own language and in a culturally appropriate manner. Even if the authorities have an obligation to provide social services in the Sámi language, in the Sámi home area it is the self-governing body of the Sámi parliament that is the key actor to ensure that the authorities realise and develop social services in the Sámi language and culture. However, this is easier said than done. There aren't so many social workers that are native Sámi or even fluent Sámi speakers. So, social work with the Sámi mainly follows the mainstream. And the Sámi are so accustomed to using Finnish when dealing with the authorities that even if there is right to use the Sámi language, most of us use Finnish when receiving services. I'd say, overall, using social services can be, or has been, difficult for the Sámi because we are used to dealing with things among our family and relatives, coping and surviving instead of seeking help from outside. It is interesting that the Social Insurance Institution of Finland (KELA) offers their home page and all the information about their services in Finland in the spoken Sámi languages. I should point out that there are three official Sámi languages spoken in Finland: Northern Sámi, Inari Sámi and Skolt Sámi. What often happens is that written Sámi is hard to understand because it can be so rigid, like a direct translation from another language, a bureaucratic language no one understands. This does not mean that the language on KELA's home page is not good Sámi in general. KELA and the Sámi parliament have tried to motivate the Sámi to use their own language when dealing with KELA. Furthermore, KELA has been told that they are responsible for providing services in a culturally appropriate way for the Sámi. But KELA does this by arguing that if you don't use the language, we don't provide the services in your language. So, now it seems that it is a requirement to use Sámi if you are a Sámi to ensure that the authorities will live up to the Constitution. It's so funny! Nothing comes without obligations it seems. Yet, the history of using Finnish by the authorities is as long as the independence of Finland

	in 1917, so even if we'd love to use our mother tongue every time everywhere, it is hard to change old habits. It's quite the dilemma there.
Leece:	Do they do extractive things like removing children from Sámi families?
Ánneristen:	When needed, Sámi children are removed from their families like any children in need of protection. But no, in Finland, there is no such thing, nor has there ever been, that the Sámi children are deliberately being removed from their Sámi families as some other Indigenous peoples have faced. I've understood that if a Sámi child is removed, the authorities try to place the child with another Sámi family or not that far to ensure that the child can speak their own language. But then again, I've also heard of cases where a child has been placed far away with no possibility to speak Sámi or maintain the connection with the Sámi relatives and life. My understanding is that it depends a lot on the social workers, and how they themselves understand the needs and rights of the Sámi people as an Indigenous people. And it is also up to the Sámi social work service users who must demand the services in Sámi language.
Leece:	Have there been state-mandated treatments of Sami communities via the social work system?
Ánneristen:	As far as I understand the question, no, there have not been state-mandated treatments of Sámi communities. All in all, equality is important in Finland and the Sámi have been treated, and still are, as any other group residing in Finland. We have no special or exclusive rights, for better or worse, in Finland, as Sámi people.
Kris:	Is there a movement aimed at language revitalisation?
Ánneristen:	We have a strong language here. So, everybody here in Karesuando, all the old and the young Sámi, we speak Sámi as our mother tongue, so we've never had the problem of losing our language. But it's a different thing in many other Sámi areas; for example, the eastern parts of Northern Finland or in cities. For those who lost the language in the boarding schools or their children and grandchildren, revitalising the language is often important. But I don't know that much about that because here in this area where I come from, we've never had that problem. I've spoken with my father and my uncles and others who have been in the

boarding schools, asking them why they didn't lose their language in the boarding schools, like so many Sámi in Finland did. My father and relatives replied that "well, if somebody said, 'don't speak', we did not understand it. We were sisters, and brothers, and cousins. We had a tight community." The schools were no match for the people here. Even when they went to school, they lived a nomad life, migrating with the reindeer. Coming from big families that were living next to each other, they kept their community and a very strong Sámi identity during their time at boarding school. They think it was the main factor in keeping the language and Sámi identity.

Satu: When did this boarding school system end? Was it in the 1970s? How was your schooling history?

Ánneristen: It was something like from the 1940s to the 1960s or1970s. I started my education in 1986 and went to school in the Inari municipality. My parents lived in the Inari municipality when I was little, and it appeared that the Inari municipality didn't have Sámi people. They were nowhere to be found. I have understood that the boarding schools impacted this 'vanishing of the Sámi' in the Inari municipality because it was not appropriate to be a Sámi publicly. Only my father and me were, or so it seemed. When I started my school, I didn't go to boarding school. I went to school and then returned back home. Nothing was taught in Sámi language except when the other children went to their Finnish mother-tongue class and I went to study Sámi as my mother tongue. There was only me and I had a teacher from Utsjoki municipality. But even if she and I had the same Sámi language (Northern Sámi), the dialects differed dramatically. So, it was a constant fight for me as a young girl against a teacher from Utsjoki who tried to get me to speak a totally alien-sounding language. In my family we speak the Sámi language – it has always been a very normal thing. There's nothing exotic about it.

Kris: But you felt this connection you talked about? Do you think the young people nowadays do not have that connection or do they have a different sense of Sámi-ness?

Ánneristen: It is not only about feeling the connection, but also living in connection. I have been fortunate to have the opportunity to live in connection with nature, reindeer, the past and ancestors, and learn from my father and with my father and other relatives. The Sámi have always been coached to modernise and maybe that's also a way of coping. You know, I think I'm very old fashioned in my thinking because I hold so very much dear those old traditions that I've gotten from my father, my uncles, my family. I hold them very dear. What being a Sámi is for others, I cannot say.

Kris: You bring up the diversity of Sámi identities as well.

Ánneristen: I'd say there's a huge difference in identities, and ways of thinking: Where do you come from? What's the history of your family and the history of the area that you come from? There are huge, huge differences. For example, we nowadays have this Sámi National Day, on 6 February. But I'm like, wow, why do we need it? While for some others the day is about waving the flag and partying, our day! For me, again, in my mind, every day is our day; we don't need just one day to show who we are. We don't even have to show who we are; we just are and we do. Because I live in this area, our way of thinking is a bit opposite to the thinking of some Sámi. For us, the elders here say that before, nobody spoke about rights, and we had it good here in Finland. But nowadays, when it's all about rights, then all of a sudden, there's the feeling that even our existence is questioned. This is not only in Finland but also in Sweden and Norway. Especially in Finland, it feels like we need to prove our Sámi-ness through DNA tests. There's always demands to prove our authenticity, while all these politics around whether we exist or not, have rights or not, is very exhausting to me.

Satu: But is this sort of an outcome of the political struggle because the Sámi are really like a minority whose issues should be acknowledged? So, the political process kind of forces some sort of uniformity from the Sámi, which is then artificial because, of course, there are many kinds of experiences, points of view, personalities and so on. This conformity doesn't do justice to individual life histories and perspectives.

Ánneristen: Exactly, that's the politics. The thing that I've noticed is that if you meet one of us, you think that OK, she or he speaks on behalf of them all. But forget about it!

Satu:	We only can speak on behalf of ourselves and maybe on behalf of our own communities.
	And that's a common story from elsewhere too. When something has happened and the suffering of a certain group of people should be acknowledged, it kind of pushes people to repeat a similar narrative – it distils it all down.
Kris:	I'm foreign and kind of ignorant about this, but what has actually been done in Finland in terms of trying to do to understand the legacy of colonialism?
Ánneristen:	Nothing. Indigenous people don't concern Finland. Finland is not a colonial state, so they say. The word colonial and colonialism doesn't suit Finland because in Finnish people's minds, the Finns are not colonisers because they have been under Sweden and under Russia. And it seems they fear that Finland's sovereignty is still threatened. In my opinion, it's about the Finns and Finland lacking self-identity, self-esteem. I'm afraid it will take another hundred years of independence before Finland is ready to accept others than Finns.
Satu:	This discussion has been going on for some time and is something that this book also tries to open up: how Finland is actually a kind of colonial place and signed up for the colonial world view early on. Although some of the chapters in this book stem from personal experiences, what is repeated in various chapters are narratives of various forms of structural oppression that people who don't fit into mainstream norms have to confront to live with on a daily basis. One question I wanted to ask you has to do with the sense of loss, as there are certain things in Sámi culture that are lost forever, and also anger, which is highly justified, maybe also with lots of sorrow infused in it. I fear that maybe Finnish society is not quite capable of dealing with this anger … but I would say, being from southern Finland, there's also ambiguity, like how to sit with this anger and sorrow? Maybe the response is often just trying to explain it away?
Ánneristen:	In Finland, there's also this lack of knowledge about the Sámi. We are here, but we are not. We pop up every now and then. Recently, during the last couple of months, we've been popping up quite a lot in Finnish newspapers. And after this, again there's silence. Over

and out, done with the Sámi again. And then we pop up again. And in the schools, they don't teach about us. You know, it's this enormous lack of knowledge about us as our own people, and not as just a small language group, because in Finland we are often considered merely a linguistic minority group. In Sweden and Norway, the Sámi are understood to be their own people. Of course, they are also Swedes or Norwegians, but they are their own people, an Indigenous people. I don't understand why here in Finland this is the hardest part for the Finns to understand. We are our own people with our own language, history, culture, future and past. About anger and being angry, I don't consider the Sámi as angry about anything, only sad that it has been and still is such a difficult thing for Finland to let the Sámi exist as Sámis in Finland.

Satu: There's also this kind of strange bias in Finnish culture regarding which Indigenous people we learn about. My boys, for example, are being taught at school about Indigenous peoples in North America. The presence of these Indigenous people has a strong niche in Finnish popular culture.

Kris: That was very striking to me when I came to Finland in 1985. Many Finnish people were fascinated by large tribal nations in the North American prairies. There were images of buffalo and Tex Willer cowboy novels at the petrol station. It was really strange to me that Finnish people really loved that stuff. And I remember seeing representations of Sámi people in comedy sketches. I couldn't get any of the cultural references, but you could still get the vibe that this isn't really nice humour.

Ánneristen: I know, I watched it when I was a young girl, and it was OK. We laughed. We were so used to it that it wasn´t a big deal that we were shown as dirty and drunken on Finnish TV. How we were represented, even if just in comedy sketches, was not kind. But what do you do? Has Finland changed since the 1980s? Not that much. There is a lot of racism in Finland, also towards the Sámi people. But it is not recognised as racism when it is towards the Sámis. This is a serious matter that should be addressed but no one in Finland seems to recognise that racism also concerns the Sámi people and it is not OK. Or they don't care – I mean the ones holding the

	power. For me, acceptance is important: that the Finns and Finland would accept us, the Sámi as we are, our own people. We are not a minority, a language minority and our language is not just some Finnish dialect. We are our own distinct people, Indigenous people with the similar right to exist as any people in the world. We don't want to be forcibly assimilated into Finns, Swedes, Norwegians or Russians.
Satu:	Do you think that the affinity between Finnish and Sámi languages contributes to the fact that the Sámi are not easily recognised as a people of their own? Does it play any role that reindeer herding is not exclusively a Sámi livelihood in Finland, whereas in Sweden it is?
Ánneristen:	Yes, I think it plays a role, but these are not the only factors. I assume that Finland's own history plays a big role. In Finland we have nothing left. Everything's been taken away, symbolically or concretely. The only thing that cannot be taken away is our feelings. In Sweden and Norway, reindeer herding is only for the Sámi people, and I think it plays a big role in this political discussion. Even in Finland, when the Finns hear about reindeer, they think of Sámi, seeing them as interconnected. But Finns cannot connect Sámi and reindeer because the majority of the reindeer herders in Finland are something other than Sámi. Traditional Sámi reindeer herding is not even recognised in Finland, not in any law, not even in everyday speech.
Kris:	So, there's no special protection like the EU has for making Parmesan cheese or champagne?
Ánneristen:	No, not for reindeer herding, nothing. And Parmesan and champagne are different things than an Indigenous people's livelihood, life, tradition and cultural heritage. Protocol 3 of Finland's and Sweden's accession convention to the EU stipulates that reindeer herding could be reserved only for Sámi, in Finland as well. But it's never going to happen. I don't believe Finland will ever even consider stipulating reindeer herding as a livelihood only for the Sámi because throughout Finland's independence this has been open to anyone who wants to be a reindeer herder. And because reindeer herding is open to everybody in Finland, the legislation, rules and protocols follow the majority's way of doing things. Mainstream practices of reindeer herding differ

	from the traditional Sámi ways of doing and thinking. For the Sámi, reindeer herding is not only a livelihood, it is everything, it is life, the past, the present, the future, the legacy, the air we breathe. When you have to follow the majority's ways, it changes, it colonises our minds without us even noticing it. It violates our cultural integrity.
Kris:	It sounds like this normative idea of equality for everyone. We're all the same. And it doesn't allow you to be who you are because we're all kind of like chugging along in this modernist system.
Ánneristen:	That's why, in my opinion, in Finland, the real Sámi will become history quite quickly.
Kris:	That's really interesting because a common theme in this book is that this normative idea of equality doesn't really fit everybody's needs because, of course, we're all quite different. It's complicated because being from North America, I value the welfare state. But then, on the other hand, there are certain things – for example, this trying to make everyone equal the same way – that seems problematic.
Satu:	And that's the obstacle for Sámi. It's not only about reindeer herding in northern Finland, especially when it has been going on like this for quite some time, so it's very difficult to take that back. In the beginning you were saying that for you, being Sámi is tied to the location where you come from and the land over there. Could you still tell us something about the importance of the land? Somehow, I think that who gets to decide about land rights is a crucial issue, especially when there are so many different kinds of interests, especially in regards to resources.
Ánneristen:	From where I come from, our goal is not owning. For us, it's not about owning land – we don't want to own anything because land is not to be owned. But I do know that owning property, owning the land is important. In Utsjoki municipality in the east, for example, they have another way of thinking, and they talk about owning the land. For us here, it's not about owning, it's about life. The very foundations of existing and existence are land. It's crucial to have access to land because the reindeer need it for grazing. And we need access to land because we are one and the same with the animals and the land.

Satu:	But is it just about states?
Ánneristen:	The nation-states of Finland, Sweden and Norway claim to own the land. This is the land of nation-states. This land is crucial for them because it holds all the natural resources. They want the gas, the oil, the diamonds. When they are all taken away, then we, the Sámi, are free because our land will have no value for the nation-states anymore. Sadly, maybe not even to us because without access to land we will not survive as our own people. That's the reality that we live in. Now, the only thing that we can do is try to negotiate, try to be heard. We have to fight for our rights first locally, then nationally, then internationally and hope for the best. Cope and survive until the end.
Kris:	What needs to happen?
Ánneristen:	What needs to happen is a structural change. Those belonging to the majority need to understand that there is a social connection between generations, a chain of structural racism and oppression that needs to be tackled to gain any real structural change. The individuals belonging to the majority need first to understand that there is this chain; second, understand that they themselves are linked in this chain; third, understand that only by breaking this chain can a change for better happen; and fourth, understand that they need to break the chain even though they themselves have not been the wrongdoers, but rather ancestors from previous generations. It is difficult to see these societal structures, and this is why I don't know if real structural change for the better will ever happen.

2

Welfare state nationalism, family reunification and forced migrants' strategies to surpass structural violence

Camilla Nordberg, Joa Hiitola, Hanna Kara and Maija Jäppinen

Introduction

This chapter investigates the consequences of the administrative restrictions imposed on family reunification processes in contemporary Finland. We shed light on the Finnish context by drawing on the notion of *welfare state nationalism*, which has been coined in the aftermath of two decades of economic crises and increasing humanitarian migration to the Global North. The notion of welfare state nationalism has been conceptualised in contemporary scholarly debates (compare Kuisma, 2007; Mulinari et al, 2009; Suszycki, 2011; Bauböck, 2016; Jørgensen and Thomsen, 2016; Keskinen, 2016; Jönsson and Kojan, 2017). Here, we refer to it in a rather broad manner as a view that suggests that welfare state benefits and/or residence should be reserved only for the 'deserving' excluding those who are not seen as productive citizens; namely, people like migrants applying for asylum and their family members.

Neoliberal transformations of welfare systems have emphasised that the productivity of nation-state residents is the key logic of welfare policies giving rise to new forms of intersectional vulnerability regimes along lines that include, for example, ethnic background, gender, class, age and disability (Nordberg, 2015; Turtiainen et al, 2020; Wrede et al, 2021). In the Nordic countries, the ideal of the respectable citizen has been built on a strong ethos of paid work, and self-sufficiency has been central to the project of the nation-state. However, in recent decades there has been a shift from structural policy measures to individualist activation policies (Berg and Peltola, 2015; Nordberg, 2018), limiting the role of the state in securing social justice and social equality (Kamali and Jönsson, 2018). This has been particularly detrimental to those categories of people who face structural disadvantage in the paid labour market due to different forms of discrimination and oppression (Ahmad, 2020).

Along with the structural transformations of the welfare state and a reconceptualisation of the state in relation to counteracting social disadvantage, nationalist populist policies have gained ground by targeting the political economy of migration. These policies often single out people with a migrant background, typically forced migrants from the Global South, as particularly unproductive and undeserving (Ketola and Nordensvard, 2018; Norocel et al, 2020; Lentin and Titley, 2011). In this way, certain categories of migrants have become the new scapegoats in the exclusionary process of nation-state building within which national belonging has always been conditional and based on different forms of cultural homogeneity and the subordination of racialised 'outsiders'. Such neoliberal and nationalist politics increasingly define state interventions and the ensuing welfare administrative practices in various ways, giving rise to systemic injustice that can be understood as *structural violence* (compare Galtung, 1969; Artero and Fontanari, 2021; also Leinonen and Pellander, 2020).

The chapter starts with an overview of the processes that inform the current welfare state nationalist policy environment. We then draw from recent empirical data to discuss how this environment constrains social justice for forced migrants in the context of family reunification and creates structural violence. Our data consist of interviews with forced migrants and social workers, as well as observations conducted in service meetings at social service agencies in the Helsinki metropolitan region. We discuss cases constructed from several different families' stories which shed light on the consequences of structural barriers that impact family dynamics, welfare service provision and immigration policy.

Transformation of the welfare state and tightening family migration policies

The welfare state is the project of nation-states and has its roots in 19th- and early 20th-century social policies. 'Society' was increasingly recognised as a source of large-scale tensions and social problems that called for and legitimised state intervention in private and family matters. In the Nordic countries, during the early years of nation-state and later construction of the welfare state, 'unruly' categories of citizens such as historical minorities, people in poverty and disabled citizens were the main targets of harsh assimilation and even elimination policies (Häkkinen and Tervonen, 2005; Nordberg, 2007; Keskinen et al, 2019).

Despite often being presented as a forerunner in equality politics, Finnish attitudes towards migration have been harsh (Keskinen, 2016; Ketola and Nordensvard, 2018). The historical trajectory of late modernisation and industrialisation, a strong agrarian influence and the unification of Church and state have all contributed to a strong communitarian understanding of belonging to one religion and one nation, resulting in a weaker influence of social democracy and solidarity than in neighbouring countries (Anttonen, 1998; Nordberg, 2007; Kettunen, 2011). Finland has a complex history of coloniality. Despite an imaginary of 'White innocence' reflecting Nordic ideas of exceptionalism, the country has had a problematic relationship with its 'othered racialised insiders' (Keskinen et al, 2019, *the Introduction to this volume*). While in early welfare state history, Indigenous Sámi people and historical minorities such as the Roma were the main targets of forced cultural assimilation and territorial exclusion, increasing transnational mobility has generated new social categories perceived as less valuable than an imagined culturally and racially homogeneous mainstream Finnish nation (Keskinen et al, 2019; Lehtola, 2021).

In Europe broadly, as well as in the Nordic welfare states specifically, the last decade has been one of increasingly tightening family migration policies. The basic human right to family life now must be earned and deserved, as family migration has gradually become more conditional (Borevi, 2015; Cochran Bech et al, 2017). In Finland, several concrete legislative changes have been introduced since 2010, including new application submission rules, income requirements and processing fees. The arrival of a larger number of asylum seekers in 2015 intensified these amendments. In 2016, income requirements were expanded to also concern forced migrants who had received status of subsidiary protection and applicants who were minors.[1] Applicants who had been granted asylum were exempted from the income requirements, but only for a period of three months. Family reunification had subsequently become extremely difficult, even impossible, for many forced migrants residing in Finland.

Our interest in the increasingly restrictive policies of family migration is rooted in research on family separation which often concludes that separation has long-lasting effects on the well-being and settlement of forced migrants (see Rousseau et al, 2004; Nickerson et al, 2010; Strik, de Hart and Nissen, 2013; Eggebø and Brekke, 2019). We subsequently investigate how structural barriers to family life manifest at different stages of the family reunification process, how forced migrants combat these barriers and how welfare service structures and actors assist or hinder these personal processes (see also Hiitola, 2019; Näre, 2020). We show how, although facing immense adversities, some of our informants can develop new strategies to support the lives of their transnational family as well as their own well-being. However, we also discuss situations where restricted family reunification policies have caused severe suffering.

Data and methods

The data in this chapter consist of observations and interviews conducted in two research projects funded by the Academy of Finland: 'Family Separation,

Migration Status and Everyday Security' and 'Ordering the "Migrant Family": Power Asymmetry Work and Citizenisation in Restructuring Welfare Professional Bureaucracies'. The first project's data set was produced in 2018–20 and includes 45 group and individual interviews with 55 migrants (18 men and 37 women) who had all received residency in the asylum process and had lived in Finland for periods ranging from less than a year to eight years. Sixteen interviewees had arrived in Finland as unaccompanied minors and were attempting to reunite with their parents and siblings.

The second data set was produced in four social work agencies in the Helsinki capital region in 2018–20. Two of the agencies were immigrant services which provide services for newly arrived persons during the approximately three-year period of 'integration', the third is an adult social work agency and the fourth provides community-based child welfare services. The data consist of observations of street-level encounters between welfare professionals and migrant service users (n=39), short reflective discussions with professionals after the observed encounters (n=31) and interviews with both service users and professionals (n=51).

The authors had joint meetings to discuss the data from the point of view of family reunification processes and different points of administrative and bureaucratic encounters during these processes. After this, authors two, three and four carried out close readings on different parts of the data, and all authors discussed together the empirical findings. In this analysis process, three main 'stories' were recognised: first, one of constant administrative obstacles; second, one of a proceeding process; and, third, one of a prolonged and unaddressed hope. In the following, we present and describe these three cases which serve as concrete illustrations of current practices and the research participants' navigation within the administrative borders of family reunification policies. The quotes presented in the text have been either transcribed directly to English from their original language or translated from Finnish transcriptions to English by the authors. All names are pseudonyms and details have been anonymised to protect the participants' identities. Some quotations have been edited to enhance readability.

Administrative obstacles in the early family reunification application process

In this first empirical section, we discuss the experience of family reunification of 'Fadi', his wife 'Amina' and their three children. The case is mainly constructed from three interviews with Fadi's family: the first two interviews with Fadi alone during the family reunification application process and the third interview with the whole family after reunification. Some details have been taken from other similar cases to better illustrate the administrative barriers and to ensure anonymity.

Fadi left his country of origin due to a personal threat in early 2015 and arrived in Finland that summer. The journey was extremely dangerous and thus Fadi's spouse, Amina, and their three children moved in with Amina's parents while Fadi attempted to secure residency in Europe. After nearly one year of waiting in Finland, Fadi received good news about his asylum claim; he acquired a residence permit based on *subsidiary protection*. Although his claim had been based on a personal threat, he did not received residency based on asylum. Fadi wanted to appeal this decision (to change it to asylum) but his lawyer advised him not to. The lawyer explained that subsidiary protection includes the right of family reunification and there is not need to appeal the decision. Fadi's asylum decision came during the spring of 2016. Little did he know that the legislation concerning income requirements would be changed on 1 July 2016, while Fadi was preparing for the reunification process of his family.

When the news about Fadi's asylum decision reached his family, they rejoiced. The children were taken out of school for the waiting period as the personal threat towards Fadi could also put his children in danger. After hearing about Fadi's successful asylum claim, they started to prepare for school in Finland by learning the Finnish language online. Although the family was already excited about their new life in Finland, Fadi faced challenges in arranging his family's travel for interviews and submitting the reunification application.

The family had to travel to the nearest designated Finnish embassy to first submit the application and later be interviewed. However, Fadi's family had difficulties acquiring a visa for legal travel. Consequently, Fadi had to rely on illegal measures and pay thousands of euros for a visa acquired from the black market for his family to access the designated embassy. Similar difficulties were described by several interviewees in Hiitola's (2019) study. For example, the designated embassy for Afghan interviewees was in India and Iraqi interviewees' families had to travel to Turkey. Travelling was impossible for many. Hence, the administrative practice designed to restrict irregular migratory movements actually ended up creating new barriers to safe and legal possibilities for asylum. In comparison with other Nordic countries, Finland has had the most restrictive policies for submitting applications (see Hiitola, 2019). Even though the situation has improved slightly, the policies still remain unclear and there are no comprehensive instructions on the Finnish Immigration Service website about these requirements or possible exceptions.

Fadi navigated the complex system and travelled to submit the application together with his family in 2016. To fund the application, travel and all the related costs he had borrowed money from several friends and relatives, taken on short-term loans and even purchased expensive mobile phones on credit and sold them for a cheaper price for quick cash. This left him severely indebted. The devastation after their family reunification application was rejected by the Finnish Immigration Service was all consuming. The grounds for rejection were that, according to the current legislation, Fadi was subject to the income requirement and thus should have a monthly income of 2,900 euros after taxes. This corresponds to around 4,000 euros of monthly income before taxes – a level above the average Finnish income. Fadi describes his state of shock in the first research interview:

> 'The suffering I passed through in Finland, never happened to me in my life, even when I lived in (a country). I prefer that I had died in (a country) rather than coming here and suffering. Do you know what happened? Once I was about to die alone at my apartment, I just didn't feel my head.'

Several events were set in motion from the rejection of Fadi's family's reunification application. His wife and two of his children were frequently moving houses and, meanwhile, Fadi struggled to find work in Finland. Fadi did find two jobs. He worked day and night to try to reach the required income, but his appeals proved to be unsuccessful. Fadi describes deep frustration with the administrative injustices:

> 'Now I feel that I am going crazy, especially when I visit the Immigration Service's website and I read what the conditions of the family reunification are. They have stated that people who received the residence permit before 1 July 2016 are excluded from the income requirement.'

While working, Fadi also arranged for his family to flee to a third country and rented a house for them during the appeal process. However, after having worked at the second job for just a few weeks, he received a decision on his appeal from the administrative court. He says: "I just wanted to get the first salary to attach my paycheck to the court, to show them that 'hey I have this job now'. But I didn't have the chance to let them know." A decision that took over a year to make, concurred with the Immigration Service and did not see grounds for Fadi's family's residency in Finland. He had to start an appeal process with the Supreme Administrative court, but the Supreme Administrative court refused to hear the case. Fadi's lawyer informed him of the decision:

> 'She informed me about it without having an interpreter via email, as I remember, and then she said that she would contact an interpreter to give me more details. When she called the interpreter, she said: "Sorry that you received a negative decision." I asked her: "What is the reason for the rejection?" She said: "The rejection has nothing to do with

your case but the request has been declined, because they take only seven per cent of the requests" … It hasn't been easy for me waiting for years and this delayed me for another three or four months.'

After applying and appealing for three years, Fadi now had to start the whole process from the beginning. His social worker was helpful, and he was able to use the online service which had been launched by the Finnish Immigration Service. However, his family's visas were about to expire in their current country of residence and his older daughter was turning 18, which could mean that she would not be included as a member of Fadi's immediate family anymore. Like most of the interviewees, Fadi explained that all of his children experienced symptoms of stress due to the extended waiting period. One of his daughters was especially suffering.

'Sometimes my daughter is having this situation; she goes to the bathroom and starts cutting her hair. I go crazy when I see that. Now she has very short hair like you (referring to the research assistant Ahmed). I would take her to the hairdresser, but she keeps doing this. Since the date of the rejection (of the application) and up to now, I have been to see them in (a country) three times. Each time I would stay for one month, because the situation of my family is miserable.'

Fadi and Amina's family's story is quite a typical story of administrative barriers that became violent when analysed from the perspectives of the family's everyday life. Finally, after three and a half years of the initial family reunification application, the family received a residence permit in the autumn of 2019. For Fadi, the legislative change in 2016 had set different processes in motion, none of which recognised Fadi's overall situation or took into account the plight of his children. The legislation itself does grant several possibilities for more lenient decision making, but these options are not utilised by the courts. Fadi's case was one among many similar stories, most of which included not just one but many injustices.

Family reunification as a proceeding process

In this section, we discuss the constructed case of 'Ammar', his wife 'Aisha' and their two children, assisted by their social worker 'Anni'. The case builds on five observations of service meetings in immigrant services with different service users in which their family reunification processes were discussed, and on the interviews with service users after these meetings. The case also draws from five interviews with social workers or social advisers in immigrant services who discussed their professional experiences of and roles in family reunification processes.

After receiving his residence permit, Ammar started the family reunification process to bring his wife and children to live with him in Finland. Due to his residence permit being based on asylum, he had three months during which he could submit the application and be exempt from the income requirement. Ammar was informed by social services that he carried the responsibility for the process which included financing it entirely, following it up, booking the necessary appointments and so forth. Social services would only assist Ammar to fill in the forms, as these were only available in Finnish, Swedish or English.

The application forms, filled in separately for each family member, were multi-page and had to be filled in carefully, and Ammar needed more than one appointment with Anni to complete the forms with the help of an interpreter. The process was stressful, as sometimes Ammar could not understand the questions or the logic behind them and was therefore unsure how to respond. Generally, Anni was unable or unwilling to assist in deciphering any difficult parts in the forms and emphasised that her support was merely technical:

> 'We really emphasise that we are not, at any point, the producers of information, of course, that it is only about helping to write down the answers in the form. So, if the service user says "I don't know" to a question, then we write "I don't know". You don't ... often service users might hope that, well, "maybe you can answer this, you know how to formulate this, or I don't understand what to answer here" ... And then, of course, we always try to say that if a question is difficult and you feel like you don't have an answer to it, then you put down "I don't have an answer to this".' (Anni)

After submitting the application, the advancement of the process and the situation of the family members were discussed at every meeting in immigrant services between Ammar and Anni. Anni inquired and advised Ammar on matters that might affect the process, such as sudden changes in the health or security circumstances of Aisha and the children, and reminded Ammar to inform the Finnish Immigration Service about any changes or offered to inform them on his behalf if he so preferred. Anni continued to emphasise, however, that she did not know about, and could not in any way influence, the actual processing of the application.

Anni (service meeting observation): So, the last time I called Finnish Immigration Service, they told me that they had not even started to process the application yet, even though it was submitted four months ago. But it's not unusual, as their processing time is nine months. But well, it's a bit difficult to

Ammar:	say, always, how much we could speed the process up. Of course, I can contact them, but I can't promise anything, at all, about what kind of effect it could have. Would you like me to send them some kind of message? I can of course do that, but … would you like me to put in a message? Yes, I would.
Anni:	Yes ok, so I'll send them an email. Whether or not it makes any difference, I can't promise you. But I can of course write to them and tell them about your situation. Would you like to tell me what you'd like me to put in the message? What would you like me to emphasise?

The waiting period was not easy for Ammar, Aisha and their children. The family lived in a third country where they submitted the application and were interviewed. Their situation was nonetheless continuously unclear and precarious, in terms of housing and finance, as well as support and care, as both Aisha and the children suffered from ill health. In Finland, Ammar struggled to offer as much emotional and material support and assistance to them as he possibly could. He was also able to travel to the third country on one occasion.

> 'There are so many concerns and so much fear. And so, Aisha needs someone to support her emotionally. But my possibilities are limited, I can't all the time talk to her and give her hope … And I worry, I worry … The process worries me a lot … And even now, I think about from where I should even get that money so that I could support her every month, that she would make a living somehow. So, even when I go to classes (Finnish language classes) here, so all the time my thoughts are there, and I can't focus.' (Ammar)

After one year and four months, Aisha and the children were reunited with Ammar in Finland. The family lived together in Ammar's one-bedroom apartment and began to settle in, learning to live together again and forming everyday routines as swiftly as possible. They were several thousand of euros in debt due to the family reunification process and struggled to pay their rent and stay afloat without developing rental debt which would in turn prevent them from applying for an apartment for a family of four. Ammar tried to deal with all the necessary arrangements but suffered from exhaustion and depression.

> 'There is the pressure, of course, that you are responsible for the family and you should take care of everything, and if you don't know how …

You cannot just put that (the ongoing family reunification application process) aside and integrate and learn the language and so on, it doesn't work like that ... that starts only when the family has arrived ... and families can develop severe debts ... so it's awkward to say that "you should use this allowance for the necessary furniture for the home". So yeah, you should, but still a year later when we go for a home visit, there's just a carpet on the floor.' (Anni)

This case highlights the lengthy, unpredictable and lonely nature of family reunification even as an ongoing process. Migrants are responsible for the process as both the financing and many practical arrangements are up to them. Practitioners in immigrant services accompany them, for example, by offering practical assistance in filling out the forms and by enquiring about the progress of the process. Yet, the practitioners often outsource themselves at a discursive level by emphasising that their assistance is merely technical and that the inquiries or statements made to the Finnish Immigration Service may not have any effect on the proceedings.

This account shows how family reunification processes cause suffering and prevent settlement. These processes also predispose the families involved to prolonged indebtedness and poverty. Even afterwards, the families continue to face severe challenges and a mismatch with the system, while at the same time they are expected to build a life in Finland: get settled, make their apartments comfortable for their families, learn a new language and find a job.

A prolonged hope for family reunification

In this last empirical section, we discuss the situation of 'Ferhat', who has lived in Finland without his family members since 2015. He still hopes to bring his elderly mother to Finland but does not know what to do, where to ask for help or whether there are realistic possibilities for family reunification.

Ferhat's case builds primarily on an observed service encounter in adult social services between him and social worker 'Minna', and on interviews with Ferhat and Minna after the encounter. Some details have been taken from other cases in the ethnographic data produced in adult social services and child welfare services to better illustrate different sides of situations with prolonged hope for family reunification but few opportunities to begin the process or receive help.

Ferhat arrived in Finland as an asylum seeker in 2015 and received a residence permit based on asylum. Ferhat has since received Finnish citizenship. He has studied in vocational training, earned a diploma and has good Finnish but has not found employment. He meets Minna in adult social services to discuss issues related to housing, employment, finances and health.

At the end of the meeting, Minna asks about Ferhat's leisure time and hobbies, and he starts to describe how missing family influences everything in his well-being.

> 'I like to go jogging sometimes, or ... Sports are always on my mind. But when you don't have a daily rhythm, you can't concentrate on it. And other things have an impact too, you know ... When you miss your family all the time. I have always hoped for a reunification. My mother is especially important (to me). Philosophers say that if a human being forgets his mother, he is not a human being anymore. This has always been on my mind.'

Minna continues asking about Ferhat's communication with his family members. Ferhat says that he is constantly worried about their safety and explains that he has tried to find information about applying for family reunification for four years already, but still does not know what to do and whether he should have a job to be able to apply.

Minna does not answer this question but moves forward to other topics. In the interview after the meeting, she explains why she did not want to continue with the theme. She says that she ignored the question on purpose because, in her understanding, it is impossible for an adult person living in Finland to get family reunification for his mother. She also justifies the change of topic with Ferhat's mental health condition: as she knows that Ferhat has suffered from depression, she did not want to continue with anything negative. In addition, she states that it is not in her expertise to give advice on these issues, and she would feel uncertain about how to do that.

Some days later, we continue discussing the family reunification issue with Ferhat in an interview. Ferhat explains that he knows family reunification is difficult, but he is still struggling to find a way. He says that during his first years in Finland, he could not think about anything else but the safety of his family members back home. He has tried to talk about the family reunification issue with social and healthcare professionals in several different agencies over the years, but still does not know the preconditions for bringing at least his elderly mother to Finland and keeps on trying.

Ferhat: I have talked about (family members and family reunification) with almost every employee (in social and healthcare services) I have met, but no one has been able to talk with me about it. I don't know, maybe they don't have the information or maybe they can't help with it ... But I hope something will be done at least, because this is really important to me. They are always on my mind.

Maija:	Do I understand right that although you have talked about your family and your hope for a family reunification, it does not really …
Ferhat:	The issue has not proceeded.
Maija:	It does not proceed?
Ferhat:	No, it melts like snow, which we have in winter, you know. It's only words.

Ferhat's example sheds light on how family reunification continues to be viewed as almost impossible under the current restrictive legislation. It seems that in social services targeted to the whole population, in which practitioners do not have special expertise in migration issues, this is the only thing that they 'know' about family reunifications. Thus, legislative requirements and their implications for family reunification are rarely properly explained to service users. Even though there is an understanding that family relations are crucial for service users and that the longing for family members influences their well-being on a daily basis, family reunification issues are seldom raised in social service encounters and remain unresolved.

More specifically, the way in which Ferhat's attempts to address the family reunification issue are repeatedly ignored reflects social services professionals' common understanding of the impossibility of family reunification for service users in adult social services. There are two main reasons for this. First, as a rule, a person who has migrated to Finland usually enters adult social services only after the deadline for making the application without an income requirement has passed. Second, typically at least one of the reasons for contacting adult social services is the need for economic support, which means that service users generally will not meet these income requirements.

Even though these practitioners conclude that assisting in family reunification issues is not part of their formal obligations and fields of expertise, street-level bureaucrats constitute the human face of the Finnish welfare state (Lipsky, 1980). This perception feeds the increasingly dominant imaginary of welfare state belonging as conditional to historical and cultural understandings of deservingness. In the midst of hopelessness, in Ferhat's case, an important point is that he has received Finnish citizenship and, thus, the income requirement no longer applies to him. But as long as Ferhat cannot find anyone to assist him in finding out the requirements and going through the procedures, he does not have the chance to even attempt family reunification.

Concluding remarks

We have created these cases from recent empirical research to show how in the family reunification processes of forced migrants, welfare state nationalist ideology materialises within administrative bordering practices that manifest for the migrants as structural violence. The cases can be thought of as demonstrating, first, a process with multiple adversities; second, a proceeding process; and, third, a process that is left completely unaddressed. In all of them, family reunification presented itself as arduous, uncertain and prolonged. People such as Ferhat, Fadi and Ammar are largely left alone to hopelessly navigate the bureaucracy. The empirical cases discussed here also reveal contradictory consequences of the existing restrictive policies; for example, in situations where administrative practices designed to restrict irregular migratory movements end up only creating new barriers for safe and legal possibilities for asylum. Furthermore, the examples show how the complicated, unpredictable and extended family reunification processes delay settlement for the migrants and their families involved and predispose them to mental health issues, troubles in family dynamics, indebtedness and poverty.

The cases previously discussed point to legal barriers to the right to family life, but importantly also to various formal and informal administrative barriers. The migrants' experiences of structural violence are reinforced by continuous changes in, and uncertainty of, legal and administrative practices that generate a prolonged state of insecurity and unpredictability. The examples illustrate how inadequate preparation of legislative changes and poor administration of these changes in practice produce structural violence that is not necessarily visible by merely analysing the legislation. This form of structural violence also increased as borders and embassies closed without adequate preparation during the COVID-19 restrictions. Moreover, while administrative barriers are located in bureaucratic policies and practices beyond the strictly legislative level, it becomes more difficult to identify the rationale behind these practices and the actors responsible for policies and practices that seem irrational and unjust (see also Artero and Fontanari, 2021).

The role of social workers proved to be limited, and at times even actively evaporated, and this arguably amplified the structural violence already caused by the legislative restrictions. Migrants that had existing contact with local social services agencies were often faced with limited assistance and advice for family reunification processes, contrary to counselling and support related to the productive spheres of the economy, such as work and education. This reflects an overall welfare policy environment in which, as a result of neoliberalisation, social exclusion has become narrowed to exclusion from paid work or self-employment (Schierup et al, 2006: 16–17). Concomitantly, the norm of employment is seen as a central criterion of the 'integration' of migrants (Davydova, 2012; Keskinen, 2016). The analysis shows how within the welfare nationalist policy frame asylum seekers are not seen as persons fleeing war, conflict or repression, nor are their family bonds and relations understood as important for 'integration' processes. That way, migrant settlement and 'integration' are approached as processes potentially resulting in a burden for the welfare state and public economy (compare Keskinen, 2016: 359).

The cases also showed how the inability of social workers and other social service professionals to effectively influence, or even be adequately informed of, the Finnish Immigration Service's decision-making processes limited their actions and, at times, made them reluctant to even touch upon these issues. This can be seen to reflect professional hierarchies within which the social work realm and mandate are seen as subordinate to immigration administration processes. In general, the cases underline a largely unquestioned understanding of family reunification processes as unintelligible and nearly impossible. Moreover, the analysis points to the troublesome dynamics of coloniality, racialisation and structural violence that materialise in normative structures of welfare policy and practice in the Finnish context and beyond (see also Introduction to this volume). The consequent helplessness of social workers in the face of migration regulations creates situations and practices that do not adhere to the ethical guidelines and principles of social work.

Note
[1] The Act was amended in 2022. The income requirement is no longer applicable to children under the age of 18 years old (https://www.finlex.fi/fi/laki/ajantasa/2004/20040301#L6P114).

References

Ahmad, A. (2020) 'When the name matters: an experimental investigation of ethnic discrimination in the Finnish labor market', *Sociological Inquiry*, 90(3): 468–96.

Anttonen, A. (1998) 'Vocabularities of citizenship and gender: Finland', *Critical Social Policy*, 18(3): 355–73.

Artero, M. and Fontanari, E. (2021) 'Obstructing lives: local borders and their structural violence in the asylum field of post-2015 Europe', *Journal of Ethnic and Migration Studies*, 47(3): 631–48.

Bauböck, S. (2016) 'Introduction to the special issue: "Solidarity in diverse societies: beyond neoliberal multiculturalism and welfare chauvinism": coping with "the progressive's dilemma"; nationhood, immigration and the welfare state', *Comparative Migration Studies*, 4(1): 1–7.

Berg, P. and Peltola, M. (2015) 'Raising decent citizens: on respectability, parenthood and drawing boundaries', *NORA-Nordic Journal of Feminist and Gender Research*, 23(1): 36–51.

Borevi, K. (2015) 'Family migration policies and politics: understanding the Swedish exception', *Journal of Family Issues*, 36(11): 1490–508.

Cohran Bech, E., Borevi, K. and Mouritsen, P. (2017) 'A "civic turn" in Scandinavian family migration policies? Comparing Denmark, Norway and Sweden', *Comparative Migration Studies*, 5(1): 1–24.

Davydova, O. (2012) 'Venäjän lännestä Suomen itään. Sukupuolittunut maahanmuutto ja haurastuneet työmarkkinat', in S. Keskinen, J. Vuori and A. Hirsiaho (eds) *Monikulttuurisuuden sukupuoli: kansalaisuus ja erot hyvinvointiyhteiskunnassa*, Tampere: Tampere University Press, pp 72–100.

Eggebø, H. and Brekke, J.-P. (2019) 'Family migration and integration: the need for a new research agenda', *Nordic Journal of Migration Research*, 9(4): 425–44.

Galtung, J. (1969) 'Violence, peace, peace research', *Journal of Peace Research*, 6(3): 167–91.

Häkkinen, A. and Tervonen, M. (2005) 'Johdanto: köyhyys, etnisyys ja etniset suhteet Suomessa 1900-luvulla [Introduction: ethnicity and marginalisation in twentieth-century Finland]', in A. Häkkinen, P. Pulma and M. Tervonen (eds) *Vieraat kulkijat – tutut talot: Näkökulmia etnisyyden ja köyhyyden historiaan Suomessa*, Helsinki: SKS, pp 7–36.

Hiitola, J. (2019) 'Locating forced migrants' resources: residency status and the process of family reunification in Finland', *Social Inclusion*, 7(4): 190–9.

Jönsson, J.H and Kojan, B.H. (2017) 'Social justice beyond neoliberal welfare nationalism: challenges of increasing immigration to Sweden and Norway', *Critical and Radical Social Work*, 5(3): 301–17.

Jørgensen, M. and Thomsen, T. (2016) 'Deservingness in the Danish context: welfare chauvinism in times of crisis', *Critical Social Policy*, 36(3): 330–51.

Kamali, M. and Jönsson, J.H. (eds) (2018) *Neoliberalism, Nordic Welfare States and Social Work: Current and Future Challenges*, London: Routledge.

Keskinen, S. (2016) 'From welfare nationalism to welfare chauvinism: economic rhetoric, welfare state and the changing policies of asylum in Finland', *Critical Social Policy*, 36(3): 352–70.

Keskinen, S.P., Skaptadottir, U.D. and Toivanen, M. (eds) (2019) *Undoing Homogeneity in the Nordic Region: Migration, Difference and the Politics of Solidarity*, London: Routledge.

Ketola, M. and Nordensvard, J. (2018) 'Reviewing the relationship between social policy and the contemporary populist radical right: welfare chauvinism, welfare nation state and social citizenship', *Journal of International and Comparative Social Policy*, 34(3): 172–87.

Kettunen, P. (2011) 'The transnational construction of national challenges: the ambiguous Nordic model of welfare and competitiveness', in P. Kettunen and K. Petersen (eds) *Beyond Welfare State Models: Transnational Historical Perspectives on Social Policy*, Cheltenham: Edward Edgar, pp 16–40.

Kuisma, M. (2007) 'Social democratic internationalism and the welfare state after the "Golden Age"', *Cooperation and Conflict*, 42(1): 9–26.

Lehtola, V.-P. (2021) 'Contested Sámi histories in Finland', in L. Junka-Aikio, J. Nyyssönen and V.-P. Lehtola (eds) *Sámi Research in Transition: Knowledge, Politics and Social Change*, New York: Routledge, pp 51–70.

Leinonen, J. and Pellander, S. (2020) 'Temporality and everyday (in)security in the lives of separated refugee families', in J. Hiitola, K. Turtiainen, S. Gruber and M. Tiilikainen (eds) *Family Life in Transition: Borders, Transnational Mobility and Welfare Society in the Nordic Countries*, London: Routledge, pp 118–28.

Lentin, A. and Titley, G. (2011) *The Crises of Multiculturalism: Racism in a Neoliberal Age*, New York: Zed Books.

Lipsky, M. (1980) *Street-level Bureaucracy: Dilemmas of the Individual in Public Services*, New York: Russell Sage Foundation.

Mulinari, D., Keskinen, S., Irni, S. and Tuori, S. (2009) 'Introduction: postcolonialism and the Nordic models of welfare and gender', in S .Keskinen, S. Tuori, S. Irni, and D. Mulinari (eds) *Complying with Colonialism: Gender, Race and Ethnicity in the Nordic Region*, Farnham: Ashgate, pp 1–16.

Näre, L. (2020). 'Family lives on hold: bureaucratic bordering in male refugees' struggle for transnational care', *Journal of Family Research*, 32(3): 435–54.

Nickerson, A., Bryant, R.A., Steel, Z., Silove, D. and Brooks, R. (2010) 'The impact of fear for family on mental health in a resettled Iraqi refugee community', *Journal of Psychiatric Research*, 44(4): 229–35.

Nordberg, C. (2007) *Boundaries of Citizenship: the Case of the Roma and the Finnish Nation-State*, Helsinki: Helsinki University Press.

Nordberg, C. (2015) 'Invisibilised visions: migrant mothers and the reordering of citizenship in a Nordic welfare state context', *Nordic Journal of Migration Research*, 5(2): 67–74.

Nordberg, C. (2018) 'Social work restructuring and paradoxes of professional identity in Finland', in M. Kamali, and J.H. Jönsson (eds) *Neoliberalism, Nordic Welfare States and Social Work: Current and Future Challenges*, London: Routledge, pp 126–76.

Norocel O.C., Saresma T., Lähdesmäki T. and Ruotsalainen M. (2020) 'Performing "us" and "other": intersectional analyses of right-wing populist media', *European Journal of Cultural Studies*, first published online, December 2020.

Rousseau, C., Rufagari, M.C., Bagilishya, D. and Measham, T. (2004) 'Remaking family life: strategies for re-establishing continuity among Congolese refugees during the family reunification process', *Social Science and Medicine*, 59(5): 1095–108.

Schierup, C.U., Hansen, P. and Castels, S. (2006) *Migration, Citizenship, and the European Welfare State: a European Dilemma*, Oxford: Oxford University Press.

Strik, T., de Hart, B. and Nissen, E. (2013) *Family Reunification: a Barrier or Facilitator of Integration? A Comparative Study*, Dublin: Immigrant Council of Ireland.

Suszycki, A.M. (ed) (2011) *Welfare Citizenship and Welfare Nationalism*, Helsinki: Nordic Centre of Excellence NordWel.

Turtiainen, K., Hiitola, J., Gruber, S. and Tiilikainen, M. (2020) 'Introduction: the changing welfare state', in J. Hiitola, K. Turtiainen, S. Gruber and M. Tiilikainen (eds) *Family Life in Transition: Borders, Transnational Mobility, and Welfare Society in Nordic Countries*, Abingdon: Routledge, pp 16–24.

Wrede, S., Näre, L., Olakivi, A. and Nordberg, C. (2021) 'Neoliberal "flexibility" and the discursive incorporation of migrant labour in public eldercare in Finland', in C. Mora and N. Piper (eds) *The Palgrave Handbook of Gender and Migration: Global Perspectives*, London: Palgrave Macmillan, pp 253–68.

3

Contesting universalism in Finnish health and social services: experiences of migrant parents with a disabled child

Eveliina Heino, Hanna Kara and Annika Lillrank

Introduction

The Nordic countries, which include Finland, are known as welfare states – nations that strive to achieve equality through the universal provision of social benefits and public services financed by taxation (Esping-Andersen, 1990). However, the Finnish welfare state has faced many challenges during the 21st century due to globalisation, economic liberalisation, an ageing population, a declining birth rate and increasing disparities within the population based on income inequality and health (Helne and Laatu, 2007; Vaarama et al, 2010).

Additionally, increasing migration has been presented as a challenge to the Nordic welfare state based on the claim that diversity within a population and presumed cultural differences pose dangers to social cohesion and public support for services (Jønsson et al, 2013; Sainsbury, 2013). In Finland, migration remains at the centre of debates concerning the limits of welfare state solidarity, especially following the general elections in 2008 and most recent election in 2023, when a nationalist conservative party won broad support. Within so-called welfare state nationalism, rights to social security are presented as inherited and, thus, belonging to those who can prove Finnish ancestry, while migration is viewed as a threat to the welfare state (Pyrhönen, 2013). The ideals of the welfare state can be employed both to promote migrants' exclusion from social security as well as to advocate for migrants' social rights, depending upon the political views of the speaker (Jønsson et al, 2013).

At the end of 2022, over 495,000 persons whose mother tongue was a foreign language[1] lived in Finland. This represents an increase from around 13,000 such individuals at the end of 1985. Therefore, in the last 38 years, the foreign language-speaking population has increased 38-fold, now representing 8.9 per cent of the entire population (Statistics Finland, 2022). Following increases in immigration, the development of the so-called integration policy also began in the 1990s. The first legislative act on migrants' integration came into force in 1999 (Act on the Integration of Immigrants and Reception of Asylum Seekers, 493/1999). The Act defined the services and benefits granted to migrants as well as the responsibilities of different authorities in promoting integration. It is possible to interpret the Nordic welfare state as promoting homogeneity in two ways: through universalistic services designed for a homogeneous population, and through integration measures focused on modifying migrants to more closely resemble the majority population, regardless of the explicitly multicultural aim within policies and legislation (Saukkonen, 2013).

The idea of 'Whiteness' is central to national identities in Nordic countries even though individual countries unevenly engaged in colonial history (Lundström and Teitelbaum, 2017; Hervik, 2019). Thus, the notion of 'race' has played an important role in the construction of social hierarchies, even if it is rarely discussed explicitly (Garner, 2014). Keskinen (2016) refers to Whiteness as a form of power, noting that within Nordic countries, individuals who are racialised are referred to as 'immigrants' or 'foreigners'. According to Garner (2014) and Leinonen and Toivanen (2014), the refusal to discuss 'race' in Nordic countries reflects an unwillingness to reflect on current hierarchies. In addition, discussions about the difficulty of integrating migrants into Nordic societies because of cultural differences can be perceived as reproducing the hegemony of Whiteness and racism, since cultures are used in a manner similar to race; namely, to justify unequal treatment (Stolcke, 1995).

This chapter analyses the accounts of 20 migrant parents of a disabled child to illustrate how their experiences within Finnish public health and social services reveal systematic limitations based on implicit bias. In our analysis, we examine migrant parents' service experiences from the point of view of universalism, in order to determine how universalism is implemented in practice. We view disability through a social model as a social phenomenon constructed within the relationship between the individual and the society (Shakespeare, 2008).

Previous Finnish research on disability has largely neglected migrant populations. Only a few studies have investigated the lives of disabled migrants or the ways migrant parents raising a disabled child perceive their interactions with public health and social services. These studies have highlighted how disability and migration are often acknowledged as turning points in families' lives. Consequently, both disability and migration render families more dependent on support and guidance from public health and social services. According to these studies, parents perceived services as inflexible, poorly coordinated and difficult to access due to language barriers and highly regulated bureaucracies. In addition, neither individuals with disabilities nor their parents were regularly included in decision-making processes with professionals. Thus, parents' interpretations of the meanings of disability and treatment often diverged from the perspectives of practitioners, resulting in bewilderment in the encounters (Päivinen, 2010; Kokkonen and Oikarinen, 2012; Vuorento and Franz-Koivisto, 2016).

We identified several international studies with similar findings to existing Finnish studies. For example, a recent British study demonstrated how disability studies and migration studies have thus far viewed the two phenomena as distinct entities (Duda-Mikulin et al, 2020; Pierart et al, 2020). Furthermore, a European study (Pierart et al, 2020: 295) spanning over five countries pinpointed barriers between legal norms and the conditions of migrant families raising disabled children. Specifically, practices within public services contributed to the experiences of inequality of migrant parents and their children.

Moreover, Norwegian (Sajjad, 2012; Tøssebro, 2012; Söderström, 2014) and Canadian (Fellin et al, 2013; Jennings et al, 2014; Khanlou et al, 2015) studies emphasised that migrant families face language barriers regardless of access to interpreters, struggle with a lack of knowledge of available services and experience arbitrariness in treatment. For example, Burns (2017) discussed how the intersections of disability and migration created complex barriers and resulted in unequal access to healthcare for disabled migrants. Similarly, Hansen et al (2017) discussed how migrant parents to a disabled child have limited opportunities for social and economic participation in society. Studies in the US and Canada have emphasised how migrant parents' understandings regarding disability may differ from definitions among health and social service practitioners (Diken, 2006; McLeod, 2012). For example, cultural or religious explanations concerning the causes of disability and an unfamiliarity with local rehabilitation services and practices may lead migrant parents to not accepting recommended treatments or treatment goals (Mortensen et al, 2014).

Disability and ethnicity represent social categories, while the ableism and racism attached to these categories produce inequality relative to the majority population. Although migrants' experiences vary, according to, for example, their country of origin, research shows that migrants face discrimination in Finland across various spheres of life (for example, FRA, 2018; Non-Discrimination Ombudsman, 2020). In what follows, we first introduce approaches to universalism. We then turn to describing the implementation of our research, after which we present and discuss our results. We conclude by discussing the implications of our findings both for social work practices and for future research.

Approaches to universalism

The concept of universalism refers to an idea or ideal as well as a way of dividing and distributing social benefits and services (Anttonen and Sipilä,

2010: 104). In the context of social policy, universalism generally refers to the services and benefits to which people are entitled and which are financed primarily through taxation (Sipilä and Anttonen, 2016).

Definitions and meanings of universalism vary according to the context. However, various definitions of universalism share the principle of equal rights to social benefits and/or services. In Finland, this means that residence permit holders including migrants are granted the same formal rights to municipal services and social benefits as Finnish citizens (Act on the Application of Residence-Based Social Security Legislation, 1573/1993). Factors such as one's life situation and circumstances (that is, parental leave or unemployment) or age (being a minor or retired) also define such rights.

Within the Nordic welfare model, the principle of universalism is often understood in connection with reciprocity, whereby everyone participates in the financing of benefits and services, and, simultaneously, everyone has access to them (Kujala and Danielsbacka, 2015). According to previous studies, countries with this model rank high on gender equality (World Economic Forum, 2018), income distribution (OECD, 2020), rule of law performance (World Justice Project, 2019), human freedom (Vásquez and Porčnik, 2019) and even happiness (Helliwell et al, 2020).

The majority of the population in Finland seems to support the welfare state (for example, Kestilä and Karvonen, 2019), although universalism has faced criticism. According to Sipilä and Anttonen (2016), the protection of middle-class incomes and an ideational move from common to individual responsibility has weakened universalism. From the neoliberal perspective, universalism is understood as ineffective and paternalistic in that it prevents individuals from taking responsibility for their own lives (Juhila, 2006). Others argue that generous benefits and extensive services have reduced the responsibility previously assigned to families, thus leading to a reduction in spontaneous unofficial support provided by individuals to one another (Kujala and Danielsbacka, 2015: 44).

In addition, many studies (for example, Hirvilammi and Laatu, 2008; Metteri, 2012; Kestilä and Karvonen, 2019) have demonstrated that regardless of its achievements, the Finnish welfare state does not always deliver its promises, and that an extensive and complicated bureaucracy creates unfair situations for many service users (Metteri, 2012). Moreover, income inequalities have widened, particularly since the 2000s (Statistics Finland, 2020).

Universalism as a general principle has been presented as opposing essentialism. As such, universalism serves to extend equality to minorities. This follows the idea that all humans are fundamentally the same and should not be stereotypically divided into different groups based on, for instance, ethnicity and presumed cultural backgrounds (Dominelli, Lorenz and Soydan, 2001). Yet, universalism is only possible if the value systems of members within a society remain uniform, service needs are largely similar and residents are perceived as members of the community (Anttonen and Sipilä, 2000).

According to Pitkänen (2006), migrants' integration into Finnish society is supported by promoting universalistic principles; that is, everyone enjoys uniform access to services and is treated uniformly. This approach can be viewed as problematic, however. As universalism stresses the sameness of people, it simultaneously limits the possibilities of discussing oppressive practices within social and health services. Keskinen (2012) has labelled this phenomenon as the *paradox of universalism*. She points out that practices thought of as universal may often turn out to be rather locally and historically constructed understandings of good practices reflecting the needs and realities of the majority population. Often, these understandings include a perception of the uniformity of a population as a norm in the society, thereby silencing other perspectives.

Mehrara (2020), in turn, has described the *paradox of equality versus equity* in universalism. In her view, equality refers to a uniform right to access and make use of services, while equity refers both to equality in access as well as in outcome. Thus, Mehrara (2020: 136) ponders how we can ensure that social rights actually exist in practice. According to previous Finnish studies, migrants face multiple difficulties in this respect. They face difficulties finding and accessing services and benefits, moving from one service to another, understanding service information, communicating with professionals and reporting experiences of unequal treatment and racism (Sainola-Rodriquez, 2009; Turtiainen, 2012; Buchert, 2015; Heino, 2018).

In previous research, these concrete everyday challenges in the use of Finnish health and social services and the theoretical discussions on universalism have typically been addressed separately (exceptions to this can be found in Keskinen, 2009, 2012; Tuori, 2009, 2012). Here, we aim to fill this gap and explore universalism in light of our empirical data. In this way, our focus lies on the structures and practices in health and social services that frame the everyday lives of migrant parents.

Data and methods

Our data consist of interviews with 20 parents of disabled children from six different countries. We contacted both public and non-governmental agencies in southern Finland that work with different migrant groups and/or disabled people. Service providers distributed an information letter regarding our research to their service users who then contacted us directly. We conducted face-to-face interviews with participants who met the following criteria: (a) residence permit holder, (b) had lived in Finland at least three to four years and (c) had a disabled child/children with a development delay or related special needs. We conducted all interviews between 2016 and 2017.

The interviewees had moved to Finland from six different countries between 1998 and 2015, with most arriving to Finland in 2009. The majority of the interviewees (n=18) lived in the Helsinki metropolitan area, while two lived in south-east Finland. Typically, the interviews took place in the interviewees' homes, in a public library or in facilities at the University of Helsinki. Parents were between 21 and 50 years of age and had moved to Finland for various reasons, including seeking asylum, employment, marriage or family reunification. Among the interviewees, 12 parents had a university degree, two had a professional education and six parents lacked any primary education. Their children were between the ages of 2 and 17 years old. Although the parents who participated in this research differed from each other, they all shared a migrant background and had a child with a disability. Thus, we aimed to analyse the similarities and differences in these parents' experiences. Our research question is:

How is universalism displayed in the parents' accounts concerning their encounters with Finnish health and social services?

In this research, we approach universalism as a principle aimed at including all residents within the social security system that provides health and social services and benefits, treating all service users (of similar services) equally regardless of their background. We approach the idea of universalism from a critical standpoint in order to promote a critical reflection of current practices and existing structures.

Our analytical approach relies on thematic analysis (Braun and Clarke, 2022). We began by searching for segments in the interviews in which the participants described challenges they had encountered in their interactions with public health and social service providers (that is, while being informed, obtaining services, using services, planning services and treatment, communicating with service providers and so on). We identified three different themes in this respect: *monolingual practices*, *standardised services* and *asymmetrical relationships*. We then elaborated upon these themes in more detail and analysed them further from the perspective of universalism. In what follows, we present and discuss our results. The extracts from the interviews have been translated into English by the writers.

Results

Monolingual practices

Finland has two official languages, Finnish and Swedish, and 16 per cent of Finnish municipalities are either bilingual or have Swedish as their primary language. Bilingual municipalities should provide services in both languages (Language Act, 423/2003). In practice, however, bilingualism is not always implemented (Regional State Administrative Agencies, 2018). In addition, the Sámi have the right to maintain and develop their own languages, culture and traditional livelihoods (Constitution of Finland, 731/1999). The Sámi also have the right to use their language and right to interpretation when dealing with authorities (Sámi Language Act, 1086/2003). Despite legislation, problems persist in the realisation of services and in the implementation of Sámi language rights. Legislation also compels professionals working in health and social services to make use of interpreting and translation services whenever necessary (Act on the Status and Rights of Patients, 785/1992; Act on the Status and Rights of Social Welfare Clients, 812/2000; Language Act, 423/2003). Overall, legislation provides a rather general framework in this respect, whereby professionals have many possibilities to define their own practices (Koskinen, Vuori and Leminen, 2018).

In our data, monolingualism – that is, the dominance of the Finnish language – emerged in many ways. Parents described facing communication problems when contacting services, finding information about services and benefits, discussing their child's disability and treatment with professionals during testing and procedures, as well as when receiving information about their child's diagnosis and test results. Interviewees described *contacting different services* as one of the most important tasks of a parent whose child is suspected of having or is diagnosed with a disability. Specifically, newly arrived migrant parents described multiple practical problems related to this theme, as illustrated here:

> 'If you don't speak the language, you'll have problems. You always have to find someone who can help, you have to call someone to translate and ask them to call the social services ... If you don't know the language ... They tell you that the next appointment is in a week or two weeks and there's nothing you can do. You have to accept everything, you don't have a choice ... You're just like a newborn baby.' (Interview 14)

In this example, the interviewee describes the experience of dependency on others caused by monolingual practices in health and social services. First, one must find acquaintances who know the Finnish language in order to contact social services. Then, the service provider will schedule an appointment, the time of which should be accepted without question. The interviewee provides a comparison of this situation to that of a "newborn baby", highlighting their subordinate position. This position was described in our data as conflicting with the moral expectation according to which parents want and are obliged to take care of their child and, therefore, capable of finding and obtaining the right services for them.

Another aspect of monolingualism revolved around *finding information about financial support and services* before and after a diagnosis. Most parents described their need for clear information about their child's disability, rehabilitation and service opportunities as well as possibilities for financial support. Information was also important during different periods of transition, such as when their child's school or treatment ended. Parents struggled to translate information for themselves written in Finnish, describing this information as overly complicated and unclear. Furthermore, they experienced similar difficulties in the sectored service system, where practitioners working in one field could not provide advice on services or benefits outside their own specific areas of expertise. For the interviewees, this led to endless, exhausting enquiries while searching for the right people and agencies in their efforts to establish communication. Here is one example:

> 'I don't know what will happen after sixth grade. I have asked the therapist and the doctors, but no one will tell me what happens after that. Maybe they don't know … I try to ask questions, but I don't get answers.' (Interview 3)

When there was no comprehensive information or functional communication, parents felt that they were "at the mercy of the professionals" – a stressful reality. Monolingualism also existed *in discussions about the child's disability and treatment*. The disability vocabulary was described as quite specific, making it difficult for parents to discuss and understand all the details. In addition, this specific vocabulary meant that not all interpreters could adequately translate details. In particular, well-educated parents attempted to find information about their child's disability and treatment in their own mother tongue, but they expected professionals to provide them with "information about possible scenarios and time frames within the Finnish system", as one parent stated.

Monolingualism also emerged *during tests.* According to the parents, their child's bilingualism and the fact that the child's mother tongue was not Finnish were not taken into account during testing, but all children were tested using the same standard tests in Finnish. Parents asked if they could be present during testing or if an interpreter could assist their child, but these wishes were denied. According to the parents, the monolingualism of the tests in many cases led to misdiagnoses. This meant that the child's developmental level was defined as lower than it actually was, which, in turn, led to assigning the child to inappropriate educational or other services. In some cases, a misdiagnosis was changed upon further examination. This required a great deal of initiative from the parents, such as writing official complaints, collecting opinions about the child's development from other professionals who worked with their child and actively opposing professionals' decisions during consultations.

> 'The mistake was that the developmental phase was evaluated as too low and [the child] was put into the corresponding group ... And the psychologist wrote that [the child] was not at the same level as others. Well, later they came and said that the problem was not about learning, that [the child] was at the same level as others, but the challenge was more with concentration, behaving, sitting down quietly in a big classroom full of children.' (Interview 1)

The phase of *diagnosis and service plans* was also described as problematic. Some parents received information about their child's transfer to special education only after a decision was made. Some parents did not receive any official information about their child's diagnosis and some parents received information only in Finnish without being able to read through it with anyone. In these cases, parents said that they felt as if they "were left hanging, not knowing what to do with it all".

Parents also described situations in which they were not properly informed about medical procedures that were done or planned for their child. Parents were not always certain whether the necessary information had been delivered to them. Alternatively, they remained uncertain whether they correctly understood the information they were provided. The following example describes how parents took their child to the hospital for what they thought was a medical check-up. However, this visit entailed a more serious procedure:

> 'I thought that they would check the ability to hear, that it was just about the ears, nothing special. So, we arrived there [at the hospital], and we had been waiting for the doctor, and suddenly a person came and said, "Well I'm the person who is responsible for the anaesthesia." Okay, and this person tried to explain to us, and said, "Well, after that I have to intubate your child and administer some special muscle relaxant." I asked, "Wait, wait, wait. What kind of intubating? What kind of muscle relaxant?" We had never heard about that ... After that, I asked the nurse with whom I had talked just a few days before, and I asked, "What do you think, that we are just some pieces of meat? We have emotions, we have feelings, we have a brain. It's impossible to do something like this, it's so impolite, it's so disrespectful."' (Interview 5)

This example illustrates how a lack of clarity about medical procedures resulted in the parents feeling disrespected and unrecognised as persons – even dehumanised. The account conveys a great deal of stress due to the unexpected situation and a loss of power. Power is reflected in multiple ways, tangible in the parents' expression of their experience of being treated as mere objects, as "pieces of meat".

Overall, it seems that the principles of universalism can legitimise practices in which professionals have no incentive or lack the necessary professional skills and means to consider possible differences regarding service users' language skills or to act upon them, thereby hampering service users' abilities to use services (also Keskinen, 2012: 131). In our data, parents described the disability of a child as a stressful situation, in which they needed informational, emotional and practical support. Yet, based on the experiences described here, the use of public services resulted in additional stress in many cases. The monolingualism characterising Finnish health and social services can ultimately be seen as a question of power, since it limits access and agency at various stages of service provision.

Standardised services

A cornerstone of universalism is that services remain equally standardised, such that the quality of the services is uniform (Sipilä and Anttonen, 2016). According to the parents' accounts, this equality proved problematic; for example, when professionals applied particular and predetermined time frames before sending children for additional tests, denied supportive treatments or when difficulties arose during attempts to combine public and private services.

Many parents began worrying about their child's development at a very early age, whereby most felt that they were not taken seriously when expressing their concerns at the child health centre. During many accounts, parents mentioned that professionals used the expression "don't worry", thereby diminishing their concerns as well as their sense of authority and knowledge regarding matters concerning their own child. Such an experience is illustrated here:

> 'I find it very hard to understand this kind of service and attitude. Maybe you could explain why I was treated that way. Is it their education, as a practical nurse or educator? Or is it because I'm an immigrant? I'm nothing? Is that why I was treated that way?' (Interview 9)

In this example, the parents discussed their experiences of being ignored when they tried to raise concerns regarding their child's development and situation. They connected the attitude they had experienced as belittling and ignoring to their status as immigrants. In the worst cases, parents were forced to wait years for referrals to see a specialist or to gain access to testing and diagnoses, services and treatment plans, leaving them thinking that "a lot of time was lost in our child's development". Excessive waiting periods caused practical problems for families, and some parents considered them "offensive".

In acute cases, during which a child had severe behavioural problems affecting the entire family, assistance remained exceedingly difficult to obtain. In desperate need of assistance, some families repeatedly consulted emergency room services. In other cases, parents stopped negotiating with public service professionals and consulted private service providers in Finland and in other countries. These struggles to access treatment representing unfair experiences were described as stressful and time-consuming, with unpredictable outcomes.

Most parents attempted to find information about their child's disability and treatment possibilities in their own language and to discuss this information with Finnish professionals. This often led to experiences of being misinterpreted or completely dismissed by professionals. In the following example, parents describe a conversation they had with a Finnish service provider. The parents wanted to discuss whether it was possible to use several supportive treatments alongside the medical treatment and to discuss different medical treatments used in other countries.

> 'We came there [to a course for parents with a disabled child], and we had a general discussion. At the end, one psychologist tried to tell every parent, every family, her own opinion about what kind of parents or family they are. And, she said to me, "You're the kind of mother who tries to use alternative, non-traditional stuff." And it was very offensive because it was such a cliché … And it is not true. Because I never would try something which is not [clinically] proven for my child.' (Interview 5)

In this example, the mother expressed her deep frustration and anger over her experience of being viewed and presented as someone who would turn to alternative and not clinically tested treatment for her child. Her views were not only dismissed by the professionals, but also, in her experience, she was categorised as a "cliché" in the sense that migrants typically try or rely upon non-Western medicine and treatment options. This extract reveals the power one service encounter with one practitioner can have in an already delicate situation.

Parents who possessed the necessary financial resources began using private sector services alongside or instead of public options. Some parents began using private services while waiting for those from public agencies. The most common private sector services parents relied on included speech and occupational therapy, massage and private day care. Parents turned to private services because they did not receive support from public agencies or because the services offered to them seemed insufficient. Some parents also described feeling diminished as parents in public service settings and sought more involvement in their child's treatment, a possibility offered by private services.

Regardless of the inflexibility in general, there were also examples of flexible solutions. For example, one family accessed a family worker who spoke their mother tongue and provided a great deal of practical and emotional support to them. Other parents were granted permission to email their social workers since they did not speak Finnish. Online tools for language translation allowed them to correspond with one another. In some cases, parents received additional assignments from their language courses in order not to lose their study place, since they had many absences due to treatment sessions for their child. Yet, these examples of flexibility depended on a particular professional who enabled and allowed diverse practices, while the system as a whole remained rather inflexible.

Asymmetrical relationships between parents and practitioners

The ideology of universalism in health and social care settings not only requires standardised service provision, but also standardised requirements for qualifying the professionals working within the services. Standardisation aims to ensure consistent quality nationwide for the services.

In this study, interviewees talked about professionals in general. Although health and social care practitioners within different spheres possess different qualifications and adhere to differing job descriptions, they all share the following characteristics: their work is guided by legislation, they combine the goals of their organisations with the service users' specific situations, they work as gatekeepers to services and they exercise decision-making power over their clients' lives.

According to the interviewees, they typically received no information or material before the service appointments, thus preventing them from preparing for consultations during which their child's treatment and service plans were discussed. Professionals had all kinds of materials with them, but these were generally not shared with the parents, even during consultations. Meetings were often perceived as short, leaving the parents feeling as though insufficient time was provided to properly discuss or justify decisions made during the consultations. One parent described these decision-making processes as follows: "It's a decision already made. It's an opinion already formed, and they have no time to even discuss it." Thus, in many cases, parents felt that they were left completely out of the discussion, such as in this example:

> 'It's like the appointment is for the child. They ask their questions and talk to the child, not to me, and all the questions are related to

the child, but no one asks me how I see this or what my part in all of this is.' (Interview 7)

In this example, professionals talk directly to the teenaged child and the parent feels left out of the discussion. While most parents felt that a child-centred approach represented good practice, ignoring parents' opinions was described negatively. Furthermore, many parents wondered whether their ethnicity, country of origin or Finnish-language deficiency resulted in differential treatment by professionals. Parents offered explanations for their experiences, ranging, for example, from professionals withholding information because "migrant parents don't understand anything" to "this will result in extra work". In addition, many parents described encounters with health and social care professionals during which they were categorised as migrants and concomitantly regarded as uneducated. One interviewee explained:

'In my experience, the staff from day care and from school never think parents can possess the same level of knowledge. Every time I was forced to explain, "Well, I am also a teacher. I am a teacher and I studied psychology. I know the subject very well. Why don't you trust me and why don't you respect my knowledge?" In my opinion, this is a very big problem here. Sometimes, people in day care, in schools, they don't believe foreigners can also be well-educated persons. Why? It's so offensive.' (Interview 5)

This example reflects a deep asymmetrical relationship between professionals and service users, and an experience of discrimination and negative stereotyping connected to a presumed lack of capacities and knowledge. Relegating parents to this position maintains and reinforces inequalities. Parents with a refugee background described their experiences in more positive ways in general, although they recognised the same practical problems as parents who migrated based on employment, marriage or educational opportunities. Among the parents interviewed, a refugee background meant that a child received no or very little treatment in the country of origin.

Conclusion

In this chapter, we examined the manifestations of universalism within Finnish health and social care services through a critical reading of interviews with migrant parents to disabled children. Based on our findings, monolingual practices, standardised services and asymmetrical relationships between parents and professionals appear to be in connection with universalistic practices that limit parents' agency in many ways while they struggle to contact, use and find information about services. This extends to their possibilities to participate in their child's testing and find information about their child's diagnoses and treatment.

Recognising and addressing the different needs of a diverse population could make current health and social care services more inclusive. Creating inclusivity relies on collaboration between service users, service providers and policy makers towards re-evaluating policy measures and devising a more nuanced application of universalism in accordance with the diverse needs of contemporary society. More concrete suggestions based on our results include the following: (1) providing parents and interpreters with information about a child's disability and the primary themes of discussion before each consultation; (2) translation of important documents, such as a child's diagnosis and treatment plans, which is possible within current legislation; (3) booking more time for consultations involving migrant parents, allowing them sufficient time to ask questions; (4) ensuring that parents have information about possible options for their child's future and services; and (5) determining where to guide parents if their doubts and questions lie beyond one's own job description or area of expertise.

According to our results, current practices in health and social services do not sufficiently take into account diverse needs, parents' knowledge about their child and differences in Finnish-language proficiency. Some parents wondered if they were, because of their migrant status, treated as uneducated and subordinate or not provided comprehensive information regarding their child. Parents' experiences can be interpreted as reflecting different forms of institutional racism. As stated in our introduction, 'Whiteness', including images of cultural, religious and (to some extent) linguistic homogeneity, remains the invisible norm against which 'migrants' are defined. This understanding appears embedded in the universalism of the Finnish welfare state.

In addition, our analysis shows that the responsibility for ensuring universalism lies heavily on practitioners as the primary service providers (also Mehrara, 2020). This shifts universalism to changing and arbitrary local-level practices, specifically with regard to the diversity of service user backgrounds and their situations. Much depends upon the time and other resources available at the local level and the interests or even courage of an individual practitioner to find flexible, sensitive and inclusive solutions and practices. These frontline workers would also need time, resources and training to critically review the system and consider how to meet needs resulting from diversity. Accordingly, Brodin and Mattsson (2014) have called for norm-critical education for service providers, which would involve professionals critically examining 'Whiteness' and reflecting upon their own prejudices.

According to Keskinen (2012), the universalist logic counterbalances the essential and hierarchical tones of 'culture speech', but also leaves little room for addressing differences and reorganising practices. Moreover, views of 'Finnishness' as static and uniform lead to welfare state nationalism and exclusion in everyday practices. Thus, there is a continuous need for more fine-grained analyses that consider diversity and varying situations as well as structural and social factors in order to achieve the primary goal of social work as a field and service that advocates for societal wellness.

Note

[1] By foreign-language speakers, we refer here to persons whose mother tongue is a language other than the officially recognised languages of Finnish, Swedish or Sámi.

References

Act on the Application of Residence-Based Social Security Legislation 1573/1993.
Act on the Integration of Immigrants and Reception of Asylum Seekers 493/1999.
Act on the Status and Rights of Patients 785/1992.
Act on the Status and Rights of Social Welfare Clients 812/2000.
Anttonen, A. and Sipilä, J. (2000) *Suomalaista sosiaalipolitiikkaa*, Tampere: Vastapaino.
Anttonen, A. and Sipilä, J. (2010) 'Universalismi Britannian ja Pohjoismaiden sosiaalipolitiikassa', *Janus*, 18(2): 104–20.
Braun, V. and Clarke, V. (2022) *Thematic Analysis*, London: Sage.
Brodin, H. and Mattsson, T. (2014) 'Lägst ned på skalan? Hälso- och sjukvårdens bemötande av äldre kvinnor som migrerat till Sverige', *Social vetenskapligtidskrift*, 21(3–4): 372–91.
Buchert, U. (2015) 'Maahanmuuttajuuden institutionaaliset kategoriat. Kuntoutussäätiö', doctoral dissertation, University of Helsinki, HELDA. http://urn.fi/URN:ISBN:978-952-5961-49-2
Burns, N. (2017) 'The human rights to health: exploring disability, migration and health', *Disability and Society*, 32(10): 1463–84.
Constitution of Finland 731/1999.
Diken, I. (2006) 'Review of research: an overview of parental perceptions in cross-cultural groups on disability', *Childhood Education*, 82(4): 236–40.
Dominelli, L., Lorenz, W. and Soydan, H. (eds) (2001) *Beyond Racial Divides: Ethnicities in Social Work Practice*, Aldershot: Ashgate.
Duda-Mikulin, E., Scullion, L. and Carrie, R. (2020) 'Wasted lives in scapegoat Britain: overlaps and departures between migration studies and disability studies', *Disability and Society*, 35(9): 1373–97.
Esping-Andersen, G. (1990) *Three Worlds of Welfare Capitalism*, Cambridge: Polity Press.

Fellin, M., Desmarais, C. and Lindsay, S. (2015) 'An examination of clinicians' experiences of collaborative culturally competent service delivery to immigrant families raising a child with a physical disability', *Disability and Rehabilitation*, 37(21): 1961–9.

FRA (European Union Agency for Fundamental Rights) (2018) 'Second European Union minorities and discrimination survey'. https://fra.europa.eu/en/publication/2017/second-european-union-minorities-and-discrimination-survey-technical-report

Garner, S. (2014) 'Injured nations, racialising states and repressed histories: making Whiteness visible in the Nordic countries', *Social Identities*, 20(6): 407–22.

Hansen, S., Wilton, R. and Newbold, B. (2017) '"There is always this feeling of otherness": exploring the lived experiences of visually impaired immigrant women in Canada', *Disability and Society*, 32(8): 1121–41.

Heino, E. (2018) *Peruspalvelukokemukset ja arjen kansalaisuuden rakentuminen venäläistaustaisten perheiden kertomuksissa*, Helsinki: University of Helsinki.

Helliwell, J.F., Layard, R., Sachs, J.D., De Neve, J-E., Aknin, L.B., Huang, H. et al (2020) 'World happiness report'. https://happinessreport.s3.amazonaws.com/2020/WHR20.pdf

Helne, T. and Laatu, M. (2007) 'Johdanto: "Hyvinvointipolitiikka" ja sen vääryydet', in T. Helne and M. Laatu (eds) *Vääryyskirja*, Helsinki: Kelan tutkimusosasto, pp 9–40.

Hervik, P. (2019) 'Racialisation in the Nordic countries: an introduction', in P. Hervik (eds) *Racialisation, Racism, and Anti-Racism in the Nordic Countries: Approaches to Social Inequality and Difference*, London: Palgrave Macmillan, pp 3–37.

Hirvilammi, T. and Laatu, M. (2008) *Toinen vääryyskirja: Lähikuvia sosiaalisista epäkohdista*, Helsinki: Kelan tutkimusosasto.

Jennings, S., Khanlou, N. and Su, C. (2014) 'Public health policy and social support for immigrant mothers raising disabled children in Canada', *Disability and Society*, 29(10): 1645–57.

Jønsson, H.V. (2013) 'Immigrant policy developing in Copenhagen and Ishøj in the 1970s', *Scandinavian Journal of History*, 38(5): 590–611.

Juhila, K. (2006) *Sosiaalityöntekijöinä ja asiakkaina: Sosiaalityön yhteiskunnalliset tehtävät ja paikat*, Tampere: Vastapaino.

Keskinen, S. (2009) '"Honour-related violence" and Nordic nation-building', in S. Keskinen, S. Tuori, S. Irni and D. Mulinari (eds) *Complying with Colonialism: Gender, Race and Ethnicity in the Nordic Region*, London: Ashgate, pp 257–72.

Keskinen, S. (2012) 'Kulttuurilla merkityt toiset ja universaalin kohtelun paradoksi väkivaltatyössä', in S. Keskinen, J. Vuori, and A. Hirsiaho (eds) *Monikulttuurisuuden sukupuoli: Kansalaisuus ja erot hyvinvointiyhteiskunnassa*, Tampere: University of Tampere, pp 291–320.

Keskinen, S. (2016) 'From welfare nationalism to welfare chauvinism: economic rhetoric, welfare state and the changing policies of asylum in Finland', *Critical Social Policy*, 36(3): 1–19.

Kestilä, L. and Karvonen, S. (2019) 'Suomalaisten hyvinvointi 2018. Terveyden- ja hyvinvoinnin laitos'. www.julkari.fi/handle/10024/137498

Khanlou, N., Mustafa, N., Vazquez, L.M., Haque, N. and Yoshida, K. (2015) 'Stressors and barriers to services for immigrant fathers raising children with developmental disabilities', *International Journal Mental Health Addict*, 13(6): 659–74.

Kokkonen, M. and Oikarinen, T. (2012) 'Kotoutumista kaikille! Vammaiset maahanmuuttajat ja kotoutumiskoulutus. Vammaisten maahanmuuttajien tukikeskus HILMA'. https://tukikeskushilma.fi/wp-content/uploads/2020/03/Kotoutumista-kaikille.pdf

Koskinen, K., Vuori, J. and Leminen A. (2018) 'Johdanto', in K. Koskinen, J. Vuori and A. Leminen (eds) *Asioimistulkkaus: Monikielisen yhteiskunnan arkea*, Tampere: Vastapaino, pp 7–18.

Kujala, A. and Danielsbacka, M. (2015) 'Hyvinvointivaltion loppu?', in *Vallanpitäjät, kansa ja vastavuoroisuus*, Helsinki: Tammi.

Language Act 423/2003.

Leinonen, J. and Toivanen, M. (2014) 'Researching in/visibility in the Nordic context: theoretical and empirical views', *Nordic Journal of Migration Research*, 4(4): 161–7.

Lundström, C. and Teitelbaum, B. (2017) 'Nordic Whiteness: an introduction', *Scandinavian Studies*, 89(2): 151–8.

McLeod, T. (2012) 'First-generation, English-speaking West Indian families' understanding of disability and special education', *Multiple Voices for Ethnically Diverse Exceptional Learners*, 13(1): 26–41.

Mehrara, L. (2020) 'Seeking the ideal of universalism within Norway's social reality', *Social Inclusion*, 8(1): 133–44.

Metteri, A. (2012) *Hyvinvointivaltion lupaukset, kohtuuttomat tapaukset ja sosiaalityö*, Tampere: Tampereen yliopisto.

Mortensen, A., Latimer, S. and Yusuf, I. (2014) 'Cultural case workers in child disability services: an evidence-based model of cultural responsiveness for refugee families', *New Zeeland Journal of Social Sciences*, 9(2): 50–9.

Non-Discrimination Ombudsman (2020) 'Selvitys afrikkalaistaustaisten henkilöiden kokemasta syrjinnästä'. www.syrjinta.fi/documents/10181/36404/Selvitys+afrikkalaistaustaisten+henkilöiden+syrjinnästä/47cdfad4-1fc5-4114-af0d-8a5d5999ffa1

OECD (2020) 'Income inequality'. https://data.oecd.org/inequality/income-inequality.htm

Päivinen, P. (2010) 'Vammaisten pakolaisten elämää Suomessa', Finnish Ministry of Interior. https://julkaisut.valtioneuvosto.fi/bitstream/handle/10024/80505/sm_382010.pdf?sequence=1andisAllowed=y

Pierart, A., Ametan, M., Gulfi, A., Albertini-Fuh, E., Liden, H., Makharadze, T. et al (2020) 'The circumstances of migrant families raising children with disabilities in five European countries: updating knowledge and pursuing new research', *ALTER, European Journal of Disability Research*, 14(4): 286–98.

Pitkänen, P. (2006) *Etninen ja kulttuurinen monimuotoisuus viranomaistyössä*, Helsinki: Edita.

Pyrhönen, N. (2013) 'This welfare of ours: justifying public advocacy for anti-immigration politics in Finland during the late 2000s', in H. vad Jonsson, E. Onasch, S. Pellander and M. Wickström (eds) *Migrations and Welfare States: Policies, Discourses and Institutions*, Helsinki: University of Helsinki, Nordic Centre of Excellence Nordwel, pp 90–137.

Regional State Administrative Agencies (2018) 'Sosiaali- ja terveydenhuollon henkilöstön kielitaidossa on parantamisen varaa'. www.avi.fi/web/avi/tiedotteet/tiedotteet-2018

Sainola-Rodriguez, K. (2009) *Transnationaalinen osaaminen: Uusi terveydenhuoltohenkilöstön osaamisvaatimus*, Kuopio: Kuopion Yliopisto.

Sainsbury, D. (2013). *Welfare States and Immigrant Rights: the Politics of Inclusion and Exclusion*, Oxford: Oxford University Press.

Sajjad, T. (2012) 'Er dere i slekt? Om slektskap og genetisk veiledning blant pakistansknorske familier', *Norsk Antropologisk Tidsskrift*, 23(1): 16–24.

Sámi Language Act 1086/2003.

Saukkonen, P. (2013) *Erilaisuuksien Suomi: Vähemmistö- ja kotouttamispolitiikan vaihtoehdot*, Helsinki: Gaudeamus.

Shakespeare, T. (2008) *Disability Rights and Wrongs*, London: Routledge.

Sipilä, J. and Anttonen, A. (2016) 'Universalismi ja sen vaihtoehdot', in M. Törrönen, K. Hänninen, P. Jouttimäki, T. Lehto-Lunden, P. Salovaara and M. Veistilä (eds) *Vastavuoroinen Sosiaalityö*, Helsinki: Gaudeamus, pp 57–74.

Söderström, S. (2014) 'Lost in translation? Communication challenges in minority families' and healthcare workers' interactions', *Disability & Society*, 29(5): 807–20.

Statistics Finland (2020) 'Income Distribution Statistics'. https://stat.fi/en/statistics/tjt

Statistics Finland (2022) 'Foreign-language population'. www.stat.fi/tup/maahanmuutto/maahanmuuttajat-vaestossa/vieraskieliset.html

Stolcke, V. (1995) 'Talking culture: new boundaries, new rhetorics of exclusion in Europe', *Current Anthropology*, 36(1): 1–13.

Tøssebro, J. (2012). 'Å Vokse Opp Med En Funksjonshemming – Et Bakteppe', in B. Berg (ed) *Innvandring Og Funksjonshemming*, Oslo: Universitetsforlaget, pp 33–56.

Tuori, S. (2009) 'Postcolonial and queer readings of migrant families in the context of multicultural work', in S. Keskinen, S. Tuori, S. Irni and D. Mulinari (eds) *Complying with Colonialism: Gender, Race and Ethnicity in the Nordic Region*, Farnham: Ashgate, pp 155–70.

Tuori, S. (2012) 'Kuunteleminen monikulttuurisuuden mahdollistajana', in S. Keskinen, J. Vuori and A. Hirsiaho (eds) *Monikulttuurisuuden sukupuoli: Kansalaisuus ja erot hyvinvointiyhteiskunnassa*, Tampere: Tampere University Press, pp 101–20.

Turtiainen, K. (2012) *Possibilities of Trust and Recognition Between Refugees and Authorities: Resettlement as a Part of Durable Solutions of Forced Migration*, Jyväskylä: University of Jyväksylä. http://urn.fi/URN:ISBN:978-951-39-4912-9

Vaarama, M., Moisio, P. and Karvonen, S. (2010) 'Suomalaisten hyvinvointi 2010. Terveyden ja hyvinvoinnin laitos'.

Vásquez, I. and Porčnik, T. (2019) *The Human Freedom Index 2019: a Global Measurement of Personal, Civil, and Economic Freedom*, The Cato Institute, the Fraser Institute, and the Friedrich Naumann Foundation for Freedom. https://www.cato.org/sites/cato.org/files/human-freedom-index-files/cato-human-freedom-index-update-3.pdf

Vuorento, M. and Franz-Koivisto, L. (2016) 'Maahanmuuttajataustainen vammainen lapsi ja hänen perheensä sosiaalipalveluiden asiakkaana', in M. Jäppinen, A. Metteri, S. Ranta-Tyrkkö and P.-L. Rauhala (eds) *Kansainvälinen sosiaalityö: Käsitteitä, käytäntöjä ja kehityskulkuja* [A Disabled Child and Their Family as a Client in Social Service. *International Social Work: Concepts, Practical Developmental Paths*], Tallinna: Sosiaalityön tutkimuksen seura, pp 104–32.

World Economic Forum (2018) 'The Global Gender Gap Report'. www3.weforum.org/docs/WEF_GGGR_2018.pdf

World Justice Project (2019) 'Rule of Law Index'. https://worldjusticeproject.org/sites/default/files/documents/ROLI-2019-Reduced.pdf

4

Homonationalism and talking back in Finnish social work with non-heterosexual people with refugee backgrounds

Inka Söderström

Introduction

This text is a story about stories. Social work is created in narratives about social work itself and about the social problems it wants to tackle. In this chapter, I aim to dismantle some of the entangled and subtle alliances between homonationalism, coloniality and social work. I ask what kind of stories and images of Finland as well as of refugees' home countries are constructed in the interviews with social workers and non-heterosexual people with refugee backgrounds in Finland. I am striving to make sense of the everyday character of colonial and homonationalist meaning-making processes that shape the Nordic ways of thinking, as well as the ways to talk back to them.

My understanding of sexuality and gender is *queer*. Following Butler (1990), I understand the categories of sexuality and gender as social structures regulated by norms that vary in different places and different times. Queer theory addresses both questions of sexuality and gender, but in this article my focus is on sexualities and how they are regulated and instrumentalised. *Queer* is also a broader theoretical, political and methodological standpoint in my research. For me, aligned with Ahmed (2018), it means seeing all cultural categories as shifting and thus challenging all kinds of social norms and forms of oppression based on them.

In this chapter, when writing about people who have claimed asylum in Finland because of their sexuality, I mainly refer to them as *non-heterosexual people with refugee backgrounds*. For me, non-heterosexual stands for any sexual identity or behaviour that is oriented only or also towards people of the same gender and is thus, in most societies, non-normative, regulated and oppressed. Sexuality and gender are categorised very diversely around the world, and imposing Western categories such as homosexual, LGBT or even queer on the research participants without knowing their identifications would be potentially inaccurate and repressive (see Wekker, 2006: 69).

I did not ask the participants how they identified; however, many of them used Western concepts to refer to themselves or their peers. None of the participants whose interviews are included in this analysis called themselves transgender or made a reference to their non-normative gender. However, in order to avoid misgendering anyone, I have decided to use the gender-neutral pronoun *they/them* for those research participants who did not articulate their gender.

As gender and sexual identity categories, like categories such as migrant, immigrant, asylum seeker and refugee, are contextual, changing and constructed by social interaction and administrative structures (Akin, 2019; Lyytinen, 2019). They do not necessarily match with the person's sense of self. That is why I avoid using words asylum seeker or refugee as nouns to describe the participants, and instead prefer talking about *people with refugee backgrounds*. It does not define the person but recalls the experience of seeking refuge, which is still very concretely present in the lives of the research participants (see Baltra-Ulloa, 2013).

The social context in my research is the Finnish welfare state, which is structured along the lines of the general Nordic welfare state model. In Finland, the term social work refers most often to public social services provided by well-being services counties and regulated by several national laws. In this chapter, when talking about social work, I mean professionalised social work practice, even though social care provided by communities, friends, neighbours and families can also be called social work (see Baltra-Ulloa, 2013: 88). Professionalised social work in Finland is operated by licensed social welfare professionals, including social workers. Apart from public sector, social services are provided in non-governmental organisations, private companies and different institutions such as hospitals, prisons and reception centres, but their role is only to supplement public social services (Ministry of Social Affairs and Health, no date).

Homonationalism and social work

What is homonationalism, then? Jasbin Puar (2007) was the first to introduce the concept in the US political context in order to analyse the discourses around the 'war on terror', where the nation's homotolerance became a sign of its modernity and a dividing line between 'modern Western states' and 'conservative and terrorist non-Western states'. Homonationalism is a discourse tightly connected to colonial and orientalist ideas about modernity/civility and backwardness/barbarity, and applied to queer politics (Puar, 2007; Schotten, 2016; Yildiz, 2017). It can be understood as sexual exceptionalism, where the West (or Europe, or Finland) is regarded to be in the front line of sexual development (Wekker, 2006: 224; Fassin, 2010; Klapeer, 2017). By reinforcing the generalised image of African and Muslim majority countries and societies as homo/transphobic, Europe can strengthen its own self-image as a liberal and progressive 'gay paradise'.

Homonationalism is bound to the idea of a nation-state and is therefore a relevant concept in Nordic social work where its roots are intertwined with those of modern Western nation-states (Lorenz, 1994: 4). According to Lorenz (1994: 4), social work's early tasks were to create internal social peace and homogeneity in nation-states through processes of inclusion and exclusion, and in doing so support the national status quo. As Clarke and Yellow Bird (2021: 3) write, 'the social worker is expected to serve two masters: the state and the client'. This 'dual mandate' makes social workers vulnerable to being subjected to serving the interests of the state – a risk that is particularly present in state systems where social work is predominantly practiced in state agencies, as it is in Nordic countries (Lorenz, 1994: 4, 59–60; Julkunen and Rauhala, 2013). In Finland, social work has been bound to the structures of the nation-state from its very beginning. According to Satka (1995: 16, 59), the most important function of early Finnish social work was to educate the working class to become decent citizens and thus build a united, physically strong and patriotic population.

Because of the profession's integral connection to nationalist movements and state building in Finland and other Western societies, social work is not separate from colonial legacies either. Colonialism, together with White supremacy, have been necessary enablers in the construction of the modern nation and social work professionalisation around the Western world (Clarke and Yellow Bird, 2021; Keskinen, 2021). Today, in the predominantly White and Westernised Finnish society, the social work practised with migrants and people racialised as non-White[1] is engulfed by questions of coloniality and institutional racism (Elfving Ström, 2021). According to Baltra-Ulloa (2013), colonial features in Western social work with migrants and racialised communities include assimilation, individualism, control, emotional distance and centring Whiteness.

Due to the complex interdependence between social work and nation-state, it is especially important that social work practitioners, researchers and students accumulate critical and reflexive knowledge about social work's colonial and nationalist histories and its current role in the internal state building. Only by doing so can social work get actively involved in deconstructing oppressive, colonial and racist systems and discourses, instead of unconsciously reproducing them (Lorenz, 1994: 59–60; Julkunen and Rauhala, 2013; Elfving Ström, 2021).

Methods

This research is based on research material consisting of semi-structured interviews with six non-heterosexual people with refugee backgrounds and 12 social workers. The interviews were recorded and transcribed. The material is constructed as part of my doctoral dissertation project, which I am finalising at the time of writing. All names of people used in this chapter are pseudonyms. My own position as a White, queer researcher with a social worker background and with no migration background has left its imprint on all phases of the research. It has left me straddling the borderlands of outsiderness and insiderness, both with participants with refugee backgrounds and with social workers.

All of the research participants with refugee backgrounds applied for international protection because of their sexuality and used social work services in Finland. I became familiar with the participants through an LGBTQI+ organisation that arranged peer support activities for non-heterosexual people with refugee backgrounds in southern Finland. I was volunteering in the peer support groups for two years and conducted the individual interviews during 2019–2020 at the LGBTQI+ organisation's premises. Three of the interviews were made with a familiar interpreter and three in English without an interpreter. I translated the quotations of the interpreted interviews from Finnish to English for this chapter. The interviews were very open and conversational. I asked about the research participant's experiences with social workers in Finland, either in reception centres or with immigrant social services. Often the story proceeded quite chronologically starting from their first meeting with a social worker. Sometimes I brought up things that the social workers had been pondering in their interviews and asked participants with refugee backgrounds to express their views.

The other part of the data consists of interviews with social workers, who were working or had worked in a reception centre or in immigrant social services, meaning public social services for refugees who were granted asylum, subsidiary protection or another comparable residence permit in the last two or three years. I recruited the social workers through two cities in southern and western Finland as well as via an open call published in a Facebook group meant for professional social workers in Finland. The interviews were conducted individually or in pairs during 2019–2020. In the interviews, I asked the research participants to talk freely about their work with non-heterosexual service users. We talked about how non-normative sexuality or gender comes up in social work encounters, what kind of support is asked for or offered and what kind of life situations non-heterosexual service users have had, among other things.

When analysing the interview data, I focused on the narratives constructed in the data. I understand narratives, or stories, as certain kinds of discourses; as ways to justify, rationalise, categorise, name, identify and make sense of the material world around us (Wetherell and Potter, 1992: 2). Discourse refers to the complex and two-way relationship between language and social practice; in discourse studies, language is seen as something that constructs the social reality. However, this does not mean that discourses as mechanisms of power would not have very concrete, material consequences (see Wetherell and Potter, 1992: 62).

In the analysis, I was interested in the colonial and homonationalist meaning-making processes that appear in social work language but also shape Finnish social work practice and knowledge production on a more general level. I leaned towards Donileen Loseke's (2003) conceptualisations about social problems work – the activity where certain claims-makers, in this case social workers, discursively construct social problems and solutions. The construction of social problems usually includes constructing images of different actors, such as *victims* of the social problem deserving sympathy and *villains* of the social problem deserving condemnation (Loseke, 2003: 77–88). I was interested in what kind of circumstances social workers cite as social problems, who or what are narrated as *victims* or *villains* of the problem and how these images are negotiated and contested by non-heterosexual people with refugee backgrounds or social workers themselves.

In every context, such as in Finland in the 2020s, certain narratives dominate, and usually they are produced and reproduced in the privileged centres of society (Juhila, 2004). The dominant narratives are dependent on time and place, and they build upon historical events, ideologies and systems of oppression – such as nationalism, capitalism and settler colonialism as the narrative foundations of White Western knowledge (Clarke and Yellow Bird, 2021: 34). The representations created by dominant narratives are often narrow. In her famous TED Talk, Nigerian novelist Chimamande Ngozi Adichie (2009) describes the danger of a single story in the following way:

> 'My roommate had a single story of Africa: a single story of catastrophe. In this single story, there was no possibility of Africans being similar to her in any way, no possibility of feelings more complex than pity, no possibility of a connection as human equals ... So that is how to create a single story, show a people as one thing, as only one thing, over and over again, and that is what they become.' (Adichie, 2009: 13:40)

In the margins, other kinds of knowledge are created. These other knowledges and discursive negotiations have the power to resist the representations constructed in the centres, to talk back to them. Talking back, as an intervention, is a concept derived from bell hooks (1989) and other Black and Indigenous feminist scholars who stood up against the dominant White and colonial discourses ruling the Western feminist activism and research back in the 1980s. Adichie (2009) calls for the same aim when emphasising the importance of telling and listening to many stories, instead of a single one. In this chapter, my goal is to reach not only the dominant narratives, the single stories, but also the many stories talking back to the dominant ones, both by social workers and non-heterosexual people with refugee backgrounds.

Narrating homonationalism with single stories

The single story of Finland as a gay haven

In the interviews, social workers constructed a narrative of Finland as a safe haven for non-heterosexual refugees. Finland was portrayed as a country where everybody can get married, everybody can walk hand-in-hand publicly and everybody can 'talk openly' about their identity – something that was regarded as an unquestioned goal (see also Yildiz, 2017; Akin, 2019). Finland with its fair legislation, open-minded population and caretaking authorities was regarded as the *solution* to the social problems of homophobia and oppression. Social workers described how they used this narrative to create feelings of safety and to share knowledge about legal rights in their meetings with non-heterosexual service users.

When social workers were talking about equality in Finnish society, the most common example raised was the equal right to marry. It was brought up several times as the only example of relevant legislation on LGBTQ+ matters, as the following quote demonstrates:

	[Talking about the social worker's meetings with a same-sex service user couple.]
Kaisa (social worker):	And then I told them that in Finland it is possible to get married[2] or register a relationship, and they were like 'wow' and 'really?', and then the discussion went very much to that theme. They invited me to their wedding and …
Inka (researcher):	Is there something else … like special support that you would have given to this case, or something else that you would have asked about?
Kaisa:	Well, maybe guidance, and then exactly to tell about the rights and that you can get married, and [laugh] … The wedding, it is somehow a symbolic thing but a very important one.

Bringing up the Equal Marriage Act as an example of tolerance appears also in one narrative of a person seeking asylum called Francis. They talked about a meeting with a social worker in a reception centre, where the social worker presented getting married and starting a family as the greatest goals for Francis' future. This made them feel welcomed and included. Probably that was the intention behind the social worker's words. As the social worker Kaisa emphasises, marriage is a "symbolic thing but a very important one". In social work appointments, marriage was frequently presented as a symbol for freedom in Finland – a freedom to follow your sexuality without the state restricting it.

However, the single story of Finland as a "country where gays can get married" sidesteps the fact that Finland was the last Nordic country to legalise equal marriage, which occurred only in 2017. The parliamentary bill was passed with an extremely tight vote count of 101:90 and 105:92, revealing extensive homophobia within the Finnish parliament (Nurmi, 2014; Tolsa, 2017). Yet, these facts did not hinder social workers from portraying equal marriage as an integral part of Finnish society. This notion is in line with Akin and Svendsen's (2017) analysis on Norway, where the Equal Marriage Act from 2009 is regarded as landmark legislation constituting the national, homotolerant 'we'. According to Mepschen et al (2010), it is typical for European countries to present gay rights as if they had been the foundation of Europe for centuries, even though the mere idea of gay rights in Europe is only a few decades old. It was less than 100 years ago when European states not only punished homosexuals by law in Europe but also exported the criminalisation into their colonies in Africa and Asia (Han and O'Mahoney, 2014).

The narrative of Finland as a gay haven was also reproduced in the interviews with people with refugee backgrounds. In their accounts, what was emphasised was the harsh contrast between the situation in their home country and in Finland. However, the more time passed, the more the single story started to fragment into critical negotiations about the safety that Finland could offer. In interviews with those who had been in Finland for several years, the relief of safety in Finland was overshadowed by fears about future residence, experiences about homophobic and racist discrimination inside and outside reception centres, and feelings of not being seen and heard by Finnish authorities. This observation is consistent with Stubberud and Eggebø's (2020) findings that queer people with migrant backgrounds in Norway talked more about racism and structural violence the longer they had been in the country.

The single story of the countries of origin as villains

In social worker interviews, the countries of origin of non-heterosexual refugees – most often certain countries in Africa and the Middle East – were portrayed as unexceptionally oppressive and homophobic. These countries were constructed as *villains* of the social problem of homophobia by social workers. The oppressive image constructed for African and Middle Eastern societies was following the logic of single stories (Adichie, 2009); it was essentialist and homogeneous, with no diversity presented between different countries or, for example, urban and rural areas. Social workers tended to speak about the countries of origin in the same context as they spoke about Finland, as demonstrated by the following quote. This construction makes Finland look like the complete opposite; as tolerant, open and safe.

Riikka (social worker): [I]t is so distressing, when you have been persecuted in your home country and forced to flee, and maybe ... have been tortured and abandoned by your community, not only your family but, say, your religious community, and you are all alone. Then that's kind of the extreme end that no one accepts you as you are, and dealing with that is the extreme. If someone in Finland is confronting this, then how much more difficult it might be for someone who is forced to leave their own country to come here.

Creating binary oppositions between Western societies and otherised, non-Western societies is a very common form of colonial and orientalist nation building. According to Said (1978), countries in the West need this kind of homogeneous, demonised and exoticised image of countries in the East to uphold their self-image as opposite to that: civilised, progressive and tolerant. The discursive character of the categories of the East and the West tend to construct them as more diametrically opposed than what they actually are (Said, 1978). This discursive logic continues to thrive. According to El-Tayeb (2011), Muslims are regarded as a general category of otherness in today's Europe. They are discursively excluded from Europeanness and employed to create a unified European identity by emphasising oppositions (El-Tayeb, 2011). During the 21st century, gay rights have become an increasingly important signifier of this Europeanness and instrumentalised to construct a difference to the homophobic Other, especially Muslim countries and people (Fassin, 2010; Mepschen et al, 2010; Akin, 2019).

As Adichie (2009) said in her TED Talk, the problem with stereotypes created by single stories is not that they are untrue but that they are incomplete. This makes the one story become the only story (Adichie, 2009). This is the case with social workers' accounts on the home countries of people with refugee backgrounds. The problem is not that the homophobia and oppression in these countries would not be true. On the contrary, the participants with refugee backgrounds told me numerous accounts of homophobic public attitudes, arrests, torture, family rejection and severe persecution that they had faced in their home countries. However, the single story of African and Middle Eastern countries as *villains* is incomplete – it is not the only story of these countries and societies. It flattens the experience and agency of the people who are born and raised there (Adichie, 2009).

Constructing the Bubble of Oppression

When creating a single story of Finland as a gay haven, Finland was not only opposed to the countries of origin of non-heterosexual people with refugee backgrounds but also to their heterosexual compatriots living in Finland. In the interviews, social workers referred to this social context as "communities", "compatriots", "people from the same country", "other asylum seekers" and sometimes also "Muslim communities" – depending on the background and social position of a certain service user they were thinking about. Social worker participants referred to these "communities" most often when expressing their concern about non-heterosexual refugees in Finland as *victims* of homophobia and oppression, and, respectively, heterosexual migrants as local *villains*. The next quotation from a social worker mirrors the idea that the reception centre constitutes a 'bubble' of oppression inside an otherwise tolerant Finland:

Anni (social worker):	And then the fact that you still need to watch out for your fellow countrymen here … I have told many that even if this is a kind of safe space camp, you know that many people here come from a very conservative society, right. And it's good to take into account that this is still a slightly different environment than the one when you step outside of the camp. This has been something that's good to talk about.

The imagined, oppressive migrant 'bubble' consisting of heterosexual migrants and racialised communities is positioned on the boundaries of the Finnish gay haven – inside it but still impermeably separated from it and threatening it. Therefore, I call this construction the Bubble of Oppression. Sometimes describing the homophobia inside the Bubble of Oppression includes the assumption that to live according to their true identity non-heterosexual people with refugee backgrounds need to jump away from their 'community' to live in mainstream Finnish society. Narrating a clear boundary between the Bubble of Oppression and the Finnish gay haven surrounding it simplifies the complex net of belongings and identities that is the reality for many queer people.

Consequently, the problem of homophobia was pushed into the margins; it was not regarded as a structural issue in Finnish society but a problem of homophobic individuals (see Røthing and Svendsen, 2010). The assumed homophobia in the 'bubble' did not endanger the image of Finland as unquestionably homotolerant, because the 'bubble' was actually not regarded to be part of Finland. This discourse indicates that while describing the Finnish open-mindedness as presented earlier, social workers were unconsciously only talking about Finnish citizens with no migration background within the family – the dominantly White majority. According to Akin and Svendsen (2017), the stereotype that all people with a migrant background are homophobic follows from two co-occurring processes in Norwegian society – a rise in homotolerance as part of the national identity, and an increase in structural racism and Islamophobia.

Talking back to single stories
The many stories of Finland

The biggest problem with single stories is that they are incomplete (Adichie, 2009), and so it is the homonationalist single story of Finland as a gay haven. Therefore, it can be talked back to by foregrounding other stories, and that is something that all social worker participants did in the interviews as well. They criticised the government for tightening the Finnish asylum law radically after 2015, as well as the Finnish Migration Service (Migri) for insensitive and years-long asylum processes, which often led to denying the applicant's sexual orientation and the need for a protection claim. Sometimes the critique was articulated very explicitly, such as when one social worker described their feelings of shame for the "inhumane asylum policies". Most often the critique was more subtle and cautious, such as in the following interview quotation:

Kristiina (social worker):	We haven't had a discussion with Migri, but *it makes me think, I hope*, when they [Migri] assess whether things hang together and how things really are, that … there wouldn't be a threshold so that in order to prove your sexual orientation you should go back and forth in the [peer-support] group or go and march in Pride.
Inka (researcher):	What kind of impression do you have about the situation right now? Is it so?

Kristiina: *I don't know because I feel – I don't know. I do not know. [silence for 8 s.]* It is so easy to prove by participating in Pride. And maybe more difficult in other ways. *So, I don't know.* But I think that maybe some training, I believe they have already had some, to be able to listen to and hear those people, and then *make the right decisions*.

In the quotation, social worker Kristiina implies that Migri makes flawed decisions but does not say it explicitly. Instead, Kristiina frequently states, "I don't know", and has difficulties with finding words. I interpret the difficulty to verbalise a critique of Finnish policies as a gesture of solidarity between Finnish authorities, and, eventually, between social work and the state – mirroring the 'dual mandate' of social work between the state and the individual (Lorenz, 1994: 4). The solidarity towards the state was particularly visible with social workers working in reception centres that operate under the surveillance of the Finnish Migration Service.

Another part of talking back to the single story of Finland was paying attention to the discrimination in Finnish societal structures and attitudes, such as racism and homo/transphobia. Only one social worker actively brought up racism as being a mental burden for service users. By emphasising racism and multiple forms of discrimination in Finnish social systems she was constructing another kind of story of Finland; a story of exclusion and othering. Apart from that, racism was not mentioned in social worker interviews. Homophobia or transphobia as structural problems in Finland were also not discussed much. A couple of social workers talked about the strong heteronormativity in social work institutions, appearing as gendering language and heteronormative assumptions. However, terms like homophobia, transphobia and discrimination were only used when talking about racialised minorities in Finland as their problems – as neatly confined to the Bubble of Oppression (see Røthing and Svendsen, 2010).

People with refugee backgrounds talked more actively and explicitly back to the story of Finland as a gay haven. For them, safety in Finland was constantly under negotiation. The relatively equal legislation, protection from authorities and more open attitudes towards diverse sexualities carried much weight, but, on the other hand, the constant insecurity about the right to stay, fear of being deported, longing for family and racism and discrimination limited their feelings of safety. Multiple, interlocking systems of oppression were very concretely present in their lives (see Fellows and Razack, 1998). A strong example of talking back was given by a participant of African descent who was gay and disabled, waiting for asylum. They related several accounts of intersecting discrimination when seeking a job, trying to visit a gay club, navigating in inaccessible reception centres and trying to find a place in the right kind of support group.

Only participants with refugee backgrounds framed racism in Finnish social structures and institutions as a social problem. For them, racism and a precarious residence status were issues that severely affected their mental health, their sense of belonging in Finland and their safety. Further, in their eyes, racism met the definition of a social problem – a condition that is 'troublesome, prevalent, can be changed, and should be changed' (see Loseke, 2003: 7). The following quote by a participant called Tracy indicates how racism is constructed as a social problem – as the main reason why Tracy is suffering and wants to travel back home:

Tracy: *Many of us are suffering from being confronted by, maybe living with the issue of racism. The way they insult you, the way they look at you, the way they treat you – we feel really bad. Maybe we don't show it, but when we are among us, the way we talk, we are really, really, really sad about the situation that we are living in. So only the fact that Africa, when they will be free … all of us would like to go back home. Because you are tired of living with this situation of being confronted by racism – we are tired of it.*

The framing of racism and other discrimination was different in social worker interviews. Social workers presented their critique of Finnish social systems usually as side notes or individual examples. The vulnerability of non-heterosexual refugees was discussed a lot, but the reasons for that were seldom found in Finnish racism and multiple kinds of discrimination but most often in the oppressive countries of origin or in ethnic minority communities. Consequently, the structural oppression in Finland, be it racism, homo/transphobic discrimination or inhumane asylum politics, was portrayed as a context but not as a social problem. It was not the reason for the suffering of the *victim* – the non-heterosexual person with a refugee background – and thus not requiring intervention (Loseke, 2003: 83). It did not shake the image of Finland as a gay heaven.

The many stories of countries of origin

The story of the refugees' countries of origin as oppressive and homophobic was very one-sided and unchallenged in social workers' accounts, but much more multifaceted in the interviews with people with refugee backgrounds. They talked back to the homonationalist single story of their countries of origin in many ways. Sometimes they were directly challenging the racist stereotypes of social workers or other authorities, as the following quote underlines. Here, a person living in a reception centre talks about how they applied for funding for a bus card to travel to the LGBTQ+ peer support meetings because of chronic health issues. They were declined funding, and after that faced stereotyping and ableist comments from a reception centre worker:

Patrice: The first time I went to the reception to complain about it [a financial decision], the female worker answered me in a loud voice that 'well, how did you manage with that in Africa then?' I have been taken to school by taxi since I was little, because I can't walk properly. And when I went back to my room I started crying. They really hurt my feelings, even in front of other people. I understand that *they probably have a bit of a weird image of Africa and about our living conditions there – they think that we are all really poor or something.* Still, I felt bad about it and I think it's not fair.

Often talking back to cultural stereotypes was more subtle and based on telling not just one but many stories about the home country. The stories of oppression, persecution and violence were counterpointed with stories of loving mothers, active and political LGBTQ+ communities and strong feelings of belonging. In this way, the research participants were talking back to the absolute construction of the contrast between their home countries and Finland, as the next quotation points out:

Dominique: I was very active there [in Cameroon]. I participated in every meeting even if it was life threatening. [LGBTQ+ activism] is very, very dangerous in Cameroon – it's not for everybody. I was thinking that I was kind of an example for the others, that you can have the courage … But you get killed very easily.
Inka (researcher): Mm, mm, yeah. It must be quite different than to act in an organisation here.
Dominique: *Actually it's surprisingly similar.* I didn't notice any other difference than the fact that we were hiding and we were afraid, and that we didn't have a place to go openly. We were very anonymous, and every meeting was held in a different place … *But otherwise it was very similar.*

In the quotation, the participant challenges my own colonial assumption that LGBTQ+ activism would be a lot different in Cameroon than it is in

Finland. In Dominique's narrative, the oppression by the state is real and life threatening ("you get killed very easily"), but it is an external context factor – and does not define the activism itself. I interpret this as an example of the rhetoric of the ordinary (Juhila, 2004), where a marginalised person talks back to stigmatising stereotypes by highlighting the similarity between themselves and people in the centre labelling them.

Another way for people with refugee backgrounds to challenge the demonised image of their countries of origin was to describe their belonging to their own country no matter what. In the next quote, research participant Tracy describes their sense of belonging to their "own place":

Tracy: No one would like to leave one's own place to come to another place. Because you [can] never be comfortable in a place which is not your own ... Like, many of us are [fleeing] because maybe we are not free to express ourselves in our country, but apart from that, [even] if we are more poor than Europe, everybody would be comfortable in one's own country. That's the fact. And I think if Africa today [accepted] it (non-heterosexuality), many of us would like to go home. Many of us.

Tracy describes how they feel *out of place* (see Ahmed, 2018) in Finland, but that is the price to pay to protect oneself from persecution. For Tracy, Finnish legislation protecting minorities and relative openness towards sexual and gender diversity do not guarantee belonging to the society because of racism, exclusion and the discomfort of living outside the dominant White, European norms. I interpret this as a strong talking back to the homonationalist idea of Finland layered on the top of development; a country that every non-heterosexual person would want to be saved by (see Schotten, 2016; Klapeer, 2017).

Fracturing the Bubble of Oppression

The hostile attitudes of other asylum seekers and especially people coming from the same country were discussed in the interviews with people with refugee backgrounds as well. They talked about homophobic harassment, death threats and emotional, physical and sexual abuse in reception centres and in private accommodation. Often the assaulted asylum seekers were left relatively on their own when trying to protect themselves. They received important support from other non-heterosexual asylum seekers in the reception centre as well as the local LGBTQ+ organisation but felt that they were largely abandoned by social workers and other staff in the centre. In these cases, the *villains* of the story were not only the assailants but also social workers failing to make an intervention. In the following quote, a research participant called Nasim talks about a situation where they asked help from a social worker after being beaten up by their room neighbour because of their sexuality:

> 'The social worker talked to me and [said]: "We heard about last night, can you tell us more?" I told about everything. She said "ok now we cannot do anything" ... They said to me: "We will change your room to that side" ... I said "no, I just want to move to another place". She said "go to [the LGBTQ+ organisation] and ask them for help."' (Nasim)

The multiple narratives about not getting support from reception centre staff indicate that the violence and discrimination in reception centres are not carried out by single, homophobic individuals (see Røthing and Svendsen, 2010) but is structural, because the structures in reception centres lack ways to actively prevent it and intervene in it. These narratives challenge the homonationalist image of Finnish authorities as protectors and fracture the Bubble of Oppression as they shift part of the responsibility for the violence in reception centres onto the Finnish authorities enabling it.

In other kinds of accounts, the oppression in reception centres was more subtle than direct physical violence. Research participants talked about their everyday strategies to remain closeted and hide their sexuality from their friends in the reception centre, while still enjoying their company. For some people, being closeted about their sexuality was routine and they did not report it as causing much inconvenience, because it was something they had been doing for their whole life. Even though they were not able to share their private issues with their friends, they could still bond with them, play football and find togetherness in having the same background and similar life experiences, as described by a participant called Patrice in the following quote:

Patrice:	With those in the same reception centre, *we often eat together and joke and have fun in a normal way, but they don't know* (about my sexuality). They really don't know. Afterwards everybody just goes into their room and that's it.
Inka (researcher):	Mm, yeah, okay. So you can hang out together, not on a very deep level, but like this everyday hanging out works out well.
Patrice:	Yeah, *we are from the same country and we joke together and have fun*. Most of us have come here

> through Greece, so *we share similar backgrounds. We talk about it a lot, like how it was and things like that.*

Stories like this bring out the importance of different intersections. Many people told me in interviews that even if they need to hide their sexuality in a reception centre, they have many other things in common with other asylum seekers that they can build belonging upon, such as the same country of origin, religion, race or shared experiences of the travel. This emphasises the importance of remembering that while non-heterosexual people might be exposed to homophobia more in a reception centre than outside, with racism it often works the other way around.

Some social workers also resisted the single story of the Bubble of Oppression by recounting stories about growing acceptance and safety in reception centres and about their non-heterosexual service users' supporting family members. However, these accounts were few and mostly presented as exceptions. The fact that non-heterosexual asylum seekers might relate to their heterosexual friends in reception centres, even more than with White Finnish LGBTQI+ people, is something that social workers did not discuss. Solidarities and identities intersect and get emphasised diversely in different people's lives, which is displayed in the variety of experiences of non-heterosexual people with refugee backgrounds. The Bubble of Oppression constructed in social worker interviews was fractured into multiple pieces, and so was the imagined (White) Finnish unity of (homo) tolerance, acceptance and safety.

Conclusion: imagining less colonial social work

In this chapter, I have investigated the entangled relationship between social work, colonialism and homonationalism. I have examined what states of affairs social workers construct as social problems and who are the *villains* and *victims*, following Loseke's (2003) conceptualisations. The dominant narrative in my interview data was a single account of a refugee who fled from their homophobic home country to come to Finland, a haven for all LGBTQI+ people. In this narrative, heterosexual migrants and ethnic and Muslim communities in Finland created a Bubble of Oppression, where all the social problems threatening queer people with refugee backgrounds, such as homophobia, were externalised. Non-heterosexual people with refugee backgrounds talked back to these homonationalist single accounts by sharing alternative stories about their countries of origin, of other asylum seekers and migrants, and of Finland. They also emphasised social problems within Finnish societal structures, such as racism and an oppressive asylum system, whereas social workers tended to externalise social issues to the countries of origin or ethnic communities of people with refugee backgrounds, upholding the homonationalist and orientalist binary thinking.

Social workers have the power to construct social problems and to demand interventions – to act as claims-makers (Loseke, 2003). Racism and homo/transphobia at the heart of Finnish social systems should be acknowledged and regarded as worthy an intervention as homo/transphobia in ethnic, religious and migrant communities and indeed the entire society. This calls for the importance of awareness of interlocking systems of oppression in social work: acknowledging all the intersecting identities and forms of oppression that influence people's lives (Fellows and Razack, 1998). It also calls for cultural humility – a decolonial approach that stresses the importance of learning from service users about the significance of their cultural background, as well as reflecting on one's own culture, social positions and power structures they are involved in (Tervalon and Murray-García, 1998). This might mean facing a regretful sea change in the collective professional view of social workers as being innocent 'agents of social justice' (Baltra-Ulloa, 2013), and instead seeing them as part of the historical system of domination that, as all other people in positions of power, need to actively strive against social injustice.

In her TED Talk, Adichie (2009: 13:36) clearly illustrates the concrete dangers of a single story: "I've always felt that it is impossible to engage properly with a place or a person without engaging with all of the stories of that place and that person. The consequence of the single story is this: It robs people of dignity." Engaging is something that non-heterosexual people with refugee backgrounds highlighted when being asked about their social work utopia. They imagined a social worker who would be available, have enough time for meetings, strip off their bureaucratic mask and feel more like a friend than an authority. They stressed how important it is that social workers really listen to service users, hear what they say and take them seriously. Disentangling from homonationalist and colonial single stories, and committing to intersectional awareness and cultural humility, will take social work closer to this kind of future.

Notes

[1] By racialisation, I refer to the social process where the notion of race and its hierarchies are constructed as part of social reality (see Keskinen, Mkwesha & Seikkula, 2021). The process of racialisation labels Black, Brown and Indigenous people outside of the realm of Whiteness and, in doing so, reinforces the norm of Whiteness. Finland is characterised by hegemonic Whiteness, and the term 'racialised' is widely used in activist, academic and social discussions to refer to the collective identity and social position of people experiencing racism in Finland (Keskinen, Mkwesha & Seikkula, 2021).

[2] By foreign-language speakers, we refer here to persons whose mother tongue is a language other than the officially recognised languages of Finnish, Swedish or Sámi.

References

Adichie, C.N. (2009) 'The danger of a single story', [video file]. www.ted.com/talks/chimamanda_ngozi_adichie_the_danger_of_a_single_story

Ahmed, S. (2018) *Tunteiden kulttuuripolitiikka*, E. Halttunen-Riikonen (tr), Tampere: niin & näin.

Akin, D. (2017) 'Queer asylum seekers: translating sexuality in Norway', *Journal of Ethnic and Migration Studies*, 43(3): 458–474.

Akin, D. (2019) 'Discursive construction of genuine LGBT refugees', *Lambda Nordica*, 23(3–4): 21–46.

Akin, D. and Svendsen, S. (2017) 'Becoming family: Orientalism, homonormativity, and queer asylum in Norway', in A. Rohde, C. von Braun and C. Schüler-Springorum (eds) *National Politics and Sexuality in Transregional Perspective: the Homophobic Argument*, Abingdon: Routledge, pp 39–54.

Baltra-Ulloa, A.J. (2013) 'Why decolonised social work is more than cross-culturalism', In M. Gray, J. Coates, M. Yellow Bird and T. Hetherington (eds) *Decolonizing Social Work*, Farnham: Ashgate Publishing, pp 87–104.

Butler, J. (1990) *Gender Trouble: Feminism and the Subversion of Identity*, Abingdon: Routledge.

Clarke, K. and Yellow Bird, M. (2021) *Decolonizing Pathways Towards Integrative Healing in Social Work*, Abingdon: Routledge.

Elfving Ström, E. (2021) 'Rasismi ja rodullistaminen: Askelmerkkejä rasisminvastaiseen sosiaalityöhön', in A.-L. Matthies, A.-L. Svenlin and K. Turtiainen (eds) *Aikuissosiaalityö: Tieto, käytäntö ja vaikuttavuus*, Helsinki: Gaudeamus, pp 164–73.

El-Tayeb, F. (2011) *European Others: Queering Ethnicity in Postnational Europe*, Minneapolis, MN: University of Minnesota Press.

Fassin, É. (2010) 'National identities and transnational intimacies: sexual democracy and the politics of immigration in Europe', *Public Culture*, 22(3): 507–29.

Fellows, M.L. and Razack, S. (1998) 'The race to innocence: confronting hierarchical relations among women', *Journal of Gender, Race and Justice*, 1: 335–52.

Finnish Immigration Service (2020) *Statistics*. https://tilastot.migri.fi/#decisions/23330?l=enandstart=588andend=599

Han, E. and O'Mahoney, J. (2014) 'British colonialism and the criminalization of homosexuality', *Cambridge Review of International Affairs*, 27(2): 268–88.

hooks, b. (1989) *Talking Back: Thinking Feminist – Thinking Black*, London: Sheba.

Juhila, K. (2004) 'Talking back to stigmatised identities: negotiation of culturally dominant categorizations in interviews with shelter residents', *Qualitative Social Work*, (3)3: 259–75.

Julkunen, I. and Rauhala, P.-L. (2013) 'Otherness, social welfare and social work: a Nordic perspective', *Nordic Social Work Research*, 3(2): 105–19.

Keskinen, S. (2021) 'Kolonialismin ja rasismin historiaa Suomesta käsin', in S. Keskinen, M. Seikkula and F. Mkwesha (eds) *Rasismi, valta ja vastarinta: Rodullistaminen, valkoisuus ja koloniaalisuus Suomessa*, Helsinki: Gaudeamus, pp 69–84.

Keskinen, S., Mkwesha, F. and Seikkula, M. (2021) 'Teoreettisen keskustelun avaimet – rasismi, valkoisuus ja koloniaalisuuden purkaminen', in S. Keskinen, M. Seikkula and F. Mkwesha (eds) *Rasismi, valta ja vastarinta: Rodullistaminen, valkoisuus ja koloniaalisuus Suomessa*, Helsinki: Gaudeamus, pp 45–69.

Klapeer, C. (2017) 'Queering development in homotransnationalist times: a postcolonial reading of LGBTIQ inclusive agendas', *Lambda Nordica*, 22(2–3): 41–67.

Lorenz, W. (1994) *Social Work in a Changing Europe*, Abingdon: Routledge.

Loseke, D.R. (2003) *Thinking About Social Problems: an Introduction to Constructionist Perspectives* (2nd edn), New Brunswick: Transaction Publishers.

Lyytinen, E. (2019) 'Johdanto', in E. Lyytinen (ed) *Turvapaikanhaku ja pakolaisuus Suomessa*, Turku: Siirtolaisuusinstituutti, pp 15–35.

Mepschen, P., Duyvendak, J.W. and Tonkens, E.H. (2010) 'Sexual politics, Orientalism and multicultural citizenship in the Netherlands', *Sociology*, 44(5): 962–79.

Ministry of Social Affairs and Health (2023) *Sosiaalipalvelut*, Helsinki: Ministry of Social Affairs and Health. https://stm.fi/sosiaalipalvelut

Nurmi, E. (2014) '*Eduskunta hyväksyi kansalaisaloitteen avioliittolain muuttamisesta*', *Yle News*, [online] 12 December. https://yle.fi/uutiset/3-7685816

Puar, J. (2007) *Terrorist Assemblages: Homonationalism in Queer Times*, Durham, NC: Duke University Press.

Røthing, Å. and Svendsen, S. (2010) 'Homotolerance and heterosexuality as Norwegian values', *Journal of LGBT Youth*, 7(2): 147–66.

Said, E. (1978) *Orientalism*, New York: Pantheon Books.

Satka, M. (1995) 'Making social citizenship: conceptual practices from the Finnish poor law to professional social work (Publications of Social and Political Sciences and Philosophy)', doctoral dissertation, University of Jyväskylä, JYX Digital Repository. https://jyx.jyu.fi/handle/123456789/26927

Schotten, H.C. (2016) 'Homonationalism: from critique to diagnosis, or, we are all homonational now', *International Feminist Journal of Politics*, 18(3): 351–70.

Stubberud, E. and Eggebø, H. (2020) 'Voldsutsatthet blant skeive med innvandrerbakgrunn', in A. Bredal, H. Eggebø and A.M.A. Eriksen (eds) *Vold i nære relasjoner i et mangfoldig*, Oslo: Cappelen Damm Akademisk, pp 107–25.

Tervalon, M. and Murray-García, J. (1998) 'Cultural humility versus cultural competence: a critical distinction in defining physician training outcomes in multicultural education', *Journal of Health Care for the Poor and Underserved*, 9(2): 117–25.

Tolsa, M. (2017) '*Suomi liittyy 23 maan joukkoon – Näissä maissa oikeus avioliittoon ei riipu kumppanin sukupuolesta*', *Yle News*, [online] 1 March. https://yle.fi/uutiset/3-9473511

Wekker, G. (2006) *The Politics of Passion: Women's Sexual Culture in the Afro-Surinamese Diaspora*, New York: Columbia University Press.

Wetherell, M. and Potter, J. (1992) *Mapping the Language of Racism: Discourse and the Legitimation of Exploitation*, New York: Harvester Wheatsheaf and Columbia University Press.

Yildiz, A. (2017) '"Turkish, Dutch, gay and proud": mapping out the contours of agency in homonationalist times', *Sexualities*, 20(5–6): 699–714.

5

Social workers' perceptions on structural challenges for minorities' social care

Kati Turtiainen and Merja Anis

Introduction

Historically, Nordic welfare societies have been rather national projects, which has had consequences for organising and delivering social rights for their citizens. Accordingly, the understanding of social work practice has been framed nationally. Social services have also been committed to a state-centred ideology of the socio-political system (Askeland and Strauss, 2014: 251). In recent decades, globalisation has impacted the national context of social work and human services. Current neoliberal policies and the rise of right-wing populism further challenge social and health services to develop practices to meet the needs of diverse populations, especially forced migrants.[1] Calls for a new orientation towards decolonial praxis have been acknowledged in social work education and the field (Clarke and Yellow Bird, 2021; Turtiainen and Kokkonen, 2020.) However, it is also recognised that the policies, social welfare organisations and their practices do not always identify and understand the specific needs of minorities' social care. There are often national or local political choices behind these challenges, especially when scarce resources are allocated, or decisions about how appropriate institutional arrangements are made. While social workers confront social problems and (social) needs of cultural or lingual minority groups, they encounter challenges, which are structural in nature. Social workers' expertise has increasingly focused on developing structures and policies, which frame the implementation of social rights.

In this chapter, we focus on the responsibility of social care services and the social work profession to develop structural and institutional conditions for service provision. By social care services, we understand that both social and healthcare services provide care for human needs. Our data concern child and family social work and child protection, but we focus on social work, as well as welfare services and policies in general.

First, we examine how the social work experts understand the structural factors of social welfare organisations hindering the possibilities of migrants and lingual minorities[2] to receive just and appropriate services. Second, we ask, what kinds of social relations are needed to improve just outcomes for clients. We found Iris Marion Young's (2011) theory of social connections and responsibility useful, since it enables the analysis of structural injustices and focuses on how single workers along with other agents can take responsibility for migrants' social care. Principally, the basis of this chapter is the understanding that Finland is committed to following the EU Charter of Social Rights as well as EU Charter on Fundamental Rights, which are included in the Finnish Constitution. These Acts guarantee basic rights to all people living in Finland, not only to residents or legal citizens. Therefore, it should be assumed that collective power is used not to exclude or degrade any groups, and that the implementation of these laws is unconditional, and not based on people's status or skills. Moreover, using this collective power is vital as a premise of justice because the need for care is the basis of human condition (Staub-Bernasconi, 2010: 17).

Previous research

Nordic social work research has pointed out that Nordic mainstream societies and welfare systems have had difficulties in taking account of ethnic diversity. Social work in Nordic countries is often described as colour-blind and universal, and therefore unable to recognise and acknowledge ethnic and racial differences and racism (Pösö, Skivenes and Hestbæk, 2013). Social work is also criticised for culturalised interpretations (for example, Anis, 2005; Kriz and Skivenes, 2010; Eliassi, 2017; Gruber, 2020) and for following essentialist Finnish and European norms and values (Berrick, Dickens, Pösö and Skivenes, 2016). In social work practice, relevant knowledge about peoples' everyday lives and the shortcomings of the service system accumulate, which gives the profession not only a unique position to analyse and influence the institution of social work itself, but also the service system in a larger framework (Eliassi, 2017; Anis and Turtiainen, 2021). Therefore, there is a need to analyse structures and institutions, which are connected to the challenges in social work with ethnic and lingual minorities.

Research shows (Hiitola, Turtiainen, Gruber and Tiilikainen, 2020) that neither service structures nor the various services always meet the needs of service users, especially the complex life situations of forced migrants. The migrant background of clients affects the expertise of service providers and, therefore, migrants may be encountered mainly as representatives of their refugee status or cultural backgrounds, and not as unique individuals. This may leave the clients' needs unnoticed and therefore clients may not receive relevant services (Anis, 2008; Turtiainen and Hiitola, 2019.) Many social workers themselves report that their expertise is not enough, and they experience their work as more challenging when they work with migrant families than the native-born Finns (Pösö, 2015).

The situation is extremely vulnerable for the families having a precarious residence permit. They do not always receive information about their rights and help for family reunification (Hiitola, 2019.) The evaluation of court cases in family reunification and transnational families is also processed differently depending on the Finnish Administrative Court (Hiitola and Pellander, 2019). The precarious situation affects the well-being of all family members. For example, children do not necessarily express their needs, but instead are loyal to and support their parents (Hiitola, Turtiainen and Vuori, 2020.)

The redistribution of power and knowledge for migrants is weak in Finnish society. Consequently, the migrants' position as active and critical citizens remains deficient (Heino and Veistilä, 2015; Nordberg, 2015). This inadequacy can be seen through the lens of unjust outcomes, caused by intentional or unintentional structural discrimination. This indicates that welfare professionals do not manage to exercise expertise, which should lead to justice for all people. However, structural discrimination has placed service providers, as welfare state professionals, into a situation where their responsibility is to mediate between the unjust state, the municipal policies and the needs of forced migrants (Kokkonen and Turtiainen, 2018). Social work has managed to restructure its position within the changing political landscape by resisting changes leading to unjust outcomes, through creative practices (for example, Nordberg, 2018).

Social work organisations strive for cultural competence, which calls for the personnel, management and leadership to reflect the diversity of the client population. This goal requires a review of policies and practices related to hiring, development, promotion and termination of personnel, as well as the distribution of power within the agency. Cultural competence means varying and even conflicting issues to differently positioned members of each organisation. Conflicts may be essential in the process of culturally competent organisational development, especially in efforts attempting to redistribute power in the workplace. Therefore, to develop culturally competent organisations, the identification, confrontation and renegotiation of these conflicts is essential (Nybell and Sims Grey, 2004.) However, DeNard, Garcia and Circo (2017) emphasise the caseworkers' vital responsibility to facilitate access to services even though the institutional-, community- and organisational-level factors may cause racial disparities.

Social connection model for building justice

We apply Iris Marion Young's (2011) social connection model for building justice, where the concept of responsibility is central. In Young's model, no groups are singled out and blamed but, instead, all agents participating in structural processes share the idea of being responsible for unjust outcomes. This theory enables us to analyse the relationship between policies, institutions and practices, which lead to just and unjust outcomes. Young's understanding of the concept of responsibility is valuable in analysing the nature of reasons, which lead to unjust outcomes.

The basis of the responsibility model is the understanding that agents have at least *a mediated connection to structural injustices*. The model implies that there should be an agreement that at least some of the so-called normal and generally accepted background conditions are not morally acceptable. These conditions could be, for example, the institutional instructions or unjust practices that civil servants follow and, by doing so, they are responsible for unjust outcomes. Young's claim is that agents (for example, social and healthcare professionals) are not judged morally or legally because the outcome of their practice is not the initial goal, even though the result could be predicted. The agent may also consider that it is virtuous or useful to follow the formally accepted rules and practices (Young, 2011: 107–8.) However, there is an ethical demand that social work practice comprehensively reflects on how practices interact with policies, as well as on instructions and the root causes of problems in order to reach the expected outcomes.

Young's (2011) responsibility model analyses typical strategies, which agents use to avoid responsibility in relation to structural injustices. The first of these strategies is the *denial of one's connection to structural injustice*. It is typical for people to acknowledge the special kind of connections that include obligations of justice for those persons with whom they can agree or with whom they feel attached, for example family members or workmates (Young, 2011: 160). It is also typical for people to deny a connection to 'distant others who act together with them in institutions and processes mediated by many other people and things' (Young 2011: 158). This is a central reason for why a responsibility-type model is necessary instead of merely assigning direct liability to other people.

The second strategy is called the *demands of immediacy of unjust outcome* (Young, 2011: 169). In social work, a broad social view is an essential part of the profession so that our actions do no harm but to facilitate justice with those with whom we do not encounter (Young 2011: 64–165.) The third strategy is the claim that *none of one's roles calls for correcting injustice*. It can be said that correcting injustices is the role of the government, or that our role is to follow the instructions of an organisation even though we know that our practice might lead to unjust consequences (Young, 2011: 166.)

The fourth strategy to avoid responsibility is *reification*, which means that products of human action in social relations are understood as material things or natural forces (Young, 2011: 154). Reification can be a socio-cognitive view, through which the reification of phenomena and subjects is understood as a natural process in which we first *simplify the world as we seek to understand it, and then seek to institutionalise those simplifications*. Reification may function as an excuse for the harm to be acceptable for certain groups or people. Reification happens, for example, in sorting people into in-groups related to out-groups, which leads to limiting opportunities and excluding some people from service provision. Therefore, in social work practice, it is morally and politically necessary to try to de-reify the understanding of social processes and their effects.

Data and method

The data contain transcribed discussions and texts. Both have been translated from Finnish to English. The main research data consist of eight peer group discussions during Autumn 2019 and Spring 2020 with three social workers and one social instructor in child protection services for newly arrived forced migrants (refugees and asylum seekers). The aim of the discussions was to reflect and build knowledge-based expertise of the team. Therefore, a researcher took part in group discussions and brought material to improve the expertise of the team. The topics arose from the peer group members since the idea of the process was to build expertise together with the researcher.

These discussions were carried out by Kokkola University Consortium Chydenius. The discussions were recorded and transcribed. General Data Protection Regulations were followed carefully, so the peer group members received a research notification and privacy notice beforehand and they provided informed consent. The final topics were discussed and agreed upon with the peer group members.

The secondary data set consists of social workers' texts on child welfare and child protection issues. The textual material was produced as part of the social workers' specialised education in child, youth and family social work. Altogether, 32 experienced social workers from two education groups (2018 and 2019), who participated in the 'special issues in multicultural social work' online course carried out by the University of Turku, gave their informed consent to use their writings for research purposes. The themes of the course consisted of multicultural and transnational issues in child and family social work. The participants wrote reflective texts based on the broad instructions and questions given by the teacher. The writings were based on the participants' professional experiences and thoughts of the social work practice, which they reflected on the theoretical study material. The texts were pseudonymised, and General Data Protection Regulations were followed in every phase of the research process.

The social workers in our research material are experienced professionals, who at the time of the data collection were improving their expertise in working with migrants by participating in the specialist education or research-based supervision. This gives our study a special context, which emphasises the awareness of the shortcomings and needs to develop working practices and service structures.

First, we analysed both data sets separately and then by comparing our results, we found several similar themes, which recurred in both data sets. The theme of structural obstacles concerning migrants' access to services was evident in both data sets. We use thematic analyses (Ritchie et al, 2014) and sought out quotes[3] where social workers wrote about the structural factors of their work, such as cooperation in their teams, offices and municipal and state agents. We also found themes where they speak about laws, policies, instructions and practices at different levels of society. The focus of our analysis is to consider how social workers understand the relations between structures and social work practices and their own role in relation to other agents and structures. We found three types of structural factors of social welfare organisations hindering migrants' and lingual minorities' possibilities to get appropriate services: first, the factors arising from the client's minority position or status; second, factors arising from the principles of treatment and instructions inside the services; and, third, the laws and their interpretation are hindering the access to the services. Next, we analyse how the shared responsibility is possible across the different levels of social work. We focus on three kinds of relationships: first, service providers must start with building a reciprocal relationship with their clients, which enables them to empower the clients in relation to power structures. The second way is advocating for migrants in teamwork, management and with other stakeholders. The third way is focusing on the structures blocking the rights from being realised.

Identifying structural injustices

Cultural and lingual barriers and normalising suffering

People's prospects of accessing services are limited if they belong to a lingual or cultural minority. According to Finnish law (Language Act, 2003/423 18§), if there is not a shared language with the service user, social and health services must provide an interpreter. In our data, social workers showed that one of their tasks is to ensure that co-workers and other professionals use interpreters. According to our data, minority languages are among the main issues that exclude minorities from services. These imagined language barriers have serious consequences to service users as is related here:

> 'I have a family where a child has neurological problems and usually the whole family is offered rehabilitation and other support. I asked why this child is not getting these services. They said: "But there is this language barrier."' (SW2)

This quote shows how the child is left without services only because of his/her language. In Finnish language, the word 'barrier' (*muuri*) means a stonewall, which gives an idea of how impossible it is to understand the communication or to provide services through an interpreter. In our data, social workers working with newly arrived refugees or asylum seekers see almost daily how clients are left without services because of their minority language. This continues to happen although many professionals in Finland have worked for decades with migrant families using interpreters to guarantee the equity of the clients, even if they have health or social issues. It seems that 'the language barrier' is understood to be so high that it is not possible to overcome it and provide rehabilitation. Consequently, in social and health services professional ethics does not apply the same way as with native-born people, if there is not a common language with the service user. The Non-Discrimination Act (1325/2014) seems not to be applied with migrants. As a consequence, treating people according to their age level also fails, if the client comes from lingual minority groups.

The interpreter, however, is only a starting point to guarantee a shared understanding of the situation. An interpreter does not help if another 'barrier' – the cultural barrier – is interpreted so that the services do not reach or help people because of cultural differences. A social worker talked about a situation where somebody has committed a serious crime against a small child.

> 'But the police officer did not do anything since the expected (sexual) crime, it is part of the culture. (I said) it has nothing to do with the culture … my hands were trembling, I was looking at my telephone and checked the number was really from from the police.' (SW2)

In this quote, the professional expertise of the police has deteriorated when child protection services receive a request to evaluate the need for child welfare services. In this case, the culture is understood not only as unchangeable but also having extremely harmful features, which are normalised in a way that the police officer assumes that it is not possible to do anything. This is an example of how reification (Young, 2011) hinders the necessary actions and causes injustice. There can be either disregard, as occurs in the previous quote, or overreactions in the work with people coming from a minority cultural background. The next quote illustrates overreaction when other services report a problem to child protection services. It is evident that it is not the child protection issue.

SW2: We received a request to evaluate the need for child protection services because it was assumed that a child (from an asylum

	centre) had a louse in her/his hair. (Every now and then there is a lice outbreak, especially in classrooms and day care centres.)
SW1:	I contacted that day care centre and said that the family has done everything properly and actually their home is super clean and there is no negligence of hygiene. They did not believe me and said, okay, but then we have to find out another solution (to confirm their suspicion that this particular child living in the asylum centre has lice).

Here the extreme reaction is visible, when the basic instructions and professional understanding are not followed in the child welfare services. Harmful behaviour is normalised and considered to belong to the client family's culture.

> 'In the autumn the child said that mother hits him/her and then we got a request before Christmas. We asked why after many months? And they said that we thought that it is part of the culture … it made me think that they have worked 30 years with refugees, and they also know the child welfare law, but now, where are the rights of this asylum-seeker child?' (SW1)

The bewilderment in assessing the situation of a child from an asylum centre is explained in the previous two examples. In the first description, the workers stigmatise the child and the family suspected of poor hygiene at home. It is not part of the social workers' expertise and daily practice to interfere in these kinds of situations. Because the child comes from the asylum centre, there was stigma and social workers were called to help. The second example shows how the parental violence is normalised and connected to the client family's culture. In situations where family violence is obvious, professionals in welfare services normally make a report to child protection services. The consequences to the lives of families are critical in each of these situations.

In these cases, language and culture are reified in a such way that the suggested services are inappropriate or are not provided at all. Reification becomes a simplified idea of 'natural' and 'stable barriers', which is taken as practice among the welfare services. According to Young's (2011: 154) theory of avoiding responsibility, limiting services is acceptable because of the previously mentioned barriers.

The reason behind not getting help can also be a reification of suffering as being a 'natural', and therefore, accepted part of refugees' lives (Young, 2011). Therefore, the children's distress or trouble is also interpreted as part of the situation, which cannot be helped and, thus, the need for support or treatment is ignored.

'It is possible that the difficult situations of refugee families are in a way accepted because of the refugee and traumatic background, which delays getting help. It is easy to think that the children have become adjusted to the situation because they have lived in that situation with the family. It is, in a way, "acceptable" to allow the children to live in harmful circumstances temporarily, or even for a longer time.' (sw 23)

The social worker's reasoning refers to a more general picture of 'refugees as traumatised and suffering others', who are seen essentially 'different' (Ahmed, 2000). This kind of interpretation makes it difficult to imagine change and a better future for the refugee families. If social and healthcare workers normalise suffering, it sounds like accepting the differences between privileged people living in safe environments and those who are suffering from the consequences of armed conflicts and wars.

Treatment principles and organisational instructions

Some structural injustices are connected to the treatment principles followed in psychiatric care. The obligations of providing care are mediated by treatment principles, which can enable the avoidance of identifying one's connection to injustice (Young 2011: 158). These principles can exclude all asylum seekers, including traumatised children, from the needed services. When psychiatric treatment is available neither to the children nor the parents, the family will eventually end up in the child protection services, where urgent measures can be needed immediately.

'As a social worker in child protection, I have noticed the challenge that in psychiatric treatment, there is the demand that the family's life situation should be stabilised, so that the treatment would be "effective". As long as the asylum process is unfinished, the family's situation is also open and in a state of ferment in many ways. Waiting to get into treatment can be prolonged excessively.' (sw 19)

'Focusing on the traumatic background of the child can be inefficient, if the parents' possibility to get support services is ignored. But the parents can get [social and health] services only in absolutely necessary situations. Often in these situations, we are already planning urgent child protection measures.' (sw 20)

When the precondition for getting psychiatric treatment is a regular life situation, the inevitable consequence is that newly arrived forced migrants do not have access to therapy. However, if the children and their parents, in the previously mentioned cases, had received psychosocial support in an early stage of their difficult situations, the urgent child protection measures would quite likely not have been necessary. The decisions are made according to general treatment principles instead of careful assessment of the child's situation and need for therapy, as well as the long-term consequences to the child.

One structural injustice, which often leaves migrants without suitable services, is connected to the principle that all clients must be treated in a similar way. According to our data, this is evident in situations where the clients are somehow categorised to be matched with services without carefully assessing their situation. Social workers explain that the basic ethical principles of their work can be neglected if the individual situations are not heard, seen and understood, and reciprocal communication is not possible.

SW2: It is said in our office, that there should not be differences in 'the script', for example, in assessing the need for child welfare services.

SI: And we need time and patience to make our services understandable so that we cannot just meet once and decide what kind of service to start with.

The instructions may leave the common understanding of the situation open if the services are not understandable to the clients. In the end, the clients' situation is not improved because it is not possible to be committed to support without understanding what it is all about.

The co-workers did not necessarily listen to the experts who work with forced migrants and agree that 'the script' should be different than working with native Finns. In this case, co-workers' personal experience and the immediacy of the relations (Young, 2011) helped them to understand the need for different ways to achieve just outcomes. So, social workers may deny their connection to injustice if the instructions are mediated by experts or managers. As Young (2011: 107–8) notes, the agents in these kinds of situation may think that it is even virtuous to follow the formally accepted rules and practices, even though it might be obvious that it causes harm to clients.

The law and its interpretation

The amendments in the Alien's Act (301/2004) and its interpretations are a massive structural issue causing problems for asylum seekers in terms of service provision. According to the social connection model of injustices, the Alien's Act causes situations where service providers do not have a clear role to provide services and correct injustice (Young, 2011: 166). Asylum seekers encounter enormous stress when they must wait for the asylum decision for a long time, sometimes even years. It is very visible in the descriptions of social workers that the main reasons for ending up in child protection services have been created because of stressful living conditions during the asylum process, not because of inappropriate parenting skills.

> 'The asylum-seeking families' need for child protection services is caused mainly by the difficult circumstances in their lives where they have to wait for the residence permit for five years or more. Without that kind of uncertainty, they would not have the need for child protection. It is particularly visible in our work, that when we receive a request to assess the child's situation and need for child protection, we can't assess merely the content of the request. We also have to take into account the living environment (waiting in the reception centre) and the asylum process, which creates the fear of deportation, and the possibility of awaiting death.' (SW1)

It is recognised in municipal services that asylum seekers are in an unequal position depending on the place where the reception centre is located. The interpretations and application of the Act on the Reception of Persons Applying for International Protection (2011/746), Social Welfare Act (2014/1301) and Child Welfare Act (2007/417) differ from area to area depending on the municipality and welfare services district, which has a major impact on the well-being and rights of asylum seekers. There is confusion about which law to follow and how to interpret it. The result is described here:

> 'In many municipalities, for example in child welfare services, there are no services (with and for parents) but emergency placement, or children are taken into institutional care – there's no services before that.' (SW2)

The municipalities do not necessarily provide anything other than emergency services to people, who do not have a domicile in the municipality, such as asylum seekers and undocumented people. However, according to the Social Welfare Act (2014/1301, §58): 'In urgent cases, or when the circumstances otherwise so require, a municipality shall see to it that institutional care and other social services are also provided for persons living in its area other than municipal residents.' This means that families are entitled to preventative services, such as family counselling, before their children are taken into foster care. 'Child guidance and family counselling' means the provision of expert assistance with child upbringing and family matters, and social, psychological and medical assessment and care promoting favourable child development. This is exactly what the families would need to make their situation tolerable for their children and themselves during the waiting period. If the parents' focus and energy is purely bound to the asylum process and insecurity, the children are suffering accordingly.

Social workers must intervene with other professionals' basic duties if their clients or patients do not have a residence permit in the municipality. This is so even though, according to other laws, the right to service provision is clear. Above all, children must get basic services and treatment as per any other children.

Therefore, it is clear that the Non-Discrimination Act (1325/2014) is violated in many ways. This Act should function as a basis of every decision. Yet, according to our data, the principles of non-discrimination are often neglected and if the client is an asylum seeker these principles are totally ignored.

The previously cited quotes indicate the understanding that organisations or professionals do not have a role to correct injustices (Young 2011: 166). If the government enacts legislation, which leads to unjust outcomes, then there are civil servants, social workers included, who justify it, leaving people without social welfare and healthcare.

Relational practices to improve clients' situation against structural injustices

Empowering clients to become agents of their own situation

Social workers state that they, as well as other civil servants in Finland, "have been trained (with the idea) that our services are reliable and the (working) practices are of a certain quality" (S1). However, after starting to work with migrants and lingual minorities, they have realised that one of their central tasks is to safeguard that the migrant families and family members receive basic services just like any other families. This aim requires investing time to build a common understanding about a client's situation and exploring the options to improve it. The first step towards improving a client's situation by militating against structural discrimination is to build trustworthy and reciprocal relationships to uncover the reasons behind inadequate service provision.

> 'And then the reciprocity, we have to ask and create a common understanding and the parents don't know the system and possibly they did not receive the basic services and then they are in a doubly vulnerable situation.' (SW2)

The double vulnerability of clients, especially asylum seekers, is raised in this discussion. It is most visible in the situation of asylum seekers because of their precarious residence permit. It means that they do not get access to all the services, as noted earlier, but they must wait for their residence permit and live with this uncertainty. Families who have newly arrived in Finland or are asylum seekers are especially dependent on civil servants. It seems that often the situation remains unclear due to the unbalanced power dynamics and lack of building a common understanding.

In these situations, the social workers say that the grounds for building trust rests on assuring the clients that they are on the same side.

> 'We have strongly expressed that we are on the same side with our clients, and we do not explain away the other workers' practices.' (SW1)

Another way of showing that social workers are on the same side as their clients is that the understanding of the situation is constructed together with the clients, and not behind their backs. This refers to the basic tenet of social work ethics; namely, to work with the clients, and not just for them (Banks, 2012).

The crucial goal in the relationship with clients is to enable them to be empowered in relation to other societal stakeholders and rights. People who have newly arrived in Finland do not know their possibilities to get services or their rights. Vulnerabilities arise mostly because they are dependent on the civil servants and the situation, not because the people are vulnerable, for example, as parents.

> 'What are we as civil servants if we do not defend the rights of our clients and help clients to understand their rights?' (SI)

The first tool of social workers to reduce structural injustices is to build mutual trust with clients so that a shared understanding of their situation is possible. It is essential to respect clients so that the decisions are transparent and made together with them. The aim of the client–social worker relationship is not only to guarantee that clients get access to social welfare and healthcare but also to enable them to know their rights and become empowered in relation to other agents.

Advocating for migrants in the multi-professional cooperation

Social workers express that their work is not only in relationship with migrants to safeguard that they receive their services, but also in advocating for their clients in teamwork and in cooperation with other stakeholders.

> 'Our work includes advocating with co-workers and other stakeholders so that we would like to enable an understanding that we are speaking

the same language. So, our work has two directions (working with service users and with other stakeholders).' (SW1)

For child protection social workers, it is ethically very challenging to get a comprehensive understanding and assess the best for the child, and this calls for multi-professional cooperation and expertise.

Child protection social workers must remind other professionals of the special situation that asylum-seeker or refugee children inhabit. Their circumstances and capabilities should be understood comprehensively.

> 'I have been worried about the help available from different actors in the service system for migrant children and youth. Unfortunately, I have participated in many school meetings where I had to remind others that the child has come to Finland just a little while ago after a traumatic journey and difficult situations in their homeland. I had to explain that the school should not expect the same ability to learn and behave as from a Finnish child of the same age, whose experiences are completely different. Also, the parents usually don't know what is expected from them, since they are in an unbalanced and powerless life situation.' (sw 27)

Social workers explain that their practice also includes advocating for their clients in multi-professional teams; for example, by explaining residence permit-related issues. The starting point for multi-professional work is a joint understanding of the situation with other stakeholders.

Focusing on the law concerning the best for the child could be a starting point in assessing service needs for children living in an asylum centre to avoid the central focus on language or culture. However, this is just a starting point for a comprehensive understanding of the situation.

Social workers share that sometimes they take a therapeutic attitude with their co-workers if the clients' situation is not understood or the reason behind the circumstances is not clearly identified. They do not agree with the idea of arguing with negative emotions but endorse enabling the co-worker to understand the situation more broadly.

> 'Once when a worker complained that this is so difficult and so challenging and her/his integration process is incomplete and there are traumas behind it all. Then you just ask: "Can you please tell more about the situation?"' (SW1)

Social workers say that it is also necessary to influence the management to understand how guidelines restrict minorities' access to services. The management is responsible for deciding who is entitled to services and what kind of services are available.

Social workers' relations to legislation

The laws and systems at the national level greatly affect social work with migrant families, as described earlier. One of the main tools is to assess injustices from a human rights perspective, not narrowly from a national point of view. The interpretation of human rights does not help people to receive adequate social welfare and healthcare services if the rights are interpreted only narrowly as law. Here our participants stated that "it is more about what is behind human rights". This means understanding the root causes of the situation, networking and advocacy work with other stakeholders, guaranteeing parents' participation in decision making and the overall processes in child welfare and protection work (Räsänen, 2020). The reference to "all that is behind human rights" crystallises the relational idea of work with migrant families.

Some concrete tools in relation to laws are needed, especially for the child welfare and child protection work with asylum seekers. When the asylum application of a family or child is rejected, one core task of social workers is to help their clients to appeal to the administrative court. Social workers are the experts in Child Welfare Act legislation, especially in terms of seeing the situation from the child's point of view. They write statements and cooperate with lawyers to ensure that asylum issues should be seen from the children's point of view.

Social workers commented that an asylum application should be evaluated using UNICEF's definition of children's rights as a yardstick, rather than the unjust interpretation of the Finnish Alien's Act. Social workers also stated that their role should be more proactive since they are aware of the child's circumstances. There could be a need for care for a child to survive, which may not be available in their home country because of war or armed conflict. Moreover, social workers are on the front line assessing the situation from the child's perspective in the family reunification processes of transnational families (also Hiitola and Pellander, 2019).

Summary and discussion

Our results show that there are social welfare and healthcare service structures in Finland that *actively* marginalise lingual and ethnic minorities. Social workers state that migrants are expected to be integrated into Finnish society but at the same time the Finnish authorities are building walls. These 'walls' well describe Young's theoretical understanding of systemic injustices, termed 'reification', which means that injustices are understood as stable and similar to material things that are impossible to change, such as a stonewall.

If minority cultures are understood to be unchangeable and not connected to individual identities, then they categorise people into in-groups (majority) and out-groups (minorities) (Young 2011: 157). Minority cultures are thus constructed as intrinsically negative and harmful. According to Young's social connection model, reification is a way of simplifying the understanding of culture and precarious social circumstances, and then using this simplification as a practice of the agency. Therefore, it renders an excuse to avoid responsibility and leave people without adequate social welfare and healthcare services or a proper assessment of their needs. These results follow the same logic as previous research on essentialist norms and values (Berrick et al, 2016), as well as culturalised interpretations (for example, Anis, 2005; Eliassi, 2017; Gruber, 2020).

Another way of avoiding responsibility is connected to institutional instructions or treatment principles where the connection to injustice is not actively identified or it is denied. These instructions can be based on services which do not acknowledge the diversity of clients and their different needs or have tools to assess these needs. This is often referred to as the colour-blindness of universal services (for example, Pösö et al, 2013). A third instance of avoiding responsibility is connected to Young's idea that correcting injustice is not the role of the agent or agency. This becomes visible if the laws are interpreted without assessing the situation based on human rights, especially using children's rights as a yardstick of the practice.

According to Young (2011: 158), avoiding responsibility takes place because the unjust outcome is mediated by many people or long physical distances. We present here that people from lingual and ethnic minorities may be left without appropriate services, even in the face-to-face practices, if the service users come from 'distant places'.

Young's (2011) responsibility model of social connections is not only about identifying the sites of injustices but also looks forward. Here, we have described three levels of social work practices, where different relations could be built to achieve just outcomes. The first is a reciprocal relationship with clients so that adequate social welfare and healthcare provision is possible. The central aim of this relationship is that clients are empowered to understand their rights and, by doing so, to minimise the asymmetrical power relations with service providers. The second relationship is with team members, other stakeholders and management to advocate for clients so that a common understanding of the entire situation and the required services is possible (for example, understanding the root causes of the problem). The third relationship is related to the nation-state and its unjust legislation. To correct these relations, social workers need human rights-based approaches. In Finland, structural social work practices are needed to correct injustices towards forced migrants that are caused by the state (see Anis and Turtiainen, 2021). Integrating anti-racist training into agency policies can challenge racial stereotypes and empower agencies to address structural-level discrimination (DeNard et al, 2017). Training in workplace settings needs to address the concepts of power, inequities and systemic racism to improve social welfare professionals' understanding of race, racism and Whiteness beyond interpersonal-level interactions (Vanidestine and Aparicio, 2019).

Notes

1. By *forced migration*, we mean a general term for people subjected to a migratory movement in which an element of coercion exists. These can be movements of refugees or asylum seekers. We also use the concept of migrant/migration when we refer to the minority position and there is no need to address the cause of movement.
2. Here lingual minority refers to clients who cannot manage with the official state languages of Finnish or Swedish.
3. In the analysis, 'SW' (social worker) or 'SI' (social instructor) in the quotes refers to the main data and 'sw' to the secondary data.

References

Act on the Reception of Persons Applying for International Protection (746/2011), available from: www.finlex.fi/en/laki/kaannokset/2011/en20110746

Ahmed, S. (2000) *Strange Encounters: Embodied Others in Post-Coloniality*, London: Routledge.

Aliens Act (301/2004; amendments up to 1163/2019 included), available from: www.finlex.fi/en/laki/kaannokset/2004/en20040301.pdf

Anis, M. (2005) 'Talking about culture in social work encounters: immigrant families and child welfare in Finland', *European Journal of Social Work*, 8(1): 3–19.

Anis, M. (2008) *Sosiaalityö ja maahanmuuttajat. Lastensuojelun ammattilaisten ja asiakkaiden vuorovaikutus ja tulkinnat* [*Social Work and Immigrants: the Interaction and Interpretations of Child Protection Professionals and Clients*], Helsinki: Väestöliitto.

Anis, M. and Turtiainen, K. (2021) 'Social workers' reflections on forced migration and cultural diversity – towards anti-oppressive expertise in child and family social work', *International Migration Crisis: Critical Social Work and Social Policy Perspectives: Social Sciences*, Special Issue 10(3): 79.

Askeland, G.A. and Strauss, H. (2014) 'The Nordic welfare model, civil society and social work', in C. Noble, H. Strauss and B. Littlechild (eds) *Global Social Work: Crossing Borders, Blurring Boundaries*, Sydney: Sydney University Press, pp 241–54.

Banks, S. (2012) *Ethics and Values in Social Work* (4th edn), Basingstoke and New York: Palgrave Macmillan.

Berrick, J., Dickens, J., Pösö, T. and Skivenes, M. (2016) 'Time, institutional support, and quality of decision making in child protection: a cross-country analysis', *Human Service Organizations: Management, Leadership and Governance*, 40(5): 451–68.

Child Welfare Act (2007/417), available from: www.finlex.fi/fi/laki/kaa nnokset/2007/en20070417

Clarke, K. and Yellow Bird, M. (2021) *Decolonizing Pathways towards Integrative Healing in Social Work*, London: Taylor and Francis.

DeNard. C., Garcia A. and Circo. E. (2017) 'Caseworker perspectives on mental health disparities among racial/ethnic minority youth in child welfare', *Journal of Social Service Research*, 43(4): 470–86.

Eliassi, B. (2017) 'Conceptions of immigrant integration and racism among social workers in Sweden', *Journal of Progressive Human Services*, 28(1): 6–35.

Gruber, S. (2020) 'Migrant families, integration, and borders in the Swedish foster care services', in J. Hiitola, K. Turtiainen, S. Gruber and M. Tiilikainen (eds) *Family Life in Transition: Borders, Transnational Mobility, and Welfare Society in Nordic Countries*, Oxford: Routledge, pp 47–57.

Heino, E., and Veistilä, M. (2015) 'Integration, recognition and security: discourses on social support by families of Russian background living in Finland', *Nordic Journal of Migration Research*, 5(2): 91–8.

Hiitola, J. (2019) 'Locating forced migrants' resources: residency status and the

Hiitola, J. and Pellander, S. (2019) 'The alien child's best interest ignored: when notions of gendered parenthood meet tightening immigration policies', *NORA – Nordic Journal of Feminist and Gender Research*, [online], 23 September, available from: https://doi.org/10.1080/08038 740.2019.1655093

Hiitola, J., Turtiainen, K. and Vuori, J. (2020) 'Enduring suffering: effects of fathers' precarious residency on family-members', in J. Hiitola, K. Turtiainen, S. Gruber and M. Tiilikainen (eds) *Family Life in Transition: Borders, Transnational Mobility, and Welfare Society in Nordic Countries*, Oxford: Routledge, pp 47–57.

Hiitola, J., Turtiainen, K., Gruber, S. and Tiilikainen, M. (eds) (2020) *Family Life in Transition: Borders, Transnational Mobility, and Welfare Society in Nordic Countries*, Oxford: Routledge.

Kokkonen, T. and Turtiainen, K. (2018) 'Social work education in Finland', in M. Kamali and J. Jönsson (eds) *Neoliberalism, Nordic Welfare States and Social Work: Current and Future Challenges*, New York: Routledge, pp 171–81.

Kriz, K. and Skivenes, M. (2010) '"Knowing our society" and "fighting against prejudices": how child welfare workers in Norway and England perceive the challenges of minority parents', *British Journal of Social Work*, 40(2): 2634–51.

Language Act (2003/423), available from: www.finlex.fi/fi/laki/kaannokset/2003/en20030423

Non-Discrimination Act (1325/2014), available from: www.finlex.fi/fi/laki/kaannokset/2014/en20141325

Nordberg, C. (2015) 'Invisibilised visions', *Nordic Journal of Migration Research*, 5(2): 67–74.

Nordberg, C. (2018) 'Social work restructuring and paradoxes of professional identity in Finland', in M. Kamali and J.H. Jönsson (eds) *Neoliberalism, Nordic Welfare States and Social Work: Current and Future Challenges*, London: Routledge, pp 126–36.

Nybell L.M. and Sims Gray, S. (2004) 'Race, place, space: meanings of cultural competence in three child welfare agencies social work', *Oxford Journals*, 49(1): 17–26.

Pösö, T. (2015) 'How the Finnish child protection system meets the need of migrant families and children', in M. Skivenes (ed) *Child Welfare Systems and Migrant Children: a Cross-Country Study of Policies and Practice*, Oxford: Oxford University Press, pp 19–38.

Pösö, T., Skivenes, M. and Hestbæk, A.-D. (2013) 'Child protection systems within the Danish, Finnish and Norwegian welfare states—time for a child centric approach?', *European Journal of Social Work*, 17(4): 475–90.

Räsänen, K. (2020) 'Ihmisoikeusperustaisuus maahanmuuttajataustaisten perheiden parissa tehtävän lastensuojelutyön lähestymistapana' ['Human rights-based orientation in child protection work with families with a migrant background'], master's thesis, Jyväskylä: University of Jyväskylä, available from: https://jyx.jyu.fi/handle/123456789/71895#

Ritchie, J., Lewis, J., Nicholls, C.M. and Ormston, R. (2014) *Qualitative Research Practice: A Guide for Social Science Students and Researchers*, London: Sage.

Social Welfare Act (491/2014), available from: www.finlex.fi/fi/laki/kaannokset/1982/en19820710

Staub-Bernasconi, S. (2010) 'Facing the dilemma between universalism and pluralism/contextualism', in D. Zavirsek, B. Rommelspacher and S. Staub-Bernasconi (eds) *Ethical Dilemmas in Social Work*, Ljubljana: University of Ljubljana, pp 9–24.

The 1948 Universal Declaration of Human Rights (UN 1948) United Nations, retrieved from the 1948 Universal Declaration of Human Rights (UN 1948).

Turtiainen, K. and Hiitola, J. (2019) 'Migrant parents talking back – stigmatised identities and doing being ordinary', *Qualitative Social Work*, 14(2): 186–98.

Turtiainen, K. and Kokkonen, T. (2020) 'Citizenship, populism and social work in Finland', in C. Noble and G. Ottmann (eds) *The Challenge of Right-Wing Nationalist Populism for Social Work: A Human Rights Approach*, London: Routledge, pp 122–34.

Vanidestine, T. and Aparicio, E.M. (2019) 'How social welfare and health professionals understand "race", racism, and Whiteness: a social justice approach to grounded theory', *Social Work in Public Health*, 34(5): 430–43.

Young, I.M. (2011) *Responsibility for Justice*, Oxford/New York: Oxford University Press.

6

Deconstructing racialised and cultural otherisation with young people through pluralistic arts-based social work

Enni Mikkonen

Introduction

Young people seeking asylum in the Nordic context are often presented in popular political and government rhetoric as potential threats who are necessary to govern and control (Hart, 2009). The nativist discourses about risk-based immigrant youth disregard young people and their communities' cultural diversities, agencies, creativity and capabilities (Jennings et al, 2008). This risk-based perspective is racialised with monolithic interpretations and is problematically skewed towards young people of colour. In contrast to this, the principles of *anti-racism*, *anti-discrimination* and *anti-oppression* provide guidance for social work – a service-oriented discipline and set of practices aimed at advocating for social justice and well-being – to engage in critical ways against perpetuating racialised boundaries (Dominelli, 2010). In spite of these orientations, there are some shortcomings in social work discussions and practices in dealing with issues of cultural and racialising otherisation of young people.

In response to the nativist racialisation and the resulting social dynamics, this chapter discusses social work research project addressing the structures of racism and bias. I aim to contribute two related challenges to the racialising of risk-based discourses. First, I examine implicit 'Western' social constructions in social work (Zufferey, 2012) and, second, I address their limitations by providing an empirical analysis of the arts-based research project with young people from asylum-seeking backgrounds in Finland (Mikkonen and Konttinen, 2022; Konttinen et al, 2022).

Research-based scholarship and acknowledgement of racialised structures and their impacts within social work itself have remained scarce (Young, 2011). In addition to this shortcoming, social workers with refugee and asylum-seeker clients are often encouraged to embrace *culturally sensitive* working methods that guide professionals to adapt their working styles to mirror the values, knowledge-systems and preferences of different clients and their specificities (Edwards, 2016). These methods tend to privilege cultural preconditions in determining social challenges. Thus, they entail a risk that racialised structures and White normativity, for example, remain unacknowledged (Zufferey, 2012). Therefore, cultural sensitivity remains incomplete in its capacity to provide tools for deconstructing complex social hierarchies and structural obstacles that social work clients of colour and of immigrant backgrounds routinely face (Jönsson, 2013).

These shortcomings in social work research and practice result in contributing to and maintaining Eurocentric and colonial epistemologies, as well as normativities and invisibilities around White dominance in professional settings (Young, 2011; Lee and Bhuyan, 2013). They can cause the erasure of the agencies of peoples of colour who are made vulnerable to institutional failures. The presence of what are in reality hegemonic cultural norms is evident in the Nordic context (Ranta-Tyrkkö, 2011; Keskinen, 2021), where refugees and asylum seekers from ethnic minorities are vulnerable to discrimination within the same contexts as where they are required to request remedy and support.

However, there are also some diversity-engaged research projects in social work that reveal how racialising discourses and systemic hegemony operate. They question the implications of these dominant values, principles and ideologies of the profession (Gray et al, 2008; Ranta-Tyrkkö, 2011; Jönsson, 2013; Ellington, 2019). This chapter builds on the Indigenous decolonial paradigm that calls for providing approaches and methods to deconstruct the hegemonic ways of knowing and knowledge-production in social work praxes and research. It aims to identify the possibilities for and challenges to pluralistic epistemologies not only through research, but also through activism and, for example, arts (Motta, 2015). I integrate qualitative, ethnographic and participatory research and suggest socially engaged and environmental arts-based methods (Kester, 2005; Leavy, 2017) to support asylum-seeking youth of colour. I engage theoretical perspectives from critical Whiteness studies (Ahmed, 2004; Young, 2011; Lee and Bhuyan, 2013; Tanner, 2015), decolonial (Mohanty, 2003; Ranta-Tyrkkö, 2011; Motta, 2015; Seppälä, 2016) and Indigenous paradigms (Gray et al, 2008; Ellington, 2019; Smith et al, 2019). This approach aims to contribute new perspectives to social work paradigm that can deconstruct racialisation and therefore is able to engage in equitable practices with all asylum seekers.

I address Whiteness not only as skin colour or a bodily feature, but also as a set of meanings, values and locations that is historically, socially, politically and culturally produced (Lee and Bhuyan, 2013). Simultaneously, 'race' is not understood as simply a biological fact but a socially constructed systemic categorisation that biological and cultural assumptions are formed as mutually conclusive (Keskinen et al, 2021). This research is premised on the anti-racist orientation and importance of challenging the risk-based and monolithic interpretations of young asylum seekers by utilising social work approaches that increase the visibility of youths' knowledge(s) and agency.[1] The research questions are: (1) what kinds of entry points can arts-based methods create for engaging pluralistic social work knowledge-production; and, (2) how can Indigenous decolonial work that integrates arts-based methods be used to deconstruct racialised and cultural otherisation, especially of young people with asylum-seeking backgrounds?

The findings suggest three interlinked arts-based entry points in social work research which can create imaginaries and epistemologies that expand social work premise beyond cultural sensitivity and deconstruct cultural and racialised otherisation: those are *movement, horizontality* and *transformation*. These entry points open creative, embodied and interactional avenues for *situational-spatial, socio-structural* and *self-reflexive/advocatory sensitivity* for social work research processes and practices. This entails epistemological spaces to examine multiple power structures critically through arts-based methods (Foster, 2012). To that end, the chapter discusses the ways in which arts-based social work research can strengthen the discipline's anti-racist stance and take it towards epistemological pluralism.

Theoretical framework: deconstructing hegemonies of social work research through arts-based methods

The theoretical framework of this study, combining critical Whiteness studies and decolonial and Indigenous paradigms, addresses racialisation as a systemic, complex process. It is sustained and perpetuated through performativity which enacts interrelationships between White normativity and those who are considered others (for example, Young, 2011; Motta, 2015; Ellington, 2019). These theoretical foundations guide social work scholars and practitioners to reflect upon the processes that they may engage and that normalise Whiteness as a dominant social discourse in institutional settings (Young, 2011; Hatton, 2016).

Critical Whiteness studies (Ahmed, 2004; Young, 2011; Lee and Bhuyan, 2013; Tanner, 2015) can help social workers to unpack, address and ameliorate the structures of 'difference'. These processes simultaneously acknowledge Whiteness as a central feature of racialisation and emerge as some of the core contributing factors that take into consideration Whiteness and ethnicity more broadly (Lee and Bhuyan, 2013). Addressing Whiteness is a complex task, including a risk of perpetuating Whiteness as a monolithic experience, yet without means to act on or to deconstruct White supremacy (Tanner, 2015). Another factor that presents challenges to this work is referred to as the phenomenon of 'White innocence', which takes place, for instance, in Finland (Keskinen et al, 2009; Keskinen, 2021). There is a tendency in society to deny the relevance of questioning the legacies and continued implications of colonialism and race in the social structures. Such positions are deflected in narratives that align Finland with the position of vulnerability, as a small nation that has struggled for its own independence only a century ago (Keskinen et al, 2009). Therefore, Finland, as a nation, and its majority White citizens, are depicted as an 'innocent' party in the history of colonisation (Keskinen, 2021).

Working through the challenges of deconstructing White hegemony shows how the processes creating racialisation are linked to the colonisation and other global geopolitical dynamics. Therefore, intersecting critical Whiteness studies with the *decolonial* (Mohanty, 2003; Ranta-Tyrkkö, 2011; Motta, 2015, Seppälä, 2016) and *Indigenous* studies (Gray et al, 2008; Ellington, 2019; Smith et al, 2019) expands the ways to dismantle hegemonies in social work. Some social work research in the Nordic context acknowledges that intellectual colonisation and Eurocentrism are prevalent in the field's knowledge base (Ranta-Tyrkkö, 2011; Jönsson, 2013). Social work has also been criticised for a tendency to disregard local, traditional and Indigenous knowledge (Ellington, 2019).

In the early 2000s, 'epistemic mobilisation' was engendered by the Indigenous scholars who argued that their erasure causes critical voids in Indigenous belief systems and knowledge bases (Ellington, 2019). Epistemic mobilisation developed a research paradigm that rebalances power and builds on pluralistic epistemologies that respect diverse knowledge bases beyond colonial construct (Ellington, 2019; Smith et al, 2019). The paradigm change has influenced social work as well (Gray et al, 2008), though it is not yet fully recognised in the 'mainstream' social work research and is particularly insufficient in the Nordic context.

I engage practical and symbolic ways to decolonise social work paradigm and to pluriversalise its epistemologies and methodologies. Pluriversal epistemologies seek to engage in equal and diverse dialogical knowledge production, recognising the entanglements of colonial power in our ways of thinking and understanding (Mignolo, 2018). They transgress epistemic borders for decolonising, de-Whitening and deracialising knowledge – and not only by crossing the borders but also by looking beyond them (Mignolo, 2018). One entry point for this epistemic shift is about hearing and revitalising multiple voices and also silence(s) without perceiving them as passivity (Motta, 2015). As decolonial approaches are often criticised for their lack of implementation (Hatton, 2016), I address art as a means in social work research to fill this gap between conceptualisation and practice.

Engaging arts-based methods

During the last decades, arts-based methods have been introduced in social work research (Foster, 2012; Honkakoski, 2017) and more generally in the social sciences (Chambon, 2007; Leavy, 2017). As a method of healing, the arts can open dialogues for questioning power structures that are embedded; for instance, in our epistemic 'blind spots' and hegemonic conditioning (Tanner, 2015). Research acknowledges, however, that arts-based methods are not inherently decolonial (Smith et al, 2019). It stands that with critical, pluriversal and decolonial considerations, arts-based approaches can offer new ways to encourage professional self-reflexivity and awareness of cultural and racialised otherisation.

My approach to arts-based methods resonates with the activist and critical social work paradigm (Foster, 2012). It aligns with *socially engaged arts* in aiming at co-creating transformation in the consciousness of participants (including researchers) and audiences (Kester, 2005). Social work and socially engaged arts commit to co-producing knowledge in dialogic processes that build on active participation, communication and interaction with communities (Hiltunen, 2009; Mikkonen et al, 2020). Socially engaged arts utilise multiple methods and art practices (also referred to as community art), dealing with issues that affect people's everyday lives (Hiltunen, 2009).

Environmental arts-based methods can bring epistemological and methodological plurality to strengthen the Indigenous paradigm in social work. They can guide social work to embrace the traditional and local knowledges linked to holistic, relational, ecocentric and spiritual ontologies (Ellington, 2019). They also can deepen our experience of place and strengthen interconnectivity of people and the environment (Hiltunen, 2009). Both socially engaged and environmental arts are often driven by the ideas of change in respect to situated and contextual matters (Leavy, 2017).

Decolonial social work research can benefit from utilising arts-based *dialogues* that combine social and environmental aspects (Edwards et al, 2016). Dialogues through socially engaged and environmental arts-based methods create processes that are physical and reflective (Katan-Schmid and Gillette, 2017) regarding emotions, thoughts and senses. In these processes, also the body is regarded as a site of learning – including the imaginaries of Whiteness or racialised bodies (Murdock, 2018). Critical Whiteness studies and the Indigenous, decolonial paradigm guide approaches in arts-based methods within social work research as *intercultural* and *intersectional* premises that create ways to 'speak back' to colonisation and racialisation (Hatton, 2016). In doing so, they aim to expand beyond mere 'speaking back' and engage in accompanying the 'universality' of social work knowledge with unique personal and local forms (Hatton, 2016). This can lead to a holistic knowledge-production process, which widens the conventional ways of knowing and deconstructs epistemic hegemonies – such as White and Eurocentric standpoints – in social work in the Nordic context and beyond.

Interdisciplinary arts-based case study with young people

This chapter builds empirically on a sub-study that was implemented as a part of an international research project: SEEYouth – Social Innovation through Participatory Art and Design with Youth at the Margins: Solutions for Engaging and Empowering Youth with Trans-Atlantic Mirroring (2020–21).[2] I, as a social work researcher, collaborated with an artist-researcher and an NGO collaborator to work with seven 18–20-year-old people from asylum-seeking backgrounds (Konttinen et al 2022; Mikkonen and Konttinen, 2022). The youths were originally from the Middle East and Africa, with residence permits in Finland. They were contacted by the NGO collaborator, who had a long-term working experience with them as a manager of a family community home for unaccompanied minor asylum seekers. His role was pivotal in gaining trust and communicating with the youths.

Planning the case study was a lengthy process and it included face-to-face meetings and online communication with the young participants[3] while engaging in critical reflection on the benefits and risks of youth participation. Together with the youths, we planned and implemented two workshop weekends in the summers of 2020 and 2021, and an arts exhibition and a keynote speech at the project's closing conference in the autumn of 2021. In this chapter, I focus on analysing the first workshop weekend, a 'camp' (in the youths' terms), which provides in-depth viewpoints on decolonising social work research.

The camp was built around five workshop sessions consisting of the themes: *identity, worries, challenges and global connection* and *future, dreams, hopes and inspiration*. Each theme was addressed in different embodied, visual and metaphoric exercises. In *the first workshop*, entitled 'Me and My Environment', the participants – including the facilitators – presented photographs and visual items to talk about themselves, with the intention of deepening the connectivity in the group via evoking memory and emotional responses (Leavy, 2017). *The second workshop* addressed the theme of 'Our Space', utilising various materials such as wooden discs, paints and coloured pencils to express one's place and position in the world. *The third workshop*, 'Let's Move Together!', created space for physical activity and freedom for the youth to design their own activities. The youth participated as workshop facilitators and chose to go for a ride on fat bikes in nature. At the end of the first workshop day, we gathered *around the campfire* in a *kota*[4] to discuss the youths' worries and challenges.

The fourth workshop, 'Forest Pond', started the second workshop day with *a path of senses*. It entailed a multisensory walk in the countryside, during which the artist-researcher guided the participants to open their senses to see, hear, smell and feel the nature around. The exercise ended at the forest pond where the youths created an *inspiration jar* from small findings in the surrounding environment. In *the fifth workshop*, 'Future', we utilised creative letter writing for the youths to imagine their futures after five years. The workshop sessions created a continuum, and each of them began with lighting a candle as a symbol of a 'global campfire' to lead into a thematic mode of the camp (this will be described in more details later on).

At the end of each session, there was a discussion in which the participants expressed their in-depth ideas and reflections. The discussions were audio recorded and transcribed, forming the primary *research data*. The secondary data included photographs, video clips, artefacts of the youths and reflective diaries of the researcher. Various forms of research data required multiple *analysis methods*, starting with the interpretive *content analysis* (Neuendorf, 2011) by open coding and thematic categorisation of the reflective discussions. I used *the ethnographic* analysis method (Behar, 1993) for interpreting the secondary data, in particular utilising the *sensory ethnography* that guides in analysing the ways the senses play a part in the performance and coordination of practices, as well as interactions with the social and material world (Pink, 2009). The *analysis framework* was formed via identifying the themes by mirroring the data to the research questions and the theoretical premises of the study.

As the study involved young people embodying marginalised positions, it is particularly important to ensure that the research does not reinforce dominant narratives that (re)create otherisation. The main *ethical premise* was to ensure that the youths' knowledge and agency were centralised and they were considered as experts and collaborators who take an active role in creating their own narratives. My duty as the researcher was to maintain an establishment of trust with the participants. An ethical approach also requires that I (and all researchers) reflect self-critically on my own position as a White academic and seek an understanding of the ways that Whiteness can create limits for knowing and knowledge production (Motta, 2015). The youths provided their written *informed consent* after knowing their participation rights (the right to withdraw from the project at any time, anonymity and safety) in an inclusive and interactive process. Chosen research methods and frameworks provide experiential, reciprocal and sensory knowledge. This guides us to create and facilitate *dialogue*, *sharing* and *co-learning* between researchers, collaborators and participants, and to produce multiple forms of knowledge together (Seppälä, 2016).

Understanding the findings through movement, horizontality and transformation for epistemological pluralism

The findings show that the arts-based methods' ability to utilise metaphorical and visual expressions can strengthen a sense of communality in research that is based on creativity, reflective dialogue and a shared space. We encountered the young people holistically, including emotions, embodiment, social relations and spiritualities – which draws from the Indigenous paradigm (Ellington, 2019). At the core of the research there was an imperative to create a safe psycho-emotional and physical space, aiming to be free from categorisations and predetermined requirements.

Through the findings, I discuss three specific characteristics in the arts-based research that entail both opportunities and challenges to tackle racialised boundaries and White dominance. These elements deconstruct epistemological hierarchies and biases in social work research: *movement* via talking, doing, walking and sensing; *horizontality* as 'being and breathing together' beyond social boundaries; and *transformation* as an internal and external (reflexive and advocatory) process aiming at social and epistemological change. These were the bases in creating the practical and symbolic ways to decolonise social work research and construct pluralistic knowledge(s).

Movement

The camp implemented arts-based exercises that were accompanied with breaks, outdoors activities, nutritious meals and attractive physical facilities around early summer greenery in the countryside. The experience included psychosocial spaces that can be interpreted as involving *interactive movement*, taking place in conversations (movement of words), actions (movement of bodies), walking (moving in place or position) and visual expressions (movement of images and imagination). In engaging in a shared movement through talking, walking, doing and sensing with the youths, the epistemic space got redistributed and the question of expertise was reconstructed. As the youths were viewed as the experts of their life contexts, they provided the content for the workshop; whereas the researchers were rather 'context providers' for a dialogic and expressive action (Kester, 2005). This all led to *experiencing together* as a part of knowledge production.

The *movement of words in time* (Chambon, 2007) and *place* incorporated the theme of a 'global campfire' that the camp was constructed around. To symbolise this theme, we lit a candle at the beginning of each workshop session for creating a still space to reflect on the social challenges, identities and the future prospects of the youths. The aim of the symbolic meaning of the 'global campfire' was, in the first place, to strengthen and create a communal, intimate and confidential atmosphere. However, it proved to provide more than that regarding knowledge production. It encouraged the youths to reflect on temporal, spatial and positional questions regarding their socio-cultural environments both in Finland and their origins. It also led us as the researchers to be learners and 'unlearners' of our own bias, and thus it widened the epistemological spheres of the research.

We also sat around the campfire concretely, in the *kota* where we wrote our worries on pieces of paper that were burned afterwards as a symbol of letting go of them. This exercise triggered in-depth discussion not only about wars, evil deeds and racism, but also identities, belonging and culture(s). The youths expressed their worries about their families back in their countries of origin – and in addressing those, the role of the NGO collaborator with a long-term, trustful relationship with them, played a crucial role. The intimate space of the *kota* around the campfire created a sense of sharing and, thus, it offered new dialogical openings for research encounters. The process also proved the power of *metaphoric expressions*, entailing the plurality of languages: non-verbal, visual and intuitive. Metaphors guided the movement of words in *time*; to memorise the youths' past experiences regarding wars and racism, and also to reflect on their current positions and future prospects, wishes and dreams.

Around the 'global campfire', we also discussed how youths on the other side of the world may face similar challenges and worries – the same macro processes impact their local contexts. Global pandemic was a prominent example of this kind of a transnational phenomenon manifesting in local ways. Transnationality also shaped the lives of these young people in very concrete ways as they had been forced to leave their homes of origin, travel through many countries and settle down in a faraway society. Traumatising memories or disruptions in one's identity in the past do not bend easily to the verbal form; that is when imagery and stories step in (Chambon, 2007). The arts-based exchanges created conceptual and imaginary movement that encouraged the youths to express their experiential knowledge beyond contextual (such as nationality and cultures) and temporal (interlinkages of past, present and future) boundaries.

Movement was also about *sensitisation*; being present and sensing the environment and other participants surrounding us. In the exercise 'Path of Senses', we walked along a path to the forest pond, stopping on the way to listen, look, smell and touch the nature around us. The purpose of the exercise was to notice silent and hidden messages, to experience holistically and maybe notice something new in the environment – thus, expand our experiential knowledge. Therefore, we stretched the spheres of knowledge beyond words; to sensing and feeling as sources of information. Sensing is something that invades our emotions, to which our body responds, dictating to our minds and leading to thoughts, maybe changing their direction (thus, learning or unlearning) (Mignolo, 2018).

In the conversational circle by the forest pond, the youths presented their connections to nature and environment as a rooting, strengthening and essential element of life, and also as a connection to their pasts and places of origin. Expanding social work encounters beyond words towards embodied, sensed and environmental spheres can help researchers and practitioners to embrace difficult topics and cross social and epistemic boundaries.

As arts-based methods allow 'half-thoughts' (Chambon, 2007), the interactive movement took intuitive, not often predetermined directions. The following conversation between a youngster (Y) and the researchers (R) illustrates the spontaneous movement of images and words. In this discussion, we were gathered around the youngster's painting on a wooden disk in an exercise where different materials – such as paints, pencils and yarns – were provided for the youth's free use. This exercise was following the discussion on 'Our Space' in the world; to reflect, with given materials, on the questions about where we come from and what is important in our own lives. The image was a colourful expression that the youngster described as:

Y: This does not tell anything. I just drew as I just wanted to draw something. Nothing came to my mind. It is not anything important. It's just like this.
R1: But it is quite colourful.
Y: This lasts.
R2: You got colours in your mind at least.
Y: Only colours.
R2: Then it is nice as it's kind of three-dimensional as there's a thick layer so it's very lively.
Y: Yes.
Y: It felt really good.

This conversation includes the idea of a 'half-thought' without a clear conclusion, which guided us not to over-interpret the painting or visual expression; instead, leave space for intuition and silence, a thought or an affect that is not clearly determined. The youth's 'participation' did not always mean clear and polished views but such notions as "this does not tell anything" or "nothing came to my mind" were valued to accept uncertainty as part of the process. Allowing space for uncertainty and silence(s) can create trustful connections that are the basis of pluriversal and decolonial knowledge-production. However, leaving the interpretations open does not mean to remain in the existing position or understanding but it also includes the possibility for a change (epistemic movement); for example, through the arts' ability to voice/visualise the 'unsayable'.

Overall, the interactional movement of words, bodies, places and positions as well as images and imaginations in the research process can bring opportunities to learn from the silent, nuanced messages and to create more multilayered understanding of plural and complicated social systems that social work addresses. Consequently, movement is an arts-based entry point to help in deconstructing the singular conceptualisations and representations of racialised young people. It can be seen as a counter act for the epistemic hegemony calling for rational, measurable and scalable information as mere valid knowledge.

Horizontality

Socially engaged arts and social work paradigm resonate in perceiving the participants as equal partners in decision making, creating synergies and communality (Hiltunen, 2009; Foster, 2012). They carry an idea of horizontality in the research relationships and epistemology. The commitment to horizontality is, however, a complex process – including social and epistemological differences and hierarchies. As building on the Indigenous paradigm to view knowledge as relational (Ellington, 2019), the work produces knowledge that is locality-specific, situational and contextual (Hiltunen, 2009). It was particularly important to critically reflect upon the socio-cultural environments that construct privileges and inequalities and that can create fissures to horizontality in the research process.

Socio-cultural environments that defined the youths' positions were reflected, for example, in their considerations on *identity*. In their visual and verbal expressions, such as paintings, drawings, writings and reflective dialogues, the youths expressed insights on their identities as being partly Finnish and simultaneously belonging to their countries of origin. One of the participants reflected on the issue as follows:

'Finnishness. I visited there [in his country of origin] and people were always talking to each other. Always … for example, you go to a shop and the cashier talks with you. They are best friends with you. Like that. But it was a bit weird to me. I would not like to share my information with them. Who are they? I don't know them. Like all that Finnish culture has impacted. Yes I am a multicultural person and I am in-between them.' (A workshop participant)

This and other participants' reflections located them as "in-between" the cultures of individuality in Finland and communality in their countries of origin. On one hand, they had found it hard that the Finnish system expected them to live alone once they turned 18, while on the other, they had adapted to a culture where strangers do not often talk to each other. Their views indicated that their identities were fluid and dynamic, locating in various ways in-between intersecting socio-cultural structures. The participants' reflections on their identities deepened the understanding of their experience of 'in-betweenness'. Even though the youths were positioned at the societal margins on ethnic, lingual, religious and cultural aspects, arts-based dialogues created connections in which those differences could be harnessed into a source of mutual knowledge-production; through learning from each other.

Horizontality meant also the requirement to embrace an *intersectional* approach to recognise the overlapping social identities (Dominelli, 2010); as all of the participants, including the researchers, could find some – intersecting – marginality in them. Acknowledging those intersecting marginalities built plural realities that encompass multiple relationships that are interpersonal and environmental (Ellington, 2019). When we engaged in an exercise of 'around a campfire', sat in a circle and reflected on our worries, in that particular moment the borders between us were rather about our skin and consciousness than otherwise governed or controlled such as in the contexts where systemic racism, nationalism and cultural biases divide us into different categories. This indicates how the research encounters were constructed in a certain time and place, requiring continuous negotiations on the research relationships.

Horizontality builds on decentralising the dominant narratives, such as those creating simplified representations of youth in the public discourse. This was done by re-telling and visualising the youths' stories and by building on their agency and expertise as the core element of the research process. Throughout the process, the participants indicated their creativity, wisdom and in-depth thinking. However, building horizontality included challenges that were based on, for example, the power imbalance in which the researchers were the resource holders in the implementation of the process. Locating my commitments to an anti-racist decolonial praxis for building horizontality was not a simple (nor fully completed) task. To do so effectively required acknowledging the structures and hierarchies of White hegemony and transgressing them in my encounters with the youths. This meant balancing between being an equal participant of the workshops and also being sensitive and acting as an instructor when the youths needed guidance, encouragement or a listener. I also meant taking a position of a learner when noticing deficiencies in my own understanding regarding the youths' worlds. Horizontality was also disrupted in situations when some of the youths indicated tiredness or challenges in expressing themselves creatively. In those cases, horizontality meant leaving space for spontaneity and inactivity as a form of the youths' agency.

Ultimately, horizontality was about being and breathing together in a shared space, which led to embodied and intuitive knowledge-production. This requires that the researchers create an epistemological space that builds on mutuality, where 'giving and receiving' is regarded as a part of knowledge production and decolonising knowledge (Motta, 2015). The NGO collaborator commented:

> 'I asked them a little that how have you felt so far. They said very good. So, completely. So relaxing. Somehow that they have a good feeling and

excellent and ... this place is great. I said to them that yes we wanted that you also receive as you participate.' (The NGO collaborator)

The excerpt illustrates how 'giving and receiving' was a question about joy and comfortableness. As the themes and the methods were in-depth and intense, it was important to ensure that there were enough breaks, food, an opportunity for the youths to decide the activities and that the surroundings and facilities supported horizontality and in-depth encounters. Thus, material, physical and environmental structures played a role in 'giving back' to the youths and in ensuring that the participation would be a strengthening and refreshing experience especially at challenging times, such as during the global pandemic. Arts-based ways to build horizontality created a unique atmosphere of sharing; 'our camp' that could engender constructive and healing impacts.

Transformation

Arts-based methods included imaginaries and reflections that created a possibility for epistemic transformation for the participants and the researchers. Transformation through physical and reflexive interaction was a two-way process: first, it was about *internal* self-reflexivity that unmasked my own biases as a researcher and aimed at decolonising minds (Motta, 2015); second, it was an *external* process to utilise arts-based ways to imagine/advocate for change and equity with the young people. Transformation as an arts-based entry point approaches knowledge as a tool for activism and advocacy.

The arts-based encounters and dialogues fostered *internal transformation* for creating intuitive and reciprocal knowledge with the youths (Motta, 2015; Ellington, 2019). In deconstructing subtle processes maintaining White hegemony and racialised structures, the focus of the analysis shifts from the 'other' to the privileged position(s) and its ontology (Young, 2011). Committing to an anti-racist orientation, however, guided us to avoid recentralising Whiteness as a dominant structure (Keskinen et al, 2021). Instead, critical Whiteness studies offered a framework for confronting and examining the reflective self for critical analysis. The embodied aspect of arts-based action created space to consider how Whiteness was performed and normalised in everyday contexts (Hatton, 2016).

The complexity of this process was seen in the biases and epistemological limits that we inevitably carry due to our positionality (Mikkonen et al, 2020). As an example of this, the reflective discussions with the youths around the campfire indicated that racism in Finland was a shared worry; but I as the researcher embodying Whiteness do not face it in my everyday life. This may cause limited knowledge regarding racialised otherisation. The discussions indicated how embodying Whiteness can lead to a lack of understanding and also the ability to comprehend what is being shared by young participants. Thus, the lens of White normativity overshadows perceptions of how world social systems operate, including racism, to the degree that comprehending another's experience with otherisation is obscured by assumptions about one's own lack of experiential knowledge.

The lens of White normativity could be deconstructed by the decolonial approach that guided internal transformation through arts-based encounters and dialogues. It included the process of 'unlearning' the epistemic privileges (Ahmed, 2004), first, by recognising and critically reflecting on the hidden and taken-for-granted 'truths' in our own understanding, and second, by seeking for ways to embrace more pluralistic epistemology. In this process, I as the researcher needed to face my own uncertainties and discomfort as sites of learning and an opportunity for change (Motta, 2015).

External transformation can be located in the integration of social work and arts which does not only help diverse peoples describe the complexities of our social worlds, but it can recreate them by imagining them in performative ways (Chambon, 2007). Through arts-based encounters in different embodied, visual and reflective spaces we could 'hear' silences as powerful knowledge that can function as driving forces of change. These silences are the products of, for example, structural otherisation and erasure, but also they can be about internalised social identities as 'others' or inadequacy in communication tools. For example, when the most silent youths started to speak around the campfire, it changed the dynamics of the workshop, which planted seeds for an epistemological shift.

Nurturing methods of self-expression that go beyond language fostered transformation that could harness the youths' agency for promoting change in novel ways. For example, when the youths' Finnish language skills were limited, they could find alternative ways of self-expression through arts-based methods. This way they could utilise their intellectual and cultural capacities beyond socio-cultural boundaries. Building the arts-based actions and dialogues based on the participants' creativity, talents, ideas and imagination was, however, a lengthy process. It required that term 'marginalisation' – which often describes youths with asylum-seeking backgrounds in the public discourse (Hart, 2009) – was deconstructed and the youths' diverse views were centralised in the discussion. This kind of a shift in roles of social work encounters does not provide closed results but open spaces for new kinds of – more pluralistic – dialogues and epistemologies.

Discussion on arts-based entry points for deconstructing cultural and racialised otherisation with young people

I now turn to discuss how the findings – movement, horizontality and transformation – can create *situational-spatial sensitivity, socio-structural sensitivity*

Figure 6.1: Deconstructing racialised and cultural otherisation with youths from asylum-seeking backgrounds through arts-based methods in social work research

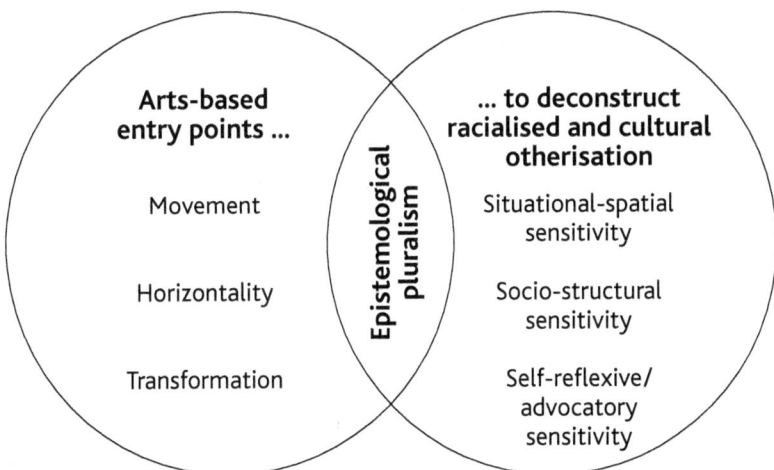

and *self-reflexive/advocatory sensitivity* which widens social work paradigm to transgress epistemic borders and deconstruct cultural and racialised otherisation (see Figure 6.1).

Movement through arts-based methods could create *situational and spatial sensitivity* for the part of the researcher. Situational sensitivity refers to recognising the interlinkages of time and place in the research process. In working with youths from asylum-seeking backgrounds, this meant being sensitive to their 'in-betweenness' on temporal and contextual dimensions; such as the meaning of their past experiences in the present and regarding their future prospects, and their simultaneous connection to their origins and willingness to belong to their current environments. Spatial sensitivity, in turn, calls for reflecting on the use of space and the experiences of exchange within the space. This leads to considering reflective and physical encounters with youths, which includes a looming question of racialised structures (Murdock, 2018). Spatial sensitivity means, for example, reflecting on the processes creating safe psycho-emotional spaces that do not guarantee a decolonising space if they are not accompanied with critical reflection on their power structures (Smith et al, 2019).

Horizontality in arts-based research requires and creates *socio-structural sensitivity* to understand processes creating otherness and privileges. The collaborative moments around the arts-based exercises with the youths included a potential to weave multiple conceptions of reality together in creative ways (Tanner, 2015). This potential builds a basis for socio-structural sensitivity that produces an understanding of intersecting social structures and identities in social work research encounters. It means sensitivity to not only the cultural aspects that have been discussed widely in social work (for example, Jönsson, 2013), but also to intersectional dimensions that – for example, race, gender, religion, language and nationality – manifest in our encounters, and the hegemonies these aspects involve. This guides us to challenge the logics of the narratives about the youths as embodying risks for unemployment, exclusion and radicalisation (Hart, 2009), which can assist social work practitioners and scholars to bring forth counter-narratives.

Movement with horizontality includes a seed for transformation that guides to engage in critical, *self-reflexive* and *advocatory sensitivity* on the part of a researcher/social worker. In this process, the experiential expertise of the young people is at the core, which can guide arts-based knowledge production that transcends the gaps between the binaries of conceptual/practical, rational/emotional, reflective/physical, subjective/objective and fiction/fact (Honkakoski, 2017). Self-reflexive sensitivity guides to not only cross the epistemological borders but also to step into the territory of pluralism (Mignolo, 2018) – where the 'truths' and ways of knowing are many, simultaneous and equal. It is the basis for advocatory sensitivity that creates collaborative and reflective spaces for promoting change, such as by presenting youths' thoughts, ideas and goals to wider audiences (such as policy makers) through performing arts and other creative methods.

The previously discussed sensitivities are interlinked and together they can create a knowledge-production process that widens social work's epistemological scope and deconstructs its hegemonies and power structures. This entails a pivotal question; on whose terms is the arts-based social work research developed and designed? Decoloniality builds on transformations and liberations of subjectivities that are tied to colonial and racial dominance – in this process, the duty of those who benefit from those structures gets highlighted (Mignolo, 2018). In these processes, researchers' and youths' knowledge bases and agencies intersect while youths can create their own meanings and act on their own terms. The researcher's role, in turn, is to be present where exchanges, disagreements, performances and transformations take place (Tanner, 2015).

Conclusion

This chapter has discussed the arts-based entry points that can bring specific qualities to methodology for deconstructing the dominant risk-based narratives about young people from asylum-seeking backgrounds. The results suggest *epistemological movement* for social work research and practice to embrace the subtle processes and structures that may reinforce the existing power structures, such as in situations when the researcher or practitioner acknowledges their privilege but remains without means or efforts to deconstruct them in practice. Arts-based entry points can create concrete and practical pathways to decolonisation and pluralism in social work – ultimately, they question the divisions between 'us' and 'them' (Jönsson, 2013), which can guide the processes of deconstructing cultural and racialised otherisation of youths.

Epilogue

> We sit in the dawn of the *kota*. Fire crackles, it burns our messages of worry and transforms them to smoke ... They transcend time and space; to imagine that similar worries may be felt in other times and places. While looking at the fire in silence, some usually quiet young people start to speak. This grows into talk about racism, evil of people, wars, religion, power. Identity, belonging, culture, dreams, wishes. This space of silence in the safeness of the *kota* grew into a moment of sharing something in-depth, powerful, which has a transformational nuance. (An extract from the research diary, 13 June 2020)

The overall theme of the arts-based camp with the youths, 'Around a global campfire', symbolised a dialogic space that combined multiple knowledges. 'Around' is a metaphor for a horizontal space where hierarchies are dismantled and silences heard. 'Global' refers to transnational connectivity, to macro structures that shape our worlds and knowing. 'Campfire' symbolises – in one of the participant's words – warmth and lightness that are the core elements of the sense of belonging. These kinds of metaphoric spaces build on ways and languages of creativity, communality and harmony (Mignolo, 2018), which can guide – with the recognition and value for differences – social work paradigm to decolonise its power, knowledge and being.

Acknowledgements

Writing this chapter has been funded by the Academy of Finland, Trans-Atlantic Platform, Social Innovation – call (decision no: 334786) and Finnish Cultural Foundation (decision numbers: 00200735 and 00210728). I thank the young contributors for providing their knowledge for the collaborative space, and Dr Leece Lee-Oliver for her critical and valuable comments on the chapter.

Notes

[1] Agency here refers to youths' ability to act on their own terms and make changes they desire to see, as through imagining valued futures, and responding to their social, cultural and economic environments (Mikkonen & Konttinen, 2022). Agency is understood as contextual and a socially constructed concept, including self-determination as well as meaningful participation and engagement of youth (Jennings et al, 2008).

[2] https://seeyouth.substack.com/

3   During the planning stages of the workshop in the spring of 2020, the COVID-19 pandemic broke out and we had to reduce the number of face-to-face meetings with the youths prior to the workshop. When the first wave of the pandemic slowed down, we were able to have one physical meeting for planning and building a sense of trust and community. We also formed a WhatsApp group for sharing thoughts and wishes regarding the workshop.

4   *Kota*, a traditional hut, has Indigenous roots and they are currently commonly – and mostly freely – used spaces in nature in Finland, gathering people around fire to rest, cook and share space temporally. In the workshop it functioned as a space that intertwined the historical and cultural aspects and built interconnectedness for creating a unique epistemological space.

References

Ahmed, S. (2004) 'Declarations of Whiteness: the non-performativity of anti-racism', *Borderlands ejournal*, 3(2). www.kent.ac.uk/clgs/documents/pdfs/Ahmed_sarah_clgscolloq25-09-04.pdf

Behar, R. (1993) *Translated Woman: Crossing the Border with Esperanza's Story*, Boston, MA: Beacon Press.

Chambon, A. (2007) 'Art works: between social critique and active reenchantment', in S. Witkin and D. Saleebey (eds) *Social Work Dialogues: Transforming the Canon in Inquiry, Practice, and Education*, Alexandria, VA: Council of Social Work Education Publications, pp 203–26.

Dominelli, L. (2010) *Social Work in a Globalizing World*, Cambridge and Malden, MA: Polity Press.

Edwards, D.M, Collins, T.M. and Goto, R. (2016) 'An arts-led dialogue to elicit shared, plural and cultural values of ecosystems', *Ecosystem Services*, 21: 319–28.

Edwards, J.B. (2016) 'Cultural intelligence of clinical social work practice', *Clinical Social Work Journal*, 44(3): 211–20.

Ellington, L. (2019) 'Towards a recognition of the plurality of knowledge in social work: the Indigenous paradigm', *Canadian Social Work Review / Revue canadienne de service social*, 36(2): 29–48.

Foster, V. (2012) 'The pleasure principle: employing arts-based methods in social work research', *European Journal of Social Work*, 15(4): 532–45.

Gray, M., Yellow Bird, M. and Coates, J. (2008) 'Towards an understanding of Indigenous social work', in M. Gray, M. Yellow Bird and J. Coates (eds) *Indigenous Social Work Around the World: Towards Culturally Relevant Education and Practice*, London: Routledge.

Hart, S. (2009) 'The "problem" with youth: young people, citizenship and the community', *Citizenship Studies*, 13(6): 641–57.

Hatton, K. (2016) 'A poetical journey: in what ways are theories derived from postcolonialism, Whiteness and post-structural feminism implicated in matters of intercultural arts research?', in P. Burdard, E. Mackinlay and K. Powell (eds) *Handbook of Intercultural Arts Research*, Oxon and New York: Routledge, pp 46–56.

Hiltunen, M. (2009) 'Yhteisöllinen taidekasvatus: performatiivisesti pohjoisen sosiokulttuurisissa ympäristöissä' ['Communal art education: performatively in the Northern sociocultural environments'], doctoral dissertation, University of Lapland, Acta electronica Universitatis Lapponiensis. http://lauda.ulapland.fi/handle/10024/61710

Honkakoski, A. (2017) 'Taiteen ja sosiaalisen työn rajalla – kohtauspaikkana draama' ['At the borders of art and social work – drama as a place to encounters'], doctoral dissertation, University of Lapland, Acta electronica Universitatis Lapponiensis. http://lauda.ulapland.fi/handle/10024/62670

Jennings, L.B., Parra-Medina, D., Hilfinger-Messias, D.K. and McLoughlin, K. (2008) 'Perspectives on participation: toward a critical social theory of youth empowerment', *Journal of Community Practice*, 14(1–2): 31–55.

Jönsson, J. (2013) 'Social work beyond cultural otherisation', *Nordic Social Work Research*, 3(2): 159–67.

Katan-Schmid, M. and Gillette, E. (2017) 'Dance for empathy: embodied practice and the physical-mental act of understanding', *Proceedings of Dance Fields Conference*, UK. www.academia.edu/31534528/Dance_for_Empathy_Embodied_Practice_and_the_Physical_Mental_Act_of_Understanding_Book_of_abstracts_Dance_fields_

Keskinen, S. (2021) 'Kolonialismin ja rasismin historiaa Suomesta käsin' ['History of colonialism and racism from the Finnish perspective'], in S. Keskinen, M. Seikkula and F. Mkwesha (eds) *Rasismi, valta ja vastarinta: Rodullistaminen, valkoisuus ja koloniaalisuus Suomessa* [*Racism, Power and Resistance: Racialisation, Whiteness and Colonialism in Finland*], Helsinki: Gaudeamus, pp 69–84.

Keskinen, S., Irni, D. and Tuori, S. (2009) *Complying with Colonialism: Gender, Race and Ethnicity in the Nordic Region*, Farnham: Ashgate.

Keskinen, S. Mkwesha, F. and Seikkula, M. (2021) 'Teoreettisen keskustelun avaimet – Rasismi, valkoisuus ja koloniaalisuuden purkaminen' ['Keys of theoretical discussion – racism, Whiteness and deconstruction of colonialism'], in S. Keskinen, M. Seikkula and F. Mkwesha (eds) *Rasismi, valta ja vastarinta: Rodullistaminen, valkoisuus ja koloniaalisuus Suomessa* [*Racism, Power and Resistance: Racialisation, Whiteness and Colonialism in Finland*], Helsinki: Gaudeamus, pp 45–68.

Kester, G. (2005) 'Conversation pieces: the role of dialogue in socially engaged art' in Z. Kocur and S. Leung (eds) *Theory in Contemporary Art since 1985*, Oxford: Blackwell, pp 76–100.

Konttinen, K., Mikkonen, E. and Ylisuvanto, M. (2022) 'Dialogues for plurality – art-based exchange for strengthening the youth's role as agents of change', in S. Miettinen, E. Mikkonen, M.C. Loschiavo dos Santos and M. Sarantou (eds) *Artistic Cartographies and Design Explorations Towards the Pluriverse*, New York: Routledge.

Leavy, P. (ed) (2017) *Handbook of Arts-Based Research*, New York and London: Guilford Press.

Lee, E. and Bhuyan, R. (2013) 'Negotiating within Whiteness in cross-cultural clinical encounters', *Social Service Review*, 87(1): 98–130.

Mignolo, W.D. (2018) 'Foreword: on pluriversality and multipolarity', in B. Reiter (ed) *Constructing the Pluriverse: the Geopolitics of Knowledge*, Durham, NC and London: Duke University Press, pp ix–xvi.

Mikkonen, E., Hiltunen, M. and Laitinen, M. (2020) 'My stage: participatory theatre with immigrant women as a decolonizing method in art-based research', *Art/Research International: a Transdisciplinary Journal*, 5(1): 104–28.

Mikkonen, E. and Konttinen, K. (2022) ' "We really have quite a lot to say …": fostering agency of youth with asylum seeking backgrounds via arts-based methods and dialogue as actions of empathy', in M. Sarantou and S. Miettinen (eds) *Empathy and Business Transformation*, London: Routledge.

Mohanty, C.T. (2003) *Feminism Without Borders: Decolonizing Theory, Practicing Solidarity*, Durham, NC and London: Duke University Press.

Motta, S. (2015) 'Becoming woman: on exile and belonging to the borderlands', in Z. Arashiro and M. Barahona (eds) *Women in Academia Crossing North–South Borders: Gender, Race and Displacement*, London: Lexington Books, pp 89–116.

Murdock, S. (2018) 'Designing for equity: social impact in performing arts-based cultural exchange', doctoral dissertation, University of California, ProQuest Dissertations Publishing. https://escholarship.org/uc/item/46p561r4

Neuendorf, K.A. (2011) 'Content analysis: a methodological partner for gender research', *Sex Roles*, 64(3): 276–89.

Pink, S. (2009) *Doing Sensory Ethnography*, London: SAGE.

Ranta-Tyrkkö, S. (2011) 'High time for postcolonial analysis in social work', *Nordic Social Work Research*, 1(1): 25–41.

Seppälä, T. (2016) 'Feminizing resistance, decolonizing solidarity: contesting neoliberal development in the Global South', *Journal of Resistance Studies*, 2(1): 12–47.

Smith, T.S., Tuck, E. and Yang, K.W. (2019) 'Introduction', in T.S. Smith, E. Tuck and K.W. Yang (eds) *Indigenous and Decolonizing Studies in Education: Mapping the Long View*, New York: Routledge.

Tanner, S.J. (2015) 'What the Whiteness project should have been: poetry as a collaborative vehicle for inquiry', *English Journal, High school edition; Urbana*, 104(4): 65–70.

Young, S. (2011) 'Social work theory and practice: the invisibility of Whiteness', in A. Moreton-Robinson (ed) *Whitening Race: Essays in Social and Cultural Criticism*, Canberra: Aboriginal Studies Press, pp 104–18.

Zufferey, C. (2012) ' "Not knowing that I do not know and not wanting to know": reflections of a White Australian social worker', *International Social Work*, 56(5): 659–73.

PART II

Naming and confronting epistemic and structural injustice

7

Silence so loud it hurts: racialisation, erasure and future-building in Finnish social work

Koko Hubara

Introduction

Before I obtained my master's degree in social work in 2020, but after I had received my bachelor's degree in the same subject in 2014, I published a collection of essays in the Finnish language (Hubara, 2017). The name of my book *Ruskeat Tytöt – Tunne-esseitä*, is *Brown Girls – Emotional Essays* in English. In the book, I talk about what it means to me to be a Brown Finnish girl/woman/mother with a working-class background in a country that considers itself purely White (not always maliciously, but just out of White normative bliss, perhaps). In the book, I write about single motherhood, Yemen/Israel/Palestine, Brown fathers, Paris and hip-hop culture, girlhood and literature among many other subjects. In one chapter, called 'Tarina Zorasta, Tonista ja pienestä jemeniläisestä kirjatoukasta' ('The story of Zora, Toni and the little Yemeni bookworm'), I describe what I call a 'Systematic White Rage' ('*systemaattinen, valkoinen raivo*'). It is phenomenological: an anger and a grief-induced pain so intense, so bright, it makes a person lose the broad scope of their vision, all but for a very sharp, white light that fills your eyes instead of tears. It's as if you're being forced to look at the sun while, simultaneously, someone (who? what? why?) violently presses their palms over your ears, nearly breaking your skull, making it impossible to hear anything or move your head. In the chapter, I tried to make the sensation comprehensible, noting the existential grip that causes a radical, physical aggression to shoot through the body. It hurts not just the ears or the head, but also my entire being, past, present – and future. I said, loosely translated, that like sleep is to death, White, bright, rage is the second cousin of structural racism and patriarchal oppression. The relentless blinding anger and frustration is born from experiencing constant microaggressions, systemic marginalisation and taunting within a home country, and in a hometown that is structurally built to militate against most of the things I happen to be, not by choice, but by the coincidental nature of the universe. I come back to this later in the section titled 'Story of arrival'.

Beginnings and consciousness

For as long as I can remember, I have been bombarded with questions about why my name is so strange, why I look so different, why my hair feels rough like a horse's mane. I have been asked whether I was adopted, or a souvenir that my mother got while travelling, or if my father is one of those criminals/rapists who come here to paradoxically *both* steal real Finns' jobs *and* live on welfare paid by real Finnish taxpayers? I could go on for pages. The last time this happened was the very month while writing this chapter. It happened in a work environment. Not to go into detail, but I've experienced actual physical violence since I was in elementary school, by both children and adults. I have been subjected to racial slurs in public spaces just for standing in line at the grocery store. I have been flat out being denied a job and an apartment because I have a foreign name. I'm not White in a space that conceptualises the nation and citizenry through White normativity. These experiences are not only mine, but also shared by my little sisters, my father and some other family members who are not White Finns. One can hopefully see why Systematic White Rage would be, if not the proper reaction, quite frankly the only possible one.

At the same time, I have wondered many times in my life if I might have a peculiar form of synaesthesia; the perceptual phenomenon where when one sense is stimulated, another sense has some type of involuntary experience. One of the most common forms of synaesthesia is the one in which certain letters or numbers or musical notes are associated with certain colours. In my case, I attach physical feelings to both theories and stories I read. I experience pain, mostly mild, in different parts of my body, depending on what I'm reading. If it's a beautiful story that I relate to, the pain is in my sternum. When I deal with or read about White supremacy, the pain is in my eyes and turns everything bright and white (as previously mentioned). When I see my White mother move in the world differently from me, but also carry the pains of racism into the domestic sphere through her proximity to Brownness, I experience a chest pain that's below and to the left of the sternum – my heart. Stomach ache is for love and sexual violence (I get those confused a lot), and so on

And when I think of social work in light of critical race theories, there is, of course, the Systematic White Light of rage generated by the generalised, historical, systemic racism that is found in academia in the world at-large, but the ache is more intense around and in my ears. It's because of a silence so loud I almost can't hear my own thoughts through it.

Finland: the best, most racist country

Finland is, according to numerous indicators, 'the best country in the world' (Statistics Finland, 2019). We are one of the happiest countries in the world (World Happiness Report, 2019), one of the most equal countries in the world (World Economic Forum, 2018) and at the top of the Press Freedom Index (World Press Freedom Index, 2019).

At the same time, Finland is the most racist country to those who come from sub-Saharan Africa (European Union Agency for Fundamental Rights, 2018: 15). An immigrant woman earns 62 cents for each euro a native Finnish man earns (SAK, 2016). Immigrants are 2.5 times more likely to become victims of physical assault than native Finns. Immigrant women are almost twice more likely to become victims of rape than native Finn women. If you take into account only women with an African background, the number is seven times more likely, and if you look at Vietnamese women, it's five times more likely (Lehti et al, 2014). Anti-Semitism, Islamophobia, far-right politics and the populism associated with them, nationalist ideologies on the rise, not just in the US, Latin America, but also in Europe, and therefore in Finland (Pelkonen, 2019; YLE, Puhe).

Usually, when I raise the matter of Finnish racism in my everyday life and sometimes at work, I'm told that the problem is that there have been immigrants in Finland for such a short time that 'we' haven't got used to them yet. And, if I would just be more patient and behave better and not cause a problem, things will get easier soon. The problem with this rationalisation is that there have always been BIPOC (Black, Indigenous, People of Colour) in Finland. The first known Black person to receive Finnish citizenship was Rosa Emilia Clay, in 1899. She moved to Finland from Ovamboland, or what is now Namibia (*Kansallisbiografia*, 2011). Finland has never been a monoculture or an ethnically homogeneous country or people, and the Sámi people, Roma people, Tatar people and Jewish people have always been a part of the Finnish demographic landscape. According to the Finnish historian Miika Tervonen (2015), homogeneous Finnishness is a myth that was created in the 1800s as a part of a larger European nationalist movement. The aim of the myth was to generate a nationalistic narrative; that is to say, a uniform story, of a White Finnish Finland, separate from a time when we ourselves were colonised by first Sweden and then Russia (Tervonen, 2015: 137–62).

BIPOC will not stop moving to Finland. Different (geo)political conflicts and the climate crisis have caused people all over the world, but especially the so-called South and East, to become immigrants and refugees. There are currently more than 70 million people who cannot live in their own homes. Around 0.04 per cent of these people (have) come to Finland through different programmes that aid and help resettle people, such as the United

Nations (Pakolaisapu, 2019). There are also many other reasons why people would move to Finland from all parts of the world: family, work, love, studies, by accident, on a whim and so on. Depending on how one counts, there were 250,000–400,000 foreign citizens or non-Finnish speakers living in Finland in 2017 (Väestöliitto, 2019). With these statistical facts, it is a little bit easier to dismantle the myth of a uniform narrative of Finnishness. What is often forgotten in both these conversations, and in research in general, is the fact that there has always been a relatively large, but completely unaccounted for group of people in Finland who are an important part of this nation: native Finn people of colour. These are people who were born in Finland, are Finnish citizens, but are racialised as non-White, and therefore as non-Finns and who didn't come here from anywhere. I am one of those people: a Finnish citizen, Finnish as my mother tongue, born in the capital of Finland, Helsinki, a person who just happens to be Brown.

Unlike in the US, Great Britain or Canada, racial or ethnicity data aren't collected in the Finland census. Therefore, it's impossible to say how many people of colour there are in Finland. The reasoning behind not collecting the data is based on protecting Finns. It is a concept that dates back before and during World War II when statistics that accounted for race and ethnicity were violently used against the people subjected to the Holocaust and other genocides (Nieminen, 2013). After the war it was decided that the risk was too great to keep such statistics – although this didn't apply to our two most marginalised visible minorities, the Indigenous peoples – the Sámi, and the Roma – who are still heavily monitored (especially the latter) and of whom much more specific data than of their native counterparts were collected until the late 1970s. Currently the census asks for place of birth, parents' place of birth, mother tongue, citizenship and some other factors. If a person has one parent that was born in Finland, they are automatically a native Finn, no matter if they're Black, Brown or otherwise POC. This is, of course, a beautiful idea that we should strive for – that every person who chooses and feels can identify as a Finn without questioning their background or appearance – but unfortunately, we are not there yet.

The story of arrival

Sara Ahmed (2012) has written that every research project has its own story of arrival. The story of racialisation and belonging in Finland can be told concretely at the level of qualitative research or, for example, at the institutional level the analysis of data reveals the realities of racialisation and inclusion/exclusion. However, there is also a personal level, what is also termed critical auto-ethnography, or examining one's inclusion/exclusion within a matrix of racialisation, patriarchal empowerment, immigration status and citizenship, that is no less important or irrefutable than the other levels mentioned. In fact, to me, the personal level is not only as important as the research or the institutional levels – it is all I have, since I am invisible in the very few statistics that exist.

I exist, by the grace of pure accident. My maternal grandfather came to Helsinki from Lapland in the 1950s; my maternal grandmother is a Karelian refugee of World War II who also settled in the capital of Finland by happenstance. Some decades before this, my paternal grandfather walked from Sana'a, Yemen, to Mandatory Palestine in the 1920s because his parents decided to go on pretty much a whim after a relatively petty dispute with another Yemeni Jewish tribe living in the neighbourhood. My paternal grandmother's (also Yemeni) family had been living in Palestine since the 1850s, and the two families met at some random Saturday night gathering. As a teenager, almost an adult, my mother, in turn, escaped the stifled Finnish post-war atmosphere to what had become Israel in 1948. Through acts of colonialism justified by the very real terrors of the Holocaust, she went to do voluntary work in a kibbutz, where my father had been placed by chance in foster care in his teens, also due to war trauma, racism and rootlessness, all of which transformed into parental mental illness as he advanced in years. My parents met on a rainy night. The streets were flooding so hard my father had to spend the night at my mother's place. Three months later they got engaged, and three months after that they were married (in Cyprus because the state of Israel doesn't recognise marriage between a Jew and a non-Jew), and another six months later, I was born, in Helsinki.

On the one hand, I personally don't need statistics. I absolutely know who I am. I also absolutely know that my lived experience is not like that of a native Finn who is White. All I need to do is look at my mother or, say, her father and the way they move in the world and see the different responses when people realise I'm their daughter and granddaughter. This is a bitter, confusing experience – a very real pain. But it is absolutely clear and true, and non-negotiable as fact.

Phenomenologies of institutional oppression

I started studying social work at the University of Helsinki in the autumn of 2006 and got my first job in child protection services the following summer. Before I became a social work student, I had studied English philology, North American studies and communications in the same university. I chose to switch majors because, as much as I loved literature and language, I felt a responsibility to use this privilege of getting a university degree towards something that would actually help my fellow human beings. (This is not to say I don't believe in the power of language and literature, and I will return to this.) I come from a family that places great value on helping others. Growing up, on more days than not, we would have undocumented immigrants, or other people in need of protection, sleeping on our floors. My grandmother literally and personally fed and clothed thousands of people in her lifetime through different charities and organisations. I felt like I couldn't just go and climb the class ladder, leave my working-class family 'behind', and do whatever I wanted. I felt a very real responsibility to use my education wisely. I chose social work with my heart, but it was very clear to me from the first day at university that it wasn't going to choose me.

Both in English philology and social work, I was repeatedly mistaken for a cafeteria worker, exchange student or a cleaning person when I was walking around campus on my way to classes. I would be addressed in English instead of Finnish. In social work I had, presumably, one other Brown person studying at the same time as me, out of probably a couple hundred students. In 2008, I wrote my bachelor's thesis on the gendered labour market that is offered to immigrants in Finland. I got a 4/5 as a grade. I was very happy with myself and felt that maybe I had found a calling in social work and social work research. I was quite disappointed when my professor, in front of all the other students, complimented me on my work saying that my thesis was so good because the theme was clearly personally familiar to me, and my experience was showing through. In my thesis, I had interviewed Estonian women who had come to Finland for one reason or another and worked as cleaning people. I am not from Estonia, as I described in the introduction of this chapter, and have never worked as a cleaning person, although I do come from a working-class family and am the first one to go to university in Finland. By then, as a 24-year-old, I had worked since I was 12, in grocery shops, as a nanny, as an aide to elderly and disabled people, even in a strip club, but never as a cleaning person. After 14 years, I still remember how my stomach sank with every word the professor said, how her voice was muffled by an intensifying ringing in my ear, and how, by the time I got home, I had a fever so high, I couldn't really see. I was ill for a week, my body completely shut down from Systematic White Rage.

Another thing worth mentioning here is that in all the years that I studied social work (on and off) between 2006 and 2020, only once, in one class, for two hours, not even a full course, did a non-White person teach me. This was in the autumn of 2019 when I attended, in my free time, a seminar arranged by Professor Kris Clarke, where visiting African-American cultural broker Devoya Mayo was teaching.

These peculiar, painful incidents are not limited to my years as a student. In a job interview for a position in social work, I was asked what my race and religion were. In another job as a social worker, my boss directed nearly all immigrant and non-White families in the area to me. Her reasoning was that I would understand the clients better because … she never finished the sentence. My clients were Chinese, Somali, Iraqi, Estonian and I didn't share a language, culture or religion with any of them. Some White Finnish clients regularly used the n-word when referring to me, and refused to have me as their case worker because I was "a foreigner".

I feel like I'm a case example of the minority stress theory, conceptualised by the American psychiatrist Ilan Meyer in the 1990s, in relation to how homophobia, stigma, stereotypes and continuous discrimination cause (mental) health issues. This same framework has later been applied to other minorities, such as BIPOC:

> The model describes stress processes, including the experience of prejudice events, expectations of rejection, hiding and concealing, internalized homophobia, and ameliorative coping processes. This conceptual framework is the basis for the review of research evidence, suggestions for future research directions, and exploration of public policy implications. (Meyer, 2003: 674)

I mentioned before that I studied social work for 14 years. That is how long it took me to get my master's, which typically is a five-year affair. I kept dropping out because I had no support from family since I was the first one to go to university; because I kept falling ill both physically with inexplicable infections and viruses, high fevers, rashes and debilitating stomach problems, as well as with depression and eating disorders, so much so that I wasn't able to leave the house and go to campus; and because I became a single mother. During this time, I also experienced what it means to be a client of social work, as a person of colour. How I would be questioned, in my own country of origin, about my language skills and 'culture' and 'religion' when seeking psychological and financial help for me and my daughter; every time I brought up experiences of racism to these case workers and therapists, they completely brushed me off and changed the subject. After years of peer support and reading an immense amount of literature, I have come to the conclusion that both endemic and structural racism, intense spells of Systemic White Rage and especially this *silence around race*, the tight-gripped palms around my skull that make my ears ring, work as tools of silencing and play a major role in why it took me so long to graduate and why I still *do not feel safe around social work.*

This really torments me: if I don't feel safe as a licensed social worker with endless privileges – language, citizenship, higher education, light skin to name a few – then how would a BIPOC client in a vulnerable situation likely feel?

The relationship between race and social work

All of the previously mentioned themes and issues – violence, poverty, marginalisation, (mental) health, (geo)political conflict and extremist movements — are connected, intersected and enmeshed in social work and its original core mission to help those in need in more ways than one (Richmond, 1917, 1922). In social work, it's common knowledge that the personal and the political are tightly intertwined; that the context in which people live affects the experiences and lives of people and communities; and that social work is not just a profession, but an institution structured by a nostalgic and racialised narrative, with policies that engender White privilege and the denial of the humanity of marginalised peoples (Pohjola, 2017).

The demographic developments previously described are inevitably visible in social work because all of society and human life is visible in social work. And I mean both in the service users and the social workers. To me, it seems that within social work, we are at least somewhat capable of talking about class when we deal with issues such as homelessness and welfare, about gender when we deal with domestic violence and day care; or ability/disability when we deal with social work in hospitals, gerontology and aid to disabled persons. But when it comes to race and racism, there is only silence. This silence is painful and dangerous.

At the end of 2020, I graduated with a master's degree in social work from the University of Helsinki. For my thesis, I researched how race (as a social construct and structural matter, not a biological issue) is comprehended and conceptualised in the teaching of social work in Finland. As data, I used the literature listed as teaching material in the curriculum for both bachelor's and master's studies in the University of Helsinki. The data consisted of 73 academic books and research reports published by the Finnish government, as well as nine scientific articles. The methodological and theoretical framework was built on an epistemological level, with Black intersectional feminism, and with critical race theory, which is a theory created within North American critical law studies by Black scholars. That is to say, quite frankly, that since statistics ignore and refuse people such as me, I ignore and refuse Eurocentric knowledge production and actively choose to centre and lean on BIPOC scholars and their ideas when doing my research or living, for that matter.

I analysed the data first with theory-based, thematic content analysis, which was followed by a content-based thematic content analysis. I then synthesised the two and named my two main findings: 'Like Two Curricula' and 'Circling Language'. Based on my analysis it can be seen that race is portrayed in the context of Finnish social work education without a clear definition of the term, which goes against the very basic rules of science: you have to be clear about what you talk and why you have chosen the concepts in use. Race is mainly addressed sporadically, implicitly and by using euphemisms such as 'foreigner', 'immigrant', 'person with immigrant background' and 'second-generation immigrant'. It is clear from the context that we are talking about non-Whiteness, when immigrants and foreigners can, of course, be, and most often in Finland are, White.

When racism and racialisation are portrayed at all, my data reflect that both are completely without any historical, contextual or critical analysis or situationalisation. If there is any connection made between social work and colonialism, oppression and racism at all, it is in brief passages in American or British teaching material – never Finnish. Although we know as fact that, for instance, child protection social work service providers played a key role in removing both Sámi and Roma children from their families and that the process of removal and placement in Finnish families or the foster care system contributed further to erasing their identities violently in the name of Finnishisation (Tervonen, 2012). The problem with trying to address the practice of silencing and erasure is that racism is perceived as something that is not a Finnish problem; moreover, it is often conjectured that considering structural racism is more of an Anglo-American curiosity. It is never challenged against the backdrop of our exceptionalist myths, which I described in the beginning of this chapter, or the concept of the so-called 'welfare state'. I put these words in quotation marks on purpose because it is clear to me that what is left of the 'welfare state' after years of deliberate, neoliberal destruction of the systems of state care is that holistic services are only meant for certain people. To be seen and deemed eligible demands demonstrations of clear reciprocity and deservingness, far more so than is usually marketed or included in discourses about Finland as one of the most equal countries in the world (Tarkiainen, 2020).

Another point of view, which exemplifies why race needs to urgently be discussed within the framework of social work education in Finland is the fact that as a part of the Nordic countries, Finland has been and is, in many ways, involved in European colonialism, Eurocentric knowledge production, White supremacy and the upholding of racist structures (Keskinen et al, 2016). Finland has never had its own official, faraway colony (Ovamboland in present-day Namibia was supposed to be one but the project was interrupted), but as a country and community we are by no means innocent or non-complicit in the imperialist projects of Europe. Most importantly, Finland has colonised, within the borders of the country, the Indigenous Sámi people, and we have accompanied the Swedish when they were colonising parts of Western Africa. Moreover, we have always leaned towards the so-called 'West' when it comes to children's literature, visual arts and advertising that reproduces dangerous and harmful racial stereotypes, along with participating in highly problematic anthropological projects and development cooperation (Vuorela, 2009; see also Gathuo, 2017). Social work has participated in these projects. One example was/ is the forced assimilation of Sámi and Roma people and, another, is the reluctance to provide social welfare to Roma families in the same capacity as to White Finnish families, which led/leads to disproportionate numbers of Roma children ending up in state custody (Tervonen, 2012). Izumi Sakamoto (2007) has stated that so-called 'Western' social work is built almost entirely on Whiteness; and Finnish social work is built almost entirely on that 'Western' social work, which is inherently White supremacist: consider the Charity Organisation Society, the Settlement Movement and Social Reformism (Toikko, 2001; Raunio, 2009). We are a part of the problem, and it is our duty to address it.

Futures

I took on the assignment to write this chapter for the following reason that, honestly, I feel alone, stuck and unsafe in the field of social work in Finland. This feeling (which by the way manifests as pain in my upper back) has led me to largely find work in other spaces, such as literature, journalism, teaching, translating other people's literary work and so on. Which is not to say that those spaces are free from the problems described in this chapter – far from it. Oppressive structures penetrate all levels, spaces and ideologies in society, especially levels and spaces of power and privilege. It's just that I've ended up in spaces where at least there are *some* words and not just total, painful silence. Spaces in which I've had a modicum of power to bend the narrative and use my voice and be heard.

Somehow still, after everything, even in my soon approaching middle-age years and having established a career as a writer, I feel a duty towards my mixed-race, working-class family, to make the best out of the ability to obtain a higher education. This duty cannot be fulfilled in any other field than social work, it seems to me. Otherwise, why would I keep coming back? Because I believe in social work. I also feel a duty towards social work itself.

Finally, I offer my last memory from my years as a student in the University of Helsinki, in the faculty of Social Sciences, Department of Social Work. I was sitting in a big lecture hall in the autumn of 2006, attending an introductory class in social sciences. The reputable and brilliant professor of social policy at the time, J.P. Roos, was giving the lecture. I don't remember the topic exactly, but I do remember him saying to us (and I paraphrase): as social scientists, you don't have to come up with solutions. It is enough that you pinpoint the problems, open conversations and debate them. I remember thinking back then, *that's silly, and so elitist, to treat people's real distress as interesting topics of conversation.* Respectfully, I still feel that way. Why wouldn't we offer solutions and opinions on solutions? Nowhere does it say that a researcher can't be an activist or a problem solver. We all know that there is no neutral, absolute knowledge, especially when it comes to social sciences. I also don't think we can afford to distance ourselves from these pressing issues much longer. The word 'work' is intertwined into our very profession and science, so we should get to work.

So, here I offer some solutions, based on both findings in my thesis but also my lived experience as both a Brown, native Finn client of social work and a social worker of colour.

1. We need to invest in research that is focused on the intersection of social work and race/racism/racialisation. The framework of this type of research needs to be rooted in decolonisation studies and critical race theory in order to truly address the issues and gain useful knowledge (Grey et al, 2013; Clarke and Yellow Bird, 2021). We have to research and reconcile the complicity of social work in the oppression of Roma and Sámi people, as well as other BIPOC in Finland. Perhaps this solution, or 'charge', could have a place on its own – especially considering the decolonial point previously mentioned and Sámi as Indigenous peoples.
2. In both the recruitment of new students and faculty members, we have to pay attention to who has access to apply in the first place. What are the thresholds that are causing people minority stress and keeping them out of higher education? Is affirmative action needed, or could there be other measures taken? It's at least a conversation to be had.
3. In teaching social work, we need to centre BIPOC knowledge, such as Black feminism and Indigenous education. In the Finnish context, social work needs to participate in gathering and creating this type of research canon and literature, invest in Finnish BIPOC scholars (also in the Finnish language, Swedish and Sámi languages, not just English) and include their (so far) few works in the curriculum. Eurocentric knowledge-production needs to be questioned.
4. Current faculty members need to be offered updated education on racism in academia, decolonisation, anti-racism from both everyday and methodological perspectives. These values need to also be translated into different strategies and action plans – and valued and measured periodically.
5. We need to be able to ask: what is framed as social work in the first place? It's one thing to speak about social work as a science, or a statutory profession (top to bottom) and another to speak about collective well-being and equality in which social work is a facilitator (horizontal, equal). We need to be able to speak about the power we have over people's lives and start dismantling it. How might this lead to a truly service-oriented approach, where social workers are in service of clients, rather than directing them to preconceived, non-racialised outcomes.
6. In the autumn of 2021, the Finnish government issued a 70-page-long 'Action Plan for Combating Racism and Promoting Good Relations between Population Groups'. In chapter 4 of the Plan it clearly states how different sectors of society can and are obligated to take concrete

measures to dismantle structural discrimination. Social services are mentioned as well. The question is: do we want to be trailblazers in showing how it can be done, or do we want to be the last ones to wake up? (See Oikeusministeriö, 2021.)

I believe that these measures can be realised relatively easily; it's more a matter of re-thinking existing resources and ways of doing than, for example, finding more funding. In the end, the common denominator to all of the previously mentioned solutions is speaking and listening. I hope to see a very active, open and critical future of social work – one that is loud not because the silence is deafening, but because the conversation around race is so lively and potent.

References

Ahmed, S. (2012) *On Being Included: Racism and Diversity in Institutional Life*, Durham, NC: Duke University Press.

Clarke, K., and Yellow Bird, M. (2021) *Decolonizing Pathways Towards Integrative Healing in Social Work*, London: Routledge.

European Union Agency for Fundamental Rights (2018) *Being Black in the EU/Second European Union Minorities and Discrimination Survey*. https://fra.europa.eu/en/publication/2018/being-black-eu

Gathuo, M. (2017) *Valkoisia valheita. Ruskeat Tytöt Media [Verkkojulkaisu, viittauspäivä]*. https://www.ruskeattytot.fi/rtmedia/valkoisiavalheita

Grey, M., Coates, J., Yellow Bird, M. and Hetherington, T. (2013) *Decolonizing Social Work*, London: Routledge.

Hubara, K. (2017) *Ruskeat tytöt: tunne-esseitä*, Helsinki: Like.

Kansallisbiografia/Suomalaisen kirjallisuuden seura [National Biographies/Finnish Literature Society] (2011) *Rosa Emilia Clay*. https://kansallisbiografia.fi/kansallisbiografia/henkilo/9823

Keskinen, S., Tuori, S., Irni, S. and Mulinari, D. (eds) (2016) *Complying with Colonialism: Gender, Race and Ethnicity in the Nordic Region*, London: Routledge.

Lehti, M., Salmi, V., Aaltonen, M., Danielsson, P., Hinkkanen, V., Niemi, H. et al (2014) 'Maahanmuuttajat rikosten uhreina ja tekijöinä' ['Immigrants as victims and perpetrators of crimes'], *Oikeuspoliittisen tutkimuslaitoksen tutkimuksia*, 265. https://helda.helsinki.fi/bitstream/handle/10138/152441/265_Lehti_ym_2014.pdf?se%20quence=2&isAllowed=y

Meyer, I.H. (2003) 'Prejudice, social stress, and mental health in lesbian, gay and bisexual populations: conceptual issues and research evidence', *Psychological Bulletin*, 129: 674–97.

Nieminen, J. (2013) *Etnisyystiedon merkitys kasvaa maahanmuuton lisääntyessä* [*The Importance of Ethnic Information Increases as Immigration Increases*], Tilastokeskuksen hyvinvointikatsaus 3/2013, Teema: Vähemmistöt. www.stat.fi/tup/hyvinvointikatsaus/hyka_2013_03.htm

Oikeusministeriö (2021) *Yhdenvertainen Suomi: Valtioneuvoston toimintaohjelma rasismin torjumiseksi ja hyvien väestösuhteiden edistämiseksi* [*Equal Finland: the Government's Action Programme to Combat Racism and Promote Good Relations*], Oikeusministeriön julkaisuja, Mietintöjä ja lausuntoja, 2021: 34. https://julkaisut.valtioneuvosto.fi/bitstream/handle/10024/163577/OM_2021_34_ML.pdf?sequence=1&isAllowed=y

Pakolaisapu [Finnish Refugee Aid] (2019) *Pakolaisuus Suomessa* [*Refugeeism in Finland*]. https://pakolaisapu.fi/pakolaisuus-suomessa/

Pelkonen, L. (2019) 'Miksi nationalismi ja oikeistopopulismi nousevat Euroopassa?' [Why is nationalism and right-wing populism rising in Europe?], [Radio Broadcast], *YLE Puheen Politiikaradio*, available from: https://areena.yle.fi/1-50125773

Pohjola, A. (2017) 'Rakenteellisen sosiaalityön paikannuksia' ['Locations of structural social work], in A. Pohjola, M. Laitinen and M. Seppänen (eds) *Rakenteellinen sosiaalityö* [*Structural Social Work*] Sosiaalityön tutkimuksen vuosikirja 2014, Helsinki: Helsinki University Press.

Raunio, K. (2009) *Olennainen sosiaalityössä* [*The Essentials of Social Work*], Helsinki: Gaudeamus.

Richmond, M. (1917) *Social Diagnosis*, New York: Russell Sage Foundation.

Richmond, M. (1922) *What is Social Case Work? An Introductory Description*, New York: Russell Sage Foundation.

SAK (2016) 'Maahanmuuttajanaisen euro on 62 senttiä' ['Immigrant women's euro is 62 cents']. www.sak.fi/ajankohtaista/uutiset/maahanmuuttajanaisen-euro-62-senttia

Sakamoto, I. (2007) 'An anti-oppressive approach to cultural competence', *Canadian Social Work Review*, 24(1): 105–14.

Statistics Finland (2019) *Itsenäisyyspäivä 2019* [*Independence Day Speech 2019*]. www.stat.fi/tup/tilastokirjasto/itsenaisyyspaiva-2019.html

Tarkiainen, L. (2020) 'Negotiated responsibilities and deservingness: a study of talk on prolonged unemployment in Finland', doctoral dissertation, University of Helsinki. https://helda.helsinki.fi/bitstream/handle/10138/320156/tarkiainen_laura_dissertation_2020.pdf?sequence=1

Tervonen, M. (2012) 'Kiertolaisia, silmätikkuja ja rajojen ylittäjiä: 1800-luvun lopulta toiseen maailmansotaan' ['Vagrants, the stigmatised and border-crossers: from the end of the 19th century to the Second World War'], in P. Pulma (ed) *Suomen romanien historia* [*Finnish Roma History*], Helsinki: Suomalaisen Kirjallisuuden Seura.

Tervonen, M. (2015) 'Historiankirjoitus ja myytti yhden kulttuurin Suomesta' ['History writing and the myth of Finland as one culture'], in A. Östman, H. Snellman and P. Markkola (eds) *Kotiseutu ja kansakunta: Miten suomalaista historiaa on rakennettu* [*Homeland and Nation: How Finnish History Was Constructed*], Helsinki: Suomalaisen Kirjallisuuden Seura.

Toikko, T. (2001) *Sosiaalityön amerikkalainen oppi. Yhdysvaltalaisen caseworkin kehitys ja sen yhteys suomalaiseen tapauskohtaiseen sosiaalityöhön* [*The Lessons of American Social Work: the Development of American Casework and its Connection to Finnish Case-Specific Social Work*], Seinäjoki: Seinäjoki University of Applied Sciences.

Väestöliitto (2019) *Maahanmuuttajien määrä [Verkkojulkaisu, viittauspäivä.* https://www.vaestoliitto.fi/tieto_ja_tutkimus/vaestontutkimuslaitos/tilastoja/maahanmuuttajat/maahanmuuttajien-maara/

Vuorela, U. (2009) 'Colonial complicity: the post-colonial in a Nordic context', in S. Keskinen, S. Tuori, S. Irni and D. Mulinari, *Complying with Colonialism: Gender, Race and Ethnicity in the Nordic Region*, Aldershot: Ashgate.

World Economic Forum (2018) *The Global Gender Gap Report.* www.weforum.org/reports/the-global-gender-gap-report-2018/

World Happiness Report (2019) *United Nations Sustainable Development Solutions Network in Partnership with the Ernesto Illy Foundation.* https://worldhappiness.report

World Press Freedom Index (2019) *Reporters Without Borders.* https://rsf.org/en/2019-world-press-freedom-index-cycle-fear

8

Transcultural mental health as the colonisation of racialised bodies: a personal insight

Fadumo Dayib and Kris Clarke

She opened the door to her apartment after two or three persistent knocks. As we entered, we were welcomed by the tantalising aroma of food. In her tentative English, she apologised for her small apartment and asked us to sit down. My colleague and I, from a Finnish mental health clinic, were paying her a home visit. My colleague, a White Finnish woman, started speaking to her in English. She had bought an assortment of fruits which she placed on the kitchen counter. She asked the racialised client to prepare a fruit salad. She rapidly barked instructions on what fruits to start with. All the while, there was no interpreter who would have translated these instructions for the racialised patient. But most importantly, there was no one who could have told her that my colleague was about to make a report that could significantly alter the course of her life in Finland. The patient did not have utensils for preparing a fruit salad. Moreover, she came from a culture where fruit salads were not the norm. However, she tentatively started by cutting a fruit but would stop midway to narrate her problems and fears. The patient was distressed and not in the right frame of mind to do anything else other than talk about her suffering and, after an hour, she had only managed to partially cut two fruits. The colleague would later return and report to the clinic that the client was unable to follow instructions and prepare a fruit salad. As such, the natural progression would be that this piece of information would feed into a larger process that would start with semi-structured interviews that address topics including the patient–clinician interaction, the cultural definition of the problem, cultural identity, spirituality and possibly an MRI. This would eventually lead to a diagnosis that the patient was either 'functionally disabled' or 'developmentally challenged' and in need of support. Without this diagnosis, the patient would not be able to continue receiving specialist care from the clinic. (Scenario 1)

Introduction

I (Fadumo) watched this scenario unfold in these services and bore witness to the emergence of hyper-racialised spaces, more than once, where power asymmetries were displayed between the Finnish healthcare providers and their racialised patients. This example illustrates one of the many psychiatric power imbalances between racialised patients navigating Whiteness in Finnish mental health services and White Finnish service providers operating from a place of power and, at times, White supremacy (Rose and Kalathil, 2019).

By stopping and narrating her painful experiences, the patient was communicating her need to be heard and given space to speak about the trauma and pain that she was experiencing. However, the colleague had one goal in mind and it was exclusively focused on executing it by any means necessary – diagnosis, treatment plan and intake into the programme. I watched apprehensively, fidgeting in my chair, my mouth dry and heart racing. Every time my colleague opened her mouth, she was also opening a wound, triggering traumatic experiences from childhood and adulthood, in the distressed patient. By the time we were leaving, every object she had touched, every path she walked and every piece of furniture she sat on was metaphorically soaked in blood. As we walked out from the carnage, my hands were curled into tight fists; it felt like we had left the service user to drown in her own blood.

As the only racialised professional at the clinic, I questioned the disempowering and epistemically violent encounters I observed and the subsequent diagnoses that were frequently detrimental to the health, well-being and agency of racialised patients. With every visit, we would rip at their vulnerabilities, open their wounds and re-traumatise them before sending them off on their own in a more fragile state of mind. I started every shift with the fear of hearing that one of these re-traumatised patients had died by suicide. The more I raised my concerns, the more there seemed to be efforts to question my credibility and competence, thereby silencing me and systematically negating my epistemic agency. At the same time, the advocacy I provided these clients was rejected. What was the difference between me and the helpless and hopeless patients sitting across from me? In this hyper-racialised space, we were in the same predicament – these newcomers and myself; me who has lived here for over 30 years.

I come to this chapter through a similar pathway that bell hooks (1994: 59) described her own route into theorising:

> I came to theory because I was hurting – the pain within me was so intense that I could not go on living. I came to theory desperate,

wanting to comprehend – to grasp what was happening around and within me. Most importantly, I wanted to make the hurt go away. I saw in theory a location for healing.

I write as a former refugee. As a healthcare professional and doctoral researcher. As a racially and ethnically minoritised Black woman who has faced and continues to face structural racism and violence every day in Finland 31 years after her arrival. I write to make sense of these professional encounters that I have witnessed.

This chapter explores the notion of transcultural psychiatry in Finland through an experiential lens. It is a collaboration between me, Fadumo, a public health practitioner and doctoral candidate, and Kris Clarke, a social work researcher. I, Fadumo, write in the first-person employing a critical autoethnographic method to explore the inner workings of the system of Finnish health and social work in the context of decolonial and social justice theories; Kris, who is a White immigrant to Finland, collaborates with the theoretical analyses that frame our collaboration. First, we outline the concept and theory of transcultural psychiatry. Second, I explore my experiential analysis as a practitioner in the *non-profit industrial complex* (a term that is discussed later) in Finland. Finally, I conclude with an examination of the non-profit social work system to consider how epistemic injustice prevails in Finnish mental health care for racialised people.

The historical context of transcultural mental health and ethnopsychiatry

We begin this theoretical discussion with the assertion that the field of psychiatry has always been a weapon in the arsenal of colonialism (Keller, 2007). For centuries, mental illness has been seen from a variety of global perspectives as a manifestation of spiritual wisdom, demonic possession or as a chronic ailment, among many other things. There is evidence, for example, that mental hospitals called *bîmâristâns*, which sought to provide medical treatment to those who exhibited violent tendencies or chronic illness, existed in ancient Arab countries as long as one thousand years ago, so mental health care has diverse ancient roots (Amad and Thomas, 2011). The rise of the lunatic asylum as a carceral activity where some people are detained in isolation from the rest of the population, but do not necessarily receive any support or treatment, is a profoundly European phenomenon that emerged during the period of the Industrial Revolution and colonialism, a time of great social change (Porter and Wright, 2003). Along with boarding schools and railroads, colonisers brought mental asylums as carceral institutions as part of the 'civilising mission' of colonial exploitation and settlement (Keller 2007: 48). Grounded in Eurocentric and androcentric Enlightenment thought, psychiatry, the science of mental illness that was born in Central Europe, has enforced ethnocentric, racist and classist social orders as it diagnosed behaviours seen as 'unreasonable' and 'uncivilised' (Foucault, 1988). Some view the psychiatric profession as the 'battered child' of medicine due to the difficult task it has to diagnose and treat people suffering from the ailments caused by living in oppressive societies, and point to how it has contributed to more humanistic views and public support of people struggling with mental distress (Greenblatt, 1975). Others like those in the anti-psychiatry movement have had much more radical critiques of psychiatry viewing it as harmful and an instrument of social control (Szasz, 2019). There is, in short, a broad spectrum of views on the profession

The debate over the validity and history of psychiatry is beyond the scope of this chapter. Here we briefly explore the scholarship of psychiatrist Frantz Fanon (1963), who documented how the structural racism and oppression of colonialism translated into the individual and collective trauma and mental distress of the colonised, and the rise of ethnopsychiatry as a method of managing the mental health of people from formerly colonised people in the heart of European metropoles. In this way, we set the stage for examining the use of these theories in how they explicate the methods that operationalise structural violence and epistemic injustice in Finnish mental health services.

Franz Fanon was a Martinican medical doctor specialised in psychiatry based in Algeria during the brutal war against French colonisers. Based on his professional experience, Fanon challenged prevailing colonial psychiatric frameworks which pathologised non-Europeans as dependent, simplistic and incapable, needing the guidance of colonisers due to their inherent inferiority (Trimbur, 2022). He argued that the structural violence of colonialism caused psychological distress, stating that 'any psychiatry that begins from a premise that normalises colonial society would thereby reinforce neurosis' (Fanon, 1988: 11). Fanon further underlined the clear link between colonial mental health as a carceral activity and the repression of the colonised:

> The truth is that colonisation, in its very essence, already appeared to be a great purveyor of psychiatric hospitals. Since 1954 we have drawn the attention of French and international psychiatrists in scientific works to the difficulty of 'curing' a colonised subject correctly, in other words making him thoroughly fit into a social environment of the colonial type. Because it is a systematised negation of the other, a frenzied determination to deny the other any attribute of humanity, colonialism forces the colonised to constantly ask the question: 'Who am I in reality?' (Fanon, 1963: 181)

The French term *ethnopsychiatrie* was first used in the mid-20th century by French professionals as a practice that combined ethnography, medicine and psychoanalysis to seek a cultural understanding of mental illness, particularly in the wake of wars and other collective traumatic events (Ellenberger, 2020: 23). Similarly, transcultural psychiatry, the term first used in the Anglophone world in 1953, brought the fields of anthropology and psychology closer together as professionals sought to create a universal framework for cultural difference in psychology (Bains, 2005). These conceptualisations were grounded in the presumption that migrants, refugees and asylum seekers – people from non-European backgrounds – had fundamentally different or 'culturalised' mental health needs than the hegemonic native White population. These racialised and culturalised populations required specialist care, with ethno- and transcultural psychiatry which reinforced the 'otherness' of people from these groups in many ways. Transcultural psychiatry, along with its French equivalent 'ethnopsychiatry', are highly contentious concepts because they are imbued with largely unexplored colonial assumptions (Antić, 2021). Emerging as many formerly colonised populations began migrating to the European metropoles after the Second World War, transcultural mental health and ethnopsychiatry sought to make sense of the 'other' residing in the heart of the empire. As Bullard (2007: 128) notes, if colonial psychiatry was based on the suppression of local beliefs, ways of knowing and healing, and diverse cultures, then the emerging specialisations of ethnopsychiatry and transcultural psychiatry firmly centred cultural difference and otherness in the psychiatric encounter, diagnosis and treatment.

Paul Gilroy (2013) argued that the role of race in the UK is directly located and entwined in the changing racialised structures of post-empire British society. In this perspective, the classic racism of the colonial period has shifted from the exoticism and backwardness of the 'uncivilised' abroad to containing a home-grown version of racialised and formerly colonised people. Indeed, policing, social services and mental health treatment have become key practices that control racialised people in Europe. Frazer-Carroll (2023) points out that it is important to analyse how mental health frameworks are deployed and what political aims they embody because definitions of mental illness often marshal biological or cultural explanations to reinforce existing power asymmetries. The rise of transcultural mental health and ethnopsychiatry in the mid-20th century thus reflects the academisation of racialised and colonial discourses on care. As Fassin and Rechtman summarise:

> Not surprisingly, Africa became the central site of the ideological tension: because it symbolised the most exotic difference within mankind, it gave birth to a mixture of racial and cultural prejudices that justified a specific regime of governance under colonial rule and later in the postcolonial world. Psychiatry and psychology played a

crucial role in culturalising racial representations and at the same time naturalising cultural specificities. (Fassin and Rechtman, 2005: 349)

Fassin and Rechtman (2005) also underline the fundamental paradox of systems of mental health services based on the French Revolution principle of equality coexisting with parallel modes of psychiatric services that create marginal services that focus on ethnic and cultural differences.

From the perspective of Finland, transcultural psychiatry arrived around the same time that the first wave of Somali refugees arrived in the 1990s (Ekblad and Kastrup, 2013). Though Finland has always had racialised and Indigenous populations, transcultural psychology was specifically developed to focus on newcomers, especially from conflict areas. There has been one textbook written about culture and medicine in Finnish, which has been foundational in the field, with chapters on a variety of issues including the use of interpreters, refugeeism and psychological trauma to the role of faith in the medical encounter (Huttunen and Pakaslahti, 2010). Most transcultural psychiatry studies have focused on addiction, depression and mental distress among Somali refugees (for example, Mölsä et al, 2014; Kuittinen et al, 2017). Perhaps the most glaring absence in this emerging field is the lack of research on the psychological impact of structural racism on racialised people. While there have been some studies of the impact of discrimination on mental health (for example, Mölsä et al, 2017; Rask et al, 2018), there is an implicit acceptance of the colonial framework of transcultural psychiatry which is problematic, if we follow Fanon's critique. It is widely recognised that recovery from mental health challenges is deeply rooted in the social determinants of health (Davidson, Rakfeldt and Strauss, 2010). Because ethnopsychiatry and transcultural mental health in Finland are fields that have generally emerged from the mental health professions rather than as community-driven efforts, asymmetrical power relations radiate through the interventions that are often created with little input from racialised people. The lack of racialised researchers in the field reinforces the normativity of the White gaze in constructing definitions and theories as well as deploying practice models.

The legacy of colonialism can be seen in the systemic racism that permeates all levels of European societies from how knowledge is produced to discrimination in the labour and housing market to differences in how patients are perceived and treated. In the field of mental health, the persistence of differential diagnoses between people racialised in European countries and those perceived as White is well documented (Bansal et al, 2022). Not only is coercive control and crisis intervention used more often with racialised people, but also disproportionate pathologisation is common (Whabi and Beletsky, 2021). For example, diagnoses of African American men with schizophrenia skyrocketed during the Civil Rights era when Black people refused to be subservient, suggesting that diagnosis can be based on the expectations of social roles (Metzl, 2010). These disparities are rooted in systemic racism and the everyday experiences of microaggressions and discrimination as well as the implicit bias and racism of many White practitioners (McKenzie and Bhui, 2007; Nazroo, Bhui and Rhodes, 2020; Williams and Etkins, 2021; Younis, 2021a). We do not know about such disparities in Finland because racial data are not collected about populations, effectively erasing useful information that could better map differential treatment. However, we do know that certain racialised groups are highly represented in the literature about transcultural psychiatry in Finland (for example, see Mölsä et al, 2010, 2014; Kuittinen et al, 2017). As Frazer-Carroll (2023: 48) has summarised: 'the psychiatric framing of illness could be used to uphold the capitalist, white supremacist and heterosexist status quo'.

Finally, it is important to underline that there is a dearth of research on Whiteness in Finnish mental health services or the experiences of racialised patients accessing transcultural mental health services without a White interlocutor. Notions of transcultural mental health and ethnopsychiatry that construct ethnic and cultural differences as a distinctive reason for specific types of mental illness among certain populations do not necessarily recognise that the toll of structural oppression on racialised patients in the form of racism, exclusion and marginalisation can cause severe mental distress. There is also a lack of inquiry about the politicisation of mental health diagnoses and how they can be used to control racialised patients.

The monetisation of mental distress: how the non-profit industrial complex operates in Finland

The arrival of refugees, asylum seekers and other migrants in the 1990s opened the door to the colonisation of newly arrived racialised bodies and lived experiences in the Finnish homeland. Employing the colonial playbook of dividing, oppressing, conquering and possessing racialised bodies, non-profit organisations and projects emerged in Finland that locally replicated the dynamics of the American plantation system where slave owners maintained control and set the agenda on behalf of racialised people (Gladden, 2022). Whether this was intentional or not, the centrality of Whiteness as a non-race became the norm of all knowledge production (Villanueva, 2018: 18).

When the philanthropic and social sectors were developed in the early part of the 20th century, the design elements were the same: bureaucracy, competition, specialisation and consolidation of power and resources. Tradition and the status quo were worshipped, resulting in conformity, formality and arrogance.

Initially, Finnish non-profit (also known as non-governmental or third-sector) organisations in the 1990s adopted policies of tolerance and colour-blindness rather than an explicitly anti-racist strategy. At the beginning of the 21st century, however, anti-racism became mainstreamed as a set of certain behaviours that reflect personal attitudes and acts rather than fundamentally challenging systemic ways that Finnish society is organised (Seikkula, 2019). The rapid leap from colour-blindness to anti-racism as personal behaviours risks erasing and sidestepping coming to terms with racial and colonial histories, and subsequently reinforcing racialised asymmetrical power imbalances (Alemanji and Mafi, 2018). These shifts have occurred simultaneously with the neoliberalisation of service provision which forced non-profit organisations to compete with one another for limited funding. In an effort to sustain their livelihoods, non-profits must often depoliticise their work to be more palatable to funders. However, the previously mentioned trends take place within the Finnish context of Whiteness and through a largely unreflective colonial framework of transcultural psychiatry. Hence, the racialised bodies, especially of migrants since the 1990s, have faced three waves of colonisation.

The first wave of colonisation started in academia with Finnish researchers in the 1990s engaging in Eurocentric migration studies and dividing up the racialised bodies and topics they would own as experts, thus consolidating their funding while treating racialised people as proprietary research subjects. This pattern, which has historical roots in how Sámi, Roma and Tatar populations have been viewed through the lens of Whitewashing, is redolent of what Kuokkanen (2022: 299) terms 'slack scholarship'; namely, closing one's eyes to the colonialism at the heart of mainstream knowledge-production on 'others'. These researchers staked out the racialised bodies they felt they owned and were extremely territorial of any outsiders entering their research plantations. This possessiveness extended to even the bodies they colonised, including potential researchers from these communities. With the acquisition of these bodies and the commodification of their misery also came power, credibility, funding and status as researchers.

The second wave of the colonisation of racialised bodies is organisations that provide services. The non-profit sector, which is always almost exclusively White in Finland, is intended to enhance citizen participation and social cohesion through smaller associations. Yet, when it comes to immigrants, these organisations often enforce White supremacy and social norms, teaching 'civility', and supporting politically defined mental health and social integration (Pyykkönen, 2007). Various non-profit organisations compete to achieve a monopoly of expertise on racialised bodies as part of the non-profit industrial complex, thus ensuring their continued existence. The US-based INCITE collective has defined the non-profit industrial complex as a form of soft control of marginalised populations through non-profit groups funded by the state as a means of thwarting radical social change (Gilmore, 2007).

The third wave of the colonisation of racialised bodies in Finland is structural and systemic. Following the definition of health researchers, 'systemic and structural racism are forms of racism that are pervasively and deeply embedded in systems, laws, written or unwritten policies, and entrenched practices and beliefs that produce, condone, and perpetuate widespread unfair treatment and oppression of people of color, with adverse health consequences' (Bravemen et al, 2022: 171). The disempowerment of racialised individuals through discriminatory practices in the housing, labour, educational and care sectors reflect systems and structures that undergird Finnish society and maintain relations of disparity and inequality which, in turn, cause the mental distress that is culturalised and monetised by largely White non-profit organisations.

Bonilla-Silva (2021) says that contemporary socio-political systems are formed in ways that reproduce racialised social orders. Here we argue that the academic framework of knowledge production and institutional organisation of the non-profit sector are shaped by these unequal structures. Racialised newcomers to Finland have found themselves enmeshed in systems that erase their humanity and discriminate against them in similar ways as historically racialised groups such as the Sámi and Roma. Kuokkonen (2022), for example, discusses how the culturalisation of Sámi peoples as ethnic minorities replicates the racial hygiene framework that has been so deeply rooted in Finnish social science. In this sense, racialised people have become fabricated as colonised subjects in Finland, where their own histories, stories and cultures are expunged, and they are subject to the prevailing unequal system of knowledge production and service provision. Maldonado-Torres (2017: 432) writes of the 'transformation of the subject into an object of scientific enquiry via specific methods' leading to the commodification, colonisation and dehumanisation of racialised people.

The clinic

The origin, theoretical foundation and referral pathways of the Finnish transcultural mental health services, sometimes referred to as cross-cultural mental health or ethnopsychiatry, are shrouded in mystery. On one hand, these specialised services only deal with racialised patients, specifically refugees, migrants and asylum seekers, who are new to Finland. On the other hand, they also cater to racialised and Finnish patients who are hearing impaired and deaf. In some ways, the services seem to be targeted at a conglomeration of the 'other'.

Patients come into contact with the clinic via three routes. The first pathway into the outpatient clinic is through referrals from doctors in primary healthcare services. The second is from a closed psychiatry ward at the hospital which combines 'foreign' patients with psychiatric problems with 'particularly demanding' patients and hearing impaired patients into a single service unit. The third avenue is via the emergency services or under police escort, which often leads to involuntary detention under the Mental Health Act (Kallakorpi et al, 2019). I worked in both the closed hospital ward and the outpatient services (a pseudonym) and base my observations on those experiences.

The clinic that I (Fadumo) worked at was a specialised clinic founded after the turn of the millennium and led by a White Finnish medical professional. Positioned as the foremost expert organisation on 'cultural competency and migrant mental health' has guaranteed it a reliable stream of state funding and created a specialty niche for its services. The clinic undertakes research which is mostly always geared towards highlighting asylum seekers and refugees as suffering from trauma. Yet no one seems to question the ethics of such research, especially when the results always justify the existence of the clinic as a segregator and stand-alone service. Because project-based funding is contingent on the intake of new patients, research and the utilisation of the services, the clinic is always under pressure to keep its numbers up. The staff of the clinic, with the exception of myself (Fadumo) for a period of time, were all White non-racialised Finns. None of these professionals had any specific professional specialisation in ethnopsychiatry, cross-cultural, transcultural psychiatry or in transcultural competency. This observation is further supported by a study by Kallakorpi et al (2018) which pointed out that Finnish professionals in ethnopsychiatry caring services generally lack transcultural competency. According to Lehti et al (2016: 22), research reveals that a 'general psychiatric assessment of a refugee patient is not very different from an assessment of a Finnish-born patient'. Considering all of this, is there really a need for this segregated and stand-alone clinic to exist? Where is the community input to develop recovery-oriented services? Can the current professionals provide the kind of care really needed with the training that they have received? A survey of psychiatric nursing staff in a province of Finland by Mulder et al (2015: 27) showed that a little over one-third reported having prejudices towards different cultures. Over half of respondents indicated that they made assumptions based on a patient's name or outer appearance, and nearly half found working with patients from different cultures to be 'demanding'. By only catering to racialised clients with staff that self-report their own bias, the clinic steers racialised people towards further alienation and segregation from society. Common illnesses and diseases experienced by racialised clients that can be treated at the primary care level are shovelled into this specialised outpatient clinic which leads to detrimental diagnoses and medicalisation. Thus, the clinic further tightens its chokehold and influence as ethnopsychiatry experts and perpetrators of White supremacy and anti-Blackness by persistently fetishising transcultural mental health as exotic and focusing on ethnicity and culture as a significant cause of mental illness in racialised people. Thus, they base their expertise on biological determinism. As is well documented, physical and mental health care institutions and services are not free from structural racism, racial discrimination, racial profiling and microaggressions, which can cause racialised people further mental distress (Cénat, 2020: 929).

The policing of racialised patients: how epistemic violence manifests

> A man sits in a public cafe. He speaks loudly on the phone in English, bangs his fist on the table and starts pacing back and forth. The more agitated he got, the louder his voice rose. A client approached the man and told him to calm down. Soon he was joined by two other clients and a waitress, all repeating the same message. This crowd was immediately joined by three burly police officers who pulled the man aside. A few minutes later, he was put in handcuffs and whisked away. Upon arriving, the police gave a report to the nurses and warned them that the man was 'defiant and resisting'. Armed with this information, the nursing team was beefed up and the man was bundled into an isolation room. Within two hours, he was involuntarily detained at the ethnopsychiatry ward on the basis of having a psychotic meltdown in a public place. During this period, he would not be allowed to move about freely, leave his room or contact anybody for almost a day and a half. (Scenario 2)

This cosy partnership between the legal, policing and medical professions is largely an unexplored terrain in Finland. In 1851, American psychiatrist Samuel A. Cartwright coined two diagnoses: dysaesthesia aethiopica and drapetomania, the latter of which was thought to explain why slaves fled and the former which was thought to explain Black people's alleged sloth and lack of work ethic. Because Cartwright believed that God made Blacks to be 'submissive knee benders', he theorised that fugitive slaves had a sickness if they sought liberation. In other words, if Black people did not want to be slaves, it was an aberration, a disease and the desire not to be slaves was pathological. According to Cartwright, practically all free Blacks were affected with dysaesthesia aethiopica. Without a 'master,' the Black person, in Cartwright's opinion, was lost (Shim, 2021). Cartwright followed 19th century 'scientific' ways of conceptualising fundamental mental and physiological differences between races, which he theorised required that Blacks be governed coercively (Myers, 2014). The origins of modern-day policing in Anglo-American nations are entwined with slave patrols that sought to find runaway African slaves and return them to their 'owners' (Spruill, 2016). Slave patrols targeted fugitive slaves who were seen as rebelling against the colonial social order, which was grounded in White supremacy. This history is significant because it also informs how predatory policing and coercive control in the Global North has emerged in its contemporary forms (Besteman, 2020). Sadly, Finland is not an exception to this rule. Schclarek, Mulinari and Keskinen (2022: 5) assert that racism in law enforcement is not an anomaly but rather a result of the interdependence of national and international power structures that shape the relationship between race, policing and geography. From the brutal suppression of riots in the *banlieues* of France to the frequent murders of Black people by US police to the detention of Aboriginal peoples by Australian law enforcement to the beatings of racialised people by security guards in Finland, the pattern of modern-day policing regimes is grounded in White supremacist ideologies that are predatory towards racialised bodies.

In Finland, racialised social control is exerted through health and welfare institutions, and is not only the function of policing. As Schclarek, Mulinari and Keskinen (2022) argue, the Finnish welfare state is a racialised entity premised on Whiteness as the fundamental marker for inclusion and belonging. Policies of colour-blindness and assimilation are officially promoted while everyday practices of policing, coercive control, repressive child protection removals and ethnic profiling target racialised minorities. There are long histories of the surveillance and control of the Sámi and Roma ethnic minority groups in Finland through restrictive laws on vagrancy and public order offences, as well as the heavy stigma placed on poverty (Pyykönen, 2015). Further, eugenicist policies and practices that targeted the reproductive rights of racialised others have resulted in practices of racial hygiene that continue to 'haunt' the social and healthcare system (Sudenkaarne and Blell, 2022).

The admission route for refugees and asylum seekers is just as traumatising as the one previously described. A negative asylum decision could be followed by an attempted suicide and escort to the ward by the police. Such an admission was often greeted by the rolling of the eyes and derision by staff. A recent study by Kallakorpi et al (2017) illustrates that Finnish nurses are often highly suspicious of racialised patients and their motives for seeking care. Nurses raised concerns about the patients' true reasons for being admitted to psychiatric wards. Some nurses were not sure whether to believe the patients' claims of persecution in their native countries or whether they really were signs of psychosis (Kallakorpi et al, 2017). This reinforces the stereotype that people experiencing mental distress are 'delusional, emotionally unstable, unpredictable, untruthful, untrustworthy, lacking all capacity for "rational" thought and invariably dangerous to oneself or others' (LeBlanc and Kinsella, 2016: 64). All of these practices result in an overarching inability to see or consider meaning in the perspectives of racialised people living in structures of systemic oppression (Collins, 2000). Finally, these practices are based on epistemic injustice, which occurs when individuals are viewed by people in more dominant positions as 'non-knowers' about their own realities and they are silenced or their perspectives are distorted by listeners (Dotson, 2011).

According to a population-based survey comparing nine regions of origin, foreign-born people (17.4 per cent) had a higher prevalence of psychological discomfort than the general population (12.9 per cent) (Robertsson et al, 2023). When drilling down into regions of origin, migrants from the Middle East and North Africa had the highest proportion of distress (29.7 per cent). While studies indicate that the foreign-born population generally under-utilises mental health services compared with the Finnish population, there are different hypotheses about the reasons. It can be due to the fact that migrants are more psychologically resilient, unwilling to use Finnish mental health services or facing barriers to accessing care (Kieseppä et al, 2020). The key factors raising the likelihood of distress among communities of foreign-born people were unemployment or economic inactivity, international protection as a cause for migration and beginner-level language skills (Robertsson et al, 2023: 5). While researchers note the increasing interest in racialised and migrant patients in transcultural mental health (Ekblad and Kastrup, 2013), there is simultaneously a lack of investment in community mental health interventions developed by racialised people and migrants themselves, as well as low recruitment of practitioners of colour. In short, the pattern of ethnopsychiatry as a profession of Whiteness persists.

A transnational European study examining how medical professionals treat immigrants in 16 different European countries indicated that there were problems with diagnosis, trust issues and a higher likelihood of exclusion (Sandhu et al, 2013). In their study on the multicultural competence of Finnish nurses, Mulder et al (2015) showed that despite the nurses' high level of cultural understanding, a third of the informants harboured prejudices towards patients with an immigrant background. Sainola-Rodriguez (2005) found that doctors in Finnish mental hospitals did not examine the perceptions of asylum-seeking patients concerning illness or care. The care was uneven and only some nurses expressed concern about these disparities. As Kallakorpi (2017: 41) notes, racism in care can be disguised as a distant attitude, impolite behaviour or direct hostility. These points are consistent with the results of a study by Kallakorpi et al (2017), which shows that Finnish nurses often do not recognise the trauma symptoms of migrant patients and are mistrustful of asylum seeking patients. The study further noted that while immigrant patients underutilise mental health services, they are overrepresented in involuntary psychiatric care (Kallakorpi et al, 2017).

It is worth noting that the structural relationship between poverty, trauma and racism and mental health is rarely deeply interrogated in mental health (Hansen et al, 2018). Racism not only drives a public health crisis on many levels but also those subjected to racist behaviours encounter disparities that affect every aspect of their lives (Wright et al, 2020). Racism is infused in the diagnostic process with racialised communities internationally at higher risk of mental illness diagnoses, longer inpatient stays, involuntary psychiatric detention and readmission (Barnett et al, 2019; Seah et al, 2021). At the same time, racialised people generally have less access to mental health services and are more likely to use crisis care (Younis, 2021). Finally, they are more likely to be medicated rather than offered talking therapy for mental illness while external risk factors such as poverty and racism are overlooked (Bignall et al, 2019). In summary, racialised people in Europe are often 'culturalised' with little attention to the multitude of symptoms that emerge from the reality of living in structures of racial capitalism.

Conclusion

The team felt uneasy whenever my observations and questions regarding the care we were providing or not providing were raised. This is not unusual because when racialised workers, who are 'both marked by difference and expected to perform a white-normed professional identity' (Badwall, 2013: 2) speak out against injustice, their mere existence becomes unsettling to the profession of healthcare, which seeks to create an image of itself as a place of Whiteness and White benevolence. My questions were seen as going against the institutional norm, an institution that was White and that provided services rooted in colonial perspectives.

To fit into this White space, the clinic and to make my White colleagues feel at ease, I went out of my way to be overly polite, to come across as unthreatening and unassuming. White fragility, a term used by DiAngelo (2018), refers to situations where when White people experience any kind of racial tension, they react with a wide range of emotional behaviours such as anger, fear, guilt, defensiveness, argumentativeness or the silent treatment. White fragility is a way that White people control social situations to preserve their racial privilege and mitigate deeper probing about how racism operates in interpersonal contexts. When broaching a subject, I fretted about how it would be heard and perceived. I policed my expressions, intonation, voice and tone so as not to be labelled as 'a belligerent angry Black woman'. After all, my responsibility was to ensure that this space stayed open for other racialised professionals wanting to join and that could only happen if I performed a dance that indicated submission and acceptance of my designated position in this White space.

When I tried to raise concerns about our work, the common response to my questioning was patronising. I was instructed not to be too emotional. My advocacy was seen as being too close to the racialised patients and not maintaining professional boundaries. The team felt it was helping the racialised patients because the diagnosis given would entitle them to receive certain benefits from the government. "We are doing good. These patients tell us that they are happy with our services." What else would these racialised patients say in a situation where power asymmetries are completely skewed? What can they say when some of them have a fear of authorities and know what going against such authorities could entail? Moreover, the personnel did not even speak their clients' language(s). Despite this, patients in the referral pathways to the transcultural mental health services were often not accorded their full legal rights, such as being provided interpretation services. This contradicts the Finnish Act on the Status and Rights of the Patients (785/1992) which states that the mother language, unique needs and culture of the patient must be taken into consideration as much as possible in their care.

The professionals were not from the cultures they were encountering and did not have access to the lived experience and knowledge of their patients (Scrutton, 2017). Yet, they had the power to diagnose racialised clients based on their own cultural practices and ethnicity using Eurocentric methods and tools. When regarding racialised people who come from societies that have been historically subjected to colonial atrocities, it is worth pondering whether a society that has a colonial legacy should have the prerogative to research and project itself on those that it has subjugated. Yet this is what the role of transcultural mental health is. It is a tool that seeks to centre and legitimise colonialism and White supremacy by pathologising, incarcerating, medicalising, diagnosing and stigmatising service users and survivors of psychiatry who come into contact with these services.

In the end, the team eventually agreed to have the Eurocentric tools updated. Some team members validated my experiences and said they appreciated the feedback given and that they also observed the same challenges that I had brought to the team's attention. One pressing concern that deeply troubled some of us was the fear that one of our patients would die by suicide after our encounters. Because our professional encounters always resulted in our patients revisiting and recounting their trauma within the allocated time, the team would have to interrupt the racialised patients and tell them that they would wrap up the discussion in their next visit. However, it was not always clear whether these patients would survive until the next appointment. I wondered why, these colleagues who saw themselves as allies, never brought up these important issues at the time. Why did they wait for me to raise them knowing that I had so much to lose? In private, they would signal that it was important to raise these matters in meetings but, at crucial moments, they would stay silent and safe.

There is a dearth of research on Whiteness in Finnish mental health services and on the experiences of racialised patients from their own perspectives about accessing mental health services in general. The lack of inclusion of racialised professionals as experts on their own communities further indicts the entire system of mental health care in Finland as constructed on the epistemic violence of Whiteness. Globally, many people who identify as psychosocially impaired, service users of psychiatry, survivors of psychiatry and by academics and professionals in the field of transcultural psychiatry strongly disagree with the idea that complex issues of living, acting and thinking can be reduced to 'mental' health and disorder that emerged in a specific socio-cultural environment. There have been concerns raised about the negative consequences of long-term usage of psychotropic medications, which are the cornerstone of modern biomedical psychiatry (Angel, 2011; Mills and Fernando, 2014). Many who oppose psychiatry cast doubt on the usefulness and reliability of diagnosis, and critique how psychiatrisation labels normal human reactions to diverse experiences as a 'mental disorder' that should be treated with medication (Bentall, 2010; Mills and Fernando, 2014). In this sense, it is important to remember that psychiatry emerged as a profession deeply intertwined with colonialism and that its contemporary statutory tools can be used to reinforce colonised social relations in the present day (Kirmayer, 2020). We close by pointing to the work of Maria Yellow Horse Brave Heart (Brave Heart and Deschenie, 2006; Brave Heart and Chase, 2016) who has underlined the significant role of colonial genocide, substantial group trauma and compounding systems of discrimination and oppression as leading to multigenerational unresolved grief and historical trauma. The tools to recover from the impact of these tectonic historical forces must stretch into changing the political realities that shape the lives of racialised people in Finland.

References

Act on the Status and Rights of the Patients (785/1992) www.finlex.fi/fi/laki/kaannokset/1992/en19920785_20120690.pdf

Alemanji, A.A., and Mafi, B. (2018) 'Antiracism education? a study of an antiracism workshop in Finland', *Scandinavian Journal of Educational Research*, 62(2): 186–99.

Amad, A. and Thomas, P. (2011) 'Histoire de la maladie mentale dans le Moyen-Orient médiéval', *Annales médico psychologiques*, 169(6): 373–6.

Angell, M. (2011) 'The epidemic of mental illness: why?', *The New York Review of Books*, 23 June.

Antić, A. (2021) 'Transcultural psychiatry: cultural difference, universalism and social psychiatry in the age of decolonisation', *Culture, Medicine, and Psychiatry*, 45(3): 359–84.

Badwall, H. (2013) 'Can I be a good social worker? Racialized workers narrate their experiences with racism in everyday practice', doctoral thesis, University of Toronto, ON, Canada.

Bains, J. (2005) 'Race, culture and psychiatry: a history of transcultural psychiatry', *History of Psychiatry*, 16(2): 139–54.

Bansal, N., Karlsen, S., Sashidharan, S. P., Cohen, R., Chew-Graham, C. A. and Malpass, A. (2022) 'Understanding ethnic inequalities in mental healthcare in the UK: a meta-ethnography', *PLoS Medicine*, 19(12): 1–36.

Barnett, P., Mackay, E., Matthews, H., Gate, R., Greenwood, H., Ariyo, K. et al (2019) 'Ethnic variations in compulsory detention under the Mental Health Act: a systematic review and meta-analysis of international data', *The Lancet Psychiatry*, 6(4): 305–17.

Bentall, R.P. (2010) *Doctoring the Mind: Why Psychiatric Treatments Fail*, London: Penguin.

Besteman, C. (2020) *Militarized Global Apartheid*, Durham, NC: Duke University Press.

Bignall, T., Jeraj, S., Helsby, E. and Butt, J. (2019) *Racial Disparities in Mental Health*, London: Race Equity Foundation.

Bonilla-Silva, E. (2021) 'What makes systemic racism systemic?', *Sociological Inquiry*, 91(3): 513–33.

Brave Heart, M.Y.H. and Chase, J. (2016) 'Historical trauma among indigenous peoples of the Americas: concepts, research, and clinical considerations', *Wounds of History: Repair and Resilience in the Transgenerational Transmission of Trauma*, London: Taylor and Francis, pp 270–87.

Brave Heart, M.Y.H. and Deschenie, T. (2006) 'Historical trauma and postcolonial stress in American Indian population', *Tribal College*, 17(3): 24.

Braveman, P.A., Arkin, E., Proctor, D., Kauh, T. and Holm, N. (2022) 'Systemic and structural racism: definitions, examples, health damages, and approaches to dismantling: study examines definitions, examples, health damages, and dismantling systemic and structural racism', *Health Affairs*, 41(2): 171–8.

Bullard, A. (2007) 'Imperial networks and postcolonial independence: the transition from colonial to transcultural psychiatry', in S. Mahone and M. Vaughan (eds) *Psychiatry and Empire*, London: Palgrave Macmillan.

Cenat, J.M. (2020) 'How to provide anti-racist mental health care', *The Lancet Psychiatry*, 7(11): 929–31.

Collins, P.H. (2000) *Black Feminist Thought: Knowledge, Consciousness, and the Politics of Empowerment*, London: Routledge.

Davidson, L., Rakfeldt, J. and Strauss, J. (2010) *The Roots of the Recovery Movement in Psychiatry: Lessons Learned*, Hoboken, NJ: Wiley.

DiAngelo, R. (2018) *White Fragility: Why It's So Hard for White People to Talk About Racism*, Boston: Beacon Press.

Dotson, K. (2011) 'Tracking epistemic violence, tracking practices of silencing', *Hypatia*, 26(2): 236–57.

Ekblad, S. and Kastrup, M.C. (2013) 'Current research in transcultural psychiatry in the Nordic countries', *Transcultural Psychiatry*, 50(6): 841–57.

Ellenberger, H.F., Delille, E. and Kaplansky, J. (2020) *Ethnopsychiatry*, 56, McGill-Queen's University Press.

Fanon, F. (1963) *The Wretched of the Earth*, New York: Grove Press.

Fanon, F. (1988) *Toward the African Revolution: Political Essays*, New York: Grove Press.

Fassin, D. and Rechtman, R. (2005) 'An anthropological hybrid: the pragmatic arrangement of universalism and culturalism in French mental health', *Transcultural Psychiatry*, 42(3): 347–66.

Foucault, M. (1988) *Madness and Civilization: A History of Insanity in the Age of Reason*, New York: Vintage.

Frazer-Carroll, M. (2023) 'Is mental illness really an "illness"?', *IPPR Progressive Review*, 30(1): 46–50.

Gilmore, R.W. (2007) 'In the shadow of the shadow state', in INCITE! Women of Color Against Violence (ed) *The Revolution Will Not Be Funded: Beyond the Non-Profit Industrial Complex*, Cambridge, MA: South End Press, pp 41–52.

Gilroy, P. (2013) *There Ain't No Black in the Union Jack: The Cultural Politics of Race and Nation*, London: Routledge.

Gladden, S.N. and Daniel, J.L. (2021) 'The plantation's fall and the non-profit sector's rise: addressing the influence of the antebellum plantation on today's non-profit sector', *Administrative Theory and Praxis*, 1–10.

Greenblatt, M. (1975) 'Psychiatry: the battered child of medicine', *New England Journal of Medicine*, 292(5): 246–50.

Hansen, H., Braslow, J. and Rohrbaugh, R.M. (2018) 'From cultural to structural competency: training psychiatry residents to act on social determinants of health and institutional racism', *JAMA Psychiatry (Chicago, IL)*, 75(2): 117–18.

hooks, b. (1994) *Teaching to Transgress: Education as the Practice of Freedom*, London: Routledge.

Huttunen, M. and Pakaslahti, A. (2010) *Kulttuurit ja lääketiede* [*Culture and Medicine*], Helsinki: Duodecim.

Kallakorpi, S. (2017) 'Transcultural psychiatric nursing of immigrant patients in Finland. A focused ethnographic study of patients and the nurses caring for them', Licentiate thesis, University of Eastern Finland.

Kallakorpi, S., Haatainen, K. and Kankkunen, P. (2018) 'Nurses' experiences caring for immigrant patients in psychiatric units', *International Journal of Caring Sciences*, 11(3): 1802–11.

Kallakorpi, S., Haatainen, K. and Kankkunen, P. (2019) 'Psychiatric nursing care experiences of immigrant patients: a focused ethnographic study', *International Journal of Mental Health Nursing*, 28(1): 117–27.

Keller, R.C. (2007) *Colonial Madness: Psychiatry in French North Africa*, Chicago, IL: University of Chicago Press.

Kieseppä, V., Torniainen-Holm, M., Jokela, M., Suvisaari, J., Gissler, M., Markkula, N. et al (2020) *Immigrants' Mental Health Service Use Compared to That of Native Finns: a Register Study*, HUS Department of Psychiatry.

Kirmayer, L.J. (2020) 'Toward a postcolonial psychiatry: uncovering the structures of domination in mental health theory and practice', *Philosophy, Psychiatry and Psychology*, 27(3): 267–71.

Kuittinen, S., Mölsä, M., Punamäki, R. L., Tiilikainen, M. and Honkasalo, M. L. (2017) 'Causal attributions of mental health problems and depressive symptoms among older Somali refugees in Finland', *Transcultural Psychiatry*, 54(2): 211–38.

Kuokkanen, R. (2022) 'All I see is White: the colonial problem in Finland', in J. Hoegaerts, T. Liimatainen, L. Henanaho and E. Peterson (eds) *Finnishness, Whiteness and Coloniality*. Helsinki: Helsinki University Press, pp 291–314.

LeBlanc, S. and Kinsella, E.A. (2016) 'Toward epistemic justice: a critically reflexive examination of "sanism" and implications for knowledge generation', *Studies in Social Justice*, 10(1): 59–78.

Lehti, V., Antas, B, Kärnä, T. and Tuisku, K. (2016) 'The assessment of traumatized refugees: clinical practices at the Cultural Psychiatry Outpatient Clinic', *Psychiatria Fennica*, 47: 17–31.

Maldonado-Torres, N. (2017) 'Frantz Fanon and the decolonial turn in psychology: from modern/colonial methods to the decolonial attitude', *South African Journal of Psychology*, 47(4): 432–41.

McKenzie, K. and Bhui, K. (2007) 'Institutional racism in mental health care', *BMJ*, 334(7595): 649–50.

Mental Health Act 1983, section 2(2).

Metzl, J.M. (2010) *The Protest Psychosis: How Schizophrenia Became a Black Disease*, Boston, MA: Beacon Press.

Mills, C. (2014) *Decolonizing Global Mental Health: the Psychiatrisation of the Majority World*, London: Routledge.

Mölsä, M.E., Hjelde, K.H. and Tiilikainen, M. (2010) 'Changing conceptions of mental distress among Somalis in Finland', *Transcultural Psychiatry*, 47(2): 276–300.

Mölsä, M., Punamäki, R. L., Saarni, S. I., Tiilikainen, M., Kuittinen, S. and Honkasalo, M. L. (2014) 'Mental and somatic health and pre-and post-migration factors among older Somali refugees in Finland', *Transcultural Psychiatry*, 51(4): 499–525.

Mölsä, M., Kuittinen, S., Tiilikainen, M., Honkasalo, M. L. and Punamäki, R. L. (2017) 'Mental health among older refugees: the role of trauma, discrimination, and religiousness', *Aging and Mental Health*, 21(8): 829–37.

Mulder, R., Koivula, M. and Kaunonen, M. (2015) 'Multicultural skills of nurses: a pilot study', *Tutkiva hoitotyö*, 13: 24–34.

Myers, D. (2014) '"Drapetomania": rebellion, defiance and free Black insanity in the antebellum United States', dissertation, UCLA. https://escholarship.org/uc/item/9dc055h5

Nazroo, J.Y., Bhui, K.S. and Rhodes, J. (2020) 'Where next for understanding race/ethnic inequalities in severe mental illness? Structural, interpersonal and institutional racism', *Sociology of Health and Illness*, 42(2): 262–76.

Porter, R. and Wright, D. (2003) *The Confinement of the Insane: International Perspectives, 1800–1965*, Cambridge: Cambridge University Press.

Pyykkönen, M. (2007) 'Integrating governmentality: administrative expectations for immigrant associations in Finland', *Alternatives*, 32(2): 197–224.

Pyykkönen, M. (2015) 'Ethically ethnic: the ethno-culturalization of the moral conduct of the Sámi and the Roma in the governance in Finland between the 1850s and 1930s', *Journal of Political Power*, 8(1): 39–59.

Rask, S., Elo, I.T., Koskinen, S., Lilja, E., Koponen, P. and Castaneda, A.E. (2018) 'The association between discrimination and health: findings on Russian, Somali and Kurdish origin populations in Finland', *European Journal of Public Health*, 28(5): 898–903.

Robertsson, T. (2023) 'Prevalence and risk factors of psychological distress among foreign-born population in Finland: a population-based survey comparing nine regions of origin', *Scandinavian Journal of Public Health*, 51(3): 490–8.

Rose, D. and Kalathil, J. (2019) 'Power, privilege and knowledge: the untenable promise of co-production in mental "health"', *Frontiers in Sociology*, 4: 57.

Sandhu, S., Bjerre, N.V., Dauvrin, M., Dias, S., Gaddini, A., Greacen, T. et al (2013) 'Experiences with treating immigrants: a qualitative study in mental health services across 16 European countries', *Social Psychiatry and Psychiatric Epidemiology*, 48: 105–16.

Schclarek Mulinari, L. and Keskinen, S. (2022) 'Racial profiling in the racial welfare state: examining the order of policing in the Nordic region', *Theoretical Criminology*, 26(3): 377–95.

Scrutton, A.P. (2017) 'Epistemic injustice and mental illness', in *Routledge Handbook of Epistemic Injustice*, New York: Routledge.

Seah, C., Johnson, J., Dueñas, H. and Huckins, L. (2021) 'Characterizing racism in psychiatric diagnoses', *European Neuropsychopharmacology*, 51: e25–6.

Seikkula, M. (2019) 'Adapting to post-racialism? Definitions of racism in non-governmental organization advocacy that mainstreams anti-racism', *European Journal of Cultural Studies*, 22(1): 95–109.

Shim, R.S. (2021) 'Dismantling structural racism in psychiatry: a path to mental health equity', *American Journal of Psychiatry*, 178: 592–8.

Spruill, L.H. (2016) 'Slave patrols, "packs of negro dogs" and policing Black communities', *Phylon (1960–)*, 53(1): 42–66.

Sudenkaarne, T. and Blell, M. (2022) 'Reproductive justice for the haunted Nordic welfare state: race, racism, and queer bioethics in Finland', *Bioethics*, 36(3): 328–35.

Szasz, T. (2019) *Psychiatry: the Science of Lies*, New York: Syracuse University Press.

Trimbur, J. (2022) '*Frantz Fanon, Psychiatry and Politics* by Nigel C. Gibson and Roberto Beneduce (review)', *American Imago*, 79(1): 145–59.

Villanueva, E. (2018). *Decolonizing Wealth: Indigenous Wisdom to Heal Divides and Restore Balance*, Oakland, CA: Berrett-Koehler.

Wahbi, R. and Beletsky, L. (2022) 'Involuntary commitment as "carceral-health service": from healthcare-to-prison pipeline to a public health abolition praxis', *Journal of Law, Medicine and Ethics*, 50(1): 23–30.

Williams, D.R. and Etkins, O.S. (2021) 'Racism and mental health', *World Psychiatry*, 20(2): 194–5.

Wright, J.L., Jarvis, J.N., Pachter, L.M. and Walker-Harding, L.R. (2020) '"Racism as a public health issue" APS racism series: at the intersection of equity, science, and social justice', *Pediatric Research*, 88(5): 696–8.

Younis, T. (2021a) 'The muddle of institutional racism in mental health', *Sociology of Health and Illness*, 43(8): 1831–9.

9

Emergent healing spaces: decolonising healing and wellness in Finland

Wambui Njuguna

I am a Kenyan American woman living and working in Finland since 2010. I'm still weaving my narrative as it unfolds in the Afro-Finnish tapestry. I was born in Kenya to a (Black) Kenyan father and a (White) Anglo-Danish mother. We moved to the US in 1991 when I was 10 years old. I finished my postgraduate studies in applied linguistics in Chicago in 2006. I spent 2.5 years teaching English in Abu Dhabi, and it was there that I began the practice of Ashtanga yoga as a healing practice. During a trip to India in 2009, I met a Finnish man and began learning the Ashtanga yoga method under his guidance.

In this chapter, I tell my own story of coming into healing spaces as a Black woman, immigrant and yoga practitioner in Finland. I begin by narrating my own journey and understanding of my practice in relation to healing spaces. I then outline some of the complexities of the Afro-Finn community. I end by discussing the challenges, and opportunities, around creating emergent healing spaces in places of pain.

There have been many challenges to integrating into Finnish society as an adult with limited Finnish-language skills. Even with my educational, class, permanent residence status, linguistic (native-English speaker) privilege and proximity to Whiteness through my White Finnish husband, the combination of my racialised and gendered identities are marginalised, silenced and erased here in Finland. There have been very few spaces where I can productively contribute all of my skills and talents to Finnish society, let alone find a moment to breathe and not have to perform to White Finnish norms. This has been true even in yoga spaces, ironically, which are supposed to be dedicated to self-realisation, self-knowledge and unity consciousness.

Despite the professional and financial obstacles I face(d) in Finland, I have had opportunities to develop. In 2010–18, I gained experience in the yoga field, travelling, assisting and teaching with my husband, a well-established Ashtanga yoga teacher both here in Finland and abroad. I was, nonetheless, always troubled by the lack of diversity in the yoga workshops and retreats. Still, my commitment and passion for the practice and what I was learning was enough to keep me engaged. In 2017, events within the Ashtanga yoga community regarding sexual misconduct from the 'guru' and some of his female students came to light. While this was shocking and disorienting enough, what really stood out to me was the failure of the senior teachers to compassionately and skilfully lead the flock away from this quagmire of power abuse and community implosion. I experienced a loss of faith and direction and needed to take time to assess the harmful, oppressive elements of narcissistic, hierarchical leadership within my South Asian lineage of Ashtanga yoga and its mostly White community. I decided to participate in further training and obtain qualifications in trauma-informed yoga. I then began to study the topic of (collective) trauma and somatic healing much more thoroughly. The key tenets of the intersectional feminist, trauma-informed, anti-racist lens in my yoga practice means linking transformative justice, as defined by people such as Mia Mingus of the Bay Area Transformative Justice Collective (2023), and adrienne maree browne of the Emergent Strategy Ideation Institute (2023), with ahimsa, the first ethical principle in yoga philosophy of non-violence; namely, doing no harm to any living thing. We may all be one on the level of absolute reality, but our different positions in society nonetheless determine who is seen, heard and valued in society. These differences do not disappear when we enter into healing and wellness spaces because the same mental systems of oppressions that maintain Whiteness, heteronormativity, casteism, fatphobia and ableism often dwell in these spaces that are supposed to be restorative.

The combination of the jarring reality of cognitive dissonance (especially when engaging in the Indigenous wisdom practices of yoga, a millennia-old art and science stewarded in South Asia, in White majority spaces) and the disheartening results of a 2018 study, *Being Black in the EU* (European Union Agency for Fundamental Rights, 2018), that documented the prevalence of everyday racism in Finnish society, made me confront questions which had been marinating in my embodied reality since I arrived in Finland. I asked myself: "Who isn't in our healing spaces? Why? Why not?" This chapter is a reflection of the struggles and challenges I, as a BIPOC (Black, Indigenous, People of Colour) person engaged in healing and wellness in Helsinki, have found when creating a culture of inclusivity and psychological safety in these spaces. Healing and wellness are industry terms oftentimes used amorphously and interchangeably to describe the goods and services that professionals offer. My understanding is that healing is often used for more specific and acute instances, such as yoga for lower-back pain or energy-healing sessions; while wellness can mean a range of holistic practices, – for example, dietary and lifestyle practices – that promote overall well-being.

Healing, of course, has deeper meanings as well. The violence of colonialism is based on deep layers of oppression that extend to the very core of our being. Societal structures of oppression reinforce ideologies of superiority and inferiority that we internalise. Rachelle Péan (2021) writes that Western medical systems that pathologise trauma cannot support healing, particularly among BIPOC, who are disproportionately impacted by systems of oppression. Péan also argues that healing from the legacy of colonialism cannot be solely individual but also requires the creation of spaces of communal healing.

As a woman who came to terms with the concept and lived reality of race in the 1990s–2000s in the US, identifying and feeling a sense of belonging in BIPOC communities in Finland has proven difficult at times. And while the range of ethnic diversity in the US is expansive and multifaceted, I haven't been able to locate a sense of Black solidarities in Finland similar to what I experienced in the US. There are many reasons for this.

Finland has always been an ethnically diverse place. The Sámi are the Indigenous population comprising about 10,000 people and their territories are in the north. Then there are roughly around 12,000 Roma people, who have been in Finland for over 500 years. If we take just these two groups alone, we see a tremendous disparity between their lived experiences and the common view that all Finns are equal. A Ministry of Justice report on the current situation of the Sámi people notes that they see themselves as a distinct people with their own culture, language and traditions, but they have serious concerns about their land rights and their lack of self-determination (Juuso, 2018). The Roma people face marginalisation and erasure, and are seen as outsiders in Finland. In a 2018 news report, a Roma man said: "It is important to me that the majority of the population sees me as a Finn, first and foremost, but also as a Roma" (YLE, 2018). These examples illustrate the struggles that racialised people face regardless of how long their communities have existed in Finland.

According to Statistics Finland (2019), the total number of people in Finland of African heritage was 54,450 in 2019. While numerically this is a rather small population largely concentrated in the Helsinki metropolitan region, it is an enormously diverse population with many different spiritual, ethnic, generational and diasporic identities. As documented in the EU Fundamental Rights Agency study (2018), 63 per cent of Afro-Finns in Finland had experienced racist harassment, which included offensive gestures, comments, threats or violence, which placed Finland at the top, with the highest level of racist incidents of the 12 studied nations. Racism is a general toxin that people of African descent must navigate, survive and negotiate, its violence outsourced and hidden in plain sight to the majority of the White normative Finnish population.

Who is allowed to declare Finnish identity?

So, who can claim Afro-Finnishness? What does it mean to be an Afro-Finn? Is it a question of whether you are born in Finland or not? Can a

Rwandan youngster born in Rwanda, who moved to Finland as a young child and acquired mastery of the Finnish language, claim Afro-Finnishness? Is Afro-Finnishness only reserved for the biracial offspring born and raised in Finland to one (White) Finnish parent and one (Black) African parent? Does it require native-speaker linguistic fluency in Finnish? Where does that leave a biracial child born to a Finnish-Swedish parent? Can a biracial native speaker of Swedish claim Afro-Finnish identity? Is it the length of time in Finland or the level of linguistic and educational assimilation that constitutes Afro-Finnishness? How do citizenship or immigration status, religious affiliation, educational and income level, work opportunities and whether one is situated in a rural or urban setting construct Afro-Finnishness? The complexity of African identities, the disproportionate burden of microaggressions and continuous structural violence pose many challenges to building trust and creating healing spaces that could bring people together.

In 2020, after the brutal murder of George Floyd and with the global uprising of Black Lives Matter (BLM), my questions became more urgent and unrelenting: "Who gets to be well and taken care of in our societies? Who gets to breathe and who, literally as well as in all the small accumulations of race-based stress and trauma, gets the breath taken away from them?"

The tricky thing about racism is that it is not always blatant like murders by the police. The more silent, insidious and benevolent that racism gets, the more difficult it becomes to name it and realise that we're all swimming in racist water and breathing racist air, all the time. This applies whether we're privileged enough to not have to be aware of it or not. In my social and professional circles, the racism I experience is supremely benevolent: it's a racism of omission. I notice the same pattern even with young BIPOC people who were born or grew up in Finland and speak Finnish fluently. This shows up in any number of ways.

One way is the lack of cultural relevance and representation in yoga among BIPOC populations. People do not see themselves represented in spaces; therefore, they will self-select themselves out of those spaces, reaffirming the narrative, already amplified by a Whitewashed media, that yoga is for thin, able-bodied White people with enough leisure time and disposable income to both afford and participate in it.

Consider any number of the following examples: the violation of personal space boundaries when people make comments about your hair or even touch it without your express consent; the need to unpack your personal histories, which often are complicated and even traumatic, in response to the often well-intentioned and curious question, "Where are you from?" Well-intentioned 'compliments' from a White person such as commenting on one's 'exotic' looks, which operates from an assumption that White is not exotic. White is the norm; White is objective; White is neutral. For any racist or assimilationist Black or Brown person, this might be experienced as a compliment, making it easier at that moment to swim in synchronicity in the racist waters. However, if one sees the world through an anti-racist lens, this objectification through the White gaze, no matter how innocent and sweet the intention, has a different impact and can be tricky to respond to, to say the least.

Due to this ongoing, chronic race-based stress and trauma which is part of the everyday BIPOC experience in Finland, both on the macro level (unemployment or unsatisfactory work, lack of housing, safety) and micro level (disrespectful comments, educating people on why a certain behaviour is harmful and so on), it's no surprise, then, that we would need to heal in spaces free from the White gaze, away from the constant psychological exertion that comes from navigating White spaces.

In a nutshell, when a small minority lives in a homogeneous, White-dominant setting, it falls on the less dominant person to observe and shape-shift their identity and mannerisms in order to survive and receive a certain level of acceptance and tolerance from the dominant majority. This is not to mention the egregious assumption that BIPOC exist to educate, often for free, the dominant group on matters pertaining to race and racism. This burden takes an enormous amount of emotional, psychological and cognitive labour. As a result, there are very few places for people of colour to feel safe to be vulnerable enough to express the full range of human emotions. I return to the example of someone White who complimented me by calling me 'exotic'. If I choose not to sing along to the same racist tune, I'll point out that it's actually not a compliment to be called exotic, not knowing how the person will react. They may get defensive. They may think I'm rude. If the discussion escalates, the person complimenting might cry, not knowing that White tears and White fragility are effective weapons in shutting me down (DiAngelo, 2018). I might get called hostile, leaning on the angry Black woman trope. Either way, it's a gamble to speak one's truth as a marginalised person in these moments. And so, depending on the day, oftentimes, the safest and easiest thing for me to do in that moment is to save myself the trouble and accept the compliment. In doing so, I am choosing to remain complicit in upholding racism but I am managing to get through my day. Either way, there's heaviness and sorrow in the choices presented before me. And the greatest sorrow lies in the obliviousness of the other person responsible for this situation.

Given that I move through the world as an unapologetically anti-racist, proud Black woman, yet have also experienced my own share of needing to survive and perform to White norms, I feel that I'm able to offer something of value to the BIPOC community here. I do this by combining my world view with my long experience in yoga, wellness and spirituality. Now, while this all sounds well and good, it's important to recognise that yoga, in general, and, in my specific South Asian lineage-based practice of Ashtanga yoga in particular, comes with 'baggage' that can make it problematic if/when presented as a partial solution to BIPOC needs. For one thing, the demographic is small. For another, while we've all been lumped together under this umbrella term, BIPOC, we are individuals with our own sense of likes, dislikes, tastes and interests, not to mention ethnic, spiritual and cultural differences. And while we are not a monolith, we are all monolithically oppressed under the yoke of White supremacy. The yoga that I have found meaning in and transformation with is derived from overtly casteist/Brahminical roots, linked with the rise of reactionary Indian Prime Minister Modi's fascism and Hindutva. This gives it a cultural and political resonance that not all BIPOC may be comfortable with, especially those who are religious minorities and have experienced religious trauma as a result of caste-based oppression. For BIPOC with Indian heritage, many may feel uncomfortable with the fact that yoga has become this tidy product, Whitewashed, commercialised, culturally appropriated and divorced from its South Asian roots for 'feel-good' consumption. More insidious is the weaponised cooptation of yoga as a form of 'soft power', making palatable the genocidal harm caused by the rise of Hindutva and the 'saffronisation' of India under the current fascist prime minister.

If we look at yoga's current consumer base, the main obstacle in mainstream yoga/wellness/spiritual communities is the lack of representation and diversity. Mainstream yoga is marketed towards primarily middle-aged, middle-upper-class, thin, able-bodied White women. Many self-identify as being good, liberal, progressive, well travelled and open-minded, so how could they possibly be racist? Even for BIPOC who have found value in their yoga practice, it can feel quite jarring and disorienting to go deep into one's yoga practice, only to encounter microaggressions in the changing room, full of supposedly friendly White people. The main takeaway from this point is that spaces that make statements before questions cannot ultimately deliver on this. For example, if a yoga studio is full of White people who see themselves as kind and open-minded, and who haven't ever had to examine and interrogate their racist ideas and attitudes claims, "This is a safe, discrimination-free space", how do they know that? What explicitly anti-racist training and implicit inner work have they done to make sure they are not replicating the same problematic, harmful racist behaviours and unexamined White privilege? To examine their unconscious and even conscious bias? We can't start from a statement of intent and assumption as it's quite final and leaves no place to go forward. Perhaps the first step is to change the statement into a question. Is this space safe for racialised and marginalised people? What can I do to make it safer? This requires further education and commitment to decolonising these so-called healing spaces from replicating the harm that swirls both inside and outside the walls of the yoga studio (Batacharya and Wong, 2018).

In my experience as a yoga practitioner who operates through an intersectional feminist, trauma-informed, anti-racist lens, I have come to see that even general liberal wellness spaces such as yoga and meditation studios operate, to various degrees, with White supremacist, anti-Black, racist norms. And right now, it falls on the shoulders of those with more privilege and proximity to power to take responsibility and address these institutionalised and personal practices, and right these wrongs; so that those with least access to and most need of healing and wellbeing can receive it. Those who are most catered to and served in wellness spaces must examine the rampant usage of phrases such as, 'We are all one', 'I don't see colour', 'Just let it go', 'You're so negative' and 'Good vibes only'. This is a toxic form of spiritual bypassing and gaslighting of marginalised people who speak up about their experiences and it happens with clockwork predictability. This type of silencing in healing spaces fosters an environment of 'hollow, (White) fragile harmony' at all costs. Since our healing spaces reflect the same hierarchies and patterns of oppression and power that the wider society operates in, these spaces will continue to be harmful, at worst, for marginalised folk and ineffective at best. While those who benefit from White privilege risk remaining in an immature arrested development stage, oblivious to their harmful behaviours rooted in unexamined Whiteness, while clinging to their innocence around racism and adamant in their demand for comfort and catering to their White fragility.

Situating BIPOC-centred emergent healing spaces

My aim as a dual heritage, Kenyan American woman, is to advocate for BIPOC-centred healing spaces. Right now, White and Black people need different things for their healing, growth and evolution. White people need anti-racism education to understand how to identify and acknowledge their conditioned racist thinking and underlying unconscious need for ownership, taking up space and entitlement to all things at all times, and to learn to be cognisant of their privilege. A great deal of unlearning must be done to hold the cognitive dissonance around being a good, kind spiritual practitioner and still operating from internalised, unquestioned racist, oppressive norms and the structures and systems they benefit from. While BIPOC need to heal in community and remember who they are when not fighting, or simply trying to exist in White supremacy. And the ways in which all systemic structures of oppression distance us from our own selves and from one another. I'm hopeful that eventually we can get to a place where we can all practise safely together and embody the ideals of yoga as and for unity consciousness. But this will involve people coming to terms with either their internalised superiority or internalised racism, contingent upon how one moves through society.

In practical terms, this has meant working with yoga studio owners towards a culture of care that is much less narcissistic and naive about the material reality of the world and society, as experienced by non-White people. This is a more complex process than simply advertising that 'everybody is welcome to our studio'. Among the main things we need to address are identifying one's social location (both as an individual and as a collective) and its proximity to Whiteness (which is the same as saying, to power and privilege); identifying who the demographic is when you think of yoga students (typically White, thin, able-bodied, cisgender, heteronormative, middle-class women); getting people to see who is being left out of wellness/healing spaces. In my consultations with yoga studio owners and individuals, we do reflective exercises on that. Journalling is a wonderful method to begin to unpack previously lauded non-truths, myths, lies and fairy tales of Whiteness.

I highlight the toxicity of spiritual bypass and toxic positivity and what those are. How jumping straight to '*We are one race, the human race*' (which is true by the way) gets coopted and weaponised to silence people who have marginalised experiences and are less protected by the status quo. We also need to think about who we accept and celebrate as the experts and authorities of yoga. If South Asian, queer and transgender, Black people are not invited and paid to teach and give workshops, something is wrong about that. What about the ableism and fatphobia that afflicts yoga spaces? All this needs to be scrutinised and dismantled. True equity and inclusion are not performative. It's not just about having a few token Black and Brown people in spaces when the underlying dynamic and unspoken norms still reflect Whiteness/White, capitalist, cis-heteronormative, able-bodied, patriarchal, Christian supremacy.

In the following, I highlight some of the initiatives I have been involved in to contribute to the overall wellness of BIPOC in southern Finland. I reflect on the challenges I have faced, and on my successes and failures.

During the autumn 2011 season, a contact of mine took me to *Moninaisten Talo* (MONIKA – Multicultural Women's Association, Finland) in Sörnäinen and I reached out to the obliging staff there with my idea: to volunteer teach Ashtanga yoga there as a way to build experience teaching yoga and make connections with people of the African diaspora. The demographic was mostly middle-aged Somali women who also came for classes at the Helsinki Astanga yoga school for some weeks. There was no issue with religion, although I didn't teach any Sanskrit mantras (chants) and focused instead on the physical aspect of the practice. While I certainly witnessed the benefit these women received and was buoyed by their enthusiasm, ultimately this set-up was not financially sustainable. I volunteered my time as a way to be in community with Black folk while offering something I know to be useful and helpful in life. However, the volunteer-based class model wasn't a priority for the commercially based model the yoga school operates in and, in the end, the classes got cancelled at the school. I did, however, continue teaching on the *Moninaisten Talo* premises in Sörnäinen.

My plans in early spring in 2020 were to offer mindfulness and meditation classes to pupils and teachers at the Montessori school in Helsinki. This had been facilitated by an Afro-Finnish acquaintance of mine. However, the COVID-19 lockdown began in Helsinki in mid-March 2020 and put these plans on hold. After the lockdown ease up, I was able to set up some in-person offerings at the Helsinki Ashtanga yoga school. In September 2020, I offered 'Dear Beloved Black Body', a weekend wellness workshop for BIPOC of African descent. This was primarily an introductory Ashtanga yoga course with the option to continue with an eight-session weekly class with me. 'Dear Beloved Black Body' was a continuation of previous offerings that I held, both on Zoom and at *Pihasali* (the owner offered me the space rent-free as a tangible gesture of solidarity). This June 2020 offering happened at the height of the BLM protest in Helsinki and due to the acute race-based stress and trauma people of Black African descent were experiencing at that time, the turnout of about 5–10 people was satisfactory. The classes were donation-based, with proceeds going to such organisations as my own COVID care initiative, Buraq, Sistah Space and Islamiqueeristi (two of which are Finnish-based).

The autumn extension of the 'Dear Beloved Black Body' weekend workshop was attended by six participants, two of whom were scholarship students from funds I had raised. After the workshop, I wanted to keep the momentum going and had set up a weekly (eight sessions) introduction to Ashtanga yoga for BIPOC. It was hard to get enough people to come to class for the first two weeks and the yoga school said they were going to drop the class from the weekly schedule. I asked them for one more week and I succeeded in bringing in seven people, over the minimum of four to five people that was required so the class stayed on the schedule. The following two weeks only two people attended per week; so I couldn't run the class officially and get paid. Since they showed up, however, I ran a shorter class and they treated me to coffee on one of those days, which was a very sweet gesture of generosity and community care gesture. While I had managed to keep the class going into 2021, the risk was that the school could cancel it at any moment due to low turnout.

After George Floyd's murder and emergence of the BLM movement, I was intentional about marketing in a way that highlighted the ladder of racial hierarchy (White on top, Brown in the middle, Black at the bottom) and got (all) people thinking not only about racism but also anti-Blackness as well. In my marketing, I had prioritised BIPOC – *only* since 2020 was such a traumatising year on matters of race. Looking back at the responses to this class, I received negative feedback from both sides of the racial divide. The school received feedback from the existing (White) demographic of yoga practitioners expressing their opinion that offering a BIPOC-only class was reverse racism and discrimination, which goes against the meaning of yoga as unity. This was to be expected and didn't take me by surprise. However, I was also tone-policed by some members of the Afro-Finnish community saying that it goes against their human value of unity and that they actually prefer the company of White people. They suggested that in the US, this kind of 'extreme' marketing can work, but in a social democratic country such as Finland, things have to be 'really chill'. While I took on board the message and reflected on my world view, that exchange was hurtful and exhausting because it revealed to me the level of internalised racism and oppression present; to go out of one's way to keep White people comfortable at all times, even among those in the work of diversity, inclusivity and racial justice. Assimilation into the dominant group is neither unity nor unifying, for anyone.

It is my wish to be able to unapologetically centre BIPOC needs here but at the moment, in order to keep the class on the roster, I have had to change my marketing of the class to include all people but that we are unapologetically BIPOC-centred. This means that no matter who attends, we begin each class identifying who we are by name, preferred pronouns and racial background. It's my wish to be able to have enough people of African descent attend but, for now, I'm struggling to simply keep the class on the schedule, so I must taper down my ideals to survive in the reality of right now; it is what it is.

From April to May 2020, I held an online three-part webinar for primarily queer, BIPOC youth of immigrant African background on the topic of 'Healing your inner child'. In exchange, the youth were featured in a short promotional video I filmed entitled 'My Yoga Is Melanated', which aims to create more visibility and representation for non-White audiences in the very White-dominated Finnish yoga scene. The key takeaway from the webinar was the generational rift between the youth and their parents in regard to the changing mores and norms around sexuality. Namely, having been raised in primarily conservative religious environments, these youth were experiencing a certain level of duress around their much more expansive and fluid sexual identities than the previous generation was generally able to tolerate and accept.

In August 2020, I worked with host Michaela Moua, an anti-racism educator and activist in Helsinki, at the Helsinki Ashtanga yoga school to lead a workshop on anti-racism as part of an Ashtanga yoga workshop that my husband, Petri, and I were co-facilitating. Michaela's contribution was the physical manifestation of the decolonising wellness vision I have had in my mind since 2018 for yoga and wellness spaces. It was relatively well attended with 14 (mostly all White) participants. It is my vision to continue collaborating with anti-racism educators such as Michaela and offer an intersectional, interdisciplinary approach to spiritual practice and sacred activism. A brave practical spirituality, rooted in compassion and courageous social action. The target demographic is the current existing one in yoga spaces and introducing the concepts that their healing work is unlearning their internalised racist conditioning. 'Decolonising Wellness' prioritises a culture of liberation 'for all of us' liberation for none of us, through karma yoga, the yoga of wise, compassionate action, to address the wrongs of societies – as opposed to yoga for escapism, self-improvement and a way to stay in shape, while remaining hyper individualised and performing well in capitalism. 'Decolonising Wellness' examines the ways in which we are complicit in the oppressive elements of society and seeks to disrupt this complicity.

Conclusion

To conclude, when I look back at my humble start in Sörnäinen at the *Moninaisten Talo* in 2011, I can see how much I have done, how far I have come and how much further the road ahead is. My efforts move in fits and starts, and I reflect that I must constantly adjust the expectations I have for myself in Finland, in comparison with the work my colleagues and peers are doing in North America. BIPOC-centric and decolonised spaces are still quite a novel concept in Finland and it is taking time for society to get on board. Some memorable comments that I have carried with me include the remark that a separate offering based on race alone is segregation and a 'new apartheid'. Others wondered how I am able to charge money for my offerings by alienating and offending the White-majority audience. A more practically minded commentator mused that perhaps the reason so few non-White people attend yoga is that the demographics in Finland are steeply slanted towards the majority-White population.

By 2021, I found myself wondering whether there is truly enough demand, interest and support in the BIPOC community for the kind of initiatives I am attempting and to what extent does my individual background influence, either positively or negatively, the response to my initiatives? While the physical BIPOC community is congregated mostly in Helsinki and southern Finland, it is numerically small, fragmented and many within it face pressing, urgent issues that a yoga class or massage treatment does not land as an accessible priority. While the wider online global community is much bigger and more diverse, there is tremendous competition with the amount of yoga, meditation and racial awareness training and offerings already available.

Reflecting on my time in Finland, I feel that I have hit a wall as a non-Finnish-speaking non-Afro-Finn who did come up in the culture or school system. I sense there is a duality of dynamic tension here when it comes to Black American culture. On the one hand, people appreciate and learn from Black American cultures globally; and on the other hand, there is also a sense of resistance because it takes centre stage in Black global identity consciousness. Take the number of people who came for the BLM protest versus the number in attendance to speak out against police brutality and to end SARS in Nigeria. What's more, I observe that Afro-Finnish identity is trying to determine for itself what it means to be Afro-Finnish, taking inspiration from Black American cultures while also soul searching for the uniqueness of Afro-Finnishness. And so I, as a Kenyan American, am both hyper visible and invisible at the same time, a pattern similar to what many Finnish-born Afro-Finns face in their country of birth as well. Despite my ongoing efforts, I am still not personally financially secure from these endeavours and wonder if I should be in the commercial sector at all. Should I go by way of grants in order to secure the finances I need to live while manifesting the vision I have around 'For Us by Us' healing spaces? Should I appeal to a donation-based, fundraiser culture of community care? I feel the main challenge I face is the fact that Finnish culture can oftentimes feel closed and insular at best and silently hostile, harsh and unresponsive at worst. I do have hope, however, in the younger generation. Finland's changing and it is exciting and hopeful to witness, while doing my small part. May I be cared for in the process as well.

It is no small task to experience healing from the toxicity of racism while the harm is constant and ongoing. From my understanding, the main location of healing must take place in decolonising the mind first. This is a radical act that not everyone will wish to embark on. As Bob Marley sang many decades ago, "Emancipate yourselves from mental slavery, none but ourselves can free our minds". As the sophistication in psychological warfare continues to refine its approaches, so too must people of African descent crave liberation and transformation. This is no small task, as it requires a tremendous amount of courage, social risk of being ostracised, misunderstood and villainised by White and non-White people alike. It quite literally means swimming upstream against all the working norms of epistemological constructs of the world.

A great deal of compassion is required for people who choose to remain comfortably colonised under the grip of structural violence. I recall the multiple trips Harriet Tubman made down into the South, risking her own freedom and life, all in the service of helping others get free. How must she have felt when enslaved people consciously chose to remain in bondage on the Southern plantations? The disappointment and rage must have tasted bitter. However, no one can want more for someone else than what the individual wants for themselves. In this way, getting free is a conscious act; a radical expression of agency, based in the deep love and care one has for oneself, rooted in a sense of worthiness that, yes, I deserve to be free.

Contrary to its name, freedom comes at a cost. Freedom is rarely, if ever, free. There is deep sacrifice and loss involved with the task of getting free. Many of us will fall by the wayside towards this somatic abolition. But so long as there is breath in my body, I face in the direction of the North Star towards freedom. As ancestor and liberator of her people, Harriet Tubman is credited to have said, "If you hear the dogs, keep going. If you see the torches in the woods, keep going. If there's shouting after you, keep going. Don't ever stop. Keep going. If you want a taste of freedom, keep going."

References

Batacharya, S. and Wong, Y.-L.R. (2018) *Sharing Breath: Embodied Learning and Decolonization*, Althabasca: AU Press.

Bay Area Transformative Justice Collective (2023) https://batjc.wordpress.com

DiAngelo, R. (2018) *White Fragility: Why it's so Hard for White People to Talk about Racism*, Boston, MA: Beacon Press.

Emergent Strategy Ideation Institute (2023) https://esii.org

European Union Agency for Fundamental Rights (2018) *Being Black in the EU*. https://fra.europa.eu/sites/default/files/fra_uploads/fra-2019-being-black-in-the-eu-summary_en.pdf

Green, K.M., Taylor, J.N., Williams, P.I. and Roberts, C. (2018) 'Black healing matters in the time of #BlackLivesMatter', *Biography (Honolulu)*, 41(4): 909–41.

Juuso, A.K. (2018) *Truth and Reconciliation Process Concerning Sámi Issues: Report on Hearings (Saamelaisten asioita koskeva sovintoprosessi Kuulemisraportti)*, Helsinki: Ministry of Justice. https://julkaisut.valtioneuvosto.fi/handle/10024/161165

Pakkanen, L. (2020) 'Joogasalit heijastelevat valkoisen vallan hierarkia' ['Yoga studios reflect the hierarchy of White supremacy'], *Maailma Kuvalehti*, available from: www.maailmankuvalehti.fi/2020/pitkat/joogasalit-heijastelevat-valkoisen-vallan-hierarkiaa/

Péan, R. (2021) 'Talks with my ancestors', *Genealogy (Basel)*, 5(1): 14.

Rankine, C. (2014) *Citizen: an American Lyric*, Minneapolis, MN: Graywolf Press.

Statistics Finland (2019) *Population Structure*. www.stat.fi/til/vaerak/index_en.html

YLE (2018) 'Roma minority asks Finns to look beyond the stereotypes', *YLE*, [online], available from: https://yle.fi/news/3-10150192

10

Intersectional knowledge practices in academia from marginal positions: *testimonios* from researchers of colour in Finland

Smarika KC, Priscilla Osei and Kris Clarke

Though social work as a profession is based on the mission of social justice and vested in non-discriminatory policies, it has historically been (and continues to be) deeply entwined with the maintenance of the nation-state, permeated with colonial ideologies, and rife with patterns of structural racism in different contexts across borders (Gray et al, 2016; Stanley, 2020). There have been increasing calls for deeper examinations of the complicity of social work in systems of oppression, specifically by examining its carceral, colonising and discriminatory practices, to gain better understanding of how social work praxes construct experts and ways of knowing (Michalsen and Williams, 2019; Dettlaff et al, 2020; Pease, 2023). Many of these critiques go beyond calls for social justice; they insist on fundamentally decolonising social work education and practices (Fortier and Hon-Sing, 2019; Khan, 2019; Sewpaul and Hendrickson, 2019), while others demand that social work profession in its current form must be abolished because it is too complicit with oppressive systems (Richie and Martensen, 2020; Maylea, 2021).

Social work is not the only academic discipline being called into question for perpetuating colonial paradigms. While universities are highly valued centres of knowledge production, they have also long been criticised as being imbued with Whiteness, racism, androcentrism, ableism and heteronormativity (Cupples and Grosfoguel, 2018). Recent movements that seek to decolonise universities have emerged from a rich lineage of intellectual, artistic and activist resistance to Eurocentrism and colonial epistemic violence. The 2015 Rhodes Must Fall movement, for example, started as a rejection of the symbol of imperialism and evolved into a broader aim to decolonise education in South Africa (Du Plessis, 2021). Scholars such as Ronald G. Lewis, Ngugi wa Thiong'o, Gloria Anzaldúa, Walter Rodney, Eve Tuck, Stuart Hall, bell hooks, Edward Said, W.E.B. DuBois, Eduardo Galeano, Amilcar Cabral and members of the Négritude movement of the 1940s are among the many examples of public intellectuals who have challenged the colonial epistemologies embedded in Western systems of higher education and the professions they shape for well over a century.

This chapter builds on the work of decolonial scholars to explore how two emerging social work scholars of colour in the Finnish academy engage in critical interrogations of the systems of knowledge while considering how their own identities inform their understandings of intersectionality in their own work. Written as a collaboration between two doctoral students of colour and their White supervisor at a Finnish university, this chapter utilises the method of *testimonio* as a decolonial approach to reflect an epistemology that starts from one's own embodied voice in critical self-reflection. The writers are at different stages of their academic careers. All have complex stories of residence in Finland that span different routes and eras of migration history, as well as a range of privileges and barriers. The White doctoral supervisor (Kris) has collaborated with the theoretical section and the two emerging scholars (Smarika and Priscilla) centre themselves through *testimonios* to illustrate their own pathways into their doctoral research and the profession of social work educators.

Epistemic injustice in the university and *testimonios*

Modern Western universities have deep roots in colonial narratives that centre ideas of progress and civilisation within Western systems. Based on epistemologies that are posited as objective and disembodied, universities have 'settled' knowledge production through the elimination of the Indigenous, for example, and by reproducing interlocking systems of oppression via institutional practices that privilege normative ideals of Whiteness, heteronormativity, sexism and ableism (Cupples and Grosfoguel, 2019). The hierarchical nature of the modern university promotes top-down approaches to knowledge production and theory building (Barongo-Muweke, 2016: 25). Despite challenges to dominant epistemologies and methodologies, the neoliberal conditions of the contemporary university increasingly fixate on quantifiable metrics as a manifestation of scholarly significance, though there are concerns that these metrics reflect more about the measure itself than the impact of the study (Fire and Guestrin, 2019). The intense focus on 'hard evidence' research has a huge impact on the processes that develop knowledge, especially in Finland where the distribution of state university funding is dependent on 'international performance indicators' leading to a market-oriented model of scholarship that favours certain fields and epistemologies over others (Lund, 2023).

In Finland, the term *sivistys* is commonly used to describe the mission of the university. *Sivistys* is defined in Finnish-language dictionaries as the cultivation of scholarly or inner development, similar to the German concept of *Bildung*, but with the further meaning of being 'civilised'. The ubiquity of *sivistys* in higher education illustrates how the civilising mission of the modern Finnish university remains embedded in Eurocentric models of knowledge production. *Sivistys* together with the prevailing market-oriented view of scholarly impact constructs an important ideological foundation for ways of understanding and conceptualising what is considered truth and the appropriate applications of that knowledge in Finnish society. While decolonial scholars have long challenged the deep structures of colonial epistemologies that have legitimised and naturalised such forms of epistemic injustice (Brunner, 2021), they would probably be hard pressed to 'prove' the scholarly impact in the narrow confines of the neoliberal university system.

Fricker's concept of epistemic injustice encompasses how systemic silencing and exclusion rooted in the dominant power structures forms the basis of ways of knowing (Fricker, 2007: 2). More pointedly, epistemic injustice is illustrated by normalising dominant ways of knowing that systemically distort or entirely exclude the knowledge systems of marginalised social groups from participating in the development of social theory and methods. The subcategory of testimonial injustice refers to instances when the knowledge of people from marginalised social groups or positions is disregarded or minimised (Fricker, 2007: 9–29). Credibility is thus embedded in the structures of social power, meaning that some people by virtue of their gender, race, accent or ability have a greater capability and social power to be trusted and believed. The double harm of testimonial injustice, according to Fricker, is not only that it sustains Western exceptionalism and Eurocentrism, but that it also causes people from marginalised positions to mistrust their own understanding of justice and truth, a point that will be taken up later. First, we examine the modern university as an institution.

Universities are hierarchical bureaucratic institutions with ranks and complex systems of gatekeepers that guard access to and advancement within its structures. Historically, admission to modern universities has been implicitly defined by social class, gender, race, age and ability. Karabel (2005) discusses how admission practices in the Ivy League, for example, were put in place in the early 20th century to limit the access of Jewish people to higher education as elite American universities sought to preserve their Anglo-Saxon Protestant heritage. In fact, the origins and recent policies of many higher-education institutions have long-standing and intentional limitations to exclude a wide range of people marginalised by social ideologies as non-normative via restrictive admission policies, lack of access and high costs. Elite academic institutions are intended to groom future leaders and develop the research and development capacity of societies. Cultivating a particular model of the normative intellectual has gone a long way to curating such highly valued knowledge as White, patriarchal and heteronormative. Struggles for civil rights in the late 20th century implanted new areas of scholarship and intellectual praxes, such as African American, Chicano, Queer and Women's Studies, which challenged the Whiteness and heteronormativity of the academy. However, by implementing diversity and inclusion initiatives, universities have also paradoxically diverted attention from how racism is reproduced in the academy. As Johnson (2020: 2) argues, diversity and inclusion policies can be weaponised to disrupt racial justice and decolonial efforts to transform institutional practices by selectively incorporating parts of dissent, while engineering a multiracial community. To reinforce the elitism of the university, administrators control who could offer 'legitimate' knowledge about racialised subjects via diversity and inclusion plans, thus reinforcing the values and goals of the neoliberal academy instead of giving space to truly liberatory efforts at knowledge production and non-discrimination (Johnson, 2020: 2). Bowman and Rebolleda-Gómez (2020: 31) further add that the individualistic focus of diversity efforts reinforces relations of epistemic injustice by fetishising individual differences and tokenising representations of diversity, while maintaining hegemonic processes of meritocracy, thus avoiding a commitment to significant transformative practices. Hence, there remains a divide between White institutional structures and practices, and performative efforts at diversity and inclusion (Ahmed, 2012).

The complexity of intersectionality in Finnish discussions

The use of the term intersectionality has expanded exponentially in contemporary research in Finland. Intersectionality was initially articulated by Kimberlé Crenshaw to identify the ways in which US legal systems failed to address or remedy employment and institutional discrimination for people who face compounded bias and discrimination, such as when race and sex and class are intertwined at the root of the actionable offence (Crenshaw, 1988). Intersectionality serves as a form of critical enquiry that centres the insight that race, gender, ability, sexuality, class and age, as well as other social categories, are not mutually exclusive and enmeshed in interlocking systems of oppression that reproduce relations of social inequality (Collins, 2017). As the term has proliferated, there has been critique that the concept of intersectionality has become deradicalised, detached from its Black feminist theoretical lens on structural oppression and replaced with a neoliberal fixation on commodifying individual difference (Lui, 2006). More troubling, the concept of intersectionality has been misused, including by feminist theorists, who focus on creating schematics of intersectional awareness to think through and even celebrate one's personal identity, while often failing to effectively implement what Crenshaw intends: that intersectional analysis serves as a vehicle for comprehending and addressing structural failure (Crenshaw, 2017).

Debates over intersectionality have deep roots in Nordic women's studies (Hvenegård-Lassen, Staunæs and Lund, 2020; Keskinen, Stolz and Mulinari, 2021) and have only migrated into the discipline of social work in the last decade (for example, Valkonen and Wallenius-Korkalo, 2016; Heino et al, 2022). Despite the ubiquity of the term, few studies deeply explore the complex and diverse genealogies of intersectionality as ontology, heuristic thinking, critical social theory and resistant knowledge practice (Collins, 2019). Carbin and Edenheim (2013) argue that intersectionality has become a consensus-builder in many Nordic discussions where diverse identities are subsumed in apolitical categories of difference and embedded in generalised non-discrimination and human rights values. The lack of critical conversation about the conflicts, discriminatory practices and relations of coloniality between, within and among different identities is not surprising when we consider the lack of diversity in the Finnish academic world generally, and specifically in the discipline of social work. Indeed, there has been fierce criticism of the Nordic feminist iterations of intersectionality as a 'Whitewashing' and 'apoliticising' term that promotes neoliberalism while failing to tackle complex questions of race and colonialism (Bilge, 2014). In response, some have pointed to how the erasure of race in Northern European societal discourse following the horrors of Nazi Germany has reproduced colour blindness in contemporary Nordic literature (Lykke, 2020). Aldrin Salskov (2020) troubled how discussions of intersectionality in a Finnish context often centre Whiteness. As Carastathis (2016) points out, the metaphor of intersectionality has often been appropriated by White feminists while women of colour remain on the margins of the academy, excluded from scholarly discourse. Reimagining Crenshaw's theory as a self-reflexive practice by White feminists illustrates what women of colour feminists have long argued about the practice of theoretical appropriation – namely, that excluding women of colour from participating in shaping the discourses lends itself to the dissolution of the power of their own theoretical tools. Intersectionality is an entry point for unveiling the metrics of compounded bias and discrimination in social structures and institutions. To have a critical conversation about the significance of intersectionality in our academic and social systems, we must broaden the circle of participants by including those whose viewpoints are also grounded in lived experience. Otherwise, we risk dismantling the power of the concept while simultaneously enhancing epistemic injustice.

Finland is often viewed as a homogenous nation on the periphery of Europe and therefore 'innocent' about issues of racism, colonialism and oppression (Wekker, 2016; Keskinen, 2019). Recent historical and cultural studies have nonetheless revealed the complexities of colonial and class relations as well as racialisation and belonging that have often been suppressed in the construction of Finnish national origin stories (Loftsdóttir,

Jensen and Kershen, 2016). In their discussion of intersectionality and the Finnish Feminist Party, Ilmonen and Rossi (2019) point out that narrative assumptions construct a 'homogenous commonplace' that renders invisible the intersectionality within Nordic identities. Because the polyvocal historical genealogy of the concept of intersectionality is not often centered in Nordic discussions, essentialised narratives of the binary between homogeneity and difference easily become accentuated.

Testimonios as a method of challenging epistemic injustice: our stories

Testimonios are first-person narratives by witnesses that describe socially significant issues (Escobar, Wilson and Garavilla, 2021). Emerging from Latin American, Chicana and Latinx scholarship and cultures, *testimonios* exist in many genres encompassing written, oral and visual formats (Strejilevich and Filc, 2015). In this chapter, we use the Spanish-language term, *testimonio*, to acknowledge the methodology's embeddedness in Chicanx/Latinx feminist studies as an alternative epistemology that gives embodied voice to self-reflexive and critical perspectives that challenge the boundaries between academic knowledge production, activism and lived experience (Cahuas and Matute 2020). Rooted in community stories that open up the impact of power relations in larger social contexts on a personal and affective level through the act of witnessing, *testimonios* challenge the epistemic violence of colonialism (DeRocher, 2018). *Testimonios* situate the researcher within a collective experience marked by marginalisation, oppression and resistance (Delgado Bernal et al, 2012 cited in Silva, Fernandez and Nguyen, 2021). Centring knowledge keepers often relegated to the margins enacts resistance against the dominance of oppressive epistemological systems that impose colonial binaries of knowers versus known. In what follows, Smarika and Priscilla, doctoral students, engage in *testimonio* to illustrate the complex intersectionality of perceptions of racialisation as they discuss their experiences of postgraduate studies. While recognising that intersectionality encompasses a variety of social identities in complex interlocking formations, for the purpose of this chapter Smarika and Priscilla focus especially on the junction of race in the Finnish academy. Kris, a White middle-aged female supervisor of the two doctoral students is in conversation with Smarika and Priscilla. First we introduce ourselves then explore common and disparate points that brought us to this work.

Setting the context (Kris)

To introduce myself, I should note that I was one of the first handful of international social work doctoral students in Finland in the 1990s. Some of my fellow students were among the inaugural social work academicians from their own counties of China and Estonia. Studying in the 1990s represented a period when Finnish doctoral education was far more flexible, less time-driven and goal-oriented than today. However, it was also a time when the academisation of Finnish social work was highly valued and the scholarly achievement of the discipline in Finland was becoming increasingly rigorous (Forsberg, Kuronen and Ritala-Koskinen, 2019).

My study group consisted of many people who, like me, had little knowledge or experience of social work but came from diverse interdisciplinary fields. At that time, I knew of no immigrant, international or racialised academics in the Finnish social work field, so many of us felt that we were navigating an unknown scholarly territory alone. Social work is a uniquely national practice throughout the world because graduates are qualified as practitioners and must have deep knowledge of local languages, laws and practices. Many of my international colleagues focused their dissertation work on issues in their own countries, thus leaving little trace of their research in Finnish social work research and practice. As for myself, I examined how the Finnish system of care for people living with HIV supported constituents with a migrant identity based on my work with the European Project AIDS & Mobility. However, after graduation, I did not feel that I had many employment prospects in Finland, so I moved to the US.

Returning to Finland as a faculty member 15 years after receiving my doctorate and after 13 years of working in California, I was struck by the continuing Whiteness and marginalisation of racialised students in the Finnish social work academic field despite the fact that processes of globalisation, the number of language groups, diverse social identities and racialised residents have expanded exponentially – along with growing socio-economic inequality, especially in the capital region. As a recent study on Finnish social work professors' perceptions on the recruitment and research of doctoral students notes, there are more transparent formal policies of admission nowadays, yet 'academically talented students, especially those who share the research interests of the recruiting professor and may even have worked in a project led by the professor, are encouraged to apply for admission to doctoral studies' (Forsberg, Kuronen and Ritala-Koskinen, 2019: 1515). The persistence of these types of old boy/girl networks in doctoral studies militates against truly diversifying emerging research voices in the Finnish social work. Admissions policies and assessments still default to normative practices, which are exclusionary. And this is a circular process because as a non-Finnish (but White) academic who has completed my doctorate and received a tenure track position in Finnish universities, I have only had older White males assigned as external examiners when deciding whether my dissertation or promotion file was worthy.[1]

Social work is a profession that touches the lives of all people in Finland at some point along the lifespan. Hence it is worth pondering how epistemic injustice operating in scholarly discourses constructed with a limited range of voices lives on through evidence-based practices grounded in a relatively narrow lens of experience. Issues surrounding representation in knowledge production are at the core of social work values and must therefore be seen as central to the profession's social justice mission (Maglajlic and Ioakimidis, 2022). The marginalisation of locally based women of colour and many other people with diverse social identities in the Finnish academy narrows them as objects of knowledge rather than as knowers (Gunew and Chakravorty, 1986).

An intersectional analysis challenges essentialising discrete social categories by centring the power dynamics of interlocking systems of oppression. As Carastathis (2016) points out, opening up the full implications of intersectional resistant knowledge practices requires an analysis of why people with certain social identities are absent from the academy. The constellation of power relations aligns in the organisation of knowledge production in universities which reinforce coloniality through testimonial injustice and the centring of Whiteness. Decolonial knowledge practices thus call for pluriversal (rather than Eurocentric universal) epistemologies and unsettling colonial projects that continue to dispossess and oppress racialised people around the globe.

Studying racialised older people with a migrant background in Finland (Smarika)

In this *testimonio*, I explore my own multiple and interlocking identities as a doctoral student of colour in relation to the people I research with; namely, racialised older women with a migrant background residing in the Helsinki metropolitan area. I want readers to know what it feels like being a student of colour doing academic research in a social work department where there are not many people like me. Writing about myself is healing and inspires the consideration of alternative perspectives on oppression through different entry points in academia (Pearson, 2010). I use reflexivity and my day-to-day interactions with my Nepalese community to explore the intersection of race, gender and ethnicity with my experience as a Nepalese social work researcher in Finland. The use of reflexivity has helped me to consider ontological and epistemological components of the self, intersubjectivity and the colonisation of knowledge (Berger, 2015).

My doctoral research focuses on the narratives of older immigrant women aged 55 and above who have migrated to Finland from non-European and racialised backgrounds. I study how these women construct and re-construct their identities after the rupture of migration, and how they find meaning and well-being in a new place. I share an insider position with my research participants as a woman of colour and a non-European immigrant. As Padgett (2008) and Kacen and Chaitin (2006) note, my insider role provides some advantages that include an easier entrée to the community, a head start in knowing about the topic and an understanding of the nuanced reactions of the participants. I identify with my research participants when they talk about belonging and exclusion. As an immigrant myself, I understand how hard it is to navigate the Finnish social and healthcare systems if one does not speak the Finnish language. I can relate to them when they talk about language barriers or difficulties to access information because even as a young, educated woman, I struggle to find information and services in Finland. Even as a highly skilled immigrant with some years of work experience, a bachelor's degree and an international master's degree in social work, I am not able to apply for my licence as a practising social worker in Finland unless I pass the official examination of Finnish-language proficiency. Hence, I can connect with what these older immigrant women tell me about their challenges of not finding work because of the lack of language fluency. I can also recognise their social and cultural constraints when they mention that they were not encouraged to study. However, I also have an outsider position as I belong to the university: an academic community which is an unfamiliar and inaccessible space for most of my research participants, and I represent a much younger generation than them. Reflexivity has allowed me to pay attention to both my insider and outsider positions, and explore how my identity assists and hinders the process of co-constructing meanings, collecting data and producing knowledge (Berger, 2015).

In doctoral seminars and conferences, my White colleagues usually ask me why I focus on racialised immigrants, and I tell them about the visible gap in research about non-EU ageing immigrants' lived experiences in Finland. Categorising them merely as immigrants does not do justice to their life stories and lived experiences if we compare them with immigrants from countries such as Russia, Sweden and Estonia because of their distinct racialised, gendered and socio-economic positions. Similarly, thinking of nations as having a monolithic class of citizens denies, and potentially erases, the diversity of citizens and immigrants there too. The intersecting identities of race, gender and ethnicity matter significantly in their lives and affect access to services. I also keep on interrogating my own positionality, privileges and experience of oppression. The issue of race and racialisation also became a recurring occurrence in my data. When I shared informally about what the data said at a conference lunch table to a few researchers, I was told that race may not be an important topic for an article and that other issues such as service needs could be more helpful in academic writing. Race, a colleague opined, may not be a big deal to people who are educated and employed. It made me think about what happens to racialised people when they step out of their institutions and workplaces where no one recognises them based on their education and professional expertise but solely judges based on their phenotype. What about people who have been successful in the White spaces of academic and work worlds but remain in marginal and precarious positions in society? I quickly realised that these can be very uncomfortable issues to discuss with people who dwell in spaces of privilege but may have little understanding of others' lived experiences.

I did my bachelor's in social work in Nepal and my Erasmus Mundus master's programme in advanced development in social work in Europe. Now I am doing my doctorate in social work in Finland. During my academic journey, there have been many instances where I have questioned my learning. In Nepal, we had quite a colonial social work education where we studied Eurocentric and North American theories and methods that had little to no relevance to the grassroots reality in Nepal. Nepalese rural and Indigenous communities are very diverse and rich with a multiplexity of identities based on the caste system, different languages, dialects and ethnicity (Yadav, 2021), yet the field of social work could not comprehend our own strengths, resources and resilience. The concepts of community organisation and decolonised social work were rarely introduced to us. Now after years of graduate school, I have a better perspective to understand the power structures and social work practice through intersectional and decolonising perspectives. I have realised that most of the narratives of the Global South are written by writers in the Global North. Nepalese people have often been the objects of development and research projects where their stories and problems are defined by others (Collins, 2009; Mainali and Saurav, 2017; Byskov, 2020). We have not had an equal standing and subjectivity to define our own reality and needs (Collins, 2009).

When I was working with an international non-governmental organisation (INGO), in the aftermath of Nepal's 2014 earthquake, I went to a mountainous, rural village for my fieldwork with some international expatriates. The earthquake had caused huge damage and obstructed the roadways, making air travel the only means of commuting and obtaining supplies. Only a handful of people could afford this means of transport in that village. Meanwhile, I noticed a helicopter arrived, loaded with books and toys for the village. Upon asking, I found out that it was intended to build a child-safe education camp by the INGO. At that moment, I questioned if that was really the main need amid the disaster and chaos when people were finding it exceedingly difficult to meet their basic needs. I am not against child-safe spaces to learn and play, but families needed support for essential food, medicines and hygiene supplies, and local people were not involved in deciding on which resources to prioritise. This example illustrates the White saviour complex where outsiders from the Global North are viewed as uniquely positioned to uplift and edify parents and children of colour in the Global South (Straubhaar, 2015: 384).

Growing up in Nepal, I was not raised or educated to discuss race or my own Brown identity. I never felt I was physically different or represented a Global South nation until I stepped out of my country for the first time for university studies. I recall recurring airport incidents with border guards, when I am often pulled aside to have a nice conversation with inquisitive agents who want to find out where I am from. As soon as they see my Nepalese passport, I receive comments such as "your English is so good for a Nepalese woman". Though I have tried my best as an immigrant in a new country to assimilate to its culture and lifestyle, it always feels strange to think about the complexity of my own belongingness. I could relate my life to a few lines from Ijeoma Umebinyuo's (2015) poem 'Diaspora Blues': 'So, here you are, too foreign for home, too foreign for here. Never enough for both.'

Friends in my graduate school ask me, "Why don't Nepalese in Finland participate more in activism?" This question has made me reflect on my own community and what we do. Most of the first-generation Nepalese I have met from my encounters in Finland are working so hard to pay their family loans or struggling to pay their bills that they have little extra time. As Collins (2009) has described, survival is such an all-consuming activity that many racialised people have few opportunities to engage in academia, activism or intellectual work. Most of the time, choosing silence is easier.

As a Brown woman, it is not easy to be vocal with the social expectations and norms around what we are supposed to be in different places. I have had instances in my own personal life when I felt my silence was preferred more than my opinion. Even when I have certain privileges based on my education, I experience some forms of discrimination and I am expected to adhere to certain social norms. In some places, I have been asked to focus on my family rather than my ambitions or career. While I see most men's career milestones are celebrated, mine have even been questioned by some. I am reminded time and again that I am a woman first.

I keep reflecting on my positionality, identity and obstacles inside and outside my own community, inside and outside academia, in the Finnish community as an immigrant woman and student of colour myself. I question my belongingness and multiple identities and how it affects me, the many times I have tried hard to assimilate, the times I have felt excluded, as a young woman of colour. I hope I can challenge some of these uncomfortable issues through my education. I trust in the process of learning. Academia has been a healing place for me for many reasons but mainly because it has helped me understand my own life alongside my intersectional positions and the interconnected lives around me. As a first-generation student, it is not easy to navigate things on our own when we are new to the academic system. Finding either funding or mentorship are challenging. However,

I am grateful for my supervisors who have included me in this space, a space where people such as me are so new. It is also a space which sometimes makes us feel like outsiders where we doubt if we have made the right decision, we ask hard questions about ourselves and we think who should we look up to in academia?

All these experiences have made me aware of how I come from a space of marginality alongside a space of privilege as a doctoral student of colour in Finland, how intersectionality has an impact on the everyday lives of my research participants and the sensitivity with which I must approach knowing and representing them. I hope that the insights that come from my research can contribute to challenging the invisibility of older non-EU migrant women in Finnish gerontological and social work research and give wings to a new social work paradigm that is truly inclusive.

Studying African mothers in the Helsinki metropolitan region (Priscilla)

I am a Ghanaian-born freelance photographer based in Helsinki, Finland, and a doctoral student in social work at the University of Helsinki. My interdisciplinary studies have been a great journey that has taken me through different countries and cultures, allowing me to observe issues that affect immigrants, particularly people of colour in Europe.

My educational journey started with a bachelor's in accounting at Valley University in Ghana. As my interest increased in financial reporting, I did my national service with the Ghana health service, which allowed me to see how cities and towns in the Greater Accra region are managed within the health sector. My desire to further my schooling in regional studies led me to do my master's degree in the Czech Republic. This experience gave me a new perspective on urban and regional development because it was from a European and transnational perspective.

My curiosity grew and I travelled to Finland to broaden my scope in natural resource management. I undertook a degree programme in sustainable coastal management. This programme gave me the opportunity to intern with the USAID sustainable fisheries management in Ghana. I felt that it was important for me as a Ghanaian and a researcher to collect stories that would help understand illegal fishing activities in the coastal communities and increase public awareness. Assisting in sensitisation workshops for fisher folks allowed me to understand how research can challenge epistemic injustice and support the credibility of testimonial justice. During this project, I took a lot of photos to support my research and that's where my interest in storytelling using photography started.

My interest in the untold stories of Africans in the diaspora was triggered years ago when I visited an asylum camp in Italy. I heard about the mistreatment of some Ghanaian asylum seekers and wondered how I could share these migrant stories someday. In Helsinki, I became acquainted with people of colour and discovered to my surprise that there was no professional photography studio space that took portraits of African families. So, I opened one in Lauttasaari and specialised in working with wedding and maternity shoots with women of colour. Spending time together during shoots meant celebrating happy occasions, but I also learned about the frustrations of my clients' everyday lives. Through this experience, I became aware of the complexities of Black African motherhood in Helsinki. Over time, we opened up to one another about the challenges that we face as Black African women living in a new country and experiencing a new culture. During maternity photo-shoot sessions, we spoke about birthing, social support, medical racism and the fear of raising Black children in a White environment. Often, my clients complained bitterly about how social workers and healthcare workers undermined their knowledge of motherhood. Who do you talk to when your body is in trouble, or when you don't agree with the services rendered? The sense of neglect and feeling of helplessness in a system barely understood was palpable. Many of their stories were heartbreaking and left me concerned. As a Black woman resident in Helsinki, who shares the same identity as my participants, I am keen on presenting our stories to depict what life is really like when we access social and health services in Helsinki, which led me to start my doctoral studies in social work.

Debates on who can conduct research with and about Black women and Black communities are common in academic discourse because of relations of epistemic injustice and the centring of Whiteness (Collins, 2022 2017; Harvey Wingfield, 2018; Walton et al, 2022). Based on my experience in the photography studio, I wondered whether Black women really opened up to talk fully about sensitive and stigmatising topics to White researchers. Do participants feel involved in and informed of the decision-making process on the direction of the research? Who decides which stories the public should know, especially when Black women are often in a far more vulnerable position in Finnish society than White women? In the following, I explore why there is a need for Black women in Finland to tell their own stories in their own way so that they can challenge the gaslighting and epistemic injustice of ways that Black women are often constructed in scholarly literature.

My doctoral research focuses on the lived experiences of African mothers as health and social service users in Helsinki. It explores Black motherhood and their perceptions of health and social services. I am at the beginning of my research journey and have been thinking about how to conduct ethical research in my community. The sister-to-sister talks in the studio are raw and deep conversations between Black women, my clients and me. However, these discussions are often confidential, dealing with issues that may be seen as bringing shame. Many feel that they might be judged by other people in the community or outside the community if these stories are not shared anonymously. Yet, I know that raising some of these conversations could shift the injustice that Black women often face in Finnish academic literature and social and healthcare service delivery. I am also aware that research on Black communities is viewed as an extension of colonisation by many Black people. It is common to hear statements such as "what you tell these researchers is what they use against us" or "they don't even do anything about the issue". So, I am personally struggling with how to present some stories to my readers (who might be mainly White readers) without causing harm to my community. Due to the mistrust in research by Black communities, I have pondered the best ways to negotiate boundaries and the ethical safeguards I need to put in place to protect my participants in the community.

This research is so important to me. I recognise my privilege of having the opportunity to conduct this study and inhabit academic spaces. Yet, I feel the dilemmas of my insider-outsider status with African communities in Helsinki. I am an insider to the population I propose to study, but I recognise my outsider status of not being a mother. During my presentations in seminars or classes, I often find myself using 'we' and 'us' instead of 'they' and 'them'. I must explore my own positionality and reflect on the complexities that an insider-outsider researcher might encounter. As a Black woman in Finland who looks forward to becoming a mother, this research is also beneficial to me, and these stories will provide me with first-hand lessons on motherhood, and differential perceptions of mothers through the lens of racialisation, in Helsinki. I am happy to be on this journey to serve the African-Black Finnish community in Finland. I believe that by empowering Black women in Helsinki to share their diverse stories of motherhood we can decolonise the ways of constructing best motherhood practices in Finland and raise the voices of Black mothers. I believe that listening to stories from Black women in Finland would not only transform academic and everyday discussions but also provide healing and support our community in dealing with issues of discrimination. Most importantly, I hope that this research can challenge the prevalent epistemic injustice that Black mothers face in research on social and healthcare service delivery, as well as provide an opening for Black researchers and practitioners to shape appropriate services that truly meet the needs of our community.

Conclusion

Dismantling the global project of colonialism starts with challenging how we understand the world through the meaningful inclusion of experiential knowledge that addresses epistemic injustice. The method of *testimonio* provides a healing path towards testimonial justice by affirming the personal stories of the marginalised as resistant knowledge that uncovers how complex intersectional social structures oppress and undermine. Smarika and Priscilla's *testimonios* offer insight into the challenges of navigating doctoral studies as students of colour who can see and also resist the social ideologies undergirding Western social work foundations. Their emerging research projects offer insights and possibilities to re-imagine and transform ways of encountering and working with the growing diversity of clients that use Finnish social and healthcare services. It also throws down the gauntlet of enacting real diversity and inclusion in research practices to the Finnish university and discipline of social work. Universities have settled knowledge production through institutional practices that have historically eliminated diverse voices and epistemologies. Returning to the radical roots of intersectional analysis may offer a way to resist the epistemic violence and Whiteness of the academy by centring decolonial struggles against interlocking systems of oppression. However, developing a robust intersectional perspective in academia cannot emerge from a monoculture. Challenging the epistemic injustice that is often so prevalent in the largely White field of Finnish social work is an important step towards decolonising social work knowledge and practice thus moving towards ameliorating the discrimination faced by many communities of colour resident in Finland.

Note

[1] It is worth noting that in my final assessment in 2023, an international scholar who identities as female and racialised became the first external reviewer that I have had as an employee of a Finnish university who did not fall into the normative categories of male and White.

References

Ahmed, S. (2012) 'Whiteness and the general will: diversity work as willful work', *Philosophia*, 2(1), 1–20.

Aldrin Salskov, S. (2020) 'A critique of our own? On intersectionality and "epistemic habits" in a study of racialization and homonationalism in a Nordic Context', *NORA: Nordic Journal of Women's Studies*, 28(3): 251–65.

Barongo-Muweke, N. (2016) *Decolonizing Education: Towards Reconstructing a Theory of Citizenship Education for Postcolonial Africa*, Hannover: Springer.

Berger, R. (2015) 'Now I see it, now I don't: researcher's position and reflexivity in qualitative research', *Qualitative Research*, 15(2): 219–34.

Bilge, S. (2014) 'Whitening intersectionality: evanescence of race in intersectionality scholarship', *Racism and Sociology*, 5: 175.

Bowman, M., and Rebolleda-Gómez, M. (2020) 'Uprooting narratives: legacies of colonialism in the neoliberal university', *Hypatia*, 35(1): 18–40.

Brunner, C. (2021) 'Conceptualizing epistemic violence: an interdisciplinary assemblage for IR', *International Politics Reviews*, 9: 193–212.

Byskov, M.F. (2020) 'What makes epistemic injustice an "injustice"?', *Journal of Social Philosophy*, 52(1): 114–31.

Cahuas, M. and Matute, A.A. (2020) 'Enacting a Latinx decolonial politic of belonging: Latinx community workers' experiences negotiating identity and citizenship in Toronto, Canada', *Studies in Social Justice*, 14(2): 268–86.

Carastathis, A. (2016) *Intersectionality: Origins, Contestations, Horizons*, Lincoln: University of Nebraska Press.

Carbin, M. and Edenheim, S. (2013) 'The intersectional turn in feminist theory: a dream of a common language?', *European Journal of Women's Studies*, 20(3): 233–48.

Collins, P. (2017) 'Intersectionality and epistemic injustice', in I. Kidd, J. Medina and G. Pohlhaus (eds) *The Routledge Handbook of Epistemic Injustice*, London: Routledge, pp 115–24.

Collins, P. (2019) *Intersectionality as Critical Social Theory*, Durham, NC: Duke University Press.

Collins, P. (2022) *Black Feminist Thought: Knowledge, Consciousness, and the Politics of Empowerment*, London: Routledge.

Crenshaw, K.W. (1988) 'Race, reform, and retrenchment: transformation and legitimation in antidiscrimination law', *Harvard Law Review*, 101(7), 1331–87.

Crenshaw, K.W. (2017) *On Intersectionality: Essential Writings*, New York: The New Press.

Cupples, J. and Grosfoguel, R. (2019) *Unsettling Eurocentrism in the Westernized University*, London: Routledge.

Delgado Bernal, D., Burciaga, R. and Flores Carmona, J. (2012) 'Chicana/Latina testimonios: mapping the methodological, pedagogical, and political', *Equity and Excellence in Education*, 45(3): 363–72.

DeRocher, P. (2018) *Transnational Testimonios: Translating Worlds, Staging Activism*, Washington, DC: University of Washington Press.

Dettlaff, A.J., Weber, K., Pendleton, M., Boyd, R., Bettencourt, B. and Burton, L. (2020) 'It is not a broken system, it is a system that needs to be broken: the upEND movement to abolish the child welfare system', *Journal of Public Child Welfare*, 14(5): 500–17.

Du Plessis, P. (2021) 'Decolonisation of education in South Africa: challenges to decolonise the university curriculum', *South African Journal of Higher Education*, 35(1): 54–69.

Escobar, G., Wilson, K. and Garavelli, C. (2021) 'Testimonio at 50', *Latin American Perspectives*, 48(2): 17–32.

Fire, M. and Guestrin, C. (2019) 'Over-optimisation of academic publishing metrics: observing Goodhart's Law in action', *GigaScience*, 8(6).

Forsberg, Kuronen, M. and Ritala-Koskinen, A. (2019) 'The academic identity and boundaries of the discipline of social work: reflections of social work professors on the recruitment and research of doctoral students in Finland', *British Journal of Social Work*, 49(6): 1509–25.

Fortier, C. and Hon-Sing Wong, E. (2019) 'The settler colonialism of social work and the social work of settler colonialism', *Settler Colonial Studies*, 9(4): 437–56.

Fricker, M. (2007) *Epistemic Injustice: Power and the Ethics of Knowing*, Oxford: Oxford University Press.

Gray, M., Coates, J., Yellow, B.M. and Hetherington, T. (eds) (2016) *Decolonizing Social Work*, London: Routledge.

Gunew, S. and Chakravorty, S.G. (1986) 'Questions of multiculturalism: an interview with Sneja Gunew and Gayatri Chakravorty Spivak', [radio broadcast] 1 January, originally broadcast in 'The Minders', *ABC Radio*, 30 August, *Hecate*, 12: 136–42.

Harvey Wingfield, A. (2019) '"Reclaiming our time": Black women, resistance, and rising inequality: SWS Presidential Lecture', *Gender and Society*, 33(3): 345–62.

Heino, E., Kara, H., Tarkiainen, L. and Tapola-Haapala, M. (2022) 'Master's-level social work students' definitions of intersectionality in relation to social work practice in Finland', *Nordic Social Work Research*. DOI: 10.1080/2156857X.2022.2130407

Hvenegård-Lassen, K., Staunæs, D. and Lund, R. (2020) 'Intersectionality, yes, but how? Approaches and conceptualizations in Nordic feminist research and activism', *NORA: Nordic Journal of Women's Studies*, 28(3): 173–82.

Ilmonen, K. and Rossi, L.-M. (2019) 'Intersectionalizing the homogenous commonplace: Finnish Feminist Party and the diversification of the story of Nordic social coherence', in J. Kuortti et al (eds) *Thinking with the Familiar in Contemporary Literature and Culture 'Out of the Ordinary'*, Amsterdam: Brill Rodopi, pp 54–74.

Johnson, M. (2020) *Undermining Racial Justice: How One University Embraced Inclusion and Inequality*, Ithaca, NY: Cornell University Press.

Kacen, L. and Chaitin, J. (2006) 'The times are a changing: understanding qualitative research in ambiguous, conflictual, and changing contexts', *Qualitative Report*, 11(2): 209–28.

Karabel, J. (2005) *The Chosen: The Hidden History of Admission and Exclusion at Harvard, Yale, and Princeton*, New York: Houghton Mifflin Harcourt.

Keskinen, S. (2019) 'Intra-Nordic differences, colonial/racial histories, and national narratives: rewriting Finnish history', *Scandinavian Studies*, 91(12), 163–81.

Keskinen, S., Stoltz, P. and Mulinari, D. (eds) (2021) *Feminisms in the Nordic Region: Neoliberalism, Nationalism and Decolonial Critique*, London: Palgrave Macmillan.

Khan, M. (2019) 'A social work perspective on Indigenous knowledges, anticolonial thought, and contemplative pedagogy: thoughts on decolonization and resistance', *Journal of Critical Anti-Oppressive Social Inquiry*, 2: 8–46.

Lui, M. (2006) *The Color of Wealth: The Story Behind the US Racial Wealth Divide*, New York: The New Press.

Loftsdóttir, K., Jensen, L. and Kershen, D.A.J. (2016) *Whiteness and Postcolonialism in the Nordic Region: Exceptionalism, Migrant Others and National Identities*, Milton Park: Taylor and Francis.

Lund, R.W.B. (2023) 'Affective alignment and epistemic polarization: the case of feminist research in the neoliberalized university', *Gender and Education*, 35(5): 437–53.

Lykke, N. (2020) 'Transversal dialogues on intersectionality, socialist feminism and epistemologies of ignorance', *NORA: Nordic Journal of Women's Studies*, 28(3): 197–210.

Maglajlic, R.A. and Ioakimidis, V. (2022) 'A call to action: voice and influence of people with experiences of social and health care in social work knowledge and social services', *The British Journal of Social Work*, 52(5): 2431–6.

Mainali, S. and Saurav (2017) *Breaking Nepal*, Kathmandu: Hami Publications.

Maylea, C. (2021) 'The end of social work', *British Journal of Social Work*, 51(2): 772–89.

Michalsen, V. and Williams, J. (2019) 'Abolitionist feminism as prisons close: fighting the racist and misogynist surveillance "child welfare" system', *Prison Journal*, 99(4): 504–11.

Padgett, D.K. (2008) *Qualitative Methods in Social Work Research*, London: Sage.

Pearson, H. (2010) 'Complicating intersectionality through the identities of a hard of hearing Korean adoptee: an autoethnography', *Equity and Excellence in Education*, 43(3): 341–56.

Pease, B. (2023) 'Facing the legacy of social work: coming to terms with complicity in systemic inequality and social injustice', in *Social Work's Histories of Complicity and Resistance*, Bristol: Policy Press, pp 219–32.

Richie, B.E. and Martensen, K.M. (2020) 'Resisting carcerality, embracing abolition: implications for feminist social work practice', *Affilia*, 35(1): 12–16.

Sewpaul, V. and Henrickson, M. (2019) 'The (r)evolution and decolonization of social work ethics: the global social work statement of ethical principles', *International Social Work*, 62(6): 1469–81.

Silva, J.M., Fernández, J.S. and Nguyen, A. (2021) '"And now we resist": three testimonios on the importance of decoloniality within psychology', *Journal of Social Issue*, 78(2): 388–412.

Stanley, J.M. (2020) 'Intersectional and relational frameworks: confronting anti-Blackness, settler colonialism, and neoliberalism in U.S. social work', *Journal of Progressive Human Services*, 31(3): 210–25.

Straubhaar, R. (2015) 'The stark reality of the "White Saviour" complex and the need for critical consciousness: a document analysis of the early journals of a Freirean educator', *Compare*, 45(3): 381–400.

Strejilevich, N. and Filc, J. (2015) 'Genres of the real: testimonio, autobiography, and the subjective turn', in I. Rodríguez (ed), *The Cambridge History of Latin American Women's Literature*, Cambridge: Cambridge University Press, pp 433–47.

Umebinyuo, I. (2015) 'Diaspora Blues', *Questions for Ada*, 175.

Valkonen, S. and Wallenius-Korkalo, S. (2016) 'Practising postcolonial intersectionality: gender, religion and indigeneity in Sámi social work', *International Social Work*, 59(5): 614–26.

Walton, Q.L., Kennedy, P.P., Oyewuwo, O.B. and Allen, P. (2022) '"This person is safe": an exemplar of conducting individual interviews in qualitative research with Black women', *International Journal of Qualitative Methods*, 21: 160940692211477.

Wekker, G. (2016) *White Innocence: Paradoxes of Colonialism and Race*, Durham, NC: Duke University Press.

Yadav, R.K. (2021) 'The doctor, development and (un)sociable monkey: an autoethnography of a social worker', *International Social Work*, 66(4).

PART III

Reimagining caring and social work futurities

11

Counter-archiving as a decolonial pedagogy of collective care

Lena Sawyer, Kris Clarke and Nana Osei-Kofi

Maybe like us you have turned a corner, entered a city square and encountered an official monument, memorial or structure, and felt erased? Or maybe encountered there a marker, that may be for some insignificant, but that for you is a potent reminder, of other collective histories, presence, contributions?

This chapter explores how we – three academics moving and living in the Nordic countries and the West Coast of the US – have engaged in embodied practices of walking and talking to challenge a colonial public archive. With colonial public archive we mean the ways that public space is marked by official commemorations (for example, statues, names of streets, squares and buildings) which reinforce the hegemony of colonialism and erase the ways the past and present continue to be shaped by colonial projects. Public space is where specific historical events and memories are celebrated and privileged, while others are erased (Mbembe, 2015). Indeed, since the early 2020s, public archives and commemoration have increasingly been a site for communities' critical re-engagement with specific colonial histories and the ways they form memory and belonging (Moulton 2021; Katz Thor, 2021). They have focused on legacies of injury, violence and death inaugurated through colonial projects and their racist knowledge systems. Here, overlapping communities of academics, activists and artists around the world have united in their localities to create practices and forms for challenging the coloniality of the public archives and the historical events and memories they preserve, as well as the injustices and struggles they bypass. This is an embodied practice where history is being re-engaged and creatively edited, as counter-narratives are formed which re-centre and re-tell colonial relations (Sawyer and Osei-Kofi, 2000; Kamaly, 2021, 2022–2023). These counter-archiving practices are not only about the past and present, but also provide a vision for the future (Rumsey, 2016; Periç, 2018; Fischer 2022).

Walking and talking with others can be a powerful way for generating collaborative and critical understandings of shared place in relation to locality, self and community (Middleton, 2018). Following Yoon-Ramirez (2021), we suggest that centring the sensory experience of walking through public space engages us in recollecting how the legacy of colonialism continues to have an impact on our being in place. Walking and talking together is a slow practice of collectively 'curiously thinking together', a decolonial practice that blends and generates new webs of meaning as it knits together seemingly disparate sites, spaces and histories, thus challenging historical erasures and distortions (Springgay and Truman, 2017; Savransky and Stengers, 2018). This is a practice that can be appreciated as decolonial in that colonialisms past and present are explored collaboratively and de-constructed and re-worked through an activity which acknowledges the violence of erasure of histories and communities (Bhambra, 2014). Through walking and talking together, the mind, soul, body and the senses combine to activate a more holistic embodied form of knowledge-making challenging colonial mind-centred forms. We argue that these practices can be understood as a pedagogy that is also a form of collective care and healing (Fischer, 2022) and that resists the Whitewashing and erasure of diverse histories (Ware, 2017).

This chapter aims to add to understandings of embodied and collaborative forms for connecting with public archives. Our work contributes to a growing literature which address the transformational potential of critical embodied engagements with the public archive (for example, Livholts, 2022). These methods have potential to develop decolonial social work education because they open up questions of power, social justice, marginalisation and social change. We argue that engaging with the public archive can be a form of collective care with transformative potential because through critically addressing the past we are also re-envisioning the future (Fisher, 2022). As an illustration of this argument, we share two such experiences of collaborative embodied walking and talking practice. This is where public space, its coloniality and erasures were critically collectively re-thought to create alternative histories in the cities of Gothenburg, Sweden, and Fresno, California, US.

Theoretical inspirations for a decolonial walking pedagogy of counter-archiving

We approached our two different cityscapes (Gothenburg/Fresno) as spaces entangled in the deep roots of local contexts of coloniality. Collective memory and sites of commemoration in our cities are buttressed by narratives and representations that elide and erase the contributions, sacrifices and suffering of marginalised peoples. This erasure contributes to the creation of a national, regional and local social memory with a skewed and incomplete understanding of the past, and which perpetuates structural oppression and dehumanisation in the present. In centring the subaltern knowledges in each of our everyday landscapes through our two different city walks, we sought to counter-archive the dominant stories of place.

Our exploration of walking, listening and talking in city spaces has been inspired by Yoon-Ramirez's (2021) pedagogical conception of walking as a sensory and relational experience. As Ramirez (2021: 118) writes, walking-sensing enables 'critically examining how embodied experiences and everyday sense of being have been shaped by coloniality ... walking-sensing can open up new and liberatory possibilities for thinking, being and sensing'.

Diverse decolonial theorisations have also informed our notion of counter-archiving in a context of coloniality, invisibility, hegemonic Whiteness and anti-Blackness (Ware, 2017; Daigle and Ramirez, 2019). Christina Sharpe's (2016) concept of 'wake work' resonated with us during this process. 'Wake work' is a concept which theorises and centres the everyday collective and individual practices of care created through Black survival, navigation and recognition of each other's lives within racist systems that perpetuate and erase ongoing Black death. She argues collective care is performed through collecting the evidence of Black survival and the myriad of everyday resistances, a practice which Sharpe calls 'wake work'. This is where our caring and mourning for the living and dead is grounded in a context where the past, present and future are fundamentally and continuously shaped by the aftermath of transatlantic slavery. Wake work as a concept resonated in understanding our practices of walking and talking in public space (Gothenburg/Fresno). Through critical and collective engagement with public archives, we created care when we recognised our own and our communities erased yet 'carried' histories (Puwar, 2021).

Sharpe's methodology of everyday collective resistances, such as through counter-archiving, are necessarily both embedded within unequal power relations but also contain potential for self and community witnessing, affirmation and healing. And it is with these perspectives in mind that we introduce you to some of the ways we have been inspired to explore and engage with our two (Gothenburg/Fresno) walking pedagogies that trouble meaning making in city space.

Lena and Nana's work on 'The Iron Well' statue in Gothenburg

Gothenburg is a city on the western coast of Sweden that celebrated its 400th anniversary as a city in 2021. It is also Sweden's second largest city with over 600,000 inhabitants in 2023 (WPR, 2023). Both historically and today the city remains one of the largest and most important Nordic ports for trade, industry and seafaring. City street names and buildings bear witness to this long history and centre not only Swedish monarchs but also commemorate and centre the city's transnational economic relations. They showcase names of central trade goods (such as iron ore, cereals, herring, sugar), capital investing economic families (such as Carnegie and Carlander) and give value to particular seafaring routes (Amsterdam, Jylland, London and

North America). Workers' labour for the extraction, processing and transport of such goods, and the destruction of the lands in terms of communities and relations between animals, plant life and humans are erased or smoothed over in the historical public archive of the city.

Commemoration of the city's and nation's economic participation and role in the transnational global economy encounters often polish over the ways violence, exploitation and racial knowledges were central to imperialism and colonialism. For example, near the city seaport stands 'The Delaware Monument'. The original statue from 1938 is said to have been in Christina State Park in Wilmington where it was presented as a 'gift' to the state of Delaware, while its 'sister' statue has rested on the dock in Gothenburg, Sweden, since 1958 (after being moved from the capital city of Stockholm). The statue is a commemoration of the 1638 establishment of the New Sweden, a Swedish colony (in the now US states of Delaware, Pennsylvania, New Jersey and Maryland). This is where Swedish, Finnish and Dutch colonisers met and traded with the Indigenous Lenape and Susquehannock peoples. The statue bears images of harmonious trading contact with Indigenous peoples who generously trade land for guns and is a good example of how the genocide is actively erased in public archives such as this monument.

Significant to understanding the erasure of Sweden's various actors and their forms of participation in the violence and dehumanisation of the transatlantic economic enterprise is how the nation has branded itself as exceptional and innocent in relation to European coloniality (Keskinen et al, 2009; Habel, 2012; Loftsdóttir and Jensen, 2012). Only recently has the city's coloniality begun to be reconsidered and re-told (Berg, 2004; Rönnbäck, 2010; Katz Thor, 2021). A movement of Afro-Swedes, Sámi, racialised minorities and other minoritised communities have been critically re-mapping and counter-archiving Gothenburg in recognition of its key role in the transatlantic trade, specifically through the production and export of iron ore from settler colonial Swedish mines, as well as through the processing and consumption of material from the Americas. This is where Gothenburg's role in a more general aspirational European imperial project of world domination is being re-traced and more publicly acknowledged.

Collaborations between artists, activists, researchers, educators and students in the city have started to make visible some of the city's colonial history. One example is a re-writing and counter-archiving in the space where Gothenburg's Court of Appeals lies, as historically it used to be called 'The French Plot' because it was on a piece of land given to France in 'exchange' for the slave-trading Caribbean Island of Saint Barthélemy. At the height of the trade in enslaved peoples, Sweden controlled the island and gained economic benefit from their exploitation. In 2021, as part of the Gothenburg Art Biennale GIBCA, extracts from the powerful poem 'Zong!' (Phillip and Boateng, 2011) were placed on the walls outside the Court of Appeals as a counter-archival intervention resisting the erasure of this history and the violence of its presence in this city space. Indeed, fragments of colonial presence are scattered throughout the cityscape of Gothenburg. Our counter-archiving work in Gothenburg can be understood as one effort to contribute to a larger movement that aims to begin to challenge and fill in the silences in public space with alternative histories and perspectives (Sawyer and Osei-Kofi, 2020).

Counter-archiving 'The Iron Well'

During the last three years, we (Nana and Lena) have been exploring Sweden's public sphere in relation to coloniality as well as to our own locations and beings. We both have a relationship to Gothenburg: we have walked the streets and encountered spaces many times in our everyday paths (Nana grew up there and has often visited because she sees this as one of her 'homes' in the world; Lena moved there in 2011 where she remains). Our work has been an organic process, and intuitively informed. By this we mean that we did not start out knowing we would eventually write and create an arts-based performance, and later record a multimodal film performance. We did not know that this process would connect us with a dynamic Swedish, Nordic and more global community of artists, activists, researchers, educators and students also interested in creating alternative pedagogies in relation to coloniality.

Our process began in 2018 by walking and talking with each other in the city and thinking together about alternative ways to communicate knowledge. As we walked together through Gothenburg we shared our own histories, our families, our own stories of migration and Black and African disaporic living and survival, as well as our own experiences of racism and commitments to overlapping and divergent feminist and Black communities in Sweden and abroad. We also felt frustrated with what we experienced to be some of the boundaries of academic life and knowledge production. During these walks we often found ourselves stopping in front of a particular statue, named '*Järntorgsbrunnen*', otherwise known as 'The Iron Well', which stands prominently in the city square called The Iron Square.

'The Iron Well' (Figure 11.1) is a 1923 bronze statue by the artist Tore Strindberg, located in a public square in the centre of Gothenburg. It contains a Swedish ship, water flowing downwards and five crouching naked women with their backs to one another. It is a public commemoration of what is called 'Sweden's Age of Greatness', when Sweden produced most of the iron ore exported to other European powers during the 1700s (and which is still true today). The five female figures represent the world based on racial hygiene concepts of racial types.

Figure 11.1: 'The Iron Well' (also called 'The Five World Parts')

Source: Nana Osei-Kofi and Lena Sawyer

During our time with the statue, we both shared our ambivalent feelings about it; its representation of Sweden, as well as the racialised 'types' of women, who crouched naked as part of the statue's base. We found ourselves drawn to and standing near the representation of an African woman. We both said we wanted her to have a name, and, in this way, our counter-archiving practice started.

We began to think about 'The Iron Well' statue and public commemoration in relation to conversations going on in other spheres and we drew connections to what we *felt* in relation to the statue as we tried to create a language to talk about this with each other. In particular, Black feminist historian and theorist Tina Campt's (2017) concept of 'listening' as a powerful methodological approach for engaging with gaps and silences in historical archives began to resonate with our own practice. Like Sharpe, Campt is also theorising a methodology of care in a context of anti-Blackness and asks us to be present through *listening* for the alternative histories of humanity and complexity that we *feel* when encountering state archives of Black life. Campt's work engages a method of embodied listening with official passport photos and prison-intake photos of Black people and analyses them as forms of state surveillance that attempt to 'capture' – that is, to dehumanise – Black life, living, humanity and complexity. She invites us to turn to feeling, and asks us to hear the alternative stories, which she argues vibrate in us, yet on another frequency, and which tell another story than that which the creator of the image wanted to tell. It is through Campt's beautiful methodology of 'listening' that we began to understand and form a methodology for understanding and creating knowledge about 'The Iron Well'. We listened: to each other, to the historical moment of the wake in which we exist and navigate, and to what had at first appeared to be disparate actions around the world in relation to public space.

Working in this way, at first, we mostly heard the violence of Swedish coloniality in the statue and the women represented there. But through time and an embodied listening, talking and thinking together we began to hear and see in the statue spaces open for counter-narratives of resilience and refusal. We heard possibility amid the fragments, and were drawn to alternative stories and different possibilities the archival facts presented. Here we were inspired by Saidya Hartman's (2008) concept of 'critical fabulation' which she describes in relation to meeting archives of coloniality where silences are acknowledged and fragments pieced together through one's own knowledge, desire and aspirations. For example, we saw the African woman's hanging toe suddenly as a sign of potential. She was kneeling, taking the knee, and ready to leap! We began to see in the statue possibility, resistance and a future (see Figure 11.2). We realised that she was not forever fastened to this space set in time. We held in her possibility for movement.

We began to hear the statue tell us other stories and ways of knowing, and we began to feel the presence of ancestors in the water flowing on and through the statue but also nearby in the port sea of Gothenburg. The sea which binds the continents, our stories and histories, and as such we began to intuitively photograph and film the ocean, the sound and image of water. In this way as we embarked on this form of knowing, we felt the presence of the ancestors with us. And as we began to prepare a gender conference presentation, we felt it important that water was part of what we called our paper performance. We brought water into the space, poured libations, called the ancestors to be with us and asked the public to join us as we created another story of the statue. Later, as we became more in contact with different art communities and activist communities, we were offered the chance (due to COVID restrictions) to film our performance, and it changed into another form, a video installation.

We turn now to discuss our reflections on, and analysis of, this exploratory collaborative practice of counter-archiving in relation to the coloniality of Gothenburg's public archive as an object lesson in how walking and talking pedagogies are a decolonial endeavour, and a practice of care. We argue that through creating a pedagogy for embodied knowledge practice we were able to critically assess Swedish colonialism and understand and even make a leap from more positivistic and colonial embedded methods of enquiry.

Figure 11.2: Leap

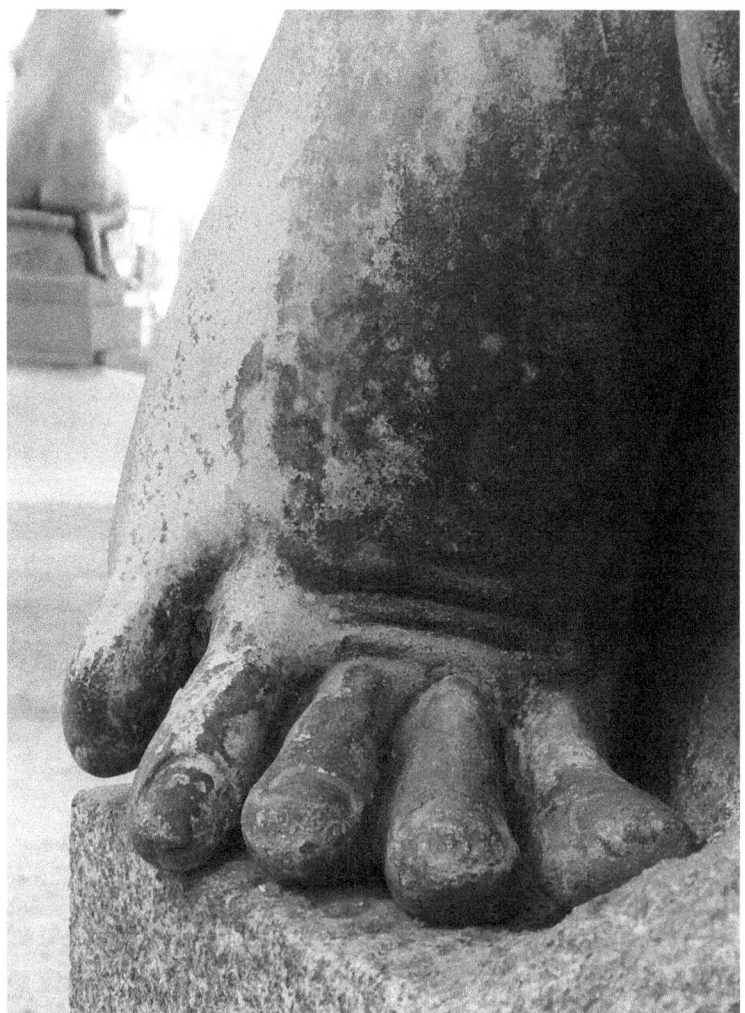

Source: Nana Osei-Kofi and Lena Sawyer

Ours was a decolonial practice in that we critically assessed the coloniality of the statue through our embodied and 'carried' knowledge (Puwar, 2021), and created a pedagogy for counter-archiving its erasures. This is a practice which led us to feel the powerful presence of our African ancestors in water; the water flowing through the statue, the sea waves moving in the harbour nearby, and which we poured as libation when we brought them into the room with us. All of these actions linked the past, present and future of Black survival and death. We understood this pedagogy to be a form of care as it encourages people to *listen* to affect and feeling in relation to public space and commemoration, and to each other: to witness, learn, listen to each other's memories, histories and understandings of place in relation to colonialism.

City walking as a decolonial macro social work pedagogy

In this section, Kris discusses how she used city walking as a decolonial pedagogy of wake work with social work students in Fresno, California, between 2009 and 2017. To orient the reader, she first outlines the local history to give a context of the place and then discusses why she developed city walks as a decolonial change-oriented pedagogy for macro practice. The experience of the walks became wake work as students learned about the hidden fragments of multi-ethnic local history. This section concludes with a discussion of the sensory experience of walking through public space as a collective and relational decolonial pedagogy that counter-archives the city (Kowalewski and Bartłomiejski, 2020).

Placing Chinatown in Fresno

Fresno is a sprawling metropolis of a half million residents situated in the territories of the Yokuts and Mono people in California's San Joaquin Valley of California. Once a complex ecosystem of wetlands and habitat of migratory waterfowl that was stewarded by the Indigenous peoples of the region, the San Joaquin Valley became the site of large-scale cattle grazing operations for hides and tallow in the 18th century. As the Spanish colonial mission system collapsed and California became part of Mexico in 1822, a rancho system emerged where vast tracts of land were owned by a handful of rancheros while Indigenous people worked in virtual peonage. In the mid-19th century, the Mexican-American War and discovery of gold in Sacramento coalesced with the ideology of Manifest Destiny, which viewed the total conquest of North America by White colonisers as the will of God, producing a systemic campaign of genocide against the Indigenous people of California (Atkins and Bauer, 2021).

These historical forms of colonisation gave rise to land monopoly, instead of small freeholds, which continues to be the main form of agriculture in the San Joaquin Valley today (Pisani, 1991). The emerging large-scale agricultural industry at the turn of the 20th century drew a multi-ethnic labour force to Fresno. From the very start, following the racial capitalism model derived from the transatlantic slave trade, Whites in Fresno strongly lobbied to maintain racial segregation in town planning with an 1874 town meeting decision to locate 'other ethnicities and disreputables to the west side' of the soon-to-be-incorporated city, making the railroad tracks the 'racial pale' of the new city (State Commission on Immigration and Housing, 1918). Chinese bachelor labourers, who made up half of Fresno's early population, came to Fresno in search of work after the completion of the transcontinental railroad seeking a safe place after being driven out of many towns in California (Pfaelzer, 2008). They settled in the central district west of the railroad line, which came to be known as Chinatown. Chinatowns throughout California emerged in cities as liminal spaces where Chinese, who faced legislative and racial discrimination, were concentrated in areas where tourism, vice and inter-ethnic mixing flourished separate from more strictly regulated and segregated residential and commercial neighbourhoods (Voss, 2020).

By the turn of the century, Fresno's Chinatown had become a vibrant multi-ethnic neighbourhood known for its nightclubs, gambling and opium dens with a police force rumoured to be on the take (Guzmán, 2012). The rough-and-tumble mentality of the emerging city produced a reputation as a 'wide-open town' with Chinatown at the epicentre of the action (Chacon, 1988). Yet, Chinatown also was home to many families with a variety of faith-based and community organisations such as the Buddhist Temple, the Mexican Baptist Church, Chinese benevolent associations, Japanese and Chinese cultural schools, youth boxing clubs and cinemas. Chinatown was one of the only places in Fresno that people of colour could shop for clothing and other goods. The first African American doctors and lawyers set up offices in Chinatown next to the street where labour contractors regularly picked up farm workers. The Chinatown District was thus a mosaic of diverse communities, cultures and social classes closely interconnected in place.

Post-war disinvestment in American cities as the role of the automobile as the primary means of transportation pushed suburbanisation. In the 1950s, Fresno Mayor Gordon Dunn, who promoted the enlargement of the police force, targeted Chinatown for demolition, viewing it as a centre of crime as he pushed for slum clearance. Within ten years, Fresno had one of the largest urban development projects in the nation through the federal Model Cities programme. A freeway was constructed between Chinatown and the residential neighbourhood of West Fresno, cutting off foot traffic to the district which affected business. Long-standing neighbourhoods rich in social capital and local history were razed and the city was reconfigured for cars as public transportation diminished with the untrammelled sprawl of the city to the north. Poverty became increasingly concentrated in West Fresno as ethnicised Whites, such as Italians and Armenians, and middle-class people fled to the newer areas of Fresno. City funding was directed to the new suburban developments as the city centre was gradually abandoned, except for government offices, and became a silent and empty place after business hours, though recent efforts at revitalisation have begun to reverse this. Nonetheless, as the oldest district of Fresno, Chinatown still retains a gravitational pull in the local imaginary as a lost collective space where nine major ethnic groups (Armenian, African American, Basque, Chinese,

Greek, Italian, Japanese, Mexican and Portuguese) lived closely together in community. This can be seen in the many efforts over the years to revitalise the area even though much of the physical history of the district is in fragments and people have scattered far and wide.

I tell this long story about Fresno because it is one that is rarely known by local students in the San Joaquin Valley. The 'tale of two cities', as one Fresno mayor once described the distinct spatial divide between the local extremes rich and poor, is often dehistoricised and not understood to be the result of deliberate structural policies by the ruling elite to invest resources in the wealthy areas of town, while the poorer and more ethnically diverse areas gradually deteriorated (Simmons, 2006). Today, there is more than 20 years' difference in life expectancy between the older and newer areas of Fresno, which shows how the disparities built into the original plan to keep 'disreputables' to the west of the growing city continue to live in local bodies (Joint Center for Political and Economic Studies, 2012).

Along with the Black Lives Matter movement and public history such as the 1619 Project, there has been growing awareness in Fresno of the need to uncover the layers of buried history and rectify historical injustice. Community members, activist groups, history teachers and media outlets such as uSpark, Community Alliance and Fresnoland have driven a reassessment of local history (Community Alliance, 2023; Fresnoland, 2023; uSpark, 2023). Several sites have been renamed in Fresno after the revelations about the anti-Semitic and racist backgrounds of the people who were had been honoured. These acts of remembering peel away the facade of Whiteness, layers of ideologies and colonial mindsets, and open up the complex historical roots of many of the deep injustices that Fresnans continue to endure.

City walks as macro social work practice

Between 2010 and 2017, I organised city walks as part of my macro social work practice course at California State University, Fresno. I was struck by how little local history had been preserved and passed on to younger generations. Fresno felt as segregated as when I was young, but there seemed to be less historical knowledge of the reasons Fresno developed the way it did because so many of the local narratives have been silenced, lost or never recorded. The extremes of poverty and wealth continue to be striking in Fresno with concentrated poverty, the lack of services and transportation, high rates of unemployment and need for benefits, poor schools and environmental injustice among the many social issues. A culture of blame, low levels of philanthropy and a mindset of 'pull yourself up by your bootstraps' still prevails, while layers of unacknowledged historical trauma and structural violence continue to drive patterns of addiction, intergenerational injustice and deprivation. Most of the Fresno State social work students came from impoverished local communities of colour and planned to practise in the Valley. Yet, they (like myself) were educated in a school system that privileged stories of the Spanish missions and local agricultural barons, with very little information about the histories of multi-ethnic communities in the Valley. The goal of these walks was therefore to explore and experience the physical and spatial landscape of the city and to collectively peel back the stories behind the disparities between neighbourhoods, and to validate the complex and hidden histories of the many diverse communities in Fresno.

Macro practice is a required course for undergraduate social work students. The goal of the course is to teach students about the larger context of social work in terms of programme development, community-based initiatives, grant writing, policy analysis, administration, organisational leadership and development. When I started teaching at Fresno State, there was a template for the syllabus that focused on these skills but had very little content on the local community. Macro practice was taught theoretically rather than experientially. I developed the city walks to bridge the gap between theories of structural injustice and lived experience.

City walks were organised on Saturdays in the autumn when the weather was not so hot, and they were open to students as well as their friends and families. We would meet in a neighbourhood at noon and walk for an hour. The neighbourhoods spanned diverse social classes and ethnicities. The idea of walking in a city generally traversed by car due to sprawl was to slow down time and to be physically present in different neighbourhoods. We usually walked with a resident from the area or a local activist. We were invited into one resident's home for coffee and got a spontaneous tour of a local fire station by enthusiastic fire fighters. The walks were an immersive and sensory collective experience of a specific neighbourhood.

I discuss the community walk in Fresno's Chinatown in detail because it was always the first walk of the series and sets the stage to understand how the city developed. Though it was a vibrant and crowded neighbourhood up until the 1950s, the vicissitudes of Chinatown are evident in its forlorn and empty buildings where there are currently only about 100 residents who live in the district and a large amount of unhoused people. Nowadays, there are efforts to gentrify Chinatown and some buildings are beginning to be renovated as office buildings as newcomers begin to buy up real estate.

Walking Chinatown

Very few students had ever been to Chinatown, let alone heard of it, even though it lies at the heart of the city. We often had to spend some time in class to clarify where exactly it was and still several students got lost, sometimes requiring many text messages to locate them. Usually, about 8–10 students turned up curious and a bit nervous as they waited on the corner of Kern and F Streets, once the bustling centre of Chinatown, but in the 2010s was rather empty and desolate. The silent streets and boarded-up buildings of the area contributed to a sense of vulnerability.

We started the walk by looking at the small memorial to Chinese labourers, who built many of the downtown buildings, which is not especially easy to find. It is a marker that commemorates China Alley and is constructed on the same bricks that Chinese labourers used to build downtown. The plaque reads (see Figure 11.3):

> In 1874, 600 people moved to what is now Fresno. Of those, 200 were Chinese, who made the brick and helped start the building of Fresno. A short time later, they were persuaded to settle west of the train tracks. They built an area of shops, which catered to all ethnic backgrounds. It was a thriving area that offered goods, services, and 'entertainment' day and night. It was the cosmopolitan area of Fresno for many years and to this day this area still has influence on the city. The brick used here came from an eighty-plus year-old church torn down in the 1970's and is thought to have been made by the Chinese settlers.

The memorial asserts the significance of the Chinatown district by pointing to its vibrancy and diversity, though it is difficult to locate it because it is hidden between a bush and parking lot. The text bypasses the issue of enforced segregation by claiming that Chinese 'settlers' were 'persuaded' to live to the west of the railroad tracks. We stopped here as a group and breathed in the loneliness and seeming insignificance of the small plaque. We talked about who actually built this city, the physical hardship of being a hod carrier and what it must have been like to be elders in this place after a lifetime of labour.

Much of the legacy of these men, who usually lived in single-room occupancy housing and were often prevented from bringing over families due to the Chinese Exclusion Act, has been erased through time. The Chinese cemetery to the west of town has been long neglected and largely destroyed. At the height of Chinatown, there were nine Chinese benevolent associations that provided social support, entertainment and funeral expenses. Only a few were still standing, though they were largely abandoned. One bore the sign that it would be renovated as part of historical preservation by the state of California, but that never happened, and it eventually burned down. Underneath Chinatown runs a series of interconnected basements known as the tunnels that were used for the storage of goods, brothels, gambling and opium dens. Allegedly, this system of underground tunnels extended all the way to city hall, though no one has ever properly mapped it. Sometimes we were able to go down into the basements by descending the steps of Ofelia's barber shop. The tunnels were dusty and empty, but we could examine large solid doors that had

Figure 11.3: Chinatown plaque

Source: Kris Clarke

peepholes and cavernous rooms. Kathy Omachi, a community activist who sometimes joined us, described how women trafficked into brothels would have to work 16–18 hours per day in small cribs underground to pay off debts incurred through migration. Many died by suicide, she said, and most could never pay the loan, though some escaped and made new lives. Here, Kathy shut the lights off and we stood silently. She encouraged us to feel the spirits of these invisible women's lives, imagine what it would be like to be trapped living in these circumstances, bear the weight of despair.

After the tunnels, we re-emerged to the street and strolled to the Azteca Theatre, built in 1948. Arturo Tirado managed the theatre and was the only venue in the San Joaquin Valley to have regular showings of Spanish-language films. It was also a venue for the leader of the United Farm Workers union, Cesar Chávez, who organised rallies at the theatre and read the 'Plan of Delano', a document written by union activists calling for the liberation of farmworkers (Historic Fresno, 2017). Next to the theatre was a nightclub known as 'La Fiesta' with an unlit vintage neon sign. At one time, there was a key shop next to the Azteca which operated as an informal social service agency and first stop for new arrivals from Mexico seeking work and housing. We discussed what it would feel like to arrive in this strange place and be directed to this little shop. What stories would the owner have and what a vast social network was situated in this small space. The fading colours of the façade and the vibrancy of the ageing neon conjured up a time of joy and interconnectedness.

We also visited the Fresno Betsuin Buddhist Temple, which was just down the street from the Azteca and China Alley, which was watched and preserved by neighbours during the Second World War. We saw the Scandinavian dairy factory, the oldest fire station in Fresno known as 'The Rock', the Mexican Baptist Church where Cesar Chávez held meetings and the Paris Cafe which was famous for its food. We also stopped in front of the Bing Kong Association (Figure 11.4), a Chinese community centre built in 1900. It had

Figure 11.4: The Bing Kong Association

Source: Kris Clarke

unique architectural features that California Governor Gray Davis promised to preserve during his term in the early 2000s, but it burned down in 2022 after being left vacant for over 20 years. We studied the many unlit neon signs that pointed to the time when, as a former resident once said, the streets were hopping until 4 am. The city walk helped students to consider the fragments of evidence of the multi-ethnic communities that breathed life into Chinatown. We discussed how these social connections were so important for wellness, solidarity and mutual aid. They were also able to see their own roots in these communities that were so rarely publicly honoured and recognised.

Social work macro practice is about advocating within larger social systems to make social change and to reimagine ways of emancipatory social work practices. Because institutions and policies are deeply rooted in the historical experiences of communities, it is essential for social workers to have knowledge of the local context of lived experience and place. City walks with the macro practice class were a way of centring local students in encounters with the public space of Fresno, sometimes in neighbourhoods they had rarely visited but which also often validated their own communities as having deep historical roots in the place of Fresno. These walks also opened up the past social justice struggles and creative ways that marginalised communities supported one another through stories. Many students reported having discussions with grandparents after these walks where elders talked about their own childhood memories of Chinatown bringing out previously untold stories of community joy, cross-cultural sharing and resistance to the various manifold levels of structural oppression in Fresno. This pedagogy allowed students to grapple with place, their own identities and how the legacy of segregation continues to have an impact on diverse communities in complex, structural ways.

Conclusion: walking, listening, talking as decolonial pedagogy

Our exploration of a sensory and relational practice of walking, listening and talking together was situated in city spaces. We used a method of listening deeply and sharing and witnessing one another's histories in a context of 'the wake' through an embodied encounter with historical fragments and/ or public commemorations (such as plaques and statues) in our city spaces. If, according to Sharpe (2016), wake work entails a *practice* that remaps the traces of our ongoing and collective resistance to the erasure of histories and existence, then our efforts to walk through our city spaces collectively looking and listening for traces of resilience and resistance in the public archive are a practice that re-politicises the local.

In this chapter we have explored counter-archiving, as a re-mapping practice, in public spaces within the city of Gothenburg and Fresno. By moving collectively through city space, we encountered public art, monuments and various geographic locations through dialogues, aiming to make visible the everyday salience of colonial history. In the case of Gothenburg, Sweden, this is a counter-archiving which challenges arguments that suggest that Sweden's involvement in colonialism was minor compared with nations such as Great Britain and France, and therefore doesn't really 'count'. We also illustrate through spatial mapping that correlating the degree of colonial power with the degree of colonial mindset of a people is a flawed view of accounting for how dominant world views of societies come into being. Sweden might not have been the largest colonial power, but the mindset of its people was no different from that of other European nations when it came to views about European superiority and the quest to gain power and control over people and resources in what we know today as the Global South.

The fragments that students encountered on city walks in Chinatown counter-archive the dominant narrative of Fresno, which is often narrowly confined to a narrative of White pioneers discovering an empty land. By walking and being present in the ruins of a once vibrant area, students were able to engage in the wake work of recognising and feeling the presence of ancestors and their structural oppressions by experiencing the space of Chinatown collectively. Following Julia Aoki and Ayaka Yoshimizu (2015), the city walks in Fresno were used as a 'spatialised, lived, sensually experienced deviations from (the absence of) abstract historical narratives'. When cities are traversed solely in automobiles with windows rolled up, there is little opportunity to engage with the lived space of the neighbourhood and the spatial-social memory of thriving districts, beloved buildings and intertwined communities. By walking through Chinatown, students were doing wake work through a decolonial pedagogy of being present in counter-archiving the local stories.

As we knit together seemingly disparate archival fragments of space and re-filled them with our own histories of these spaces and their significance, we engaged in an intimate form of social care. This is a practice of care that is relational and links communities, such as those between academic disciplines, civil society organisations and activists. We found that these kinds of pedagogical forms have potential to bring together people within cities where connections can be fragmented. This has particular relevance for the field of social work, but also other disciplines, as it shifts spaces and places for learning from inside the university to embodied engagement with the city spaces and communities. It highlights the fact that learning comes from reflecting on our collective being in specific local spaces in the world we share.

Questions for readers

- How do you see yourself, your communities, your history when you walk around in your city, town, area?
- How is history represented, seen or felt when you walk in your city, town, area?

- Are there statues, plaques or other official history markers that you encounter during your everyday walk in your space? What, whose or how do they tell this history? Do you identify with this? Feel included? Invisible?
- Are there 'archival fragments' you see, feel, hear when you walk around in your city, town, area?
- What histories do they tell, remind you of?
- Have you walked with someone else in your city, town, area and they have told you a history about a particular place, space, marker that was new to you?
- If you use Campt's understanding of 'listening' what do you 'hear' inside yourself in relation to particular spaces in your city?
- Have you ever entered space and felt and heard other histories than those commemorated?
- Have you thought about how different histories reflect local power relations, in what ways?
- What ways can you think you make this history visible to the public?

References

Aoki, J.' and Yoshimizu, A. (2015) Walking histories, un/making places: walking tours as ethnography of place', *Space and Culture*, 18(3): 273–84.

Akins, D.B., and Bauer, W. (2021) *We Are the Land: a History of Native California*, Oakland, California: University of California Press.

Berg, M. (2004) *Förlåta men inte glömma. Röster om rasism, nationalism och det mångkulturella samhället i Namibia. Och i Sverige*, Stockholm: Carlsson.

Bhambra, G. (2014) *Connected Sociologies*, London: Bloomsbury.

Campt, T. (2017) *Listening to Images*, Durham, NC: Duke University Press.

Chacon, R.D. (1988) 'The beginning of racial segregation: the Chinese in West Fresno and Chinatown's role as red light district, 1870s–1920s', *Southern California Quarterly*, 70(4): 371–98.

Community Alliance (2023) https://fresnoalliance.com

Daigle, M., and Ramírez, M.M. (2019) 'Decolonial geographies', *Keywords in Radical Geography: Antipode*, 50: 78–84.

Fischer, J.M. (2022) 'Urban walking as a practice of care: sensorial activism in Durban, South Africa', *Journal of Cultural Psychology*, 3: 165–74.

Fresnoland (2023) https://fresnoland.org

Guzmán, C. (2012) 'Race, citizenship, and the negotiation of space: Chinese, Japanese, and Mexicans in Fresno, California, 1870–1949', PhD dissertation, Santa Cruz, CA: University of California.

Habel, Y. (2012) 'Challenging Swedish exceptionalism? Teaching while Black', in K. Freeman and E. Johnson (eds) *Education in the Black Diaspora: Perspectives, Challenges and Prospects*, London: Routledge: pp 99–122.

Hartman, S. (2008) 'Venus in two acts', *Small Axe*, 12(2): 1–14.

Historic Fresno (2017) *The Azteca Theatre*. http://historicfresno.org/nrhp/azteca.htm

Joint Center for Political and Economic Studies (2012) *Place Matters for Health in the San Joaquin Valley: Ensuring Opportunities for Good Health for All. A Report on Health Inequities in the San Joaquin Valley.* www.nationalcollaborative.org/wp-content/uploads/2016/02/PLACE-MATTERS-for-Health-in-San-Joaquin-Valley.pdf

Kamaly, H. (2021) 'Spår', *Ord&Bild: Urban konst*, (3–4): 51–9.

Kamaly, H. (2022–2023) *Behold, We Are Here*, Konstinstallation: Lunds Konsthall.

Katz Thor, R. (2021) 'Minnen och monument: Förhandlingar om sårbarhet och sörjbarhet i det offentliga rummet', *Glänta*, 1: 5–15.

Keskinen, S., Tuori, S., Irni S. and Mulinari, D. (2009) *Complying with Colonialism: Gender, Race and Ethnicity in the Nordic Region*, London: Routledge.

Kowalewski, M. and Bartłomiejski, R. (2020) 'Is it research or just walking? Framing walking research methods as "non-scientific"', *Geoforum*, 114: 59–65.

Livholts, M.B. (2022) 'Immaterial monuments, narrative inequality and glocal social work. towards critical participatory community art-based practices', *British Journal of Social Work*, 52(2): 776–95.

Loftsdóttir, K. and Jensen, L. (2012) *Whiteness and Postcolonialism in the Nordic Region: Exceptionalism, Migrant Others and National Identities*, London: Routledge.

Mbembe, A. (2015) ' "Decolonizing knowledge and the question of the archive". Africa is a Country', contributed by A. Okune, Platform for Experimental Collaborative Ethnography, Platform for Experimental Collaborative Ethnography. https://worldpece.org/content/mbembe-achille-2015-"decolonizing-knowledge-and-question-archive"-africa-country

Middleton, J. (2018) 'The socialities of everyday urban walking and the "right to the city"', *Urban Studies*, 55(2): 296–315.

Moulton, A.A. (2021) 'Black monument matters: place-based commemoration and abolitionist memory work', *Sociology Compass*, e12944.

Perić, S. (2018) 'Ice as a counter-archive: permafrost, archival melt and climate futures', *Public (Toronto)*, 29(57): 163–70.

Pfaelzer, J. (2008) *Driven Out: the Forgotten War against Chinese Americans*, Berkeley: University of California.

Philip, N.M. and Boateng, S.A. (2011) *Zong!* Middletown, CT: Wesleyan University Press.

Pisani, D.J. (1991) 'Land monopoly in nineteenth-century California', *Agricultural History*, 65(4): 15–37.

Puwar, N. (2021) 'Carrying as method: listening to bodies as archives', *Body and Society*, 27(1): 3–26.

Rönnbäck, K. (2010) 'Socker och slavplantager i svensk historia', in L. Müller, G. Rydén and H. Weiss (eds) *Global Historia Från Periferin: Norden 1600–1850*, Lund: Studenlitteratur, pp 97–115.

Rumsey, A.S. (2016) *When We Are No More: How Digital Memory Is Shaping Our Future*, London: Bloomsbury.

Savransky, M. and Stengers, I. (2018) 'Relearning the art of paying attention: a conversation', *SubStance*, 47(1): 130–45.

Sawyer, L. and Osei-Kofi, N. (2020) '"Listening" with Gothenburg's Iron Well: engaging the imperial archive through Black feminist methodologies and arts-based research', *Feminist Review*, 125(1): 54–61.

Sharp, C. (2016) *In the Wake: On Blackness and Being*, Durham, NC: Duke University Press.

Simmons, A. (2006) 'The worst of times on Fresno's south side poverty sharply divides California City', *Washington Post*, [online] 11 June. www.washingtonpost.com/archive/politics/2006/06/11/the-worst-of-times-on-fresnos-south-side-span-classbankheadpoverty-sharply-divides-california-cityspan/f8086949-1992-49ae-81a5-8cd2d6ed16aa/

Springgay, S. and Truman, S.E. (2017) *Walking Methodologies in a More-Than-Human World: WalkingLab*, London: Routledge.

State Commission on Immigration and Housing (1918) *Report on Fresno's Immigration Problem*, Sacramento: California State Printing Office. https://www.loc.gov/item/18027173/

uSpark (2023) www.usparkvalley.com

Voss, B. (2020) 'Interethnic relationships in nineteenth-century Chinatowns: new perspectives from archaeological research and missionary women's writings', in C. Rose and J.R. Kennedy (eds) *Chinese Diaspora Archaeology in North America*, Gainesville, FL: University Press of Florida, pp 109–38.

Ware, S.M. (2017) 'All power to all people? Black LGBTTI2QQ activism, remembrance, and archiving in Toronto', *TSQ: Transgender Studies Quarterly*, 4(2): 170–80.

World Population Review (WPR) (2023) https://worldpopulationreview.com/world-cities/gothenburg-population

Yoon-Ramirez, I. (2021) 'Walking-sensing as a decolonial art and pedagogical practice', *International Journal of Education through Art*, 17(1): 115–33.

12

Post-professional social work? Decolonising social work professionalism through the engagement of community health workers

Saana Raittila-Salo

'To me, community [health] work means helping others in the community ... I feel as if I am the focal point in the community ... and those from the community look at me as if I were the eye of the whole neighbourhood because I know that if anything happens, they will consult me.'

(Hélvia)[1]

Community health workers are the lowest cadre of healthcare professionals, who typically come from local neighbourhoods and have little or no formal training (WHO, 1989). Community health workers' programmes are widespread in African, Asian and Latin American countries and in the US, with programmes dating back to the 1950s. As estimated by the WHO (2011), more than 1.4 million community health workers are deployed around the world. In this chapter, I focus on Indigenous community health workers and volunteers in the Chamanculo neighbourhoods in Maputo City, Mozambique, because they have deep experiential knowledge of the social environment of the peri-urban areas, as well as the collective adversities shared between residents. This chapter presents a case study that examines community health work in an NGO-led project in the Chamanculo neighbourhoods, where community health workers provide services through health promotion, finding patients and enhancing access to health clinics. Using a decolonial lens, the invisible labour of these health workers went unrecognised by the supervising NGO and Western funders. This project shows that Indigenous health workers also address social problems, community disputes and other health-related social issues.

Community health work has been widely researched, but social aspects of community health work have rarely been studied. Matthew et al (2017) have explored, as a model, community health work which supports culturally responsive social work in US Latinx communities. Spencer et al (2010) have suggested that community health work should be incorporated into social work. In both cases, they pursue similar values such as social justice. Other studies address – albeit more briefly – community health work in social work, seeing it as relevant to public health social work (Lu et al, 2018) and framing community health workers as para-social workers (Linsk et al, 2010). The questions I pose in this chapter are how Mozambican community health workers' practices challenge social work professionalism and how important local Indigenous health workers' social interventions are to the successful integration of social work as a practice within local communities.

This chapter is structured as follows. First, I present the context of community health work in Mozambique and engage in the debates around popular social work and the downsides of professionalism. Second, I discuss the history and concept of post-professionalisation and frame the contemporary post-professional times as an opportunity to deconstruct social work professionalism. In the results, I examine how community health workers in Maputo, Mozambique, deviate from traditional notions of professionalism and how they intervene in social problems. In closing, I discuss what Nordic countries can learn from the decolonial model of community health workers' engagement in social problem solving and conclude by highlighting the need for paraprofessional training to deploy lay practitioners.

Community health work in Mozambique

In Mozambique, community health worker programmes and projects are divided along the lines of a rural-urban divide. Government-deployed community health workers live in remote villages far from health clinics; therefore, their tasks include basic curative service provision, such as treating malaria and testing for HIV and tuberculosis (Give et al, 2019; Källander et al, 2019). In the Chamanculo neighbourhoods, where health clinics are nearby, there is no need for training on curative tasks – nurses can perform them if the people in the community are aware of the services available and are referred or accompanied to health clinics in a timely manner. The difference is also that the rural government programmes provide a full four months of paraprofessional training for the volunteers (Muula et al, 2006; Rustagi et al, 2015), while the peri-urban NGO projects may provide only one or two weeks of formal training. All community health workers in Mozambique are paid volunteers (referred to as 'activists') since they receive less than the minimum wage. In recent years, community health workers receive an average monthly salary of 21 US dollars (Macuácua et al, 2019), whereas the national minimum wage was around 51 US dollars per month.

In the NGO that is the focus of this study, the level of remuneration ranged between 20 US dollars and 67 US dollars, depending on the project.[2]

Mozambique has been hard hit by the HIV/AIDS and tuberculosis epidemics. On a national level, 2.1 million Mozambicans are HIV-positive (UNAIDS, 2020), while Mozambique is one of the few countries failing to create a decline in the rates of tuberculosis (García-Basteiro et al, 2017). In Maputo, 17 per cent of the population is HIV-positive (Andrade and Iriart, 2015), and coping with illness is complicated by poverty, lack of opportunity and unemployment. Municipal health clinics in Mozambique are largely run by nurses and the lack of trained healthcare workers in Mozambique has augmented task shifting from higher professional cadres to less-trained personnel – from doctors to nurses and from nurses to community health workers. For these reasons, the roles and tasks of community health workers are very different in Mozambique compared with those deployed in more affluent healthcare systems in other country contexts. Personal ties and social networks of extended families and neighbours may become notable assets as peri-urban residents seek to survive and cope with the adversities of urban living (for example, Hansen and Vaa, 2004). This is the context in which Mozambican community health workers operate, working within local communities and using existing assets and resources.

Popular social work and the downside of professionalism

As Mlotshwa et al (2015: 2) point out, community health workers are employed as 'ordinary community members', but they oftentimes generate 'an identity of superiority associated with professions … which distance them from their communities'. Other scholars have identified similar challenges that follow as community health workers are 'professionalised' (Nading, 2013; Logan, 2020). Among the supporters of the role of community health workers as social advocates, professionalisation seems a way to make their practice more manageable – or, as Nading (2013: 91) states, professionalisation can move community health workers away from a political orientation, towards a more technical approach to their work.

Based on this earlier research, there seem to be two conclusive options for preparing community health workers: to maintain those who have strong personal and community ties as lay people and community representatives, or to opt for more rigorous paraprofessional training. With respect to the first option, the concept of *popular social work* may be useful in favouring the first alternative of community-embedded work by lay people. Popular social work refers to social work practised outside the state-directed welfare system, by activists and community members not part of a 'recognised' profession (Lavalette and Ioakimidis, 2011). Lavalette and Ioakimidis (2017: 120, 123) suggest that popular social work is a social work that is 'flexible, open, reliable, non-stigmatising and non-conditional' and 'genuinely grassroots'. It can take place in NGOs, community groups and associations, since to become a 'popular social worker' formal qualification is not required.

Debates around the concept of popular social work have recognised the need to question what is meant by social work historically and internationally as the profession expands in the Global South (see McDermott, 2014; Lavalette, 2015). Popular social work stays true to the values of the social work profession – such as equality, human rights and human dignity – but refrains from defining social work based on higher-education qualifications. This is not to say that anyone can 'do' social work or be a social worker, or that we should rely solely on community-based and popular forms of social intervening (Lavalette and Ioakimidis, 2017). Rather, the authors remind us that state-directed services are not the only context in which social work can be practised.

Addressing social work globally, and in contexts where there are few professionally trained social workers and very few social work placements in the public sector, popular social work as a concept can help us to unravel professional hierarchies between the Global North and the Global South, and potentially employ a complex, community-based system of care that integrates and creates networks between local non-professionalised community workers alongside professional service providers. In what follows, I propose a community-driven model of non-professional (or lay people's) intervening that stays true to the ideals of popular social work, but engages a decolonial reorientation by evening out professional, paraprofessional and non-professional practice in relation to the current tendencies of post-professionalisation.

Post-professional social work

'Post-professional' carries two different meanings. It may refer to a transition in the study of professions shifting away from functionalist theories, or to actual historical changes in Western societies affecting professions in the second half of the 20th century (Burns, 2019). I am interested in the future of social work as it has been affected by the actual changes and the possibility of understanding and creating best practices using a decolonial model. Indeed, state-directed social work has been challenged, since the 1970s at least, by professional decline following proletarianisation and de-professionalisation (Randall and Kindiak, 2008). For Kritzer (1999), three elements are leading to the post-professional transition: the formal professions' loss of exclusivity, specialisation and the segmentation of abstract knowledge, and an increasing use of technology that enables the public outside of professions to access information that was previously possessed by professionals. One main outcome of this process of post-professionalisation would be that previous expert-provided services will be increasingly provided by 'specialised general professions or nonprofessionals' (Kritzer, 1999: 720).

In the field of social work, Ranta-Tyrkkö (2011) points to the problem of how Western theory today continues to rank higher than Indigenous or local knowledges. I think there is a parallel between the monopoly of Western theory and prevailing modernist ideas of professionalism as the exclusiveness of professional-expert knowledge obtained through tertiary education directs who can be in the position of social intervening – only after acquiring qualifications. Post-professionalism challenges these monopolies of expert knowledge, which have maintained skill hierarchies in modern societies (Derber et al, 1990). Hence, Derber et al (1990) discuss 'democratisation of knowledge' as marking the post-professional society.

The post-professional transition entails renewing professional identities (see Burns, 2019) but it also calls into question established methods and ways of practising a profession. In Nordic social work, for example, community-based working methods are marginalised (Roivainen, 2004); however, the post-professional transition might be used as an opportunity to strengthen community practices. To start inventing new community-based working methods in social work in the Global South and beyond, I agree with Fielding (2016: 51) that practitioners' skills need updating – that, in fact, practitioners affected by the forces of post-professionalisation 'are not being deskilled' but 'instead, they are using new skills'. This *upskilling* or *reskilling* rather than 'deskilling' would best describe the skills adaptation needed to decolonise the idea of professional social work and to enable professionals to pair up with non-professionals. Decolonising social work practices, thus, entails those professionalising trainings to integrate and learn from community-based practices and the community leaders who carry them out.

Historically, social work was once viewed as a semi-profession without the status equal to a full profession, such as medicine or law (Etzioni, 1969; Toren, 1972) but it has eventually reached that professional status through higher-education qualifications (Sewpaul, 2010). This has been celebrated but from an opposite point of view, Sewpaul and Henrickson (2019) criticise the science base of social work as stemming from one-sided striving for professional recognition and status. They refer to the contemporary situation as 'positivist professionalism' that colonises social work by dismissing community-based practices in favour of what is considered to be more 'scientific' and manageable practice. Even nowadays, paraprofessionals and untrained lay practitioners work widely in the healthcare sector in Africa, Asia and Latin America – which calls for a re-evaluation of the legitimising processes of inclusion and exclusion of some practices as deserving to be called social work.

On the one hand, the fragmentation and technocratisation of social work has been alarmed as it 'permits complex social work tasks to be undertaken by less highly skilled practitioners at lower rates of pay' (Dominelli and Hoogvelt, 1996: 52). On the other hand, however, employing para- and non-professionals may be seen as an opportunity for post-professional social work. Randall and Kindiak (2008) view the post-professionalisation of social work as a consequence of professional decline caused by *proletarianisation* and *deprofessionalisation*. In fact, the grip of capital leads to 'factory-like' working conditions and bureaucratisation (Oppenheimer, 1972), and managerialism, fragmentation of expert roles and government regulation of professions shrink the latitude of social workers to exercise their exclusive expert knowledge and authority over the governed populations (Haug, 1972; Randall and Kindiak, 2008).

This decline and loss of professional dominance of the certain field of knowledge and practice – that has arguably already affected social work professionalism during the post-professional period – could be tackled, according to Randall and Kindiak (2008) by expanding the scopes of social work practice or by restratification within the profession. Through the process of restratification, social workers would need to take up more managerial and supervisory roles, while broadening the scope of social work could create a niche for paraprofessionals and non-professionals. This type of repositioning of social work is not new in the history of the profession. As Payne (2015) has noted, social workers in the early days 'professed' expertise of certain areas of practice that previously were not included in social services or social care. Counselling could be viewed as an example of claims-making, where advice-giving – which lay people do very well – has become professionalised (see Halmos, 1965). As a continuation, to resist the loss of professional authority, I suggest that community interventions by lay people and community members should be claimed and recognised by the profession.

Methodology: an ethnographic case study of an NGO-led project

The research data sets were gathered in 2018 during a three-month period of fieldwork. The main methods of data collection were participant observation and individual semi-structured interviews with community health workers. The community health work project focused on HIV/AIDS, tuberculosis, child malnutrition and gender-based violence; other topics were covered in health promotion, such as hygiene and methods of contraception. Fourteen community health workers were recruited to participate in the study, based on their own interest. They were recruited among 25–30 community health workers actively working in the NGO; hence, approximately half of the community health workers participated in interviews. Convenience sampling was used by the selection of the first people who expressed interest to participate in interviews. The interviewees were six men and eight women, were 19–36 years, and had less than three months up to 11 years' experience working as community health volunteers.

The research data mainly consist of individual in-depth interviews (two persons were interviewed in a group discussion) and field notes from participant observation. An open story-inducing (or narrative) interviewing style was used as a practical way to collect personal histories of the successes and failures of health interventions involving the community. The interviews were conducted in the NGO facilities, in interlocutors' homes and on the porch of the house where I was staying. The interviews were conducted in Portuguese, tape recorded and transcribed by a research assistant, and only quotes used in the research report were translated into English. A written informed consent was obtained and the intended use of the data and my role as an observer-researcher was thoroughly explained to the community health workers, the NGO and the residents, who received us in their homes.

The study was conducted at the University of Helsinki, Finland, and it followed the ethical guidelines of the Finnish National Board of Research Integrity (TENK). In Finland, ethical review may only be obtained for studies that deviate from common ethical procedures (such as informed consent) or involve threat to safety or mental harm, among other research designs that are precisely defined as requiring an ethical approval (TENK, 2019). This study did not meet the national requirements for research to be examined by an institutional review board.

Results: foundations for decolonising Nordic social work

The following frameworks: Closeness, Reciprocity, Recognition and Social Intervention are used by community health workers to provide insights into certain decolonial entry points for shifting Nordic social work practices by both utilising local and socially accepted Indigenous workers and reshaping the organising structure, and workers, within Nordic social work systems. In this study, community health workers are not viewed only as auxiliaries of service extension – or, as 'another pair of hands' for the nurses (Walt, 1990, in Scott and Shanker, 2010). Instead, because they know the social context and living conditions of the peri-urban areas, they are seen as bringing supplemental value to their work as local community members. This position of being an insider and a peer, arguably, suggests a different type of professionalism and social intervention than that generally followed by formally trained social workers.

Reconsidering professionalism

Based on my analysis, I suggest that, in Chamanculo, Maputo, community health workers engage with patients and communities with three entry points that shape and encourage good working relationships and positive outcomes, including that they were assumed to be closer to the patient than nurses and doctors; there is a sense that they help, which is perceived as reciprocal; and community health workers benefit personally through gaining status, recognition and good fame, which enable them to advance the interests of the community from a position of leadership. These differences render the encounter with the 'client', or the patients and community members, highly meaningful.

Closeness

In Maputo City the slum-like residential areas expand far and wide around the narrow 'cement city' of contemporary Maputo, but the area is not referred to as a slum; rather, it is viewed by locals as a normal place to live, given that in Maputo, 75 per cent of the population lives in informal settlements (UN-HABITAT, 2019). Community health workers understand the notions of health and illness, as community members and as locals. Like those who they were helping, community health workers struggled to make ends meet – they also turned to neighbours for financial and other support when in need. Yasser laments:

> 'If there are a lot of people in activism [unpaid work], only doing that thing, [she] does not work, doesn't do anything, she is just stuck in activism. Now, if they don't have any remuneration [or it is too low], how is the person going to be presentable in the community ... how are they going to be presentable, where are they going to find soap, Colgate [toothpaste], to be presentable there in the community.'

Some community health workers had experienced break-ins, fires and floods in their houses and had neighbours as the first helpers on site; they drew from these experiences in their work. For others, personal experiences with health problems had motivated them to pursue community health work. Helder says:

> 'I inclined to tuberculosis because when I was starting to work, I lost someone because of that disease. The moment when they were alive, I didn't know any symptoms or signs [of tuberculosis] ... One year later the person passed away ... In that [moment] I fell in love [with community health work]. Because I couldn't help the person I lost, I prefer to help another person.'

In this way, community health workers in Chamanculo were tied to local community structures of mutual aid and were at the receiving end of norms of reciprocity and solidarity. Community health workers live in the communities which they serve, adding an element to their work that is different from professionals at health clinics, or social workers. By virtue of being community members and volunteers, acting as what would be viewed as 'professional' does not concern them and, more importantly, this different role allows them to approach community members with ease.

Because they shared the same living environment with patients and had experienced similar adversities in life, community health workers could turn their personal experiences to their advantage in oftentimes sensitive, difficult conversations. Trained social work professionals could have personal experiences of social problems and life situations that they could discuss with their clients, but it would often be considered strictly unprofessional to bring that up – unlike professionals, community health workers as lay people were, on the contrary, expected to be close to and personal with the beneficiaries.

Reciprocity

Through their personal connections, community health workers gained access to intimate social networks that are closed to the trained professionals. They were able to build a personal network during their working time – as part of the job, they patched up missing pieces in the social fabric of the community to the benefit of the patient or client. They could and did, however, use their networked connections to their own advantage. Community health worker Helder tells the story of one family he had helped, and uncovers how he might, eventually, expect a service in return. Helder recounts:

> 'Yes, I gain experience and [better] condition also because there are those patients that, because they are accustomed to corruption, when you do something, they even end up wanting to pay you. So, I always choose to deny. I tell the patient, "The money you want to give me, save it. After three years I may need your help, and then you will help me."'

Expectations of receiving money or other support in the future from a patient or other beneficiary could be interpreted as unprofessional, but it should not be expected that the work community health workers undertake for their community is strictly altruistic. The pay is low, so personal encounters with other community members could become important to the volunteering experiences – as emotional encounters, with warm feelings, but also as a means to pursue their own interests and the perceived interests of the community.

Closeness and reciprocity lead to long-lasting relationships. The relationship building started from the community health work encounter but could sometimes continue as a friendship when community health workers conducted follow-ups. Community health workers kept in touch with the beneficiary families by phone calls and text messages, and paid them irregular visits. Carolina explains: "Sometimes I have nothing to do. I go and ask how they [the family and the patient] are, how is their health, how is her health." In the same way, Miguel recalls: "He [the patient] went back to the treatment and thanked me. Still today I come to pay them a visit or send a message, and he says that everything is fine."

Recognition

The objectives of the project – such as finding people who had stopped taking HIV or tuberculosis medication, and providing health promotion – did not seem to affect the community health workers quite like the interpersonal work and the something extra, the informal support they provided, often taking the form of social interventions. Although social problem solving, care and support were not part of the assigned tasks of community health workers, these practices focusing on the social aspects of health and social problems seemed to bring most satisfaction and joy to community health workers. Moreover, social intervening seemed to result in good fame and recognition, unlike health promotion and other assigned tasks. A community health worker, Mônica, who was widely known and recognised in her neighbourhood, described how her work as a community volunteer had gained her a good reputation. This is depicted in her description of how she imagined her own memorial:

> 'So, [in my work] I get out of it gaining fame. People will look at me like a great thing in the world, even when I lose my life, they will come to bury me. [They] will say that I did this and that, and even more.'

Of course, working in a certain job does not necessarily result in positive recognition. However, arguably because of the positive halo effects of volunteering or because the community health workers knew more than others about health, illness and related topics, they were often called on for advice beyond their expertise. Community health workers were often (but not always) well received, respected and listened to.

Social interventions: examples from the Chamanculo neighbourhoods

Community health workers' position as recognised community members gave them access to social resources but also social obligations beyond their assigned tasks as lay health workers. Many community health workers in Chamanculo told stories of how they helped other community members outside the working hours – even if a neighbour came knocking on their door at night, they felt obliged to do what they could do, in their trusted position, to address their concerns. Moreover, according to one community health worker, compared with nurses who have a more medicalised view of health, the community health workers swiftly address the social aspects of illness. In the following, my aim is to present the diversity and complexity of the social work and community work intervening; these are not officially included in community health workers programme goals, but community health workers in Chamanculo engaged in these regularly and recalled them in the interviews joyfully and with pride.

Finding support from the family

In the Chamanculo neighbourhoods, physical distance to health clinics is rarely the main problem in access to healthcare. Instead, the negative service experience and the feelings of not being heard and treated with respect were frequently mentioned. It is not uncommon that a patient checks-in at the hospital early in the morning and does not receive attention the same day. Within the context of restrained public resources in health and social services, it is unsurprising that community health workers, patients and family members dealt with social problems within the local community.

The stigma of communicable diseases, such as tuberculosis, is especially high. However, in Chamanculo, neighbours were suspicious also of people with non-communicable disease, disabilities or who were simply frail. The following is an illustration of how community health workers took the opportunity to raise awareness in the local community to reduce stigma on frailty in old age. They met an older woman with respect and affection, demanding others to do so as well. Helder says:

> 'There are those discriminating neighbours. Last week, I met a sick patient and took her home. She could not walk so I had to support her from the torso. So, people looked [at us] with that air of contempt. This lady said that if no one brings something to eat, she can spend two, three days without eating, but she was living with a family. But since that day I went [to her home] with her, I took advantage [of the situation] and educated the others who live there, and [one] Friday she said, "Thank you very much, son, since the day you came, I already have the right to breakfast and dinner. They already treat me well, already talk to me. At least in my social life I cannot complain."'

Repeatedly, community health workers tried to find material resources and support for patients and their families within their personal social networks. As Helder recounts, intervening in a situation in which an older woman did not receive food from her family sometimes for days, seemed rather easy; community health workers visited, discussed the issue with the family and family members easily changed their behaviour towards the woman, and attended to her needs.

In another example, community health workers worked with a young man who could not adhere to HIV medication because he did not have enough to eat to regularly take the medication. Studies have suggested that antiretroviral treatment (ART) can cause hunger – or make it feel worse than usual (Kalofonos, 2010). The adolescent explained his difficult family relations to the community health workers who started mapping his personal network to find sources of support. Mónica describes the conflict in the family: "[He] undergoes treatment but he abandoned the treatment simply because … the stepfather does not let him have meals properly because he says he is not his son so practically there is no way to take the medicine." Mónica continues to explain how they advised him to rely on extended family, particularly his grandmother who could offer her grandson extra meals on a regular basis:

> 'Once he said he had a grandmother close by, we educated him to go grandma and explain to grandma [imitates what he would say] … It was what we left to him [as an advice]. Stopping the medication is not the solution either, not taking medication practically means dying; that is, killing yourself personally.'

Suppose one did not have 'anyone'? In Chamanculo, there is a local helping system in place. Support organised by the *chefe do quarteirão* (a local leader voted to look after what is happening in the quarter) could be utilised by the community health workers if it turned out that a patient lacked established social support networks for material support. *Chefe do quarteirão* collected, for example, handouts from neighbours for funeral costs, if a family could not arrange a funeral. First, however, families in need turned to closest neighbours.

Helping structures in shared living environments

In Chamanculo, at every turn, I was told that one should regard their neighbours as their 'closest family', because the actual family often lived far away in rural areas. This thinking was visible in moral codes of helping one's neighbour, which community health workers – as Indigenous to the communities – knew and could utilise to the benefit of patients and their families.

As in other peri-urban neighbourhoods, Chamanculo consists of shared living spaces like small yards and compound living; social life is organised on levels of physical proximity. Households may comprise many families, or families may live in separate households. Compounds with many households in a small living space, with shared yards, are common. In the fieldwork I wondered whether living physically close to another family had any effect on relationship building and interactions. The closest circle of family and neighbours, however, often failed to meet the needs of the patients. This was especially difficult with stigmatised illnesses, such as HIV/AIDS and tuberculosis. Miguel tells the story of a single-parenting father who fell ill and was rejected by his brothers living in the same compound. Then community health workers lectured the brothers and others living within the compound, on community norms of helping the person and his children:

> 'So, we had to intervene in the way [of] talking with the family, with the brothers also, in the way that [we explained] that the patient there could be any one of them ... So, we talked to the brothers, agreed with the brothers that from their necessities they should support that person. He is not in that condition because he wants. Life put him there. They who left the same womb [need to] help him out of these conditions. But not only [did we talk] with the brothers but also the neighbours. We talked to all the neighbours to say, "Look, you must do something to help him. It doesn't have to be much."'

The closest neighbours living in the compound organised themselves to provide food for the family – one offering rice, another salt and oil, and other food products, so that the children could leave the hazardous working conditions of the streets of the city centre since, following their father's illness, they had started to collect plastic to support their family. The father recovered from the illness and the family's life returned to as it was, thanks to the help from the closest neighbours. In a way, neighbours are the 'the closest family' that can help in times of crisis – but in times of prolonged illness or social problems the support systems may fail, leaving families in need of outside help in rebuilding the relationships of reciprocity.

Lessons from Mozambique: unravelling skills hierarchies of social service professions

Social work in Africa has been criticised for it does not mirror the needs of the local people (for example, Mathebane, 2020), which, I argue, is partly due to the exclusion of non-professionals' caring, helping and social interventions from the professionalised ideal of social work practice. While this chapter promotes lay practitioner involvement in social work, advances in state-directed social services and higher education in social work are desired in Mozambique, and in similar contexts, where few social workers are trained and employed. Still, the need for qualified social workers with bachelor's degrees should not delimit what social work can be. As Cox and Pawar (2012) note, social work may become a lost profession, easily replaced by other, more 'flexible' professions if (paraprofessional) training does not adapt to local needs.

In concurrence, this chapter demonstrates that community health workers bring immense potential to social work through their personal ties, ideas of closeness and reciprocity, and community leadership, which all deviate from mainstream ideas of professionalism. This deviation from what is generally considered as 'professional', I argue, adds to community acceptance of and the feasibility of the community health workers programmes. Even in Nordic country contexts, community health workers as members of the local community, which they serve, could work alongside qualified social workers to establish strong links between health and social problems – promoting culturally relevant practices that recognise and therefore rely on, and compensate fairly, community health workers as peers, equals and as 'insiders'.

Adapting community health work to the context of Nordic countries through paraprofessional training and volunteering could enrich community-based social work practice. Community health workers can intervene in community dysfunction, family disputes and social problems, such as substance abuse (Glenton and Javadi, 2014). They do not only provide auxiliary health services, such as health promotion, nor only tackle barriers to care; they can also, potentially, help build social networks and trust in local communities (Nxumalo et al, 2016). In Finland, community health workers were employed in local communities in the North Karelia project in 1972–97 as opinion leaders and unpaid volunteers to deliver health promotion on cardiovascular health (McAlister et al, 1982; Kottke et al, 1984). The goal in framing Mozambican community health work as social intervening and problem-solving is to enrich community-based social work practices currently on the margins of social work in Nordic countries, yet that do exist (see, for example, Roivainen, 2004).

In the practical sense, decolonising Nordic social work practices entails revitalising community-based social work, perhaps following the community volunteering models of the established public health interventions of the North Karelia project – but this time setting social work aims and goals to substitute health promotion. Some models exist globally, such as the South African social auxiliary workers programmes, to employ paraprofessional (see, for example, Zibengwa and Bila, 2021), but until now, the engagement of Indigenous community volunteers in social services has not been widely researched or tested in practice. The decolonised model of community engagement proposed here would tap into the primary skills – the neighbourly relationship building, conflict mediation skills and insights into health disparities and signs of social distress – that community health workers can put forward in partnerships with professionally trained social workers. More research is needed to determine whether social work-focused supervision and training could also support community health workers in their current practice globally to address health through its social determinants.

Conclusion: towards post-professionalisation

Post-professionalisation – or the full-scale reshaping of the modernist ideas about professionalism (Kritzer, 1999), which started during the second half of the 20th century – challenges social work's expert knowledge, professional status and practitioners' authority over clients (see Randall and Kindiak, 2008) unravelling skill hierarchies in the society (Derber et al, 1990). The reframing and reimagining of Mozambican community health work as social intervention work, which is suggested in this chapter, is compatible with the post-professional push towards inventing professions anew. New forms of social work professionalism rise continuously in the Global South and in the peripheral North. I suggest in this chapter that the involvement of community members in social work should be encouraged. This inclusion of lay people in a more community-driven social work could be seen as a form of Indigenous, popular and culturally relevant social work. Mozambican peri-urban community work may function as an illustration of such efforts to include previously othered community interventions by lay people and paraprofessionals within the scope of social work. If community health workers' practice is labelled as (paraprofessional) social work, their efforts at social intervening may be better noticed and appreciated. Partnerships between community health workers, programme management and paraprofessional education in social work should be further developed to explore the potential of lay practitioner-led community interventions.

Notes

[1] All interviews were conducted in Portuguese, and all interlocutors were local residents of Chamanculo neighbourhoods employed as community health volunteers. Pseudonyms are used throughout the chapter.

[2] Meticals are converted to US dollars based on the exchange rate of January 2021.

References

Andrade, R.G. and Iriart, J.A.B. (2015) 'Estigma e discriminação: experiências de mulheres HIV positivo nos bairros populares de Maputo, Moçambique', *Cadernos de Saúde Pública*, 31(3): 565–74.

Burns, E.A. (2019) *Theorising Professions: A Sociological Introduction*, Cham: Palgrave Macmillan.

Cox, D.R. and Pawar, M. (2012) *International Social Work: Issues, Strategies, and Programs*, California: SAGE.

Derber, C., Schwartz, W.A. and Magrass, Y. (1990) *Power in the Highest Degree: Professionals and the Rise of a New Mandarin Order*, New York: Oxford University Press.

Dominelli, L. and Hoogvelt, A. (1996) 'Globalization and the technocratization of social work', *Critical Social Policy*, 16(47): 45–62.

Etzioni, A. (1969) *The Semi-Professions and Their Organization: Teachers, Nurses, Social Workers*, New York: Free Press.

Fielding, S.L. (2016) 'Empowerment evaluation, postprofessionalization, and oligarchy: a retrospective', *Journal of Applied Social Science*, 10(1): 44–54.

García-Basteiro, A.L., Ribeiro, R.M., Brew, J., Sacoor, C., Valencia, S., Bulo, H. et al (2017) 'Tuberculosis on the rise in southern Mozambique (1997–2012)', *European Respiratory Journal*, 49(3).

Give, C., Ndima, S., Steege, R., Ormel, H., McCollum, R., Theobald, S. et al (2019) 'Strengthening referral systems in community health programs: a qualitative study in two rural districts of Maputo Province, Mozambique', *BMC Health Services Research*, 19(1): 263.

Glenton, C. and Javadi, D. (2014) 'Community health worker roles and tasks', in H. Perry, L. Crigler and S. Hodgins (eds) *Developing and Strengthening Community Health Worker Programs at Scale: a Reference Guide and Case Studies for Program Managers and Policymakers*, USAID Maternal and Child Health Integrated Program. https://www.mchip.net/sites/default/files/mchipfiles/MCHIP_CHW%20Ref%20Guide.pdf

Halmos, P. (1965) *The Faith of the Counsellors*, London: Constable.

Hansen, K.T. and Vaa, M. (2004) *Reconsidering Informality: Perspectives from Urban Africa*, Uppsala: Nordic Africa Institute. http://urn.kb.se/resolve?urn=urn:nbn:se:nai:diva-103

Haug, M.R. (1972) 'Deprofessionalization: an alternate hypothesis for the future', *Sociological Review*, 20(1), 195–211.

Källander, K., Counihan, H., Cerveau, T. and Mbofana, F. (2019) 'Barriers on the pathway to survival for children dying from treatable illnesses in Inhambane province, Mozambique', *Journal of Global Health*, 9(1): 010809.

Kalofonos, I.A. (2010) 'All I eat is ARVs', *Medical Anthropology Quarterly*, 24(3): 363–80.

Kottke, T.E., Nissinen, A., Puska, P., Salonen, J.T. and Tuomilehto, J. (1984) 'Message dissemination for a community-based cardiovascular disease prevention programme (the North Karelia Project)', *Scandinavian Journal of Primary Health Care*, 2(3): 99–104.

Kritzer, H.M. (1999) 'The professions are dead, long live the professions: legal practice in a postprofessional world', *Law & Society Review*, 33(3): 713–59.

Lavalette, M. (2015) 'Once more on "popular social work": a reply to Des McDermott', *Critical and Radical Social Work; Bristol*, 3(3): 425–31.

Lavalette, M. and Ioakimidis, V. (2011) 'International social work or social work internationalism? Radical social work in global perspective', in M. Lavalette (ed) *Radical Social Work Today: Social Work at the Crossroads*, Bristol: Bristol University Press, pp 135–52.

Lavalette, M. and Ioakimidis, V. (2017) '"Popular" social work in extremis: two case studies on collective welfare responses to social crisis situations', *Social Theory, Empirics, Policy and Practice*, 13(2016): 117–32.

Linsk, N., Mabeyo, Z., Omari, L., Petras, D., Lubin, B., Assefa, A. et al (2010) 'Para-social work to address most vulnerable children in sub-Sahara Africa: a case example in Tanzania', *Children and Youth Services Review*, 32: 990–7.

Logan, R.I. (2020) '"A poverty in understanding": assessing the structural challenges experienced by community health workers and their clients', *Global Public Health*, 15(1): 137–50.

Lu, J.J., D'Angelo, K.A., Kuoch, T. and Scully, M. (2018) 'Honouring the role of community in community health work with Cambodian Americans', *Health and Social Care in the Community*, 26(6): 882–90.

Macuácua, S., Catalão, R., Sharma, S., Valá, A., Vidler, M., Macete, E. et al [The CLIP Working Group] (2019) 'Policy review on the management of pre-eclampsia and eclampsia by community health workers in Mozambique', *Human Resources for Health*, 17(1): 15.

Mathebane, M.S. (2020) 'Quizzing the "social" in social work: social work in Africa as a system of colonial social control', *Journal of Progressive Human Services*, 31(2): 77–92.

Matthew, R.A., Willms, L., Voravudhi, A., Smithwick, J., Jennings, P. and Machado-Escudero, Y. (2017) 'Advocates for community health and social justice: a case example of a multisystemic promotores organization in South Carolina', *Journal of Community Practice*, 25(3–4): 344–64.

McAlister, A., Puska, P., Salonen, J.T., Tuomilehto, J. and Koskela, K. (1982) 'Theory and action for health promotion illustrations from the North Karelia Project', *American Journal of Public Health*, 72(1): 43–50.

McDermott, D. (2014) 'The two souls of social work: exploring the roots of "popular social work" – popular or radical social work?', *Critical and Radical Social Work*, 2(3): 381–3.

Mlotshwa, L., Harris, B., Schneider, H. and Moshabela, M. (2015) 'Exploring the perceptions and experiences of community health workers using role identity theory', *Global Health Action*, 8(1).

Muula, A., Hofman, J. and Cumberland, M. (2006) 'What motivates community health volunteers in Mecanhelas district, Mozambique? Report from a qualitative study', *Ghana Medical Journal*, 38(1): 24–7.

Nading, A.M. (2013) '"Love isn't there in your stomach": a moral economy of medical citizenship among Nicaraguan community health workers', *Medical Anthropology Quarterly*, 27(1): 84–102.

Nxumalo, N., Goudge, J. and Manderson, L. (2016) 'Community health workers, recipients' experiences and constraints to care in South Africa: a pathway to trust', *AIDS Care*, 28(4): 61–71.

Oppenheimer, M. (1972) 'The proletarianization of the professional', *The Sociological Review*, 20(S1): 213–27.

Payne, M. (2015) *What Is Professional Social Work?* (2nd edn), Bristol: Policy Press.

Randall, G.E. and Kindiak, D.H. (2008) 'Deprofessionalization or postprofessionalization? Reflections on the state of social work as a profession', *Social Work in Health Care*, 47(4): 341–54.

Ranta-Tyrkkö, S. (2011) 'High time for postcolonial analysis in social work', *Nordic Social Work Research*, 1(1): 25–41.

Roivainen, I. (2004) 'Local communities as a field of community social work: Nordic community work from the perspective of Finnish community-based social work', *Nordisk Socialt Arbeid*, 24(3): 194–206.

Rustagi, A.S., Manjate, R.M., Gloyd, S., John-Stewart, G., Micek, M., Gimbel, S. et al (2015) 'Perspectives of key stakeholders regarding task shifting of care for HIV patients in Mozambique: a qualitative interview-based study with Ministry of Health leaders, clinicians, and donors', *Human Resources for Health*, 13(1): 18.

Scott, K. and Shanker, S. (2010) 'Tying their hands? Institutional obstacles to the success of the ASHA community health worker programme in rural north India', *AIDS Care*, 22(2): 1606–12.

Sewpaul, V. (2010) 'Professionalism, postmodern ethics and the global standards for social work education and training', *Social Work/Maatskaplike Werk*, 46(3): Article 3.

Sewpaul, V. and Henrickson, M. (2019) 'The (r)evolution and decolonization of social work ethics: the global social work statement of ethical principles', *International Social Work*, 62(6): 1469–81.

Spencer, M.S., Gunter, K.E. and Palmisano, G. (2010) 'Community health workers and their value to social work', *Social Work*, 55(2): 169–80.

TENK (2019) *TENK Guidelines | TENK*. www.tenk.fi/en/tenk-guidelines

Toren, N. (1972) *Social Work: the Case of a Semi-Profession*, Beverly Hills, CA: Sage.

UNAIDS (2020) *Mozambique. Overview*. www.unaids.org/en/regionscountries/countries/mozambique

UN-HABITAT (2019) *UN-HABITAT County Programme Mozambique 2018–2021*. https://unhabitat.org/sites/default/files/documents/2019-05/hcpd_2019.pdf

Walt, G. (1990) *Just Another Pair of Hands: Community Health Workers*, Buckingham: Open University Press.

WHO (1989) *Strengthening the Performance of Community Health Workers in Primary Health Care: Report of a WHO Study Group [Meeting Held in Geneva from 2 to 9 December 1987]*. World Health Organization. https://apps.who.int/iris/handle/10665/39568

WHO (2011) *World Health Statistics 2011*. www.who.int/whosis/whostat/EN_WHS2011_Full.pdf

Zibengwa, E. and Bila, N.J. (2021) 'The roles of social auxiliary workers in drop-in-centres: addressing the biopsychosocial needs of children living with HIV', *Social Work*, 57(2): 193–213.

13

Decolonising mindfulness, mindful decolonisation and social work futurities

Michael Yellow Bird and Holly Hatton-Bowers

Wendell Bell (nd) is quoted saying that, 'The future, of course, is still being made: it is what people can shape and design through their own actions. To act intelligently, people need to know the consequences of these actions, of others' actions and reactions, and of forces beyond their control'. When we think of the future, we are challenged to consider how our actions and the consequences of our actions shape future generations. Futures studies focus on understanding possible, probable and preferred futures (Inayatullah, 2012). A goal of futurist scholars is to 'discover or invent, propose, examine and evaluate possible, probable, and preferable futures' (Bell, nd). As social workers, it is important that we understand that allowing the future to happen without our input and actions places us at the mercy of chance and a futurity of unpredictability, risk and lost opportunity. We live in a world that is deeply challenged by many existential threats. Our rabid partisan politics is driving greater divisions among us encouraging hate, mistrust and fear, while gender, sexual and racial violence continues unabated. Global poverty, hunger, disease and the lack of clean water, especially since the beginning of the COVID-19 pandemic, have demonstrated the sharp divisions between us and resulted in the disproportionate deaths of marginalised peoples. Our continued colonisation of the planet has pushed many species to the brink of extinction, upsetting the delicate balance between all creatures and ecological systems we depend on for life. Engaging in decolonisation is no longer an option, metaphor or abstraction; it is something that we must fiercely engage in if we want our future generations to survive the harm and suffering that we are collectively causing. Decolonisation is the dismantling of colonisation by understanding the extent to which we, and the world we live in, have been harmed, controlled and silenced by colonialism (Clarke and Yellow Bird, 2021). Perhaps there has never been such an urgent need as now for collective compassion, caring, truth-telling and '"praxis"—action and reflection upon the world in order to change it' (hooks, 1994: 14).

In this chapter we aim for Finnish social workers to understand the importance of mindfulness as a tool of healing and improving well-being. At the same time, we advocate for a decolonised approach when infusing mindfulness into education and practices for social workers. Much of mindfulness has been coopted by neoliberal forces that do not seek to address structural inequalities. Specifically we argue that (1) mainstream mindfulness interventions can support social work values and healing practices and that mindfulness helps heal and improve well-being; (2) mindfulness has also been coopted, privatised and colonised by the forces of neoliberal capitalism (Purser, 2019) and is being used to 'pacify feelings of anxiety and disquiet at the individual level rather than seeking to challenge the social, political, and economic inequalities that cause such distress' (Carrette and Kind, 2004: 22); and (3) mindfulness must be decolonised by moving towards a mindful decolonisation paradigm that uses mindfulness principles and frameworks but adds practices designed to engage practitioners in systems change. In the social work field, the forces of neoliberalism and colonialism have and continue to perpetuate a narrative of dehumanisation and violence for Indigenous and marginalised people (Sinclair, 2004; Gray et al, 2008; Midgely, 2011; Gray et al, 2013; Clarke and Yellow Bird, 2021). Mindful decolonisation can guide our efforts

> at rehumanizing the world, to breaking hierarchies of difference that dehumanise subjects and communities and that destroy nature, and to the production of counter-discourses, counter-knowledge, counter-creative acts, and counter-practices that seek to dismantle coloniality and to open up to multiple other forms of being in the world. (Maldonado-Torres, 2016: 10)

This understanding prepares us to cultivate and promote truth-telling, intelligent and calculated resistance, healing and planetary rebuilding (Clarke and Yellow Bird, 2021).

In the following sections, we begin by defining mindfulness, share some its benefits for individuals, groups and relationship building with the natural world, and present evidence of how mindfulness improves the health and well-being of social work students and professionals. We next discuss how mindfulness has been colonised and limited to individual healing and transformation rather than a force for systems change and how we believe that by adding principles and practices of mindful decolonisation it can serve as a vehicle for structural transformation. We conclude by sharing two mindful decolonisation meditation practices and future directions for mindful decolonisation and social work futurities.

What is mindfulness?

Mindfulness as a practice refers to maintaining present-moment awareness, presence of mind and wakefulness (Goldstein, 2013). It is a way of intentionally and non-judgementally directing our attention to what's happening, what we are doing, to be curious and give ourselves permission to live fully and completely in the present moment (Kabat-Zinn, 1990). Many people practise mindfulness to become more present, compassionate and less judgemental. Some practise to relieve their stress, quiet their fears and heal their traumas; others to enhance their personal potential or become mindfulness teachers (Yellow Bird et al, 2020). Staying in the present moment helps to reduce stress, harmful rumination and distraction while increasing our awareness that can soothe knee-jerk responses and lead to calmer and kinder states (Purser, 2019). Engaging in mindfulness practices involves maintaining a sense of compassion, interest, friendliness and openheartedness towards the experiences we are having whether they are pleasant or unfriendly (Kabat-Zinn, 2003). When we focus on our attention in this mindful way, we are also encouraged to refrain from self-judgement and judging others, to respond authentically and proactively instead of reacting and strengthen our connection to our core selves (Wagner, 2019). Being open and non-judgemental can help us see things in a more balanced way, be less critical and appreciate the strengths in others and the difficult lessons of life.

Mindfulness has its roots in Eastern spiritual traditions with many teachings and knowledge having been imparted by Gautama Buddha who was a spiritual teacher who lived in ancient India (c. 5th to 4th century BCE). However, mindfulness has also been a part of many Muslim, Christian, Jewish and Indigenous Peoples' spiritual traditions for thousands of years. Mindfulness has grown in popularity in the West and is practised to reduce suffering and promote well-being (Baer and Krietemeyer, 2006) and make our lives meaningful (Siegel, 2010). Schools, universities, hospitals, prisons, mental health clinics, military, police, small businesses and major corporations have integrated mindfulness into the work they do and the services they provide. Although reliable statistics are hard to find, it's generally estimated that between 200 and 500 million people around the world engage in meditative practices.

Mindfulness is practised as a way for practitioners to develop 'positive qualities such as awareness, insight, compassion, and equanimity' (Baer and Krietemeyer, 2006: 4). Empirical research finds there are many individual and interpersonal benefits to practising mindfulness. These benefits include higher self-compassion (Beshai et al, 2016), improved stress regulation (Heckenberg et al, 2018), reduced blood pressure (Pascoe et al, 2017), lower depressive symptoms (Ma et al, 2019), decreased anxiety (Zhou et al, 2020), healthy emotion regulation (Frank et al, 2015) and improved quality of life (Edwards, and Loprinzi, 2018). Mindfulness practices can also improve our relationship with and responsibility to the natural environment.

Historically, across difficult cultures humans have connected mindfully with nature to heal and cultivate physical, emotional and social well-being. As Van Gordon and colleagues (2018) write:

> We interexist with nature (and all other phenomena) to the extent that it is impossible to assign boundaries. Our minds and bodies are embedded within the natural world such that when we breathe in, nature breathes in with us, and when we breathe out, nature also breathes out. We are of the nature of nature; it exists in us and we exist in it. (2018: 1655)

Moreover, 'the cultivation of mindfulness and nature connectedness can help to ensure that the symbiotic relationship we create with nature is one that is mutually beneficial, rather than mutually destructive' (2018: 1658). A recent critical review of the empirical research describes how mindfulness is associated with sustainability, prosocial environmental behaviours and connectedness with nature (Thierman and Sheate, 2021); however, the research examining mindfulness practices and nature as a way for societal transformation is just emerging and will benefit from a mindful decolonisation approach.

In part the previously described benefits emerge from practising mindfulness meditation. Sogyal Rinpoche (1992: 61) says practising mindfulness meditation accomplishes three things: (1) 'all the fragmented parts of ourselves, which have been at war, settle down and dissolve and become friends' and 'in that settling we begin to understand ourselves more and sometimes have glimpse of the radiance of our fundamental nature'; (2) it 'defuses our negativity, aggression, and turbulent emotions, which have been gathering power over many lifetimes'; and (3) it 'unveils and reveals your essential Good Heart, because it dissolves and removes the unkindness or the harm in you. Only when we have removed the harm in ourselves do we become truly useful to others.' In other words, practising mindfulness meditation can support our personal, interpersonal and collective well-being.

One of the ways that empirical research is used to demonstrate the effectiveness of mindfulness meditation is through neuroscience, which shows positive benefits for brain health. Some research finds changes in areas of the brain involved in attention (Yakobi, Smilek and Danckert, 2021) self-awareness, self-regulation, memory and executive functioning (Boccia, Piccardi and Guariglia, 2015). A recent meta-analysis reported that meditation was associated with structural changes to grey matter, which is involved in neural plasticity; however, the authors cautioned that additional longitudinal data are needed along with larger samples and more rigorous study designs (Pernet et al, 2021). In a recent study of people participating in an eight-week mindfulness intervention, neuroplastic brain changes were not evident (Kral et al, 2021). However, previous research finds that longer-term meditators have different changes in emotional parts of the brain compared with beginning meditators. Expert meditators show less activation in the amygdala than novice practitioners. The amygdala is the part of the brain associated with our fear, startle and freeze response, cortisol regulation and emotion-related behaviour (Ressler, 2010). This evidence suggests there is a 'dose-response effect' and that these eight-week interventions may not be long enough for these neurological changes to manifest (Goleman and Davidson, 2018).

Although limited, the emerging empirical research examining mindfulness among social work students and professionals finds promising evidence that mindfulness-based interventions are associated with personal and interpersonal aspects of well-being. Empirical research finds that mindfulness-based interventions are associated with reduced stress (Roulston et al, 2018; Maddock et al, 2021), promoting social worker well-being (for example, satisfaction, self-compassion; Roulston et al, 2018; Maddock et al, 2021) and emerging evidence that it can reduce implicit bias (Wong and Vinsky, 2021) and may promote anti-oppressive social work practices (Maddock et al, 2021). However, it is unknown how long these benefits are sustained, and greater attention is needed in how these practices are taught. Inclusion of self-compassion and compassion practices is often taught in these mindfulness-based interventions and may be a core aspect of supporting social worker well-being and their work.

Decolonising mindfulness

The individual and interpersonal benefits to those who practise the present secular Western forms of mindfulness are well established. However, many are now beginning to regard mindfulness in the same way that Karl Marx described religion, the 'opiate of the masses' (Turnbull and Dawson, 2006). Mindfulness critic David Forbes (2019) argues that Western secular mindfulness 'does not bring the self into question; it has no moral worldview; and it is not a soteriology – a way out of human suffering – just a way to help the self cope and adjust' (2019: 27). Mainstream mindfulness is also criticised for having been colonised and 'stripped of its history and cultural tradition' (Forbes, 2019: 24). To be inclusive, secular and more readily accepted by a Western audience, mindfulness often does not include spiritual practices (Forbes, 2019), nor does it focus on our need for constructive, critical and wise judgements about our responsibilities beyond ourselves. Although many individuals practise mindfulness meditation to feel calmer, more relaxed, to reduce anxiety and to regulate emotions more effectively; only a small number are reported to practise mindfulness for spiritual reasons (Pepping et al, 2016).

The predominant focus of teaching mindfulness to support individual well-being and stress reduction, although important, has limited the ways that mindfulness can lead to collective actions to bring about structural change by eliminating systemic bias and racism and the colonisation that has been perpetuated in the field of social work. As Stanley, Purser and Singh (2018) write: 'Critics of mindfulness contest the extent to which mindfulness, as a therapeutic or social movement, is a revolutionary force for individual awakening and liberation, or a conspiracy to enslave individuals to consumer capitalism, by making them individually responsible for their own suffering, distress, and well-being' (2018: 5). There are concerns that teaching mindfulness without explicit attention to the ethical and spiritual aspects of mindfulness may lead to people to simply learn to cope with systemic harm. Pursar (2019) writes: 'I am skeptical. Anything that offers success in our unjust society without trying to change it is not revolutionary – it just helps people cope' (2019: 7).

Decolonising mindfulness by intentionally including ethical principles and spirituality may be necessary for sustained systemic changes within the social work field. As Hanh (2013: 56–7) writes:

> There is a revolution that needs to happen, and it starts from inside each one of us. When we change the way we see the world, when we realise that we and the Earth are one and we begin to live with mindfulness, our own suffering will start to ease. When we're no longer overwhelmed by our own suffering, we will have the compassion and understanding to treat the Earth with love and respect. Restoring balance to ourselves, we can begin the work of restoring balance to the Earth ... There is no difference between healing the planet and healing ourselves.

When one begins to practise mindfulness with acknowledgement of our interdependence with all living things, then true healing can occur.

Additionally, practices acknowledging how historical violence and harmful social work interventions have contributed to Black, Indigenous and People of Colour (BIPOC) lives is challenging, often painful work, but also important for healing and change. We need compassionate awareness and action to be able to deeply commit to our work to look inwards and outwards as, 'Many of us feel the pain in our hearts, spirits, and bodies, and suffer with those who are most directly harmed, but as we deepen our capacity for mindful inquiry, we experience more than empathy and compassion' (Magee, 2019: 295).

The following are ways that we can begin to actively engage in decolonising mindfulness in social work: (a) Regard mindfulness as an effective approach that can be used to reduce individual suffering and improve personal well-being and understand that mindfulness can and should be much more; (b) study how the appropriation, commodification and colonisation by neoliberal forces market mindfulness for profit and self-care rather than a tool for decolonisation and resistance; (c) examine the colonisation of social work, the historical and current traumas resulting from colonisation, and use mindfulness practices to engage in reflection and compassionate exploration of how to heal and contribute to systemic change; (d) incorporate decolonised mindfulness practices to fit the cultural and diverse needs of students and communities to facilitate learning, growth, compassion and action. Students and communities should work together to co-create the mindfulness practices that reflect their own cultures, identities and need for change; (e) train social workers to develop their own decolonised mindfulness methodologies and practices to use in their own personal and professional development; and finally, (f) re-incorporate spirituality into mindfulness practices to help students 'seek and express meaning and purpose in their lives and the way they experience their connectedness to the moment, to self, to others, to nature, and to the significant or sacred' (Puchalski et al, 2014: 643).

Social work professor Edward Canda and colleagues (2019: 3) believe that 'spirituality is the heart of helping. It is the heart of empathy and care, the pulse of empathy of compassion, the vital flow of practice wisdom, and the driving energy of service'. Intentionally engaging in the spirituality of mindfulness engages the mind–body–spirit connection for seeing our interdependence and can lead to making wise judgements in the present and for the future.

Mindful decolonisation and social work futurities

> What will the future bring to the field of social work? Futurists argue that our future, 'largely depends on the choices that people make and the actions they take today' and that our wise judgements are informed by 'systematically studying possible, probable, and preferable futures' (Bell, nd) and 'in order for decolonisation to be successful it must begin in our minds'.
>
> (Yellow Bird, 2013: 293)

As we consider the future of social work, we must challenge ourselves to reflect, discuss and identify the best ways to create our desired future. We can begin this journey with mindful decolonisation, which is an important futurist social work paradigm that uses decolonised mindfulness meditation practices to confront and dismantle the destructive and unsustainable processes, effects and structures of colonialism. Such an approach aligns with the Finnish Social Welfare Act of 2015 which challenges social work education, research and practice to 'enact structural social work and address community – and structural-level social issues beyond individual cases' (Matthies, 2022). Decolonising mindfulness approaches seek to bring about the social-justice thinking, policies and practices needed to foster and put into place such structural and community changes.

How can decolonising mindfulness in Finnish social work happen? In educational settings, such as schools and universities, curricula can include mindfulness practices as a way to be more present, open and aware in learning about the ancestral harms that are often perpetuated in the social work field and engage in truth-telling. For example, there could be a better understanding of how children have been removed from families due to not fitting into normative cultural beliefs and identities. In practice settings, social workers can engage in mindful decolonisation practices to build on the strengths of individuals and communities, promote emotional and social intelligence, strengthen emotional and behavioural regulation and enhance personal and societal activism and resilience. Mindful decolonisation uses mindfulness principles and frameworks but adds practices designed to engage practitioners in *systems thinking and change*. It allows and encourages constructive and wise judgements of what has happened, what is happening and what will happen to help practitioners develop a sense of concern and responsibility to change the things we can change. Our encouragement of engaging in these wise judgements can broaden our mindfulness practices not only for individual health and well-being, but also to understand how these wise judgements affect others and solidify our commitment to be good ancestors to future generations.

Begin today to prepare for tomorrow

As a way to begin engaging in mindful decolonisation we offer the two mindful decolonisation sitting practices (Yellow Bird, 2021). These practices can be used for self-care, to promote well-being and inspire optimism for social workers involved in the struggle for individual, community and societal compassion, justice and healing. It's important to remember to bring a sense of curiosity, openness and hopefulness as you do these practices. The framework of these practices is adapted from a core Buddhist meditation practice called *Anapanasati*, meaning 'mindfulness of breathing'.

A. Observing and confronting colonisation practices

	In-breath	Out-breath
1.	Seeing the colonisation of the mind Shortened to (Colonised mind)	Teaching liberation Shortened to (Liberation)
2.	Experiencing colonised emotions (Colonised emotions)	Releasing unskilled emotions (Releasing emotions)
3.	Awakening to systemic oppression (Systemic oppression)	Dismantling domination (Dismantling)

	In-breath	Out-breath
4.	Establishing myself among the ruins of colonisation (Ruins)	Rebuilding the destruction caused by colonisation (Rebuilding)

Instructions: To begin with this mindfulness practice it is important to remember that attitude is everything. The Buddha once said, "what you think you become". Therefore, it is important to understand that in this practice you are putting yourself in a frame of mind to open up and invite yourself to *see, analyse and confront colonisation* through your social work practice. If any thoughts, emotions or images arise during this meditation that are overwhelming, you can choose to stand and feel the sensations of your feet on the floor.

Setting your intentions. Please find a comfortable sitting position. Relax your body, sit up straight, lay your hands on your lap, gently lower your gaze or close your eyes and silently and mindfully repeat to yourself, three or four times: "*I am meditating in order to decolonise all oppressive systems to end the suffering of all sentient beings*". You can later change your affirmation to better reflect how you see yourself engaging in systems change. When you have finished your affirmation, begin focusing on your breath and relax any tension you have in your body. As you breathe in and out, spend several minutes focusing on your breath, the content in your mind and any feelings or emotions that are arising. Allow them to pass and continue watching your in-breath as it enters your nostrils and circulates throughout your body and leaves on the out-breath.

Observing colonisation. When you are ready, and using your own language, on your in-breath silently say to yourself "*seeing the colonisation of the mind*". This phrase is intended to help you understand how your, or any mind, can be colonised by external forces. On the out-breath silently say to yourself "*teaching liberation*". This phrase refers to liberating your mind from colonised, unhelpful thinking. On the in-breath repeat to yourself "*experiencing colonised emotions*". This wording may allow you to experience colonised emotions such as fear, self-doubt, inferiority, anger or others that have been imposed upon by external colonising forces. On the out-breath say to yourself "*releasing unskilled emotions*", which allows you to give back the emotions that are not of your making. Pause and, if needed, repeat this phrase a few times. If your emotions are overwhelming, you may want to stand. Feel the sensations of your feet on the floor. As you stand notice that you are safe and have the support of your breath, the ground and your surroundings. Take a few deep breaths and notice the strength that is within you.

Confronting colonisation. Now breathe in and on the out-breath silently say, "*awaking to systemic oppression*", which is meant to widen your understanding of the harms created by colonising systems. Breathe in again and on the out-breath silently say, "*dismantling domination*". In saying this phrase, you are awakening the ways you might go about undoing the colonisation of dominating structures. Breathe in again and on the out-breath silently say, "*establishing myself among the ruins of colonisation*", which refers to mindfully locating yourself in the struggles of marginalised and oppressed groups, and now breathe in again and on the out-breath silently say, "*rebuilding the destruction caused by colonisation*", which refers to working directly with communities using mindful decolonisation practices to transform society. All the previously mentioned phrases can be shortened once you learn and integrate the meaning into this meditation practice.

Reflection

This meditation can be deeply moving so it may be helpful to take a minute to settle in a moment of silence. For many of us, we may experience difficult, painful and challenging feelings. We may also experience feelings of strength and feel grounded to confront colonialism. After settling, note what emotions, thoughts and sensations came up for you. It can be helpful to write or draw what came up for you during this practice.

B. Fierce loving-kindness practices

1. May I thrive with ease in the struggle for change.
2. May I embody courage and action in the face of fear/uncertainty.
3. May I find serenity in resistance.
4. May I find satisfaction in my pursuit of justice.

Instructions: First identify and repeat your affirmations (3–4 times) of why you are doing this practice: "*I am meditating in order to increase my positive energy to take care of myself in order to do this work.*" In a comfortable sitting position bring awareness to your body, mind and the emotions you are feeling, allowing yourself to acknowledge and release them. It may be helpful to breathe in the feelings and on the out-breath silently say, "*let go*".

Giving myself fierce loving-kindness. Begin by taking a few deep breaths and try and let your mind rest on the sensations of breathing in and out. If it is helpful gently close your eyes or lower your gaze. Now, silently repeat each of the previously mentioned phrases as you breathe in and out.

Reflection

When you have finished both practices, share your experience. If you are in a group setting, share with those who are practising with you. Some questions to reflect upon are: What did it feel like to do the exercises? What came up for you? Do you think the practices can help prepare you to engage in more strategic, compassionate and fervent decolonisation activities? How might you teach these practices to the people and communities you work with? What habits, behaviours or conditioning do you need to move past or break through to be of great service in your work, your communities and to the planet?

References

Baer, R.A and Krietemeyer, J. (2006) 'Overview of mindfulness- and acceptance-based treatment approaches', in R.A. Baer (ed) *Mindfulness-based Treatment Approaches: Clinician's Guide to Evidence Base and Applications*, London: Academic Press, pp 3–27.

Beshai, S., McAlpine, L., Weare, K. and Kuyken, W. (2016) 'A non-randomised feasibility trial assessing the efficacy of a mindfulness-based intervention for teachers to reduce stress and improve well-being', *Mindfulness*, 7: 198–208.

Boccia, M., Piccardi, L. and Guariglia, P. (2015) 'The meditative mind: a comprehensive meta-analysis of MRI studies', *BioMed Research International*, 419808.

Canda, E.R., Furman, L. D. and Canda, H.-J. (2019) *Spiritual Diversity in Social Work Practice: the Heart of Helping* (3rd edn), Oxford and New York: Oxford University Press.

Carrette, J. and King, R. (2004) *Selling Spirituality: The Silent Takeover of Religion*, London: Routledge.

Clarke, K., and Yellow Bird, M. (2021) *Decolonizing Pathways Towards Integrative Healing in Social Work*, London: Taylor and Francis.

Edwards, M.K. and Loprinzi, P.D. (2018) 'Comparative effects of meditation and exercise on physical and psychosocial health outcomes: a review of randomized controlled trials', *Postgraduate Medicine*, 130(2): 222–8.

Forbes, D. (2019) *Mindfulness and its Discontents: Education, Self, and Social Transformation*, Halifax, Canada: Fernwood Publishing.

Frank, J.L., Reibel, D., Broderick, P., Cantrell, T. and Metz, S. (2015) 'The effectiveness of mindfulness-based stress reduction on educator stress and well-being: results from a pilot study', *Mindfulness*, 6: 208–16.

Goldstein, J. (2013) *Mindfulness: a Practical Guide to Awakening*, Boulder, CO: Sounds True.

Goleman, D. and Davidson, R.J. (2018) *Altered Traits: Science Reveals How Meditation Changes Your Mind, Brain, and Body*, New York: Penguin.

Gray, M., Coates, J. and Hetherington, T. (2013) *Environmental Social Work*, Abingdon: Routledge.

Gray, M., Coates, J. and Yellow Bird, M. (eds) (2008) *Indigenous Social Work Around the World: Towards Culturally Relevant Education and Practice*, Aldershot: Ashgate.

Hanh, T.N. (2013) *Love Letter to the Earth*, Berkeley, CA: Parallax Press.

Heckenberg, R.A., Eddy, P., Kent, S. and Wright, B.J. (2018) 'Do workplace-based mindfulness meditation programs improve physiological indices of stress? A systematic review and meta-analysis', *Journal of Psychosomatic Research*, 114: 62–71.

hooks, b. (1994) *Teaching to Transgress: Education as the Practice of Freedom*, New York, NY: Routledge.

Inayatullah, S. (2013) 'Futures studies: theories and methods', *There's a Future: Visions for a Better World*, 36–66.

Kabat-Zinn, J. (1990) *Full Catastrophe Living*, New York, NY: Delacorte Press.

Kabat-Zinn, J. (2003) 'Mindfulness-based interventions in context: past, present, and future', *Clinical Psychology: Science and Practice*, 10: 144–56.

Kral, T., Davis, K., Koronay, C., Hirshberg, M.J, Hoel, R., Tello, L.Y. et al (2021) 'Non-replication of structural brain changes from mindfulness-based stress reductio: two combined randomized control trials', *medRxiv*, 21258762.

Ma, L., Zhang, Y. and Cui, Z. (2019) 'Mindfulness-based interventions for prevention of depressive symptoms in university students: a meta-analytic review', *Mindfulness*, 10: 2209–24.

Maddock, A., Mccusker, P, Blair, C. and Roulston, A. (2021) 'The mindfulness-based social work and self-care programme: a mixed methods evaluation study', *British Journal of Social Work*, 00: 1–18.

Magee, R.V. (2019) *The Inner Work of Racial Justice: Healing Ourselves and Transforming Our Communities Through Mindfulness*, Canada: Penguin.

Maldonado-Torres, N. (2016) 'Outline of ten theses on coloniality and decoloniality', *Fondation Frantz Fanon*, [online]. http://frantzfanonfoundation-fondationfrantzfanon.com/article2360.html

Matthies, A. (2022) 'Next-generation modelling of community work and structural social work in Finland', *Nordic Social Work Research*, 12(2): 229–42.

Midgley, J. (2011) 'Imperialism, colonialism and social welfare', in *Colonialism and Welfare*, Cheltenham: Edward Elgar.

Pascoe, M.C., Thompson, D.R., Jenkins, Z.M. and Ski, C.F. (2017) 'Mindfulness mediates the physiological markers of stress: systematic review and meta-analysis', *Journal of Psychiatric Research*, 95: 156–78.

Pepping, C., Walters, B., Davis, P. and O'Donovan, A. (2016) 'Why do people practice mindfulness? An investigation into reasons for practicing mindfulness meditation', *Mindfulness*, 7: 542–7.

Pernet, C.R., Belov, N., Delorme, A. and Zammit, A. (2021) 'Mindfulness related changes in grey matter: a systematic review and meta-analysis', *Brain Imaging and Behavior*, 15: 2720–30.

Puchalski, C.M., Blatt, B., Kogan, M. and Butler, A. (2014) 'Spirituality and health: the development of a field', *Academic Medicine*, 89(1): 10–16.

Purser, R. (2019) *McMindfulness: How Mindfulness Became the New Capitalist Spirituality*, London: Repeater.

Ressler, K.J. (2010) 'Amygdala activity, fear, and anxiety: modulation by stress', *Biological Psychiatry*, 67(12): 1117–19.

Rinpoche, S. (1992) *The Tibetan Book of Living and Dying*, in P. Gaffney and A. Harvey (eds) San Francisco, CA: Harper San Francisco.

Roulston, A., Montgomery, L., Campbell, A. and Davidson, G. (2018) 'Exploring the impact of mindfulness on mental wellbeing, stress and resilience of undergraduate social work students', *Social Work Education*, 37(2): 157–72.

Siegel, D.J. (2010) *Mindsight: the New Science of Personal Transformation*, New York: Bantam.

Sinclair, R. (2004) 'Aboriginal social work education in Canada: decolonizing pedagogy for the seventh generation', *First Peoples Child and Family Review: A Journal on Innovation and Best Practices in Aboriginal Child Welfare Administration, Research, Policy and Practice*, 1(1): 49–61.

Stanley S., Purser R.E. and Singh N.N. (2018) 'Ethical foundations of mindfulness', in S. Stanley, R. Purser and N. Singh (eds) *Handbook of Ethical Foundations of Mindfulness: Mindfulness in Behavioral Health*, Cham: Springer.

Thiermann, U.B. and Sheate, W.R. (2021) 'The way forward in mindfulness and sustainability: a critical review and research agenda', *Journal of Cognitive Enhancement*, 5(1): 118–39.

Turnbull, L. and Dawson, G. (2006) 'Is mindfulness the new opiate of the masses? Critical reflections from a Buddhist perspective', *Psychology in Australia*, 12(4): 60–4.

Van Gordon, W., Shonin, E. and Richardson, M. (2018) 'Mindfulness and nature', *Mindfulness*, 9: 1655–8.

Wagner, P. (2019) 'Meditation and mindfulness: methods for lasting peace', *Gaia*, [online]. www.gaia.com/article/meditation-vs-mindfulness-methods-mindsets-for-lastingpeace?gclid=EAIaIQobChMIkda1m9rc9AIVD4nICh14PgudEAAYASAAEgKApfD_BwE

Wong, Y-L.R. and Vinsky, J. (2021) 'Beyond implicit bias: embodied cognition, mindfulness, and critical reflective practice in social work', *Australian Social Work*, 74(2): 186–97.

Yakobi, O., Smilek, D. and Danckert, J. (2021) 'The effects of mindfulness meditation on attention, executive control and working memory in healthy adults: a meta-analysis of randomized controlled trials', *Cognitive Therapy and Research*, 45(44): 543–60.

Yellow Bird, M. (2013) 'Neurodecolonization: using mindfulness practices to delete the neural networks of colonialism', in *For Indigenous Minds Only: a Decolonization Handbook*, Waziyatawin and M. Yellow Bird (eds) Santa Fe, NM: School for Advanced Research Press.

Yellow Bird, M. (2021) 'Siíŝu' tooxuun awi'ooxiik (the mind that is calm is beautiful): an Arikara mindfulness curriculum for youth', *Engaged Mindfulness Teacher and Facilitator Training Course*, Deerfield, MA: Engaged Mindfulness Institute.

Yellow Bird, M., Gehl, M., Hatton-Bowers, H., Hicks, L.M. and Reno-Smith. D. (2020) 'Defunding mindfulness: while we sit on our cushions systemic racism runs rampant', *Zero to Three Journal*. https://www.zerotothree.org/resource/journal/perspectives-defunding-mindfulness-while-we-sit-on-our-cushions-systemic-racism-runs-rampant/

Zhou, X., Guo, J., Lu, G., Chaoran, C., Xie, Z., Liu, J. et al (2020) 'Effects of mindfulness-based stress reduction on anxiety symptoms in young people: a systematic review and meta-analysis', *Psychiatry Research*, 289: 113002.

Conclusion

Kris Clarke, Leece Lee-Oliver and Satu Ranta-Tyrkkö

The chapters in this volume, *Decolonising Social Work in Finland: Racialisation and Practices of Care*, identify how colonial structures, systems, knowledge and ways of being still influence society and social work practices in Finland. The contributions point to the need for critical reflection by practitioners and policy makers in the Finnish welfare state on the ways that coloniality is embedded in the narratives, logics and policies in the universal welfare state, standardising Whiteness, heteronormativity, saviourism and dominance. Through richly nuanced explorations of case studies, the first chapters in this collection respond to the systemic and subtle ways that policies and practices in the Finnish welfare state perpetuate structural violence on those seen as being 'other'. In pointing out the myriad ways that asylum seekers, refugees and immigrants inhabit precarious circumstances amid welfare state nationalism and homonationalism, the authors call for a more emancipatory Finnish social work praxis where social workers confront the silences surrounding the limitations surrounding social workers' responsibilities.

Indeed, years of financial crises and policies of austerity have created a harsh climate for social work in Finland, and throughout the world, to fulfil its mission to promote social justice. Some have described a tectonic shift in many countries in the Global North from the welfare to the workfare state, in which a person's worth no longer rests on their social citizenship in the community, but is reduced to their ability to work and survive conditions of economic insecurity (McDonald, 2006). Kantola et al (2022) describe a Finland where people are increasingly categorised as 'winners' and 'losers', existing in sociopolitical bubbles separate from other groups of people in society. In these circumstances, where the common humanity of all residents is challenged through the enactment of policies intended to punish those deemed as unworthy, the silence of social workers can be a defensive – or even trauma – response to working in neoliberal circumstances where heavy workloads, burnout and micromanaging prevail. Current trends in Finland follow what Loh and Hu (2014) have described as the erosion of professional autonomy through coerced complicity with neoliberal management. The increasing use of punitive eligibility policies that often withdraw support from the most vulnerable in social work restricts social workers' ability to enact socially just decisions rather than simply procedurally correct ones. The challenge facing Finnish social work, as these studies show, is to resist coerced complicity and to actively mobilise the advocacy skills of the field to manifest the profession's commitment to a more equitable Finland. This requires that social workers speak up and engage in making social change on many levels.

Scholars and practitioners of colour in the second section of this volume draw attention to the manifold barriers they face as racialised people entering the Finnish academy and social work labour force. In troubling the epistemic injustice of prevailing Whiteness, these authors make visible the multiple challenges that they face and reveal the potential they hold for transforming Finnish social work policies and practices. In broadening the narrow definitions of social work, these contributions show how mental well-being and healing require more inclusive approaches that challenge the narrowness of constructions of Finnishness, colonial epistemologies and neoliberal definitions of social support. By dismantling structures of systemic oppression, reckoning with the past and deconstructing the power dynamics of Whiteness, heteronormativity, misogyny and ableism often central to constructions of Finnishness, the potential for an emancipatory social work emerges which could incorporate diverse voices, identities and viewpoints as a starting point. Reaching this point, however, requires recognising and taking seriously the everyday challenges that these authors describe as racialised students, practitioners and residents of Finland.

Racism has been in the headlines in Finland in 2023. The Finnish government, a coalition of neoliberal, far-right and smaller political parties, was recently forced to renounce racism due to a series of political scandals. It released a programme of anti-racism in August 2023, which called for criminalising Holocaust denial, outlawing the use of symbols such as the hammer and sickle and swastika, and proactive measures to enhance equality in schools. The fundamental contradiction of constructing such a programme without troubling notions of Finnishness and belonging or reckoning with the past makes the exercise a rather empty performative act. Notions of Nordic exceptionalism, which have emerged from the idea that Finland and other northern European countries have not been involved in colonialism and thus represent progressive universal welfare states, elide the fact that White innocence, White fragility and a growing culture of winners and losers has been a form of branding that is increasingly at odds with the local realities. Challenging racism in Finland thus requires more than statements and plans; it calls for action to enact a fundamental reimagining of how we live together with diverse identities in a broader and more complex Finland. Here, Finnish social work can lead the way as a profession enmeshed in people's everyday lives and as an advocate for social change, if we take up the challenge to first start with ourselves.

Finally, the contributors in the last section of the book present examples of how social work education and practice could embrace emancipatory praxes to confront and revolutionise our colonised ways of thinking and being. Exploring our local cityscapes, understandings of professionalism and how that we think holds the potential to reimagine new ways of being and acting as social workers, citizens and human beings. Far from being on the fringe, these approaches represent directions that the field of social work could take to further grow and develop in challenging epistemic injustice, enhancing inclusion and moving towards a liberatory praxis for all.

Decolonisation holds great promise because its frameworks and practices enable people to dismantle the logics of colonialism, imagine futures and implement new praxes that centralise human dignity and ecological sustainability locally and globally. Indeed, everyone around the world could gain from making our societies fairer and more equitable despite our cultural differences. Becoming more aware of the power dynamics of oppressive ideologies and taken-for-granted attitudes and practices – for example, where colonial legacies such as misogyny, racism, ableism and homophobia are manifested – can also liberate oppressors. But these goals cannot be achieved until a process of decolonisation is started where the wrongs done are acknowledged, amends are made and lessons are learned. Rather than any kind of a simplistic and short-term 'woke agenda', this process demands learning how to live with one another and support one another in ways that recognise the dignity and worth of each person – a core social work value.

Rightly so, Indigenous and liberation activist scholars question the efficacy of engaging in decolonial work. We are a long way, in Finland and other Westernised countries, from the sustainable systems of Indigenous reciprocity that existed for millennia – the critique that we as human societies cannot return to the historical contexts where those practices were cultivated and practised. This collection does not propose a decolonial return of that nature. Rather, the works herein acknowledge that many Indigenous societies exist around the globe and retain their relationships to place, sociopolitical ways of organising, wellness practices and mutuality. Thus, it is important to acknowledge that in the vast diversity of peoples in the world, there is much that we could learn from cross-cultural engagement. As such, decolonisation as a practice responds to coloniality as a complex factor in the ways that we exist, think and construct welfare systems. It critiques how coloniality shapes how we understand social justice and the logic and reasoning. It also demands looking closely at the 'beneficence' of social policies and practices, which often were constructed on structural and epistemic injustices. It is important that we in social work and other human service fields are willing to comprehend what we actually do together with service users, and how we see the world, and whether we are prepared to see the world from others' perspectives and engage in genuine dialogue.

Decoloniality is not a vague futurism. Rather, as this collection demonstrates in myriad ways, it is a practice that requires practitioners to imagine and design pathways for learning, engaging, revising and responding to the everyday ways that colonial ideology is rooted in systems of welfare. The precarity of the service users differ, despite the fixedness of racialisation, so place and context matter. As the authors show in the context of Finland, decolonial approaches can enable social workers to seek out the wisdom of those most impacted and uniquely aware of the machinations of domination thus fulfilling the fundamental mission of the profession to enhance social justice. Decoloniality also relies upon place-based and situated knowledges, which necessarily disrupt the power and dominance inherent in both governmental and university systems. Part of the challenge is incumbent upon each student and practitioner of social work, and human being, to recognise coloniality and act in a liberatory way.

References

Kantola, A., Aaltonen, S., Haikkola, L., Junnilainen, L., Luhtakallio, E., Patana, P. Et al (2022) *Kahdeksan kuplan Suomi: Yhteiskunnan muutosten syvät tarinat* [*Finland in Eight Bubbles: Deep Stories of Social Transformations*], Helsinki: Gaudeamus.

Loh, J. and Hu, G. (2014) 'Subdued by the system: neoliberalism and the beginning teacher', *Teaching and Teacher Education*, 41: 13–21.

McDonald, C. (2006) *Challenging Social Work: the Institutional Context of Practice*, London: Palgrave Macmillan.

Index

References to endnotes show both the page number and the note number (231n3).

A

ableism 68, 189, 196, 271
Act on the Application of Residence-Based Social Security Legislation (1573/1993) 69
Act on the Integration of Immigrants and Reception of Asylum Seekers (493/1999) 67
Act on the Reception of Persons Applying for International Protection (2011/746) 115
Act on the Status and Rights of the Patients (785/1992) 175
Action Plan for Combating Racism and Promoting Good Relations between Population Groups (2021) 157–8
activation policies 49
Addams, J. 14
Adichie, C.N. 89, 92, 93, 94, 101
administrative bordering practices 61
advocacy 117, 137, 140, 174, 270–1
African social work, learning from 2
Afro-Finns 184–5, 190, 191, 192–3, 206–7
ageing society 11, 247
ahimsa 183
Ahmed, S. 85, 98, 113, 127, 138, 150–1, 198
Akin, D. 91, 94
Aldrin Salskov, S. 199
Alien's Act 301/2004 114, 119
alternative healthcare 76
Anapanasati 263–5
ancestors 39, 48, 66, 193, 223, 263
anger 147
angry Black woman trope 174, 186
anti-Blackness 170, 188, 190, 219, 222
anti-immigrant rhetoric 13
anti-psychiatry 164
anti-racist stances
  arts-based social work 126–7, 137
  and 'colour-blindness' 12
  education for White people 188
  Finnish government 3, 271
  future-building 157
  healing spaces 183, 186–7, 192
  non-profit industrial complex 168
  training 121
anti-Semitism 149, 227
Anttonen, A. 68–9, 70, 75
Aoki, J. 233
archiving 217–36
arrival stories 150–1
arts-based social work 125–44
assimilation 50–1, 87, 155, 172, 185, 191, 205
Assmuth, L. 10, 11
asylum seekers
  Alien's Act 301/2004 114–15, 119
  and child protection 113, 115
  family reunification 51, 52, 58
  policies 11
  sexuality 85, 94, 98–100
  structural injustice 111
  transcultural mental health 172
  young people 125–44
  see also migration; refugees
austerity 270
auto-ethnography 150–1, 163

B

Baer, R.A. 258
Baltra-Ulloa, A.J. 86, 87, 101
Bandung Conference 19
basic services 116
belittling attitudes 75
Bell, W. 256
bias, recognising 132, 137
  see also positionality
bilingualism 72
biracial children 185
Black American culture 193
Black intersectional feminism 157
Black Lives Matter (BLM) 185, 190, 193, 227
Blell, M. 18
Blumenbach, J. 3, 5
boarding schools 16, 41, 42
body as a site of learning 129, 133
  see also embodied practices
Bonilla-Silva, E. 169
border changes 10
border controls 11, 61
Bowman, M. 198
Brave Heart, M.Y.H. 176
Bravemen, P.A. 169
breathing exercises 263–5
Brodin, H. 79
browne, a.m. 183
Bubble of Oppression 93–4, 95, 98–100
Bullard, A. 165
Burns, N. 68
Butler, J. 85
bystanders/neutral, Nordic societies as 8

C

Campt, T. 222–3
Canada 68
Canda E. 262
Carastathis, A. 199, 202
Carbin, M. 199
care, children taken into institutional 16, 41, 115, 155, 156, 263
Carrette, J. 257
Cartwright, S.A. 171
case study methods 130, 242–3
census data 150
Chaitin, J. 203
Chamanculo, Mozambique 237–55
Chambon, A. 132, 133, 134, 138
child protection services 111–12, 113, 115, 118, 119, 155, 172
Child Welfare Act (2007/417) 115, 119
child-centred approaches 78
children's rights 119, 120
Chinatowns 226–7, 228–9
Christianity and colonialism 3, 18, 189
Chydenius Consortium 109
citizenship 12, 60, 149, 150, 153, 270
city walking 225–32
civilising mission of colonialism 3, 163, 197
claims-makers, social workers as 101
Clarke, K. 2, 14, 87, 89, 105, 152, 157, 163, 200–2, 225–32, 256, 257
Clay, Rosa Emilia 149
climate crisis 13, 37, 256, 272
closeness (community health workers) 244–5
co-construction of meaning 203, 262
coercive sterilisation 18
co-learning 131
collective care 218, 219
Collins, P. 205, 207
colonialism
  binary Western/other 92
  Christianity and 3, 18, 189
  civilising mission 3, 163, 197
  colonial epistemologies in universities 195–8
  'colonial matrix' 17
  colonial public archive 217
  in Finland 7–8, 17–18, 44, 128, 149, 155, 199–200, 271
  genocide 150, 176, 220, 225
  healing from 184
  homonationalism 86
  nation-state building 87
  and psychiatry 163, 164–5, 166, 176
  slavery 3, 167, 171–2, 193, 219, 220, 225
  Sweden 219–25, 233
  violence 183
  'White innocence' 128
coloniality 5

colour-blindness 12, 106, 120, 168, 172, 188, 199
communality 135
communitarianism 50–1
community art 129
community health workers 237–55
community-based social work 241, 250–1
compassion 192, 193, 256, 258, 260, 261, 262
conditionality in welfare policies 51, 60
Constitution of Finland 39, 40, 106
content analysis 131
counter-archiving 217–36
COVID-19 61, 133, 142n3, 190, 256
Cox, D.R. 250
Crenshaw, K. 198, 199
critical auto-ethnography 150–1, 163
critical embodied engagement 218
critical fabulation 223
critical law studies 154
critical race theories 148, 154, 157
critical social work paradigm 129
critical Whiteness studies 79, 127–8, 137
cultural barriers and structural injustice 110, 111, 120
cultural competence 107, 170, 173
cultural humility 101
cultural identity 161
culturalised social work 106, 120
culturally sensitive working methods 125–6
Curtis, C. 20

D

data analysis 52, 71, 88–9, 109–10, 131
'Dear Beloved Black Body' workshop 190
decoloniality 5, 140
decolonisation
  adaptive nature of 15
  decolonising social work in context 16–19
  definition 1–2
'Decolonising Wellness' 192
dehumanisation 10, 15, 74–5, 154, 169, 220, 222, 257
democracy 17–18, 241
DeNard, C. 107
Denmark 7
de-professionalisation 240–1, 242
deracination 36
Derber, C. 241
deserving/undeserving tropes 49, 50, 60, 155
deskilling 241
detention under Mental Health Act 170
development aid 9
dialogues (arts-based) 129, 131, 132, 138
DiAngelo, R. 174, 186
dignity 101, 240, 272
disability 66–84, 95, 247
discourses 88–9

diversity and inclusion initiatives 198
doctoral research in Finland 201
Doctrine of Discovery 17
Dominelli, L. 242
dual mandate of social workers (state-client) 87, 95, 107
Duda-Mikulin, E. 68

E

Edenheim, S. 199
education
  boarding schools 16, 41, 42
  mindful decolonisation 263
  professional imperialism 14
  special education 74
Eggebø, H. 91
Ellington, L. 126, 127, 128, 129, 135, 136, 137
El-Tayeb, F. 92
emancipatory practice 270–2
embassies 53
embodied practices 133, 136, 217–18, 222–3
emergency services 115
employment 54
empowerment of clients 116–17
English 152, 157, 161
environment 258–9, 261, 272
  see also climate crisis; nature, connection with
environmental arts-based methods 129, 133
epistemic justice 163–4, 172–3, 196–9, 200–8, 271, 272
epistemic violence 15, 162, 175, 200
equal marriage 90–1
Equal Marriage Act 90
equality 69, 70, 155, 240
  see also inequalities
erasure 36, 147–60, 184, 199, 217–20, 232
  see also silences/silencing
Esping-Andersen, G. 66
essentialism 69, 106, 120
ethical guidelines/principles 62, 108, 111, 114, 131, 170, 243, 261
ethnography 131, 242–3
  see also critical auto-ethnography
ethnopsychiatry 163–7, 169, 173
EU Charter of Social Rights 106
EU Fundamental Rights Agency 183, 184
eugenics (race hygiene) 16, 17–18, 169, 172, 221–2
Eurocentrism 126, 129, 154, 155, 163, 168, 175, 195, 197
European identity 92
European Union 11
European Union Agency for Fundamental Rights 149
evidence-based practice 16, 196, 202, 260

exceptionalism 9, 11, 51, 155, 220, 271
exoticism 186
expertise 17, 107, 241, 242
extreme right politics 2–3, 149

F

failure to act 99
family reunification 49–65, 107, 119
'Family Separation, Migration Status and Everyday Security' 51–2
family separation research 51
Fanon, F. 164, 166
far-right politics 2–3, 149
Fassin, D. 165–6
feminist research 14, 89, 154, 157, 183, 198, 199
Fielding, S.L. 241
fierce loving-kindness practices 265–6
Finnish Administrative Court 107
Finnish colonialism 7–8, 17–18, 44, 128, 149, 155, 199–200, 271
Finnish Constitution 39, 40, 106
Finnish Feminist Party 200
Finnish Immigration Service 49–65
Finnish language 40, 72, 157, 166, 182, 185, 203
Finnish Migration Service (Migri) 53–4, 55, 56, 58, 62, 94, 95
Finns Party (*Perussuomalaiset*) 11
Floyd, G. 185, 190
Forbes, D. 260
forced migration 92
  see also asylum seekers
Forsberg, Kuronen, M. 201
Foster, V. 127, 128, 129, 135
Foucault, M. 164
Frazer-Carroll, M. 165, 167
Fresno, US 218, 225–32, 233
Fricker, M. 197
funding 170
futures, importance of 19–21, 262–3
futures studies 256–69

G

Garner, S. 67
gatekeeping role 14, 77
'gay haven' story of Finland 90–1, 93, 95
gender 10, 69, 85, 86, 95, 154
genocide 150, 176, 220, 225
Ghana 206
Gilroy, P. 165
Global South 13, 14, 204, 240, 241
globalisation 12, 15, 105, 201
Gothenburg, Sweden 218, 219–25, 233
Greenland 6

H

half-thoughts 134
Hanh, T.N. 261

Hansen, S. 68
happiness indexes 149
Hartman, S. 223
healing 182–94, 218, 256–7, 261
health services 72, 75–6, 78, 79, 207–8, 237–55
hegemonic cultural bodies 5
hegemonic cultural norms 126
hegemonic Whiteness 10–14, 18, 67, 101n1, 125–44, 219, 271
Hemminiki, E. 18
Henrickson, M. 17, 241
heteronormativity 16, 95, 189, 196, 197, 271
hierarchies
  of knowledge 14
  professional social work hierarchies 62, 240, 241, 249–51
  racial hierarchies 3, 5, 6, 8, 11–12, 67, 87, 190
Hiitola, J. 53, 106, 107, 119
Hill Collins, P. 15
Hiltunen, M. 129, 135
history of social work profession 16, 18, 87
Hölscher, D. 17
homonationalism 85–104
Hoogvelt, A. 242
hooks, b 89, 162–3, 256
horizontality 135–7, 140
Hortelano, P. 12
Howe, D. 14
Hu, G. 270
human rights 51, 61, 66, 106, 119, 120, 240
Hutcheon, L. 5
hyper-racialised spaces 162

I

identity 92, 161, 184–5
see also national identity
Ilmonen, K. 200
INCITE collective 168–9
income requirements 60
Indigenous societies
  California 225
  in census 150
  colonisation of 5–6
  community health workers 237, 238
  community-based social work 250–1
  decolonial paradigm 126
  forced cultural assimilation 51
  helping structures 248–9
  Indigenous knowledge paradigm 15, 36, 128, 132, 135, 157, 183, 241
  lack of knowledge about Finnish 45
  mindfulness 258
  place-based theory and praxis 272
  reciprocity 272
  removal of Indigenous children 16, 41, 115, 155, 156, 263
  trade with 220
  see also Roma; Sámi
individualism 69, 135, 198, 257, 260
inequalities 69, 201
information provision 73
informed consent to research 131
infrastructure 7, 13
in-groups and out-groups 120
inherited rights to social security 66
insider/outsider status 8, 11, 50, 88, 184, 203, 204–5, 208
  see also 'othering'
institutional oppression 151–3, 197
institutional racism 79, 87
'integration' processes 12, 16, 52, 61–2, 67
interactive movement 132, 134
interconnectivity 13, 37
intercultural premises 129
interdependencies 13, 87, 261
interdisciplinary research 130–1, 201
interpreter services
  duty to provide 110, 111
  family reunification 55, 56
  mental health services 161
  migrant parents with a disabled child 72, 73, 79
  research methods 88
  rights to 175
intersectionality
  in academia 198–200
  arts-based social work 136, 140
  Black intersectional feminism 154
  commonalities between certain characteristics 100
  healing spaces 183
  intersectional vulnerability regimes 49
  multiple discriminations 95
  need for research in 157
  Nordic women's studies 199
  testimonios 200–8
interview methods 52, 70–1, 88, 242–3
Ioakamidis, V. 239–40
'Iron Well' statue, Gothenburg 219–25
Islamophobia 94, 149

J

Jensen, L. 8
Jewish communities 149, 151
Johnson, M. 198
Jönsson, J. 126, 128, 140, 141

K

Kacen, J. 203
Kallakorpi, S. 170, 172, 173
Kantola, A. 270
Karabel, J. 197
Kaye, H. 4

Keeling, K. 20
KELA (Social Insurance Institution of Finland) 40
Keskinen, S. 5, 6, 7, 8, 11, 12, 14, 15, 50, 51, 62, 67, 70, 87, 126, 128, 137
Kindiak, D.H. 242
King, R. 257
knowledge
  ancestral 223
  beyond language 138
  BIPOC scholarship 154, 157
  co-construction of meaning 89, 203, 258, 262
  colonial epistemologies in universities 195–8
  'colonising knowledge' 1–2
  control of 'legitimate' 198
  democratisation of 241
  deracialisation of 128
  discursive negotiations 89
  embodied knowledge 136, 218, 223–4
  epistemic justice 163–4, 172–3, 196–9, 200–8, 271, 272
  'epistemic mobilisation' 128
  epistemic violence 15, 162, 175, 200
  evidence-based practice 16, 196, 202, 260
  experiencing together 132
  hegemony of Western knowledge in Global North 14, 89
  hierarchies of 14
  holistic knowledge-production processes 129
  Indigenous knowledge paradigm 15, 36, 128, 132, 135, 157, 183, 241
  mutual epistemological spaces 136
  objets of knowledge versus knowers 202
  pluralistic epistemologies 14–16, 126, 128, 140
  pluriversalising knowledge production 14–16
  rationality 135
  reconstruction of suppressed 15
  redistribution to migrants 107
  relational knowledge 135
  respect for parents' 78
  'right knowledge' 17
  sensory information 133
  situated knowledge 19
  testimonios 200–8
  'unlearning' 133, 138, 188
  White Western narrative foundations 89
Kokkola University Consortium Chydenius 109
Konttinen, K. 125, 130
Kovach, M. 15, 16
Krietemeyer, J. 258
Kritzer, H.M. 240–1, 251
Kuokkanen, R. 168, 169

L

land 47–8, 184, 225
language
  assistance with asylum form filling 56
  asylum seekers 53, 56
  barriers to disability services 67, 71–5
  barriers to mental health services 175
  barriers to social work practice 203
  diagnosis of disability 73–4
  English 152, 157, 161
  Finnish language 40, 72, 157, 166, 182, 185, 203
  foreign mother tongue as measure of migration 66–7
  lingual barriers and structural injustice 110–16
  mental health 173
  monolingual practices 71–5
  official languages 40, 71–2
  parents with disabled children 71–5, 79
  Sámi 39–42, 45, 46, 72, 157
  translation services 72, 79
  use of mother tongue 76, 77
  see also interpreter services
Language Act (2003/423) 110
Lavalette, M. 239–40
Lehti, V. 170
Lehtola, V.-P. 6, 7, 51
Leinonen, J. 67
Lipsky, M. 60
listening 101, 158, 222–3, 232
localisation of training 250
Loh, J. 270
Lorenz, W. 87, 95
Loseke, D. 89, 96, 100, 101

M

macro practice courses 228
Magee, R.V. 261
maiden allegory 35
Maldonado-Torres, N. 169, 257
Maputo, Mozambique 237–55
Marley, B. 193
marriage 90–1
maternity services 207
Matthew, R.A. 237–8
Matthies, A. 262
Mattsson, T. 79
McDonald, C. 273
meaning-making processes 89, 126, 203, 258, 262
meditation 258, 259–60, 263–5
Mehrara, L. 70, 79
memorials/commemoration in public spaces 217–36
mental health 59, 61, 96, 153, 161–81, 258
  see also stress
Mental Health Act 170

Index

Mepschen, P. 91
meritocracy 5
Merivirta, R. 7
metaphors 133, 141
Metkat menopelit (*Funny Set of Wheels*, WSOY, 2010) 9
Meyer, I. 153
microaggressions 185
middle-class 17, 69
Midgley, J. 14
Mignolo, W. 1, 5, 128, 133, 140, 141
migration
   culturalised mental health needs 165
   and disability 66–84
   family reunification 49–65
   history of 10, 149
   immigration policy 11
   'integration' processes 12, 16, 52, 61–2, 67
   migrants as 'undeserving' 50
   non-heterosexual refugees 85–104
   non-profit industrial complex 167
   racialised older women 202–6
   structural challenges for social care 106–7
   structural injustice 110–16
   transcultural mental health 172–3
   see also asylum seekers; refugees
Mikkonen, E. 125, 129, 130
mindful decolonisation 257–60
mindfulness 256–69
Mingus, M. 183
minoritisation 5
minority stress theory 153
Mlotshwa, L. 239
modernisation 38–9, 50
Moninaisten Talo (MONIKA – Multicultural Women's Association, Finland) 189–90, 192
monolingual practices 71–5
moral judgement 108
Morley, C. 20
Motta, S. 126, 127, 128, 131, 136, 137
Moua, M. 191
movement (arts-based research) 132–5, 140
Mozambique 237–55
Mulder, R. 170
multicultural social work 109, 135
multi-professional cooperation 117–19
Muslims 92, 93
mutual aid 232, 244
mutual epistemological spaces 136
mutual understanding between social worker and client 114, 116

N

Nading, A.M. 239
Namibia 155
narrative 85, 88–9, 90–100, 133, 149, 200–8

national identity 10, 17, 36, 67, 94, 149–50, 200
national security 11
nationalisation 7
nationalism 4, 18, 50, 61, 66, 87, 149
nation-states
   homonationalism 87
   legislation 119, 120
   nation-state building 50
   Sámi 48, 49
   and social work 195
   and the welfare state 50–1
nature, connection with 38–9, 258–9, 261
neoliberalism
   mindfulness 257, 261
   neoliberalisation of service provision 105, 168
   social exclusion 61
   and universalism 69
   universities 197, 199
   and the welfare state 155
   welfare state nationalism 49, 50
   workfare state 270
Nepal 204
neutral, Nordic societies as 8
NGOs 130, 133, 204, 237, 238, 239, 240, 242–3
Non-Discrimination Act (1325/2014) 111, 116
non-profit industrial complex 163, 167–9
'Nordic exceptionalism' 9, 11, 51, 155, 220, 271
Nordic welfare state model 86
Norway 43, 45, 48, 68, 91
nostalgia 11

O

official languages 40, 71–2
older people 11, 202–6, 247
Omachi, K. 230
'Ordering the "Migrant Family"' 51–2
organisational instructions 113–14
Orientalism 3, 17, 86, 92
Osei-Kofi, N. 219–25
'othering'
   binarisation 92
   in colonialism and imperialism 3, 168
   and hegemonic Whiteness 10, 127
   history in Finland 51
   and national identity 17
   power structures 12
   referring all non-White clients to a non-White social worker 152–3
   structural violence 270
   transcultural mental health 165, 169
   us and 'others' 2, 17, 141, 208
   young people seeking asylum 125–44
   see also insider/outsider status
'out of place' 98

P

Padgett, D.K. 203
paid work 49, 61
paradox of universalism 70
paraprofessional training 250
Pawar, M. 250
Payne, M. 242
Péan, R. 183–4
Pease, B. 13, 15
peer group discussions 109
peer support 153, 243
performativity 127, 138, 198, 223, 271
personnel policies 107
Pierart, A. 68
Pitkänen, P. 70
place-based theory and praxis 14, 132, 217, 272–3
pluralistic arts-based social work 125–44
pluralistic epistemologies 126, 128, 140
pluriversalising knowledge production 14–16, 128, 202
police 16, 18, 111, 165, 170, 171–4
popular social work 239–40
populism 50, 105, 149
positionality 136, 137, 168, 196, 203, 205
postcolonialism definition 5
post-professional social work 237–55
Potter, J. 88–9
Pötzsch, T. 12, 16
poverty 16, 172, 173, 226, 227
power
  asymmetries 78, 120, 136, 165, 168, 175
  collective resistances 219
  colonialism 4
  coloniality 5
  critical examination through arts 127, 129
  cultural humility 101
  deconstruction 271
  of diagnosis 175
  emancipatory practice 272
  Global North 13
  intersectionality 202
  racist power structures 12
  redistribution to migrants 107
  researcher-researched 136
  and universalism 75
  White superiority 3
  Whiteness 67
private service provision 76
privileged narratives 89
professionalised social work 17, 86, 87, 239, 240, 241, 249–50
pro-Nazi groups 2–3
prosenttiliike (per cent movement) 9
psychiatric care 113–14, 161–81
Puar, J. 86
public health services 67, 250
public spaces 217, 219–25

Puchalski, C.M. 262
Purser, R. 261
Pyykkönen, M. 7, 168, 172

Q

queer theory 85, 191
Quijano, A. 17

R

race
  colour-blindness 12, 106, 120, 168, 172, 188, 199
  definition 154–5
  racial theories 8
  social construction of race 126, 154
  and social work 153–6
racial hierarchies 3, 5, 6, 8, 11–12, 67, 87, 190
racial hygiene praxis 16, 17–18, 169, 172, 221–2
racial segregation 225–6, 229
racialisation
  and colonialism 5
  as complex process 127
  Eurocentrism 168
  hyper-racialised spaces 162
  nativist discourses 125
  need for research in 157
  in Nordic societies 67, 155
  transcultural mental health 161–81
racism
  anti-Blackness 170, 188, 190, 219, 222
  benevolent/of omission 185
  and disability 68
  erasure 147–60
  eugenics (race hygiene) 16, 17–18, 169, 172, 221–2
  Finland as most racist country 149–50
  Finnish government's renunciation in 2023 of 271
  Finnish social binaries 2–3
  hegemonic Whiteness 67
  and homophobia 91, 93
  institutional racism 79, 87
  law enforcement 172
  and mental illness frameworks 164, 166–7, 173–4
  migration 70
  multiple stories of Finland 95
  myth of no racism in Nordic societies 8
  need for interventions 101
  people with refugee backgrounds 95–6
  racist harrassment 148, 184, 186
  racist power structures 12
  researcher positionality 137
  as a social problem 96
  social worker framings of 96
  structural racism 94, 147, 153, 155, 163, 164, 166, 169

yoga 187–8
see also White hegemony; White supremacy
radical nationalism 18
Randall, G.E. 242, 251
Ranta-Tyrkkö, S. 7, 16, 126, 128, 241
Rebolleda-Gomez, M. 198
Rechtman, R. 165–6
reciprocity 69, 116, 120, 245–6, 272
recognition of practitioners 246
refugees
 family reunification 49–65
 mental health services 170
 non-heterosexual refugees 85–104
 structural challenges for social care 105–24
 structural injustice 111
 transcultural mental health 166
 see also asylum seekers; migration
reification 108–9, 111, 112, 119
reindeer-herding 36–7, 39, 47
Reiter, B. 15
relational knowledge 135
relational practices 106, 116–17, 245–6, 250–1
research methods 51–2, 70–1, 87–90, 109, 130–1, 242–3
researcher positionality 136, 137, 168, 196, 203, 205
residence permits 53–6, 58, 69, 115–16, 117
reskilling 241
resource exploitation 13, 48
respect 117, 246
'respectable citizen' ideal 49
responsibilities 112, 120
restratification processes 242
rhetoric of the ordinary 98
Rhodes Must Fall 195
Richmond, M. 14, 154
rights
 children's rights 119, 120
 human rights 51, 61, 66, 106, 119, 120, 240
 right to family life 51, 61
 rights to social security 66
 Sámi 72
 social rights 70, 105–24
 understanding 117, 175
right-wing populism 50, 105
Rinpoche, S. 259
risk-based perspectives 125
Rodney, W. 4
Roma 7, 8, 51, 149, 150, 155–7, 168, 172, 184
Roos, J.P. 156
Rossi, L.-M. 200
rules and practices of social work 108, 113–14
Ryynänen, S. 14

S

Said, E. 3, 17, 92
Sainola-Rodriguez, K. 173
Sakamoto, I. 156
same-sex marriage 90–1
Sámi
 Finland's ethnic diversity 184
 forced cultural assimilation 51
 as Indigenous societies 35
 issues in contemporary Finland 35–48
 language 39–42, 45, 46, 72, 157
 policing 172
 racialisation and erasure 149, 150, 157
 rights 72
 settler colonial practices 6–7
 Sweden 220
 transcultural mental health 168, 169
Sápmi (the Sámi land) 6, 35
Satka, M. 87
Sawyer, L. 219–25
Schclarek Mulinari, L. 172
'script, the' 114
seasonal migrant labour 13
sectored service system 73
security (national) 11
SEEYouth project 130
Seikkula, M. 11, 12
self-government 36, 39–40, 141n1, 184
self-reflexivity 129, 137, 140, 196, 199, 202, 265
self-sufficiency 49
sensitisation 133
sensory ethnography 131, 133
sensory experiences 219
service-oriented approaches 157
Sewpaul, V. 17, 241
sexuality 85–6, 99
Sharpe, C. 219, 232
silences/silencing 138, 147–60, 162, 188, 189, 221, 222, 270
 see also erasure
simplification of the world 109
single stories 90–100, 101
Sipliä, J. 68–9, 70, 75
situational/spatial sensitivity 139
sivistys 196–7
'slack scholarship' 168
slavery 3, 167, 171, 193, 219, 220, 225
Smith, L.T. 1, 15, 16
social connection model for justice 106, 107–9, 120
social construction of race 126, 154
social democracy 51
social determinants of health 166
Social Insurance Institution of Finland (KELA) 40
social justice
 academia 195

arts-based social work 125
city walking 232
mindful decolonisation 262
movements 9
role of state 49
social connection model for justice 106, 107–9, 120
social work practice as 6, 101, 202
social workers as 'agents of social justice' 101
structural injustice 108, 110–16, 120
see also epistemic justice
social model of disability 67
social networks 245–9, 250
social rights 105–24
Social Welfare Act (2014/1301) 115, 262
socially engaged arts 129
socio-cultural environments 135, 176
socio-structural sensitivity 139–40
solidarity 95, 232, 245
Somali refugees 166
South Africa 195
sovereignty 18, 36, 44
spatial sensitivity 139
speculative fiction 20
Spencer, M.S. 238
spirituality 24, 132, 184, 186–7, 260, 261–2
standardised service provision 75–7
Stanley, S. 261
state-centred social services ideology 105
state-client dual mandate of social workers 87, 95, 107
Statistics Finland 184
statues 219–25
stereotypes 45, 69, 92, 96–7, 136, 155
stigmatisation 16, 98, 172, 247
stories 85, 88–9, 90–100, 133, 148, 200–8
street-level bureaucrats 60
stress 55, 74–5, 114–15, 153, 258, 260
Stringberg, T. 221
structural challenges for social care 105–24
structural injustice 108, 110–16, 120
structural racism 94, 147, 153, 155, 163, 164, 166, 169
structural violence 50, 55, 61, 62, 99, 164, 185, 193, 195, 227, 270
Stubberud, E. 91
subsidiary protection 53
Sudenkaarne, T. 18
suffering, reification of 112
Suoranta, J. 14
surveillance 95, 222
Svendsen, S. 91, 94
Sweden 7, 43, 45, 48, 155, 219–25
Swedish Democrats (*Sverigedemokraterna*) 11
Swedish language 71–2, 157, 185
synaesthesia 148

Systematic White Rage 147, 148, 152, 153
systemic oppression 271
systemic racism 121, 136, 148, 166–7, 260
systems thinking and change 263

T

Tamale, S. 1
Tatar people 149, 168
teachers of social work 152, 157
technocratisation of social work 241–2
Tervonen, M. 149
testimonial injustice 197, 206
testimonios 195–213
textual analysis 109
thematic analysis 71, 110, 131, 154
therapeutic attitudes 118
Toivanen, M. 67
tokenism 189, 198
training 121, 152, 157, 250
transcultural competence 170
transcultural mental health 161–81
transdisciplinary practice 6
transformation 137–8
translation services 72, 79
trauma
  arts-based social work 133
  counter-archiving 227
  healing spaces 183, 184
  mindfulness 258
  structural injustice 113, 118, 270
  transcultural mental health 162, 173
  treatment principles in psychiatry 113–14, 120
trust 116, 117, 130, 133, 173, 247
Tubman, H. 193
Tuori, S. 70

U

UK 68, 165
UNICEF 119
United Nations resettlement programmes 149–50
universalism 66–84, 106, 120
universities 195–213
'unlearning' 133, 138, 188
upskilling 241
Urry, J. 19
US 68, 86, 172, 184, 191, 197, 198, 206, 225–32
us and 'others'/them 2, 17, 141, 208
  see also insider/outsider status

V

Van Gordon, W. 258–9
victims/villains 89, 91–3, 96, 100
Villanueva, E. 167
violence
  in colonialism and imperialism 4, 183
  genocide 150, 176, 220, 225

healing 261
homophobia 99
parental violence 112
principles of non-violence 183
structural violence 50, 55, 61, 62, 99, 164, 185, 193, 195, 227, 270
Swedish coloniality 223
visas 53, 55

W

'wake work' 219, 225, 232, 233
walking and talking pedagogy 217–19, 221, 225–32
welfare state
  conditionality in welfare policies 51, 60
  Nordic welfare state model 86, 105
  racialisation 155
  as racialised entity 172
  universalism 66–84
  welfare state nationalism 49–65, 66, 80
  to workfare state 270
Western concepts around sexuality and gender 85–6, 87
Western mindfulness 260
Western social work 155–6
Western theory in social work 241
Westernness and Finnishness 2
Wetherell, M. 88–9
White benevolence 174
White Finns 8–9
White foreigners 155
White fragility 174, 186, 188, 271
White hegemony 10–14, 18, 67, 101n1, 125–44, 219, 271
'White innocence' 11, 51, 127–8
White normativity 10–14, 126–7, 138, 147–9, 168, 174, 185, 197, 207
White privilege 154, 187

White saviour complex 18, 204
White supremacy
  erasure and silencing of others 148, 155, 156
  in Finland 3, 16
  healing spaces 188
  homonationalism 87
  oppression of BIPOC 187
  policing 172
  transcultural mental health 162, 167, 170, 175
Whiteness as a non-race 167
Whiteness as a set of meanings 126
Whiteness as central to national identity 67
White-passing Finns 2
Whitewashing 168, 185, 187, 199
winners/losers 270–1
winters 37
workfare state 270
working classes 87, 152
working with clients (versus working for) 117
Wright, K. 18

Y

Yellow Bird, M. 6, 14, 16, 87, 89, 105, 157, 256, 257, 258, 262, 263
'Yellow' race 8
yoga 182–3, 185, 187–92
Yoon-Ramirez, I. 217, 219
Yoshimizu, A. 233
Young, I.M. 106, 107–9, 111, 112, 113, 114, 116, 119, 120, 125
young people seeking asylum 125–44

Z

'Zong!' (Phillip and Boateng, 2011) 220–1

www.ingramcontent.com/pod-product-compliance
Lightning Source LLC
Chambersburg PA
CBHW051530020426
42333CB00016B/1862